ROGUE ELEPHANTS

ONE PR GIRL'S FIGHT THROUGH THE HUMAN JUNGLE

To Jane.

Best wishes

Jane Hunt

BY JANE K HUNT

Dedication

This book is dedicated to all the people who have enriched my life and career and provided me with such an interesting and intriguing story to tell. It is especially dedicated to my parents and my Nan for all their unswerving support, to my wonderful son (for putting up with a mother who is often in a parallel universe) and to my grandmother and grandfather, who are long passed away, but who taught me the joy of being funny and witty, from a very early age.

It also dedicated to the uniquely gifted and entertaining Dr Anil Seal and to Mr S in Sri Lanka, for their invaluable life advice. I would also like to thank Manchester's Hilton for giving me such spectacular, truly unforgettable and confidence boosting moments that I never wanted to end.

One final note of thanks must go to my primary school teacher at Claremont junior School in Blackpool, Mrs Hamer, just for teaching me 'there is no such word as 'can't'.

Definition

Rogue elephant:
1. *A lone, vicious wild elephant that separates from the rest of the herd. Elephants can be docile, but they can become aggressive and violent without explanation. At times domestic or wild elephants can become extremely dangerous to humans. This may be connected to sexual behaviour or a demonstration of dominance, but the reasons are not exactly clear. Elephants are known to turn for no reason at all and, after this, can attack anything and anyone that is in their way. They are even more dangerous when you do not appreciate how to avoid them.*
2. *A human whose behaviour is aberrant and resembles that of a rogue elephant.*

Chapter 1
DEMONS, A GENIUS & A BUDDHIST

I'd like to say that I planned my 'glamorous' career in PR, but the truth is that I planned that as much as I strategised anything else in my lifetime. Perhaps that's why one of my favourite quotations is that of the enigmatic John Lennon, who said, 'Life is what happens to you while you're busy making other plans'. And, in turn, perhaps that's because, at the age of 2, I could do an impersonation of The Beatles famous 'wooooooo', with an impressive sideways shake of the head and emphatic vocal accompaniment.

I was well and truly a child of the swinging sixties, growing up in an age of flower power, love and peace and a challenging of the boundaries of acceptability. By April 1990, I was reliving this in the Maracanã in Rio watching Paul and Linda McCartney in concert and still shaking my head with a 'wooooooo'!

'Give me a child at the age of 7 and I will give you the man', said the Jesuits and maybe that's true of women too. In my formative years, I spent many hours a day in the very large hotel owned by my Nan near Blackpool's Gynn Square, in a prime position on the North Promenade of the then much more sane resort than the one we know today, complete with furriers in Queen Street and a true family resort feel. At the time, 'The Ingledene' was second in size only to 'The Imperial', so she had numerous staff, all of whom spoiled me rotten, took me out, as a cute toddler with Shirley Temple blonde curls, and taught me how to interact with people from many walks of life.

I even grew to love those with Glaswegian accents, who would take me to Lewis's department store and allow me to be photographed with a monkey, or astride a Push-me-pull-you – my earliest appearances in photo shoots. Not surprisingly, Kathy from Glasgow was my favourite waitress, but I also named one of my two tortoises 'Frank' after one of the chefs in the kitchen. 'Frank' was a headbutter. His namesake was merely a chef and, although I know only too well that chefs can be crazy, I'm sure I never saw him headbutt anyone!

Somewhere along the way, however, I lost this early personality and my school years were not particularly happy ones, for a variety of reasons surrounding my weight, bullying and other factors. I became awkwardly shy, blushed at the slightest thing and withdrew into my schoolwork, at which I excelled. By the time I was 19, I was borderline anorexic and saved only by the fact that my cousin had also suffered anorexia and knew the signs.

In the 1980s, when I was graduating, nobody even talked about PR, or made you aware of its existence on the career spectrum. As a career, it wasn't even on the map, or at least not where I was – made in Blackpool, educated in Fleetwood, enhanced in the 'rabbit warren' of New Hall College, Cambridge and refined at Trinity College, hotbed of spies rather than spin.

Back then, if you were a woman, you were enthusiastically informed at school about the world of the svelte, made-up-to-the-nines airhostess, or the much-needed role of the nurse. By the time I was in the hands of the career service at University, I was told I could be a journalist or a top advertising exec, if I was a hound with the scent for the kill, or had a daddy with contacts in Covent Garden. When it came to PR, as my hero Yoda would say, 'there was no try': it wasn't even referenced.

Perhaps this is why I stumbled through my history degree at Cambridge with absolutely no idea what I was going to do when I left, or maybe I didn't. Maybe my heart was then happily ensconced in the world of academia and my spirit too scared to venture beyond that safe, cosy, book-filled world.

I went to Cambridge by accident. My school, Fleetwood Grammar School, was desperate to try to get some of its students into Oxbridge, so put its highest achievers into 'Oxbridge lessons'. Me being me, I ducked out of that. If I wanted to go anywhere, which was highly debatable, as I didn't want to leave the security of home, I had thought that the University of Sussex was my best bet, as my uncle lived in Rottingdean. My sights were set on an American Studies course and so I never attended the 'Oxbridge' lessons, despite having achieved the best O' Level results in the school.

Instead, while others learned all the tricks to get into Oxford and Cambridge, I thoroughly enjoyed myself in pottery classes for five full weeks of sixth form, until the 'Oxbridge' lessons organisers realised that I should have been swotting for the Oxbridge entrance exam.

They dragged this free spirit into 'Oxbridge' lessons at the final hour, with one lesson to go. I think I'd escaped until then, because an amalgamation of schools had taken place that summer and everything was up in the air. Once coerced into the class, with just two pottery ashtray dishes and one small bowl to my name, or rather my initials carved into the base, I was forced to go on an away trip that took in both Oxford and Cambridge. As the lesser of two evils, as it was smaller, more intimate and I liked the river and The Backs, I chose Cambridge and sat the entrance exam.

It was truly sod's law that all those students who'd been in the class for weeks failed and I, with an eye on Sussex and one Oxbridge lesson under my belt, passed – or at least got put into the 'pool'. The college I had named (by largely sticking a pin in the list) didn't want me and put me up for grabs by other colleges. I was plucked from 'the pool' by New Hall – a college that hadn't really been on my radar and about which I knew nothing.

New Hall was Cambridge's equivalent in today's world to a squashed 'Gherkin' and when I refer to it as the rabbit warren, this is because it was described as such 'both architecturally and sexually' in a guide to the University, out at the time. It was there to champion the cause of the underprivileged at Cambridge – women – and I warmed to it when I discovered that my interview was with the amazing American, Dr Zara Steiner, wife of the renowned academic, George Steiner. Somehow, I convinced Dr Steiner that I could be a successful student at New Hall, despite my humble grammar school roots and I joined the new intake that October.

That's a bit misleading actually, as I lived in New Hall (first sharing a room with a very strange girl who still wore knee length socks, played a wind instrument and only talked in monosyllables), ate in New Hall, rowed for New Hall, but was never supervised in New Hall – not once in 3 years. For anyone worrying about my fate with the girl with the knee socks, I begged for another room after a few weeks and was transferred to a room in D block. Sanity was restored, though by year 3, the knee sock wearer was ripping up letters a younger student had left for her regarding possible changes to the music society and stuffing all the little pieces into the girl's pigeon hole in the porters' lodge! I must count my blessings!

For those who don't know the Cambridge system, you attend lectures and then have in-depth tuition, often one-to-one, with a supervisor, who informs your learning, sets and marks essays and advises on reading lists. As a Cambridge college, New Hall was much smaller than others and only had two history tutors, who obviously couldn't between them specialise in all periods of history. One was a medieval history tutor and the other specialised in modern history. Me being me, I decided to study those eras which fell between their areas of expertise.

My decision to root myself between 1500 and 1900 meant I had to be farmed out to other supervisors in other colleges. Thus began my life as the eternal itinerant gipsy, nosying around other colleges, getting to know the moods of various head porters and seeing how the aristocratic students of other colleges like Magdalene lived, or rather lolled, as only members of the higher echelons of society can, on the pew type benches in their porters' lodge.

In my first year, I was supervised at Selwyn, Magdalene and Emmanuel. My Selwyn tutor was thoroughly nice and re-taught me everything I had learned at school about the Stuarts, reinforcing my love of the rather dashing Prince Rupert (is it mad to be in love with a figure from history?)

My Magdalene tutor, on the other hand, was a little obsessed with religion and witchcraft, but totally honourable in allowing me to dry out in front of his fire, after a complete drenching when riding my bike to his supervision one day. The lesson didn't commence until I had stopped dripping!

The Emmanuel tutor, on the other hand, was a bit of an oddball and very detached, but luckily I only had to attend five supervisions with him. I certainly never ever fell in love with Emmanuel as a college. This could never have been said of St John's, through which I would deliberately walk, to then cut back to New Hall, just so that I could see the Bridge of Sighs and dream of being a student there (which was totally impossible as women were not admitted!) To get around this problem, I seemed to find as many male friends as possible at St John's, so that I could visit them and make believe that the admissions policy had changed!

My bike was my best friend as a result of this wandering minstrel lifestyle, with numerous miles covered during the course of a week, not to mention the very steep hill back up to New Hall from Cambridge town centre, which was quite a challenge when dangling two heavy Sainsbury's carrier bags from the handlebars after the weekly shop! I also cannot stress how many times I left a backless, sling-back shoe at the traffic lights at the bottom of the hill when setting off on green – a rather embarrassing situation necessitating backtracking to retrieve said sling-back shoe!

I had initially put my foot down, in both sling-backs and trainers, and declared in typically capricious style that there was 'no way' I was going to take my bike to Uni and cycle around – in other words stating that I wasn't going to conform to type. That steely resolve lasted all of a week, with humble pie taking the form of a telephone call to my father begging him to bring my bike down, as the skin was literally peeling from the balls of my feet!

Things were about to look up however, as my second year presented more possibilities than the first and that started with what I consider one of my best life decisions – ticking the box alongside the 'Expansion of Europe' option for year 2. In all honesty, I didn't know what to expect with this theme, but it sounded exciting and full of the glamour of exploration – something that had always fascinated me since I found some dusty, old school books of my father's about such ships as the 'Santa Maria' and strangely named explorers like Fernão Mendes Pinto, who smacked of mystery, intrigue and potential roguish behaviour.

When I went to the first lecture on this topic, no supervisor had been found for me. The New Hall historians seemed to be floundering when it came to suggesting someone. I changed all that and made the decision for them, having been left in absolutely no doubt that there was one, and only one, tutor for me.

I vividly recall awaiting my first lecture on 'The Expansion of Europe' in 'The Seeley', an architectural nightmare that was the ultra-modern history faculty in Cambridge, constructed mainly of glass and so a hothouse in summer and a building that forced me to buy Albert Steptoe fingerless gloves in winter, just to survive sitting and making notes. A fair few students had gathered for this lecture and we were all crammed like sardines in a second-floor lecture room, watching the clock tick the minutes past the appointed hour when the lecturer, simply a name on a piece of paper to me at this point, Dr Anil Seal, should have arrived to start the address.

I'm not sure what monsoon wind blew him into the room that day, papers and notebook tucked under his arm, beige corduroy trousers and a vivid patterned shirt comprising his garb; a lit cigarette dangling between his fingers, making it hard for him to put his papers on the lectern. He had the features and mannerisms of Mick Jagger, a way of pronouncing his words that simply entranced me and the wildest hair and look in his eyes. For someone so visually off-the-wall, compared to the typical staid Cambridge don, he was a total enigma, on the one hand emitting a 'take me as I am' message and on the other seemingly very self-conscious that his unique 'look' was very much not the norm.

I had gone to this lecture with another New Hall history student – a mature student who would go on to work on BBC sport at a high level, but who had a way of looking at people with a permanent grin on her face. Unfortunately, she was wearing this smile as Dr Seal caught her eye. 'What do you think you are looking at', he barked, causing every student to leap out of their seat in an instant and my friend to turn a deep shade of purple. I have to say that this simply added to the fascination of this relatively short and slight human dynamo for me and I wasn't at all perturbed by it. In fact, this may have been the moment when I realised that I find the maverick and the quixotic totally entrancing and perhaps even addictive. I don't think I 'do' stereotypical or staid.

I had already decided that I couldn't resist watching this man's every move even before he went on to set the wastepaper bin on fire. However, that was what swayed it for me as he stood there flapping around with a naughty schoolboy grin on his face and an air of mischief that was verbalised with a few choice swear words and a shrug of the shoulders, as smoke started to rise!

I simply knew that I couldn't be supervised by anyone less unconventional, non-stereotypical and brilliant. The lesson that I had reinforced in my mind that day was that genius is next to madness and that the journey is so much duller, if you don't encounter a genius in your life. To this day, I count my blessings that I had Dr Anil Seal in my life and can firmly state that my life has been much richer for it.

I instantly informed Dr Steiner that I wanted to be supervised by Dr Anil Seal at Trinity College. I recall a furrowing of the brow and could detect a sharp intake of breath, almost conveying, in words unspoken, that I would be Daniella straying into the lion's den. As I was known for being outwardly shy and unassuming, I think she thought that I would be eaten up in the first ten minutes of any supervision, but on the other, I think that she thought it would never come to that and he would never accept me.

I waited on tenterhooks for the decision and I was summoned to attend a meeting with Dr Seal, in his rooms in Trinity. It was snowing, but I wore a lovely dress that my mother had made, which had quite a full skirt and was bright pink. I arrived at Trinity and sought out his rooms, up a winding staircase in the famous and stunningly graceful Neville's Court, en route to the Wren Library. Once I had left the grandeur of the courtyard, my journey continued up an ageing timber staircase, with creaky stairs and a beautiful window halfway up the ascent, complete with leaded panes and a stunning Cambridge view.

I entered the room to find around 40 students in there, all of whom seemingly belonged to Trinity. I recognised some from the history department, but where the others had been hiding, goodness knows. There was a trio I did recognise – real trendsetters, always dressed in the latest fashions, sporting way-out hair and hanging out together in the coffee bar like a little elite clique. The room was too packed for me to take in its inner essence, but it had the feel of somewhere vibrant, yet learned, somewhere totally unique and enchanting, with an amazing chaise longue, on which some of the students were lolling.

There was nowhere for me to sit, so I joined quite a few others on the floor and waited and waited and waited as one student after another was addressed, given their instructions for the term and dismissed from the room. One by one, they all departed, leaving me, sitting with my wide skirt splayed out across the floor and Dr Seal sitting on his sofa. He flashed his eyes around the room and alighted on me. To this day I remember the words, 'You're not one of my Trinity ladies', cascading down to me with his unique style of pronunciation.

'Come, come', he urged, inviting me to actually leave the floor and sit in a more orthodox fashion. I swear I felt as if I was Anna being summoned by the King of Siam. At that point, I noticed the little miniature soldiers situated in an alcove of the wall, the exquisite furnishings of his room, the sight of a massive, wall-sized bookcase packed with jewels of academia and antique furniture that undoubtedly told its own story of the expansion of Europe.

At this point, the news was bestowed upon me that I could be jointly supervised with a male student from Jesus College called Dave, who also wished to study with Dr Seal. I felt truly blessed to have been accepted, even on this shared supervision basis and soon made Dave's acquaintance. We became quite good friends, which had the advantage, or disadvantage, depending on how you look at it, of introducing me to the delights of C.U.S.T.O.D.Y – the Cambridge University Society for the Tasting of Diverse Yogurts – of which he was a leading light!

I remember being invited to the Christmas awards of this offbeat society and tasting everything from turkey yogurt to the ultimate award-winner of that year, the Crunchie yogurt! To say one felt a little sick after the whole experience is a bit of an understatement. However, I had passed Dave's initiation ceremony and consequently he returned the favour by completely throwing himself into the fancy dress spirit of the St Trinian's party, which I gave that year, which coincided with the arrival of Madness in the charts and naughty boys from nasty schools breaking all the rules, along with gym-skirt wearing girls, which included myself. I even managed to bring my Fleetwood Grammar School hat into the costume, having only ever worn it on my very first day at school and been bullied by a fifth former, who said I must have woodworm in my head, to be wearing such a monstrosity! As it happened, within weeks, I was told that Dr Seal would supervise me alone and my association with Dave dwindled.

So it was that I learned all about Dr Seal's amazing life, the old green Mercedes, which he still drove because of an emotional attachment to it, as it once got him to the bottom of Greece in a hurry, his amazing network of contacts, from Indira Gandhi to columnists on the national press, his Indo-Hungarian parentage and his dreams for scholarship schemes for Commonwealth students wishing to study in Cambridge.

He was, as one might have expected, invariably late, or exceedingly late, for my supervisions and, in turn, the sessions could take hours, but I never minded one bit, no matter how dark the road on the way back to New Hall, or how long the wait sitting on the stairs. Look for the benefit in everything and you will find it and so it proved, because if you sat on the stairs halfway up his flight and looked through the leaded window, you could see where the original glass fitters had etched their names into the glass centuries before. History was all around me, taking me to a place I had never thought possible in my first year.

I grew up under the tutelage of Dr Seal, who took me under his wing and made me feel very much one of his Trinity ladies, even if my time in that honoured institution, at that stage of my Cambridge existence, was very much borrowed and always resulted in Cinderella having to return back to the New Hall pumpkin. Despite his fiery nature, I never felt anything but admiration for him. Nothing I have achieved in life would have been possible without him. The debt of gratitude I hold to this amazing don is immense and my bookcase still holds his book, 'The Emergence of Indian Nationalism'.

To this day, I will count his advice as some of the best that anyone has ever imparted to me, particularly memorable phrases such as, 'Nothing is ever all black or all white, but usually a little bit grey around the edges' and 'For goodness sake stop pussy-footing around and take your feet off the ground and jump'. That one was bestowed on me in the middle of a really non-committal essay that I had written about the Boer War, but was actually a life tip for me, which I immediately realised.

To his credit, Dr Seal was the one who also once said, 'You have a really hard time trying to look your age'. I am delighted to report that this particular trait has served me very well!

If truth be told, I fell far too much in love with the Indian sub-continent. Entering Anil's room was like being transported to another time and place, enriched by his most recent tales of trips to Delhi and to Goa, where he had a beach house, from which he would watch the Arab dhows sail past. Sometimes, he would talk of laying on the beach, being judged as to where he should be placed in the Indian caste system, according to the colour of his skin. Supervisions were incredible, vibrant, enchanting, full of life drawn from another culture and an escape from everything else in my life. I would literally float on air having spent time with Dr Seal, feeling like a princess or a Maharani, rather than who I actually was.

I learned all about the chapatti theory of the Indian mutiny, had my mind changed about the role of the sepoys, was introduced to the political ambitions of Jinnah and tutored on the impact of Mahatma Gandhi, by someone with links to his descendants. It was an amazing adventure, whether I was focusing on life in busy Calcutta, or the life of the Raj's ladies sipping tea in Srinagar.

With this vibrant Indian fix filling my veins each week, my life changed completely, even beyond Trinity College. In my first year, I spotted a male student, who would cycle around Cambridge with a big black overcoat flapping in the wind. I was totally transfixed by his wild Heathcliff looks – a mix of Sylvester Stallone and a young Paul McCartney. No matter where I went, he would spookily seem to appear, even arriving by the coffee machine in the geography department on a freezing February morning, when my friend had decided to post several Valentine's cards. Incredibly, at a college disco in my second year, I was dancing away when tapped on the shoulder and invited to dance with someone else, rather than myself. It was 'Heathcliff' and he transpired to be a medical student at Fitzwilliam College.

The third piece in the jigsaw of the life by the age of 21, when I can honestly say that I had everything I ever wanted with the two A's (Anil and my medical student), was slotted into place during the summer holidays between my second and third years. That summer, my family spent a month in Sri Lanka, not even a well-known place on the tourist map, but a destination in its infancy, offering fabulous tour and beach holidays at a good price.

A most peculiar thing happened to me by the luggage carousel at Colombo airport, while reaching out for my battered green (and amazingly small) suitcase, for one who now doesn't know the meaning of travelling light! A large brown hand had already grabbed my luggage and, as I stood up from my grasping and lurching-forward-for-suitcase position, I came face to face with our tour guide, Mr S. I experienced a really strange sensation, when I looked him in the eyes and Mr S would undoubtedly say that it was fate. It felt as if our stories would be entwined in some strange way. And so it proved.

That holiday changed who I was and how I viewed the world thereafter. The tour party was packed with colourful characters, from three gays from Brighton, to two spinsters, who clearly had their heart set on Mr S. We had three tour guides, who would each assist us at the many points of cultural interest at which we stopped, but it was mainly Mr S who would take to the crackling microphone in the old, classic bus that rattled us around the island, with exhaust pipe shaking and a strange vibration of the back seat, on which my family had taken up residence.

Maybe it was his soothing tones that would send us to sleep back there, or the rhythm of the bus carriage on the wonky back axle, or maybe just the heat and dust of a Sri Lankan summer approaching monsoon season, but whatever it was, it never detracted from the experience, whether we were slamming on the brakes to stop on a remote jungle road and ask a villager if he would let us all take an impromptu, bareback elephant ride, or cracking open coconuts in some rural plantation.

Again, Mr S was truly fascinating to me, whether looking me in the eye, as if trying to make me blush while he talked about lotus leaves as a form of contraceptive, or urging me to eat fiery Sri Lankan curry, rather than joining the 'pariah' omelette table of non-curry eaters! In his flowery Sri Lankan shirt, his description of the Buddhist faith made perfect sense to me, while his charm, personality and vibrant outlook wooed the spinsters, the gays, the straight members of our party and myself alike. We were, undoubtedly, all under his spell.

Little wonder then that the majority of us – other than my Nan, my mother and one of the gays – decided to tackle the health and safety nightmare that was the hill fortress of Sigiriya. To say I have never been more terrified in my life of any 'challenge' put before me is an understatement, but to also say that, if Mr S was going to the top so was I, is a truism.

If you don't know the story of Sigiriya, let me explain. Sigiriya stands for 'Lion's Rock' in Sinhalese and it is one of the eight world heritage sites of Sri Lanka. In its lifetime, it has been a monastery, a fortress and a complex city built into a massive, granite rock that is simply daunting. It stands 180m high and consists of various 'levels' – moats, walls and gardens at the base (where I left my mother) and where the local kids were swarming around in their usual manner asking for bonbons and telling me I looked like Princess Diana! From there, one finds a lower palace the next level up, then the Lion Gate and the mirror wall with its famous frescoes on a mid-level terrace. Finally, and only for the very intrepid rock climber, the remains of an upper palace are found on the flat top of the rock.

It was explained to us that we could quit at any stage and wait for Mr S to come back to reclaim us, but all the ladies were vying to get to the top with him, myself and my sister included. As we began the first stage of the ascent we lost one of the gays, as he froze halfway up a vertical metal ladder and had to be 'rescued' and taken back to ground level. I think this was purely due to the nature of the sheer climb, whereas I was climbing directly above Steve the metallurgist, who decided to add a running commentary to this part of the ascent, by telling me that he didn't like the look of the metalwork, which looked decidedly unsafe and downright dodgy! As his travelling partner, Steve the transport policeman, was in hot pursuit on the steps, he didn't get the option to quit either, despite his metallurgy insights.

After our first drop out had been rescued, we continued, getting a false sense of security as we came to the frescoes and caves, which seemed to offer little danger. It was all uphill from there, however, literally walking up a shiny smooth rock face with nothing to stop us from sliding off the edge and just a few worn footholds, or rather grooves in the granite purporting to be footholds, already occupied by children looking to make pocket money, by offering to assist the mad tourists climbing up this health and safety nightmare.

How we made it up to the palace at the top goodness knows, but how we made it back down again is even more of a puzzle, the propensity to slip and slide off the edge being even greater and all the footholds now occupied by either those travelling up or the wannabe guides offering assistance for a few rupees. The views from the top of Sigiriya were incredible, but the real kudos was in having been one of the few survivors to get that far and proved my worth to Mr S! One thing's for sure – nothing would ever possess me to do it again, however much safety standards may have improved over the years.

As we moved on in our rickety tour bus to Kandy and the Temple of the Tooth, we experienced all the joy of leaving our shoes on board and trailing through the dark streets of Kandy through cow dung and other refuse to see the famous 'tooth'. We eventually returned to the tour bus filthy, smelling of cow dung and in no mood to put our shoes back on!

Next we were off to the hill country where, one evening, we all took to the rather cold hotel pool. Maybe this was the start of my demise, however, as the next stop was the English hill station of Nuwara Eliya, where we would experience dinner in the colonial hill club, where waiters would be dressed in full costume and white gloves and where the ambience would be that of life in colonial Ceylon. We had travelled through the tea plantations and had the afternoon at leisure in the small town, the main feature of which was a botanical garden-style park. I can remember feeling intensely cold in the park, almost chilled to the core, but nobody took any notice. We went back to the hill club and started to dress for dinner, being advised that the evening would commence with traditional Sri Lankan music and dance at the neighbouring hotel.

I can recall entering a large room, literally spinning before me, but I sat down and hoped things would become less hazy. Then they started

– the drums, the interminable drums, banging and beating and driving me dizzy and faint, losing the will to live as each beat rang out and cymbals crashed and feet stomped. I stood up and remember saying, 'It's the drums, the drums', as I staggered out of the room. Nobody raised an eyebrow, the rest of my family transfixed by the same colourful costumes and headdresses whirling around the room that were driving me to distraction.

The reception area was completely empty as I staggered into it, but I remember it being composed of white and cream marble and there being a green chaise longue, on to which I collapsed, holding my head and closing my eyes to stop the room spinning. My moment of relative calm was rudely interrupted. A bony finger poked into my flesh and I opened my eyes to see a witch-like creature staring down at me. 'Arrack, Arrack', she muttered in a kind of incantation-like way, as she continued to poke at me and stare.

I realised that she thought I was drunk on the hugely alcoholic and potent local Sri Lankan drink made from fermented palm sap, so I shook my head and muttered, 'I've not had any Arrack'. I am not sure whether I screamed in the end as the poking continued, but to my rescue came my knight in shining armour, Mr S, who made his appearance in the nick of time. He swept me up and started to virtually drag me to the door, calling one of his colleagues to summon assistance. Together, the three of us started to head back to the hotel.

I am not sure how many times I was sick en route, but it wasn't good, particularly in a colonial hill club. Allegedly, I left a trail behind me all the way up the beautifully polished wooden floor, probably exquisite teak or mahogany! Mr S got me back into my room and started telling me that he continuously worried about me as I ate like a mouse and never finished a meal. 'This is why you are so ill, because you don't eat', he kept stressing, as we waited maybe an hour before the cavalry arrived, the musical performance having ended and my family finally realising I was missing!

I never had the pleasure of seeing the waiters in their white gloves and colonial costumes. Everyone else went to dinner, leaving me in the bedroom still being violently sick. A very sweet member of staff kept appearing and kept saying, 'Do you want anything to eat Madam', which I clearly didn't, but for some reason, in true Paddington Bear mode, I kept replying, 'Marmalade sandwiches', the only thing I ever want to eat when I am really ill.

We got past midnight and there were worried faces all round. In the end, a doctor was called, though goodness knows where they found him, as we were literally in the wilds of Sri Lanka. The newly found doctor examined me and determined that I had to be moved for urgent medical attention.

It was by now about 1am and I had to get up and get dressed in whatever anyone could find to put on me. I had my nightdress, my father's silk dressing gown, a pair of slippers and goodness knows what else – a mishmash of clothing that had been hurriedly put together to try to keep me warm. I may have been ill, but I wasn't totally out of it and remember the deep embarrassment of encountering the two Steves in the corridor, both looking at me as if I was going to die, or at least be forever known as being a walking fashion disaster!

Four of us – myself, my father, the guide and the doctor – piled into the tiniest little car and started to drive, in the middle of the Sri Lankan night, up hill roads that had no lighting, no markings and certainly no road surface given the bumping that resulted. We seemingly climbed up and up, with no real explanation as to where I was being taken and just a constant repetition of one phrase by the doctor, 'I want you to know that I am not a witch doctor: I trained at The Middlesex'.

I may have been semi-dazed and not entirely compos mentis, but I was in a better state than the rest of the people at the place to which I was taken. 'Aren't they all wearing straitjackets' was the first thing I said to my father, having sat staring at the scene for about 10 minutes. I don't think he even replied, just nodding his head and wearing a look on his face that said he had hoped I wouldn't realise.

Strange shrieking and wailing punctuated the silence as staff led various straitjacket-wearing people around. I looked down at my terrible garb and reflected that I probably didn't look out of place in this hilltop mental asylum.

Asking to use the bathroom was a very big mistake and I will never forget the bath full of brown sludge that awaited me as I entered the room. I returned to my father looking white and telling him I'd never seen anything more revolting. By this point, the non-witch doctor, who had trained at The Middlesex, had informed me that I had a severe infection of the colon, which needed urgent injections and that this was the only place for miles that had the necessary medication. I didn't argue, duly receiving injections, which I was told would probably make me very drowsy and weak.

I suppose we must have escaped the sanatorium at some point after that, but I don't remember the return journey back down the mountain roads. I just recall getting up the next day and being told that the tour party had to move on. The other breaking news was that Mr S had decreed that I should leave my place on the back seat and spend the final three days of the tour sitting next to him on the front seat. I could feel the daggers in my back from the two spinsters two rows behind!

To say that these were three days that changed my entire life is probably an understatement. Although very weak after the asylum visit and the injections, I somehow managed to stay awake better on the front seat than I had on the back and had literally hours to learn all about Mr S and his life. We talked endlessly about his Chinese wife and his children, about his life in Colombo and, more importantly, about my life. He probed into areas such as why I didn't eat, why I lacked confidence, what I wanted to do with my life and much, much more. He had noticed and observed so much that I didn't ever communicate verbally and having truths relayed back to you is quite something when you are just about to turn 20 and starting out in life.

There were more stunning and unspoilt sights to see, but I had to take it slowly and was always informed that I should remain seated at the front. Time was ticking down to the end of the tour, with what was to follow being 2.5 weeks on the beach in Bentota. The conversation started to change, beginning with a discussion about the Tamil Tigers and their fight for political recognition. Mr S began to tell me about Jaffna, located at the top of the island and a bit of a Tamil stronghold. He firstly explained that he would be heading there with his family when the tour ended. Then, as the hours passed, he suddenly asked me to go to Jaffna with them, rather than going to Bentota.

This was a true bolt from the blue. It was explained to me over and over again that he wanted me to see more of Sri Lanka, spend time with a Sri Lankan family to see the true character of the country and also get over all the things that he felt were holding me back – primarily my lack of confidence and anorexia, I guess. I was truly flattered, but at that point in time did something that has been a trend throughout my life: I thought what other people would say. I couldn't expect my family to let me go off to Jaffna, with what was virtually a complete stranger, when they had paid for me to have my holiday with them in Bentota. I knew that I simply couldn't ask them and that they wouldn't understand, even if I tried to explain.

Despite being asked several times to re-consider and join Mr S and his family in Jaffna, I had to decline and so it was that I had to say good-bye to this spiritual man in a hotel lobby in Bentota, collecting my case from him and dying a little inside as the Jaffna dream faded from sight and the tour bus rattled out of sight for the last time. What I did have in my possession was a business card, which I treasured in a black wallet for many years, never throwing it away or forgetting where it was. That would prove as significant as the legacy of my time in Sri Lanka.

Chapter 2
THE RAJ, THE RAVING MAD &
ROMANCING

B y the time I returned to Cambridge for my third year, I was well and truly fired up by the history of Asia, so little wonder then that I threw myself into my Indian history studies with massive amounts of enthusiasm. My supervisions were as entertaining and captivating as ever and I was now living in a delightful, modern house in the grounds of New Hall, accessed by a woodland path, which ran behind the library.

Following my lectures from Mr S, I had begun to eat a bit more, to the extent that I even attempted a meal that I received free-of-charge for doing library duty once a week.

My other main modules for this year concerned public perceptions of Queen Victoria, as conveyed by the Victorian media, and a literally novel module, which studied perceptions of the industrial revolution conveyed through literature of the time. This was so revolutionary that one of our lectures was screened on ITV's 'World in Action', on which my left arm appeared – one of many body parts to have been shown on TV over the years!

When I look back, both of these courses were, in their own ways, about PR: public relations of the early Victorian kind and astute messaging on the behalf of authors/propagandists of their time. Both courses were really interesting, though having to deal with microfiche machines to view 'The Times' of 1901 or some other Victorian year was an absolute nightmare, involving reels of film, technical skills when it came to loading it up and lots of the patience that I just don't have! Students have it very easy these days!

I boldly decided to apply for a scholarship, which would enable me to study at the University of Michigan. I shared this idea with Anil, who offered to write a reference. This was absolutely glowing and when the judging came round in February, I was awarded the three-year scholarship. The issue with this was that I was by now wholly in love with India and the idea of becoming a research student, studying under Anil. My whole life was now pretty wrapped up with him in some way or another. He had firstly asked me to set up a network of readers for a blind African student at Trinity and I, and the others that I recruited, would go and read to him on a rota basis. Furthermore, he had introduced me to his secretary, with a view to me becoming a friend to her daughter, who had suffered brain damage having contracted meningitis as a five year old. Consequently, I found myself taking this young woman to the cinema, or out for a coffee, or spending time at her home.

Additionally, I would sometimes be invited to special occasions organised by Anil. One was particularly memorable, as it fell out of term time, but I had stayed on for a few days and ambitiously decided to cycle down to Trinity in a long evening frock. Halfway through my journey, the frock caught in the chain and I was virtually catapulted over the handlebars, ending up in a heap on the floor – not a particularly auspicious or glamorous start to the evening, but maybe the word 'catapult' was rooted in my brain for eternity! It was to become the name of my PR consultancy.

Things went from bad to worse, as the menu included scallops, which I had eaten with gay abandon in America in the past, but which suddenly decided to become one of the fish dishes to which I am highly allergic. This allergy had affected me since being a child in relation to salmon, but gradually more and more things were disappearing from the 'green list' and becoming decidedly red-listed.

I spent the whole night throwing up and wishing I had never gone out. This was really the first sign of an allergy that would greatly affect my diet and my life in years to come.

So with one thing and another, when awarded the scholarship, I had changed my mind and wanted to stay in Cambridge as one of Anil's PhD students. I explained this to him and I think he was pleased. He began making all sorts of plans as to what I could study for my thesis and even started talking about me living in a new flat that he had built in New Delhi, as I would have to spend time studying history there, as well as in Cambridge.

Things just moved on so fast that year. I started seriously seeing 'Heathcliff' on a regular basis, heading out to some of the weirdest pubs in Cambridge, where typically there was some sort of music scene that was rock, punk or heavy metal orientated. These were typically the 'town' rather than the 'gown' establishments and actually quite rough. That was him though – wild, unrestrained, unpredictable, hooked on playing his keyboards and playing gigs in various small venues – the complete opposite to me at that time.

During my third year, I also took up a new hobby. By this time I'd done the rowing thing, having been a hopeless bow and hating having to get out on the river at 6.00am in the freezing cold in winter, having already had to cycle out to the boathouses. Catching a crab just made the whole thing a lot more painful.

My friend and I had also auditioned to appear in a production of 'Zigger Zagger', as we felt we really should tread the boards and the footie theme appealed to me. Luckily, we didn't have any success, as goodness knows how that would have turned out. It was a definite 'don't call us' moment and one which proved that my future career was not going to be on the stage, despite all my formative years spent in the Winifred Clarkson School of Dance in Blackpool and my gold medal for character dancing!

My main interest of year three was that of writing for the University newspaper, 'Stop Press', edited that year by Gideon Rachman. If I recall correctly, the journalist Andrew Rawnsley was also writing for it. We would meet in a pub on Monday lunchtime, to have our stories allocated and then depart and get the story together before submitting it to Gideon.

I loved writing for 'Stop Press'. It gave me my first buzz of seeing my words in print and I suppose laid the foundations for my future career in PR. One of my first stories was about a cat, which had got into a sub-station and caused a loss of power to virtually the whole of Cambridge.

Another was about my boyfriend's band – victims of instrument theft. My most challenging, however, and the story that nobody put their hands up for at the editorial meeting, concerned the infamous porter, 'Bob the Beast', who had terrorised undergraduates for years. Bob was about to retire and someone had to interview him, to find out how he'd earned his name!

I must admit that I went to interview 'Bob the Beast' with a fair degree of fear and trepidation in my heart, but well armed with the questions I wanted to pose. As it turned out, he was reasonably amiable, or at least didn't bark at me in the way I had expected. Once my story was filed, I had truly earned my stripes with the 'Stop Pressers'!

Things were always very strange in our college house, in which around 10 of us lived. One of the most surreal events came about when a flatmate had her heart broken when her fiancé called off their wedding. This was February and the wedding had been set for September. To get over the pain of it all, she decided to throw a medieval party in the house, turning one of her maroon velvet bridesmaid's dresses into a robe worthy of Guinevere or Maid Marian and making herself a very impressive conical hat. My 'grinning friend' chose to turn herself into a knight and covered herself in a most remarkable way with tin foil. I think I just went as myself and was a wench!

The best news underpinning this party was that the broken-hearted girl had already bought all the champagne and other booze for the wedding. Believe me, every drop of the wedding alcohol was drunk that night by we bawdy strumpets, many of us ex-members of the rowing club, where getting legless was part of the initiation ceremony!

As the spring term came round, one of the most important things for me to do was to get myself some May Ball tickets, having not been to a May Ball in either of my first two years, though I had had my chance with a student from Queen's in my first year and had hoped that a friend of mine, Nick, might invite me in the second year. He didn't, though he did stagger up the hill with broken ribs to come to a Christmas dinner with me, so give the man some credit.

While all these thoughts about buying two May Ball tickets, and who to go with, were flying around my head, as it was hardly 'Heathcliff's' sort of do, a strange thing happened. Valentine's Day came along and I received a black card, in a black envelope and addressed in silver ink. The lyrics to the Dire Straits song, 'Romeo and Juliet', had also been beautifully written out on the card in silver ink. I was absolutely dumbfounded. What happened next explains why I opted for a career in PR, rather than detective work!

I knew for sure that 'Heathcliff' wouldn't have done anything as romantic as this! Jumping to conclusions, which I am allegedly very good at, I got it into my head that it might be a guy in one of my lecture classes, who I'd been chatting to quite a lot just prior to this occurrence. In good Mata Hari style, to test out this theory, I manufactured a ridiculous conversation with him as he was trying to do his satchel up. 'Are you in dire straits by any chance?' I simpered, looking knowingly into his eyes. I gave him a good 10 seconds to reply and remember a totally blank look crossing his face, in utter bewilderment at my completely random question.

'I don't think so', he eventually said, still looking bemused. With my great powers of detection, I instantly knew that my romantic missive had nothing to do with him, as he departed the room nervously, looking over his shoulder to see if I was following him!

Having failed with suspect number 1, the suspense was killing me. I couldn't think of anyone else to approach with my bizarre 'dire straits' conversation, so decided to put a message in 'Stop Press'. It read 'Dire Straits declare yourself!' Within about a day of it being printed, I received another missive in my pigeonhole, this time gold ink on green card. On this occasion it was a verse from U2's 'New Year's Day'. I was even more nonplussed, so had to resort to yet another advert asking for the person to reveal their identity.

Racing away with your imagination is a sure way to end up with a massive disappointment on your hands and so it proved. It transpired that the card was from a sort of friend of mine, P, who I had met when my friend and I travelled with the team to watch the very first Rugby League Blues match in Fulham. P was a leading light in the squad, but the truth was that after our trip, it was with Nick-with-broken-ribs that I struck up a friendship. Both P and Nick were in my beloved St John's at the time, but by now Nick had graduated and taken up a career as a policeman. He dropped out within weeks, but was still in line to potentially be a spy, by virtue of an interview with MI5 and the fact that he spoke Russian!

I was supposed to have sussed that P had danced with me to the tune of New Year's Day, but to be honest, I couldn't even remember dancing with him. Perhaps his affection sprung from the fact that, having discovered he was ill the previous summer, I had bought him this thing called an Ugly Mug. That had proved an unfortunate purchase, or so I thought, as he had looked at it and, I'm pretty sure, thought I was being incredibly rude about his appearance.

Having made such a song and dance about discovering my admirer's identity, I had to do some serious backtracking after the declaration, but 'Heathcliff' rode to the rescue, suddenly deciding to abandon leather trousers and jacket for the night and dress up in tux and dicky bow. It was somewhat unfortunate that my tickets were for the St John's May Ball. I do recall that poor 'Dire Straits' was left stranded alone by the side of the dance floor for half the night. It was not the last time I would witness that blank expression and look in his eyes, as I shall reveal later.

As it was, however, the evening went swimmingly, maybe the most memorable highlight being the fact that I found myself the only one twirling around in the middle of a dance floor at 3am, as I was determined we would both make it on to the Survivors' Photo (which we did). 'Heathcliff' was looking worse for wear and sitting on a chair by the edge of the dance floor, when the American rocker, Steve Gibbons, who'd headlined, suddenly strolled up, grabbed me and said, 'Are you coming back with me then honey?'

I can swear that I'd never seen the laid back 'Heathcliff' move as fast, as be wrestled me out of the rocker's grasp with the words 'No she's ****ing not!'

So the May Ball Survivors photo showed us surviving at 6am and we carried on surviving for quite some time, with me spending virtually a whole summer at his north Leeds home, admittedly having to listen to him playing the piano for half of it! The most life-changing thing he did for me that summer was to get me eating curry. Being a medic and destined to start being a junior doctor, he took it upon himself to nurture me into the curry-eating world by taking me to the dodgiest curry house in Bradford and treating me to a vindaloo! He claimed it was essential, if I was to go to India and I did kind of see the logic in that, so the omelette-eater pariah turned curry eater after all, allowing him to force feed me the vindaloo until I could actually start to appreciate it! I have stayed in love with curry ever since, however revolting the curry house was and however sick I felt a little later!

Things were made much easier after the August of that year by my 21st birthday present. I actually had two 21st birthday celebrations, a garden party in Cambridge in the June and then my family party in August. I think all garden party attendees will vividly remember the phenomenal punch. I'd taken lots of advice and soaked strawberries for hours in a concoction of alcohol, before adding them to the mixture of yet more alcohol. To say I was as pleased as punch with it was an understatement as well as a pun – it was lethal! The daughter of Anil's secretary had been allowed to come to the party, but I was busy circulating around, so left her in the charge of two housemates. To my horror, when I returned, I found they'd allowed her to dig the alcohol-primed strawberries out of the punch and eat them!! She was virtually paralytic, incapable of standing up and totally giddy. Lots of water came to the rescue, as I tried to sober her up, while chastising my less-than-attentive housemates!

On my real birthday, I was given my true pride and joy – the only car I've ever felt emotionally attached to – Sophie. Sophie was a navy blue Ford Escort and was so named because her number plate contained SFV. She became my new best friend in Cambridge as, having graduated, I could apply to have a disc and become a car owner in Cambridge – something only allowed to an undergraduate if they had special needs.

I was on tenterhooks that summer waiting for news of my grant for my PhD studies and praying that I would still be in Cambridge. Eventually, the news came through from Anil and I was advised that I could become one of his 'Trinity ladies' at long last and have a room in a Trinity-owned graduate house opposite the rugby fields. Before I knew it, I was packing my bags again, this time into Sophie, and heading back to Cambridgeshire, parking a car, and not a bike, on a road I had cycled down thousands of times between The Seeley and New Hall. My heart was set on becoming an eternal student and growing old in the University Library.

The large student's house was a really odd place to live and I had to get to know a whole bunch of complete strangers, none of whom I had encountered as an undergraduate, as most had studied at Trinity. I soon met my next door neighbour, Jonathan and a tall, lanky and very blonde guy called Kevin, who had the attic room on the third floor. Jonathan and I were on the main landing area of the second floor and then there were other rooms down a very narrow, dark corridor, which also led to the bathroom. On the bottom level there was Adam and then Ginny, a veterinary student. I can't recall who was originally in the room below me.

I suppose the strangest aspect of the house related to its housekeepers. They were an elderly couple, who at times were joined by their porter son. He was a good laugh and coerced Kevin, Jonathan and myself into a darts team comprising porters and graduates. I was the only girl! We used to head out to various pubs around Cambridgeshire and take on whoever were our opponents in the 'league'. It wasn't very serious, but we had a reasonably good time doing it, even though, by this point, Kevin was becoming a major irritant to me. All these years later, we are still in touch and nothing much has changed on that front!

While the son was easy to get along with, his father was a little trickier to deal with. Dementia had set in, leaving him totally confused for the most part and, most definitely at night, believing that he was still a Trinity porter. I often wonder if J K Rowling modelled Argus Filch on him, as the synergy is amazing. Luckily, his behaviour was reported by one of the boys first, or I might have screamed the house down. The tip-off was that he went round by dead of night, trying to open everyone's door, believing he was on locking up duties at college. This being the case, he had barged into someone's unlocked room, while they were sleeping and frightened the living daylights out of them. His other disturbing trick was to loiter in the very dark corridor between my landing and the bathroom, so if you came home late at night, you stood a chance of him leaping out of some doorway and saying, 'What time do you call this then?' or, 'Bit late isn't it', in a very spooky voice. Various strategies to get into the house without him seeing had to be adopted, as the alternative was truly terrifying.

Doorknob trying wasn't the only thing to keep me awake at night in the second term. A returning student, who had just landed back in Cambridge from India, moved into the room below mine and the first time I saw him he reminded me of a Bolshevik refugee,who'd spent a very cold winter in the wilds of Siberia. He had wild, wayward hair, dark-rimmed glasses and a black serge overcoat that I'm not sure I ever saw him take off. A scarf would be wound madly round his neck too, completing the look and feel of what I suppose you would today say was a prisoner of Azkaban, just to keep the Harry Potter theme going.

Anil realised that this student (A) was moving into our house, so suggested that I try to get to know him, as he had been working in New Delhi on his Indian history PhD. That was a total impossibility, as any conversation even vaguely approaching normality proved completely out of the question. He came and he went from his room with hardly a word to anyone, only returning very late into the night or early in the morning, but always ensuring that I, in the room above, knew the hour. His return would be accompanied by wild banshee type wailings, a throwing of items around the room, which would crash into the walls and sounds that were sub-human. I would have to put my pillow over my ears at times, as it was so disturbing, but the explanation was even more unnerving.

I discovered the reasons for all of this from Anil, having shared the A 'returning home' scenario with him. He informed me that A had suffered a severe case of hepatitis when in India and it was thought that it had made him a little mentally imbalanced. The care might also not have been too clever, or at least that is what I was led to believe. Lying there in bed and listening to the sounds of someone, who had suffered this fate in a country where infections were almost inevitable, literally made my blood run cold. I told myself that there was no way I wanted to end up like poor, unfortunate A.

This was the first seed of doubt in my mind about my research. Anil had produced an absolutely wonderful topic for me to study, combining literature with history and some of the most significant events in the history of the sub-continent. My task was to explore the historical

26

background of the 'Raj Quartet' by Paul Scott, with specific reference to 'The Jewel in the Crown'. This was to encompass everything – the culture of the Anglo-Indians and the colonials, the politicisation of India under Mahatma Gandhi, the ambitions of Jinnah, the role of Mountbatten and much more.

It was fascinating stuff and there were absolute tomes to wade through, in the form of records relating to the partition of India. My time was split between The Seeley, the UL (the University Library), the South East Asian Studies department, close to Queen's College and over the bridge from where they held the birdman contest each year, and the India Office in London.

Going down to London was a bit of a drag, usually entailing a stay in a pretty seedy hotel (all that could be afforded), with a tin of cold ravioli and a tin opener, to save money on food. I would then trek off Waterloo underground station via Tube the next morning and walk over the bridge to the India Office. Getting there early was a must, as formal requests for documents had to be submitted at the counter and these then took hours to appear. The later your arrival, the longer the interminable wait. You then had only a few hours to work on these massive research resources, before having to hand them back.

Anil informed me that he wanted to get his Commonwealth grant scheme for foreign students off the ground and he would be away for substantial periods of time. He wasn't joking and his absence was much felt. However, he had given me a strategy to follow, which was to make friends with some of his older research students and pick up tips from them about how to approach things. The two names he recommended were both males whose names began with R. I will refer to them as R1 and R2.

I seem to recall meeting R1 fairly conventionally in the library and then going out for a few drinks with him in the evening. I found his company truly charming and his insights very valuable. If there was one thing R1 taught me, it was that life as an academic was hard, with years of being virtually penniless and then no guarantee of a position within the University.

The R2 experience was somewhat different. Having been told by Anil to seek out this person, I had to first discover who he was and didn't have much to go on. It took me a while, but some divine inspiration cascaded down on me one day, when I was working in the South East Asian Studies department. I became aware that a bespectacled individual with a mass of black wavy hair and a beige corduroy jacket was he.

I went over to where he working and tentatively introduced myself. I explained that I was one of Anil's research students and told R2 that Anil had suggested I get to know him, particularly as he would be back in India at the same time as I was destined to be there. Having made my introductions, I went back to my table and carried on studying. A short time after this, R2 approached and asked if I fancied going to lunch. I said that would be nice, thinking a trip to the nearby pub was on the cards. Instead, we walked further than I had expected, ending up at what was then one of the best restaurants in Cambridge, Angelina's.

This restaurant had always been way beyond my student budget, so I had never eaten there. It was naturally very quiet, partly because of its price tag and also because this was a lunchtime, mid-week. It all felt very uncomfortable sitting there amid the pristine white tablecloths and silver cutlery, with a waiter all to ourselves, who was clearly thinking what an odd couple we were. I began to fret about the bill that might result and which I would presumably need to go halves on. That thought was removed from my head when my 'host' told me to select whatever I wanted. I actually felt even more uncomfortable at that and tried to focus on the white doyleys and pristine tablecloths, rather than my lunch companion.

I left the restaurant feeling very much in his debt and really didn't know how to take my leave, having been treated to such a luxury. He was extremely courteous, but I still felt extremely awkward and that awkwardness just stayed with me thereafter, every time we met, whether he was instructing me on how Indians poured tea and when they added the milk, or inviting me to see Indian dance troupes performing at the theatre. By now, I was attempting to learn Hindi in the University language lab, as the countdown to Delhi was on. To be honest I never got much beyond 'my name is Jane' – mehra nam Jane-heh – but it was all becoming real.

Encounters became more numerous as he embraced the idea of taking me under his wing when I reached New Delhi. I almost felt that he wanted to be a substitute Anil. The more my new life in New Delhi was mentioned, the more I worried about it, even sweated cobs about it, thinking how he would literally be the only person I knew out there and there would be no real escape, no pretending not to be in when he knocked at the door and no excuses to be made as to why I couldn't do something. Exit strategies had already been devised when he came calling on me in my digs – very easy-to-do for him, as he lived fairly close at hand. I dreaded opening the door at times, as it meant being trapped.

Things came to a head when he suddenly invited me to dinner at his flat, much to the amusement of some of my housemates, who had noticed what was happening, or had encountered him wandering around the house when I wasn't in. I didn't like to hurt his feelings and refuse this invitation, but deep inside, I was absolutely dreading it. I felt like a fly walking in to a spider's web and literally had to psych myself up to going down there, having no idea what to expect.

What I most definitely hadn't expected was to find a dinner table all beautifully laid up for a feast and a sitar player sitting cross-legged on a cushion in the corner, playing his instrument throughout the meal! I found this immensely disconcerting and every time I tried to catch the sitar player's eye, to try to communicate that there was nothing going on here and there was no need to create a romantic mood, he would cast his eyes away and ignore my visual pleas. I ate like a mouse, feeling that I could be sick at any moment and too distracted by the craziness of the whole situation to have any appetite at all. My stomach was churning more with each note emanating from the sitar! The only thought running through my head was that this was the future that I was seeing: myself and R2 having numerous uncomfortable rendezvous like this, when I was a poor little English girl trying to cope with the pressures of living in New Delhi.

After a while, with the sitar player still doing his thing and R2 hardly having said a word during this splendid occasion, as if words would ruin the seductive mood being set, I felt compelled to jump out of my seat. I made some feeble excuses and was escorted down the stairs and out to the front gate, from where I could still hear the sitar player carrying on regardless. I could feel a lurch towards me coming on from R2, so swiftly took a step away and turned on my heels, scampering up the road as fast as I could! I hardly saw R2 after that night, so never explained my horrendous rudeness, induced by panic!

Following this incident, the pressure on my mind was huge. I had A screaming blue murder every night in the room below, was coming up with strategies to avoid R2 like the plague, couldn't talk to Anil because he was overseas and had the nagging doubt planted by R1 that all of this would be for nothing.

I nearly didn't have to make any decisions on my future, however, thanks to an appalling incident on the A1 when travelling back home for Christmas. I had half the contents of my room in the back seat of Sophie, with a pile of coat hangers on top of all the boxes and cases. The weather was absolutely foul, with heavy rain making it hard to see much of the road. I was travelling reasonably fast in the third lane, when I suddenly lost all control of the car, which started to veer at a great speed right across the two inner lanes and on to the hard shoulder. I just couldn't seem to stop it and started heading up a steep, grass embankment, trying to steer the car the other way, but knowing that I was virtually tipped up, with the roof on the grass and, at this point, with coat hangers flying round my head. Immediately, after that, I came down from the embankment, as if in slow motion, and headed straight across all three lanes of the A1 again. This time I ended up at the central reservation, where I finally got control and somehow managed to again get across all lanes back to the hard shoulder.

I just burst into tears, wondering how on earth I had survived. I got out in the pouring rain to find my back tyre completely punctured. I was totally shell-shocked and started walking up the hard shoulder, suddenly becoming aware that a lorry had pulled up ahead of me. As I reached it, the driver told me to jump in, which I did without even considering what the consequences of that might be. He told me he had heard about what had happened on his CB Radio, with a lorry driver heading in the opposite direction describing the incident. He had looked out for me, to see if he could help. He said he could take me to a truck stop further up the road, which he dutifully did. Without his assistance, goodness knows what might have happened.

I was given tea with copious amounts of sugar, to try to treat the shock, and someone rang my father. He had only come out of hospital a short time before, having had a leg operation, but he somehow managed to drive all the way to Newark to get me. The car had to be transported back, as it was in a terrible state, covered in mud and grass from roof to doorsills. Nobody really knew what damage had been done. As it transpired, there was very little damage, other than the tyre, thanks to all the rain and mud on the embankment. When the tyre was inspected, it contained a metal bar about a foot long and 1.5 inches wide, which must have been flipped up by the front tyre and pushed straight into the back one. My father still has that bar somewhere.

I lived to tell the tale, but inside I was caving in. I couldn't sleep for worrying about the research, life in New Delhi and the risk of hepatitis and then the fears over ever finding a post at the University. I knew I couldn't go ahead with it, but the problem was that I had to break this to Anil.

I had to wait until he was back from one of his overseas trips. He was his usual ebullient self, late for our meeting, although by now I could get into his rooms without sitting on the stairs. He was full of life and started telling me how the flat he was developing for me in New Delhi was coming along. I had to stop him and start to explain and, once I did, it all came pouring out. He was silent and I could tell that I'd dropped a bombshell. It also really hit me that I was going to lose all those precious moments, dashing around in the green Mercedes that once got him to the bottom of Greece in a hurry and hearing about his latest adventures in various far-flung places. The pain was immense.

May came along and as a good social secretary to the Graduates' Committee, I had organised the end-of-term court party – drinks in the corner of Neville Court. This was across the courtyard from Anil's rooms and took place the night before I was due to leave. We'd already sort of said our goodbyes, but I knew it wasn't enough and I had to do more. I looked up at his window and thought I saw him looking down into the courtyard. I left the drinks party and headed up the staircase that had come to mean so much to me during my years at Cambridge.

At the top, the door to his room was ajar, so I knocked and he came to see who was there. I was carrying some chocolates I had bought for him, but what I presented were my tears and I knew at that very moment that this was probably going to be the hardest thing I had ever done in my life, leaving him in that room, walking back down that staircase and out into the great unknown, with no real idea of where I was heading, or what I could be. I thought my heart was going to break into tiny pieces. I left a trail of teardrops on those beautiful stairs, as I looked at the glaziers' initials scratched into the glass for the very last time in my life. It was time to move on.

Chapter 3
GRADUATES, GEISHAS AND A GOPHER

I was floundering once I left Cambridge. Floundering on the Fylde Coast, with not an idea in my head of what I could do for a job other than pursuing a career in journalism. For that reason, I applied for the trainee reporters' scheme operated by both the Blackpool Gazette and the Lancashire Evening Post and received an interview at both.

Weirdly, there were massive front-page news disasters in each area on the days of my interviews at the respective papers. Despite this, my interview with the editors still went ahead, but there was a subdued mood in both newsrooms. I recall both editors asking whether I would feel comfortable knocking on the door of a relative of someone, who had died, to ask them for a quote and a photo. In both cases, I lied to myself and said this wouldn't bother me. One of the editors asked whether I would go through a file marked confidential, if left in someone's office alone and on the trail of a news story. Again, I think I said I would.

My answers must have been good ones, because I was offered a place at the training school and a position on the Fleetwood newspaper, on which young journalists cut their teeth. Times were hard, however, with the country in a recessionary dip. Before I even got a chance to take up the position, the training programme was suspended and I had no role to go to. Had it not been for this situation, I would probably never have entered the world of PR.

My mother took charge. She brandished the evening school course list and told me I should go and sign up for typing lessons, so that I could get a job as a secretary. I had no choice but to go along to do this, Blackpool and Fylde College being just a few fields away behind our house. I didn't want to study on this course one little bit, but had, in all honesty, lost the will to fight.

When I arrived to enrol, the tutor looked at my form and then introduced herself as the mother of a friend called Jackie, who had been at Cambridge with me as an undergraduate. Although Jackie and I had completed our degree course at the same time, she had been a year above me at school and had been forced to take a year out by King's College. She had worked in the library and was apparently doing the same again, being unable to get a job. Her mother informed me that she was enrolling for a full-time graduate secretarial course and suggested that I do the same.

I had been reasonably friendly with Jackie at Uni, given that she was the only other person who had come from Fleetwood Grammar School. She had studied English at King's and had a fiancé called Paul at Downing College. They had an up and down relationship and I had been delighted that, during one of the downs, I had inherited the ticket to the prestigious King's College carol service, which would have been destined for him! Tickets for that were like gold dust, so I had always found his timing exquisite!

Jackie had also introduced me to a friend of hers called Michael, who studied Economics at King's and also had the privilege of wearing the glamorous purple scarf that I coveted in preference to my black, blue, red and yellow New Hall monstrosity. For quite a while, I had called him 'The Snow White Man', as I had first encountered him when locking up by bicycle in the bike stands between King's Parade and Cambridge market, no doubt during one of my many trips to the Andy's Records' market stall, which was an absolute magnet for me. Little did I know that my lucrative patronage would underpin the growth of a big East Anglian music empire in years to come!

The reason for calling him 'The Snow White Man' was that he had been en route to the cinema with Jackie to see the Disney classic on that day. Jackie had never given him a name and it really amused him to be called this. The introduction was to prove so valuable to me in the coming years.

On this basis, I didn't mind the idea of enrolling for the full-time course with Jackie, who I discovered had now finally broken up with Paul. I went home and informed my mother, who seemed highly satisfied.

The graduate secretarial course ran from a Monday afternoon to a Friday lunchtime each week in term and wannabe PAs and executive secretaries came from all over the country to study on it. I can't say that the goal of being a PA was at any time in my sights, while studying on this course. In fact, there were bits I absolutely detested, in particular Monday afternoon 'Office Practice'. To me, 'Office Practice' featured the most mundane tasks you could ever imagine doing in the course of a working day – learning how to put a roll in the adding up machine, understanding the principles of filing, even changing the words on a rubber stamp. I was always bored out of my skull during this lesson and yet terrified of the teacher at the same time. My mind would wander continuously and I would literally watch the clock ticking down the two hours of hell that we had to endure.

The same teacher taught typing, but was never as omni-present in the typing class as she was when dealing with the myriad of mediocrity in the 'Office Practice' lesson. Once we had learned how to touch type and use all of our fingers to type without looking at the keyboard, using 'The Quick Brown Fox' methodology, it was actually a breeze and all about speed. That I could do, the competitive side in me coming out each typing lesson, to enable me to record the top or joint top words per minute (wpm) typed in the allocated time.

Similarly, I found shorthand exciting, as it was like learning a language. I soon developed a very quick shorthand speed and again treated that as a sort of cycling time trial, whizzing my pencil across the page as fast as I could, to get everything logged in code, before proceeding to transcribe it back into English.

As for the rest of the course, it was just a passing of time for me, with no real purpose. I just wanted to get through the week and play badminton in the college's sports hall on Friday lunchtime, before packing up for the weekend.

Earning some form of income was pretty important and, at this point, my sister was a waitress in the restaurant of a pub colloquially known as 'The Vic', which was (and still is) on the main road leading into Cleveleys.

This was a really traditional and very large pub, mainly serving local residents and not particularly trendy at all. However, it transformed itself on Friday nights with the influx of some pretty fit young guys, including Tony who had been the school heartthrob in the sixth form. On a Sunday night, it just became a completely different venue, packed to the rafters with people piling in from all over the place to listen to the live band.

I went along for an interview with T the manager, a quirky, older and single guy, who had a strange turn of phrase, but was actually very fair and kind. There was also a manic chef and the Queen Bee barmaid, who had been there years. My sister wasn't old enough to work in the bar, but I was, and that was where I was placed.

I did have 'previous', which probably assisted this successful acquisition of a job, as I had spent my second Christmas holidays from Uni working at a really trendy pub at the time called 'The Buccaneer'. That had come about because the previous year my father had banned me from working in a pub and forced me to become a Christmas postman. That was probably the only year that the Fylde Coast had about two feet of snow, leading to me having to deliver post in my red jeans (so my mother would be able to find me if I got stuck in a snowdrift) and being forced to leap over walls and gates, taking my life in my hands, because I couldn't open any gates thanks to the snow!

I loved working in the bar – I think it was probably in my blood from my days in and around the bar at my Nan's hotel. I treated serving as a challenge too, preparing as many drinks in a round as I could at once, totting everything up perfectly in my head, working out the change like clockwork and moving on to the next customer. I did work the bar like lightning and my tip jar was always heaving, as I did it all with a friendly exchange with the customer, while working my magic with the pouring and the totting up. Others viewed my tip jar with immense envy, as I really coined it in and I had some customers, who would only be served by me, which was very flattering.

The manager caught on to this really quickly, but had other ambitions for me than those I shared for myself. One of his constant turns of phrase was delivered about every two weeks when he would ring me at home and say, 'Jane, you're so sophisticated'. There was then always a pause. After a few seconds he would say, 'So, I was wondering if you would work in the cocktail bar tonight'. This was an invitation I always declined, having no wish to be stuck upstairs in the restaurant, losing out on my precious tips.

I think I managed to escape this fate because I did acquiesce to his other phone calls and would regularly cave in to work extra shifts, though I was really contracted to do Friday night, Saturday lunchtime, Saturday night and Sunday night. If not dragging me in for extra weekday shifts, he would suddenly ring and ask me if I would open up for him at 7pm, or work in 'The Vaults' on occasions, this being the sportsman's bar at the back. At times, he had me working nearly every night of the week.

Having been given this job, I convinced Jackie that she should join me, though she didn't do the Saturday lunchtime shift. That was something I could really have done without as well. The place was either as dead as a dodo, with myself, the chef and the manager trying to amuse ourselves until 2.30pm came along, or else hosting a couple of regulars perched on barstools and a few diners, who had wandered in for some pub grub.

The restaurant wasn't open at lunchtime, so that was the one occasion that I had to serve food. I absolutely hated doing that, having none of the waiting-on skills my sister had developed. I dreaded taking food to the table, because the chef would load up my arms with plates and there was a lot of carpet to traverse before any tables were reached. I knew disaster was only one topple away and so it proved. One Saturday lunchtime, the chef had intricately balanced four plates on my arms, for me to take to a table a long way from the bar. The long anticipated topple happened just as I reached it. One plate of scampi and chips went, followed by the other three, leaving a mound of fried food under the table and around the feet of the diners. I was absolutely mortified and got to my knees to try to retrieve the scampi, at which point, I was literally barged out of the way by the manager, flying under the table as if trying to leap on top of a bouncing rugby ball, as he headed towards the food.

'Never mind the scampi. Never mind the scampi', he urged like a man possessed. 'Just make sure you retrieve the tartar sauce packets'. He simultaneously dived into the piles of chips now deposited on the floor and came out triumphantly with four plastic packets. The diners' mouths literally fell open, as did mine!

As I was so 'sophisticated' and, consequently, frequently given the honour of opening up on a Saturday and Sunday night, I naturally managed to make the acquaintance of the almost resident alcoholic – always there to watch the till, while I went down for the ice. I have no idea how I felt about this, but he frequently asked me out, telling me that the person I was by then seeing was absolutely no good for me and that they had come to blows several years before and been sworn enemies since.

I definitely had my fan club. Another older guy lived opposite the entrance to Blackpool and Fylde College and he began to spookily tell me what time I had arrived for lessons, whether I'd been earlier than normal on certain days, or later on others. I suppose these days you would call it stalking, but I'm not sure that term had been invented then. I didn't mind too much, as he gave me massive tips!

There was also an older chap, who was almost blind and who was one of my Saturday lunchtime crew. He would seat himself at the bar, as one of the few things he could see was the illuminated beer pump. When talking to him, I realised that I was actually performing the role of a social worker.

While Jackie missed out on a lot of this colour that punctuated the day and early evenings, she most definitely shared the Sunday night experiences. I can't now remember the name of the band that played every week, perhaps because I could never actually see them from the bar! Literally, customers were packed in like sardines in this massive pub and, with no exaggeration, would be waiting for drinks, standing four deep, along every inch of the very long bar.

The stock of glasses would run out one hour into the evening and we would be scouring the shelves for that odd schooner that could maybe carry a whisky, or a traditional pot tankard that might be OK for a pint. It took courage to go out glass collecting, but if you summoned it up, it was literally a case of playing sumo without the suit, barging your way through the queue and then getting down on all fours to crawl under tables, where you would invariably find around 30 pint glasses all stacked up. Short skirts were not the best of ideas on a Sunday night!

You can imagine how many tips I earned on this night of the week, my speed of service during those periods when glasses were available being wholly appreciated by the queue. My regulars would always make a beeline for me, knowing that I could probably pour their drink while doing another order at the same time. I think I actually thrived on the adrenaline rush of Sunday nights, setting myself different challenges to accomplish, despite the incredible pressure.

The band was hugely popular, playing a variety of current and ret-ro classics, some of these being anthems such as 'Glad All Over' and 'Daydream Believer'. When we had no glasses to serve drinks in, we'd all just smile and sing along, maintaining the mood of the queue while we desperately waited for someone to get back on to their feet and emerge with 30 pint glasses retrieved from under a table!

What we all loved about the band was that they always played the same song as last orders passed and we were into drinking up time – a great bonus for us, as we never had time to check the clock. The song they always played at this point was Lulu's 'Shout' and the minute we heard that 'Weah-eh-eh-eh-eh-eh-eh-eh-ell'............. we all breathed a quick sigh of relief before pogo-ing up and down to the 'You make me wanna shout' bit.

Somehow, we'd managed to get through another night without being lynched and it was time to party, with the bar finally shut and no more glass seeking-out required for at least another week, once all were col-lected and put through the washer.

This mix of machination, mediocrity and mayhem filled my week from September to the following January, when things took another turn. By then, I had managed to achieve a typing speed of 120wpm and short-hand of 100wpm, which was pretty good in just a few months and the top grades in the class. As I'd remained on the mailing list of the Cambridge careers service, I received their latest appointments round up – just those appointments that recruitment consultants had reserved for Cambridge students. A position that talked about a Japanese firm in the City needing an executive secretary had caught my eye and I had sent in an applica-tion form. I was offered an interview in January.

Snow fell heavily just before my interview. I remember walking along the City pavements, slipping all over the place in my interview heels and hoping that I wouldn't take a tumble before being seen. Gresham Street, where the employer, New Japan Securities, was based, runs parallel with Cheapside, on which St Paul's Cathedral is situated. The nearest Tube station to the office was Bank and, indeed, the Bank of England was just a short hop away. The area is rich in social, political and financial history and the marbled, impressive buildings seemed to whisper of their secrets on that freezing cold January morning in the snow.

The main thrust of my interview centred around two main necessities – my ability to make green tea and my shorthand speed. I had no qualms about the second of these and duly produced my certification. When it came to the former, I adopted the 'how hard can it be' viewpoint and confidently declared that I would have absolutely no trouble making green tea. With this bright and breezy attitude to everything, I sailed through the interview and was appointed 'Executive Secretary' to the Chairman and directors of this Japanese stockbroking company, starting in February.

The main issue with this was, of course, accommodation, but you only need to know one person that you can camp out with and I did – the Snow White Man! By now, Michael was living and working in London, having sold out on his Marxist principles and his working class, Coventry upbringing to become an equities expert in The City. He was actually working a stone's throw from Gresham Street and living in a rather less than salubrious flat on a smallish ex-council estate in Southwark, which to outward appearance smacked of a set you might have seen featured in 'The Sweeney'! It was very grey, very concrete and very scary getting to and from it by dark: a walk that entailed passing under a railway bridge with very little lighting and many a scary shadow.

The flat had one bedroom only so my 'accommodation' was a blow-up bed on the floor of the small lounge, which Michael dutifully pumped up for me every night with a foot pump. I was continuously reminded that the flat was virtually under the arches of the railway line by the sound of trains rattling up the line and a station announcer, who would rudely awake me each morning. While 'squatting' here, I soon made the acquaintance of one of Michael's friends from Coventry – a dental student called Brian, who instantly annoyed me when I asked him to repeat what he'd said by saying, 'I'm not surprised you can't hear me with that crap in your ears'. As this referred to my favourite earrings of the time – fuchsia pink, chunky glass danglers – I was not amused and remembered this exchange with Brian for years after, much to Michael's amusement. He did have something to offer, however, namely passes to the canteen at Guy's, where he was studying dentistry. The food was good and cheap, so we couldn't really have asked for more.

I was extremely lucky to have parked myself upon Michael, as he knew exactly what it took to find a bedsit in London and imparted this knowledge to me. The trick involved situating oneself somewhere with some essential ingredients at hand – a very central Tube station, a phone box (we didn't have mobiles back then) and a newsagent or newspaper stall. Having pondered this at length with Michael, we determined that where I should be loitering, at around 11am each day, was 'Embankment', which had all three factors required for being ahead of the game when it came to flat hunting.

Good flats were at such a premium that the trick was to nab the very first edition of the 'Evening Standard' as it hit the newspapers stands, even before the string was cut on the bundle. What was then required was very fast speed-reading, to identify possible flats within the budget. These then had to be circled, before running to the phone booth and starting to dial all the prospective flat owners, so as to make appointments to view. Ideally, viewing would be achieved within the hour, hence the reason why I had to be situated at a 'useful' Tube station. From Embankment, I could hop straight on to the Circle, District, Northern and Bakerloo lines, thus reaching many different possible locations on the periphery of London, where flats were likely to be found, very quickly. There was definitely method in Michael's madness.

Naturally, as Bank sat on several of these lines, Embankment was a pretty good place for me to be situated, but to this day, there's something about that Tube station that I don't like. It doesn't have the windswept desolate attractiveness of Tottenham Court Road, or the buzz of Oxford Street: nor does it have the quirkiness of Covent Garden or the almost rural feel of Green Park. However, it served its purpose.

Day after day, I made appointments, going to see accommodation when I could by day, but then heading off in the evenings, if necessary. I saw a flat right by Chelsea FC, where I would have had to share with a single man living on his own and then one in Richmond, which just wasn't suitable. Michael then decided to accompany me at an evening appointment in Putney, where this time it was a single female looking for a flatmate.

This woman was the archetypal 1980s Yuppie, living in a fairly small flat, but one with exquisite furniture and not a thing out of place. The flat actually seemed too small for two people to share and how that would have worked goodness knows. As it was, this landlady didn't grasp the situation from the moment we arrived, somehow believing that Michael and I were trying to rent the room as a couple, no matter how much we tried to explain that this was not the case. She seemed to be floating around in a cloud of something – maybe some elicit substance, or maybe just a bubble, as she was totally devoid of any sense of reality. 'So what time would you be starting work?' she asked me in a refined, upper-class accent that could only be pronounced by someone, who hardly opened her mouth to speak. I replied that I would start work at 9am, at which she threw her hands up in horror and declared, 'Oh, darling, that is SO uncivilised'. Michael was killing himself with stifled laughter in the chair behind me, reverting to his Marxist principles, particularly when she then asked him what time he would be starting work. Once again, in unison, we reaffirmed that we were not a couple and he was only there as a friend helping me out. It was like talking to the wall. We both left there in fits of giggles, leaving the 'landlady' in as equally a confused state as the one in which we had found her and still floating around in her bubble.

I was beginning to get a little desperate now. I hadn't yet started work, but the date was looming and I was still having my bed blown up for me every night by Michael, getting to know every intonation of the platform announcer's voice and becoming more and more frightened every time I returned to the flat in the darkness of January evenings. I'd already encountered a few undesirables under the arches and really didn't feel that safe.

Luckily, things were about to change. As usual, I had based myself at

Embankment, but on this particular day, I spotted an advert that stated that a large Victorian house in Tufnell Park was looking for a sixth flatmate for a room that had become spare. I consulted the map and found out that Tufnell Park was on the Northern line, so ideal for getting to Bank every morning. I wasn't sure about living with such a large number of people in the house, but as the single people looking for a co-habiting plus-one that I'd encountered were all very odd, I was beginning to think that there might be safety in numbers. I made the call.

I was invited to immediately head out to the house for an interview. I discovered that Brecknock Road, on which the house was situated, led up from the Tube station and that the house was just a few minutes walk away. The exterior of the house was very imposing, with three sedate floors, plus a basement flat. It seemed pretty grand compared with some of the places I'd seen and when the door was opened by the landlady, Fiona, I got quite a feel-good factor about it.

I was taken into the kitchen to find a sleepy-looking, bearded guy, probably aged in his late 20s, in a grey flannel sweatshirt and sweat pants seated at the kitchen table. The kitchen and lounge area were open plan and my interview was seemingly to take place at the table. The guy uttered a 'hello' in a broad Scottish accent and was introduced to me as Dougie. The line of questioning was very relaxed and mainly conducted by Fiona, with Dougie chipping in now and again. I just answered honestly, explained my background and the job I had got and just tried to suss them out a bit.

Fiona was probably in her late 30s or early 40s and very trendy, sporting red-framed spectacles and a neck scarf and bright blouse. Her blonde, shoulder-length hair was cut really well and she seemed very bright and intelligent. She explained that she owned the entire house, but lived in the basement, so effectively the house belonged to those renting rooms.

I left my interview feeling hopeful, but knowing that she had others to see. Later that day, I received a good news phone call, informing me that I had made it past stage one of the interview process, but that really she wanted the other flatmates to meet me, as all would have to agree if I was the right choice.

Once again, Michael accompanied me to this interview and again caused confusion, with everyone assuming, yet again, that we were an item. On this occasion, I met Will, a lawyer in Holborn, Glenn, a New Zealander and an accountant and Jane, who was an accounts clerk, as well as seeing Dougie again, who explained that he was a floor producer at TV-am, working on the Good Morning Britain programme with Anne Diamond and Nick Owen. For this reason, he had to get up very early in the morning and then sleep in the afternoons. The final flatmate, Jo, was not present, but it was explained to me that she was also a Kiwi and part of the production team on 'World of Sport'.

Various questions were fired at me and it was a little intimidating, but I got through it and, later that night, was told that I had passed the initiation ceremony and could move in, if I wanted to.

My room was the smallest in the house, but then I was the newbie. It was situated on the top floor and was the furthest room from the front door, overlooking the back yard of the house, with the view available being obtained through a classic sash window. There was not much floor space, once that allocated to the bed was taken out of it, but it seemed right for me and I accepted the invitation to move in. I was to learn that this was a very fair and democratic household, but also one that fostered a very strong bond between flatmates.

That bond was impressed upon me the moment I moved in. It was explained to me that the house tried to do things together as much as possible on Friday and Saturday nights, but that it was really a house regulation that everyone participated in curry night, which took place every Sunday. Every week, there was a different rota in operation, so one person ordered the curries, another drove off to fetch them, someone laid the table and then, after the curry ceremony had taken place, someone did the washing up. I was instantly relieved that I had been put through the Bradford curry ordeal and could participate in this ritual.

As it was, we did do an awful lot together on Friday and Saturday nights too. There was an unofficial rota for going down to the off-licence, just around the corner from the Tube station, for when the house de-cided to stay in. There were then frequent trips to pubs, particularly on Saturday nights, when we would pile into two cars and go out to venues like 'The Highwayman' in Hampstead and other popular North London spots. We used to frequent a nightclub in Muswell Hill and a really nice place in Highgate, near to the famous cemetery in which Marx is buried.

I think we all genuinely cared about each other's social life and did what we could to share as much as possible, without feeling strangled by the household. There was a really good buzz in the house, which that year inspired me to make an FA Cup Final cake for the boys, to go along with some popcorn and other treats that I'd won in a competition. My lovely chocolate cake collapsed as I tipped it out of the tin, so I transformed it into a hedgehog cake, much to Will's amusement!

I found myself using my flatmates for different things. The first one who took me out anywhere was Jo, on the first Sunday after I'd moved in. She decided to take me to the trendy Camden Market, which I wasn't that keen on, my lasting impression of it being rubbish, that had been left in the gutters, swirling around my ankles. Things were about to get worse when we encountered a tramp, who had died in the entrance to the Tube station. Funnily enough, I was never quick to make a beeline to Camden Market.

Will became my handyman, with my sash window requiring constant attention – and that's not a euphemism! I also bought myself an exercise bike, which I just about managed to squeeze into my room. Will kindly assembled it for me.

Jane seemed to spend less time in the house than the others, so I didn't really have a role for her and, to this day, I am not sure what role Glenn fulfilled. Glenn was the oldest person in the house, in his 30s at the time, and to me he always looked like the TV character 'Magnum'. He was not only gorgeous, particularly when walking round the kitchen with just a towel round his waist, but also really kind, funny and charming. He would engage me in conversation, while I was ironing my knickers, or chirpily remind me of the golden rule of the scout movement in NZ – 'Be a tidy Kiwi'. He was often out windsurfing in the London docks and worked right down by Victoria, so was often late back. Given all the circumstances, I never thought it possible that he could be a love interest.

I definitely knew the role that Dougie played. I would often be the first home from work, due to the ease of hopping on the Northern Line, so as I arrived back, Dougie would have just about emerged from his afternoon slumbers. He was addicted to 'Brookside' and would usually be found lolling around on the beanbags in the lounge/kitchen area. I would seat myself at the table and he would utter a few sentences to me, or wind me up in a really cheeky-chappy way, though he wasn't one for that many words, being really quite intense.

Somehow, and I have no idea how it started, we developed this little game that we would play when I came home. It involved me sitting at the kitchen table and using the tablemats like a Frisbee, trying to hit Dougie as my target, as he darted around the room from beanbag to beanbag trying to make for cover. We would dissolve into fits of laughter during this game, which I admit was neither mature nor rational, but a hell of a lot of fun!

What I hadn't really realised when acquiring this room in Brecknock Road was that just around the corner lived one of my housemates from University – the girl whose wedding had been called off and her champagne drunk at our medieval party. By now, she was working at the Girl Guides Association in North London and her flat was literally just a few minutes walk away from my new abode.

While this was all terribly handy, there became a bit of an issue with this. On my way to work, I seemed to encounter all manner of strange people in the Tube station. One was a Peruvian guy, who used to come and sit next to me on the platform and tell me all about his seven brothers and sisters. The other was a ginger-haired, bearded Aussie, who began to stalk me!

Literally, wherever I went in the local vicinity, I used to bump into him. If I went to the Tube station, he would be there waiting for me. He soon sussed out where I lived and seemed to lurk by the gate and worst of all, he lived two doors away from my friend. That meant that if I wanted to go and see her, I had to take my fate in my hands and risk him spotting me. He invariably did spot me and would come rushing out into the street to talk to me, which just made my visit to her pointless, because by the time I'd despatched him, I had no time to chat to her.

My spirits were raised somewhat when he told me that he was going to Amsterdam for the weekend. I sort of thought there was a part invitation in the conversation we had about this trip, but I didn't respond, doing my usual thing of talking politely to him, rather than risking upsetting him. I put this down to my schoolteachers at Fleetwood Grammar School, where girls had outnumbered boys by 3 to 1. At Christmas, we would have formal dances, comprising mainly country dancing with a few other things chucked in. It was drummed into we ladies that, if a boy asked you to dance, it was rude to refuse – all very Pride & Prejudice and Mr Darcy, but probably responsible for a lot of the woes in my life.

I breathed a sigh of relief over the weekend that I knew he was away. I could actually go out of the house and not have to look over my shoulder and I managed to go and see my friend without any fear of being hijacked en route. It was hugely relaxing and I half hoped that he would have found a new love interest in Amsterdam and that would be that. My landlady shattered my faith in this eventuality a few days later.

'Jane', she said, in a quizzical voice that immediately made me sit up, 'This very strange Australian chap came looking for you earlier on, but when I told him you were out and asked for his name, he said you didn't know it'. Even at this stage, I was hugely embarrassed, as this conversation was taking place in front of all of my other flatmates and I had not breathed a word of my stalker to any of them, for fear of them ribbing me about it. Things were about to get worse.

'The thing is', continued Fiona, 'He came to bring you a gift, which was a little bizarre'. By now, my heart was pounding, dreading what this gift could have been. I wanted to head her off at the pass, but also wanted to know what on earth had gone on. In total shock, I sort of spluttered out, 'What was it?' as Dougie's eyes alighted on me questioningly.

'Well', continued Fiona, 'He had it tucked under his arm and I think he was hoping to woo you with it. It was a whole Edam cheese'.

To this day, I can still remember the guffaws that rang out in the room and the sight of cushions being shoved in mouths to stifle laughter. I think there were comments that accompanied Fiona's declaration, such as, 'That's the Aussies for you', from my Kiwi flatmates and I think that just made the whole thing even more embarrassing. I must have turned as red as his Edam cheese at that moment in time and couldn't decide what was worse – being told about the damn cheese, or being presented with it! I don't even like Edam cheese!

After that, I resolved that there was no way I ever wanted to encounter him again, especially while the ball of Edam was still on the loose. To avoid him, I started going to work extra early and then getting off at Mansion House, instead of Bank, so that the walk was a little longer and I wouldn't arrive too soon at Gresham Street. I also adopted a very useful technique, if a little whacky one, of putting up a very large umbrella, if I wanted to visit my friend, and scurrying past his house with the umbrella facing his window, so he couldn't see who was under it. Thankfully, I avoided him for weeks, and although I had a note pushed through the door about a 'gift' from Amsterdam, never went to collect it. I think he finally got the message.

The other key thing to tell you about my time in Tufnell Park relates to someone who washed up on our shores one day, out of the blue. Jo, as I have said, was a Kiwi working on 'World of Sport', but she had previously worked on New Zealand TV. One day she suddenly announced to the house that she had a friend called Philip, who was English and with whom she had worked in NZ. He was now coming back to look for work in England and needed somewhere to crash. She wanted to know whether we would object, if he slept on our sofa for a while.

Having been through the blow-up bed situation at Michael's and been truly grateful for what he did for me, I was hardly likely to refuse this request and, as the only time that I saw any objection to any prospective newbie being when Will wanted his policeman friend to move in, the others were hardly likely to say no either.

As a result, Philip breezed in one day and explained how grateful he was to have this temporary accommodation. He explained that he would be going out for interviews as much as possible and hoped to be able to find somewhere else soon. He seemed like a thoroughly decent chap, so I quite liked having him around, but was always intrigued as to why he carried a little suitcase with him. When I asked about this, it was explained that it was a little friend that he had for his TV work called 'Gordon the Gopher'. It sounded strange at the time, but he was quite quirky, so I didn't really question it.

During the time that Philip was in residence, I maybe saw more of him than most. As he wasn't always out on interviews, he was usually around when I returned from work. I have always had a terrible problem with locating my keys and would sometimes leave them behind, when setting off for work, meaning that I would have to ring the doorbell, hoping that Dougie would be up and about and ready for another instalment of 'dodge the drink mat'. However, when Philip was there, it was he who was usually first to the door and he would do the same thing each time – open it, see it was me, and then shut it again saying, 'No milk today, thank you'. I used to find this terribly amusing!

I rather took Philip under my wing in a way, well in one sense anyway. Having returned from New Zealand, he used to seem to get an awful lot of packages and parcels sent to him, which would invariably end up miles away in a collection office in Holloway. As I had Sophie and sort of knew the way to Holloway from the curry run, I used to volunteer to either take him to get the parcels, or collect them on his behalf, picking up all packages for Philip Schofield!

At this point, I had absolutely no idea that the guy kipping on the sofa, whose parcels I would collect, and who would slam the door in my face when I came home, would one day be the megastar and A-lister that is Philip Schofield, TV presenter. I can recall him coming back one day and saying that persistence had paid off and he had been offered a role in something called the Broom Cupboard and, after that, I think he stopped sleeping on the sofa. Little did I know the impact that Gordon the Gopher would make on the world of TV. Despite working in PR for so many years, I have never seen Philip since our days in Tufnell Park.

But, while all of this was going on at the house, there was, of course, my job at New Japan Securities and my new lofty position as 'Executive Secretary' to the Chairman, Mr O, his deputy, Mr A, and three other directors. As I had to work for the whole board, my desk was in the centre of a hub, from which one could reach the offices of Mr O and Mr A the boardroom and the training room. The other directors, Mr T, another Mr O and Mr M, worked on the Bond and Equity floor, which also had a large administration section. Almost everyone who worked in the administration area was Japanese, bar a lady called Dorothy, who had once been the Executive Secretary before falling ill. My immediate predecessor in the role was also still around, having transferred on to the Equity desk.

It was fortunate that she was still there to 'induct' me, as she quickly made me come to terms with the fact that my new employers could at times be unpredictable and forgetful. She urged me to keep every single instruction I was given, whether typed or handwritten, in a file – advice that would prove invaluable, as it turned out.

On the other hand, Dorothy was there to guide me in the art of making Japanese green tea, or at least she tried! Having so confidently stated that I would have no problem in brewing up this delicacy, I am convinced that I never once made the perfect cuppa for my bosses, their meeting guests or other honoured visitors. On a day-to-day basis, the green tea had to be served in little plastic beaker cups. When guests came, they too sometimes had these, but were usually treated to posh china. I think that's what threw me, as I could never seem to get the consistency right, no matter how hard I tried. Invariably, my little plastic cups would only ever be half drunk, to my total dismay, as I really did try very hard. Somehow, however, I escaped punishment!

To be honest, I got away with blue murder – much to the amazement of other members of staff. While Mr O was a lovely, kind and gentle man, who caused me no problem at all and Mr A was quite fiery, but still very supportive, I was warned to pay great attention to Mr M, who was in charge of all things office-related. I was told that Mr M only tolerated English staff because he had to employee some English nationals to keep the office running smoothly. I was also advised that he had the worst temper imaginable and nobody, but nobody, could stay on the right side of him for long. Add to this the fact that he was a workaholic, so always stressed, it was a combination with disaster written all over it.

I saw many an employee reduced to a gibbering wreck by Mr M, but I wasn't one of them. I think initially this was down to the fact that the Japanese directors were delighted to have a secretary with a degree from Cambridge, though I was less than delighted to find a member of the Bond department, with a lesser degree, earning so much more. This was despite the fact that he was called Christopher Deane, which amused me greatly, as I would frequently think of him performing the Bolero in tight purple lycra!

From there, however, I think I truly pulled it off when it came to handling my relationship with Mr M. It didn't really take that long for something to start niggling him, if the truth be told. What niggled him about me was the fact that I was unwittingly and, through no fault of my own, upsetting the system of Japanese protocol that Mr M felt should reign supreme in the office.

This started because Mr O seemed to greatly appreciate my speedy typing, general efficiency (down to all that dire office practice no doubt) and my shorthand, though demanding a high Pitman speed was pointless on their part, as they couldn't actually speak English fluently enough to really put sentences together in less than a couple of minutes. My shorthand skills soon evaporated. What was appreciated, however, was my ability to finish off sentences for them and get the gist of what they wanted to say and then create the prose to suit! Mr O must have truly valued this and this is where the trouble set in early on.

It all revolved around the attachment of 'san' as a suffix to my name. Mr O would wander over to me, within Mr M's hearing, and say 'Jane-san, please will you write me letter', or whatever it was he wanted. It was always Jane-san this and Jane-san that. This drove Mr M absolutely insane, to the point that he would be almost purple in the face and shaking, when saying to me, 'It is not right. You must NOT allow him to call you Jane-san. It is sign of respect. Not good for secretary'. At that, I would retort, very calmly, that Mr O was my boss and that it would not be right for me to tell him what to do and that, if Mr M had an issue with it, he should be the one to tell Mr O. Not surprisingly, that never happened, so Jane-san stayed Jane-san, causing constant irritation every time the name was used.

This was not all. In general, Mr M really did not like 'English ladies and gentlemen' and never put up any pretence to suggest otherwise. We all knew this for a categorical fact thanks to the number of times we would hear things such as 'English ladies and gentlemen like sitting on desks too much' (something he hated), 'English ladies and gentlemen eat too much', 'English ladies and gentlemen like to talk too much', etcetera etcetera.

He also had a massive bugbear about untidy desks – a particular

failing of 'English ladies and gentlemen'. All of this led to much bitter-
ness within the office, to the extent that the guy who ran the Bond department, and I exaggerate not, would fly British flags on his desk on VJ
day, to celebrate the Allied Forces victory over Japan in the Second World
War, just to wind up Mr M! At times, it was like being at school!

When the Tokyo Stock Exchange was closed for a Japanese public
holiday, there was little for anyone to do in the office until Wall Street
opened. These days were truly bizarre, as Mr M would present all of the
'English ladies and gentlemen' with a duster and polish and order us to
clean our desks until America woke up! Now believe me, there's only so
many times you can polish a desk and it doesn't take that long!

I am not sure how I decided upon my strategy with Mr M, or what
made me think it would work, as he was hugely intimidating, though
diminutive in size. Somehow or other, I decided to call his bluff and see
how he would react. I think it started thanks to a combination of two
of the aspects of office life detailed above – the sitting on desks and the
cleaning of desks on a Japanese national holiday. He caught me sitting
on the edge of a desk talking to one of the English Bond dealing guys
and, perhaps feeling he couldn't shout at the much-honoured Jane-san,
decided to mutter something under his breath about, 'English Ladies and
Gentlemen like sitting on desks too much'. To this, I quickly retorted that
I was actually cleaning the desk with my dress because I knew it was a
Japanese holiday and hadn't yet been given a duster. I clearly recall the
noise of a sharp intake of breath being taken by all those English staff in
earshot. Mr M said nothing for about 30 seconds and then broke into the
broadest laugh and uttered something like, 'Executive Secretary is very
funny'. From this point on, this was my strategy with him, as I was sure
that all the man wanted was a little laughter in his life.

As I worked for all the directors, though in fairness my role for Mr
T mainly involved, 'Writing letters to bloody landlord', as he put it so
eloquently, and trying to sort out a longstanding dispute that he had
over a garden fence, I was frequently taken to lunch by one or the other
of them. Mr O and Mr A invariably took me to Japanese restaurants and I
can vividly recall Mr A teaching me how to use chopsticks and introducing me to the delights of Teriyaki chicken. Mr M, however, had lived in

America and, for all his criticism of the English, felt himself to be very westernised. His favourite restaurant was one called 'The Baron of Beef' where he liked to tuck in to a good roast dinner, so he nearly always took me there.

These lunches were somewhat strange affairs, given the language barriers and the constant feeling that they had been arranged out of some sense of duty to the 'Executive Secretary'. With Mr M things were different and he would often tell me of his dream to return to America and to be a cowboy. To that, I pointed out that he would be too short to ever be able to mount any horse owned by John Wayne. This again made him crease up with laughter and he repeated this back to me countless times back in the office. When an instance like this occurred, however, he would typically laugh for ages, then consider that he shouldn't have done that and end with a stern sounding, 'Jane, you are too familiar!' I loved that.

It was only several months down the line that I discovered that my lunches with Mr M were a fairly new departure and that he very rarely bothered to ask anyone out to lunch. I think there was a real feeling of incomprehension on the part of other English staff, who could not for the life of them understand how I managed to get along with him – and so famously at that. I don't think they understood that what we had was true banter, quite intellectual at times, but playing to Mr M's good command of English and understanding of Western life. Literally, nobody else indulged in banter with him and I think that's what he liked, above all. I think I humanised him and tapped into his real self, rather than the automaton and dictator that he appeared to be for most of the time.

There was one way in which I know I wound him up greatly, but the more I knew that it wound him up, the more I did it. It all revolved around my dresses. Being blonde, I have always loved to dress in pink and red and, at the time, had a particular favourite dress in my wardrobe, which happened to be pink. I absolutely loved to wear that dress and, at first, got away with it, until Mr M came over one day and muttered, 'Pink not good colour for lady. Pink is geisha colour'. The day after that, I wore a blue dress and, to make a point, he came bombing over to me almost the moment I'd walked down the office and declared in a booming voice,

'Blue very good colour for lady. Blue not geisha colour!'

I just looked at him quizzically and said, 'But I like wearing pink Mr M: it goes better with my hair'. I am not sure he understood the concept of that and I left him a little open-mouthed. I carried on, not only wearing my favourite pink dress, but also other pink items from my wardrobe, just to make my point.

When not dealing with all these strange cultural gaps in comprehension, I had various functions to fulfil. My very first job of the day, at around 8am, was to go to the fax machine positioned close to the Bond desk. For hours prior to my arrival, this would spew out endless material on one continuous fax roll, which would by now be laying in a concertina shape all over the floor, yards and yards of it stretching out across the carpet and all of it in Japanese. My job was to cut up this roll into sections and then copy each section for each of the directors. The trouble was, of course, that I had no idea what any of it said, so my scissor action was completely random and could have completely destroyed the sense of the communication, particularly if I then dropped the cut up sections on the floor and lost the order in which to copy them, according to where they had been placed on the roll! That was pretty easy to do, as the moment I appeared at the fax machine, one of the Japanese Bond dealers, Mr Y, would appear at my side and try to engage in conversation, invariably, at some point, uttering the phrase, 'Muggy weather isn't it', this totally distracting me from my chopping and sorting. Despite the numerous flaws in my fax gathering and scissor action, nobody ever complained, so it can't have been too bad! But then they never complained about my horrendous green tea either!

A major role of mine was actually performed outside the office. As one of the leading Japanese stockbrokers in The City, with a big head office back in Japan, we received numerous visitors from Tokyo – probably at least two a week. Every single time that a guest was on their way, I was despatched to the top jeweller's, Mappin & Webb, down on the end of Cheapside, to buy a gift – this usually being specified as cufflinks. Should the guest be a little higher up the ladder in terms of their status, we could upgrade to cufflinks plus a tie pin and I was once also told to buy a tea service, until I pointed out that it wasn't the easiest of items to cart back to Japan.

I swear that I could have made 'Cufflinks sold by Mappin & Webb' my specialist subject on 'Mastermind', given the time that I had to spend choosing them and the number of pairs that I bought. I was definitely one of the shops 'regulars' and knew every pattern, design and style of cufflinks that the shop sold. Making sure I didn't give the same pair of cufflinks to someone, who had already visited, was a skill in itself!

News of 'visitors from Japan' was met with enormous joy in the office, as it always meant an after-work drinks and buffet reception, to which we were all invited to shake hands with the guests. They usually departed shortly after that, leaving 'English ladies and gentlemen' with what was effectively a free bar for the night and pretty decent nosh too.

When not out buying cufflinks, making green tea, listening to boardroom conversations in Japanese that would suddenly include the English words 'Execootiv Securterry' (always a time to duck) and organising the rota, journeys and schedule of the company chauffeur (who completely detested my attention to detail when it came to his working day), I was most often to be described as the lesser-spotted-social-life-planner. I spent numerous days each month organising golf tournaments, speaking to Gleneagles about bookings for the directors and their guests, organising golf days for the Japanese stockbroking fraternity, which was called what sounds like the "itchy-moshu-kai" to our ear and finding out where golf sessions could be booked. When not ensconced in the world of golf, I was organising theatre tickets, making reservations at restaurants and then also booking flights, airport transfers, tours, afternoon teas and a whole lot more for the 'visitors from Japan' who needed something to sit alongside their cufflinks!

These requests for entertainment, golf, travel and restaurant bookings came in from every director, making it truly hectic. Only a strong organisational strategy and the help of the Japanese travel agent that we used, who had an office near St Paul's, made it feasible to do and, as directed by my predecessor, I filed every scrappy little bit of paper that details had been scrawled upon, when I was being given the brief.

For many months, this did not prove necessary, but one morning I had just arrived at my desk when the usually mild-mannered head of

Equity, Mr O, came storming up to me with a purple face and angry glare. He thumped his fist on the desk and said, 'Guests from Japan arrive at hotel and have no room'. My heart began to sink, as he continued to rant and rave at me. I spun round on my chair, reached for the file-bible that contained all my tiny bits of paper, filed according to who had given them to me and when, and retrieved the original instructions. To my total relief, I discovered that I had been asked to book the rooms for May and not for April, as he was now saying was the case. I shoved the note in front of him and a look of total remorse fell across his face. He went back to his desk like a dog with its tail between its legs.

Within the hour, he was back, thrusting tickets to a concert at The Barbican at me. I explained that it really wasn't necessary to give me tickets, but there was no deterring him. Before I knew it, I was lined up for some violin recital that the whole of the Equity department were attending – a rare Anglo-Japanese outing. For months, I could ask anything I wished of him, had him rush to open the door for me, even if he was way off it as I was approaching it, and he even went into raptures about a new swimsuit I had just bought and was showing to the receptionist! Mr O the second had lost face and was trying to make amends for it for months afterwards.

Despite all of the office politics and intricacies of life in Gresham Street, I did enjoy working there. My only niggling doubt was that I should be doing something more with my degree and that ate at me every time I talked to other graduates – typically men – working on the Bond and Equity desks. However, there were perks to the job – luncheon vouchers, the arrival every day of a very cheery Japanese delivery man, who brought in Japanese lunchboxes for those who wanted them and really good friendships with fellow English females, who I would go to lunch with in the sound of Bow Bells. There was then the location, so very close to the Barbican, whose library I joined and, of course, the shops of Cheapside. There was even a builder from Ilford working on a site nearby, who rushed out and asked for my telephone number on three separate occasions, though he never once rang me up, unless my housemates didn't pass on the message!

There was always something going on in the office, as proved to be the case when we got a new arrival from Japan. I was probably the first friendly face he met in the office and after that he seemed to get very attached to me. He was treated to English lessons in one of the offices close to my desk and would immediately come and talk to me afterwards to practice. I tracked his progress quite carefully and laughed to myself the day I got the 'muggy weather isn't it' phrase that was delivered to me every day by the fax machine. It was obviously a milestone in the learning schedule, as the weather was anything but muggy. This newcomer's attachment to me soon also exacerbated the annoyance that Mr M felt about my Jane-san title, as the new recruit picked up on Mr O's lead and also started calling me Jane-san!

One day I arrived at the office to find that all hell had broken loose, as Mr M had collapsed at his desk, having done his usual workaholic thing and stayed there virtually all night. Luckily, it was only a scare, but I did broach the subject of how hard he worked and tried to get him to understand that it wasn't good for his health.

After this, our visits to the Baron of Beef started to involve another topic – the further education of his daughter. Mr M was torn between sending her to a University in America and getting her into Oxford, so started to draw on my Oxbridge insights, as a means of guiding her decision-making in the right direction. Eventually, he asked me if I would talk to his daughter and put some advice to her in a letter. I did so and felt very honoured to have been asked.

To me, life in the office became the accepted normality, but I suppose to outsiders it was anything but. I rather liked the fact that I worked for the same firm as the Japanese wife of 'Johnny Fingers', the piano player with the Boomtown Rats. One of my friends at school had been rather obsessed with Bob Geldof and so we had been to see them on a couple of occasions. To now be working with Yoko was a bit of a feather in the cap – even more so than living with Philip Schofield at the time. Yoko had the kudos of being the wife of a rock star: Philip hadn't made it yet. There is perspective in everything.

However, a reinforcement of the fact that maybe life was a little different in this role was delivered when my sister came down to London. I took her to a faster-food Japanese restaurant towards St Paul's – being now pretty au fait with all the Japanese restaurants in London, not just in the City, but also in North London, where I was sometimes taken in the evening for my Executive Secretary meal treats.

As we were sitting at the table, I was amazed to see Mr A, Mr M, Mr T and about five other Japanese staff from the office trooping in. It must have been an impromptu thing, as I certainly hadn't booked it for them. They immediately spotted us and came bombing over to the table, all giving a courteous bow as I stood and introduced each of them to my sister. They then proceeded to move further into the restaurant. I looked at my sister and she was in hysterics. 'What's the matter?' I asked. '

'Well, for starters, they're all wearing the same raincoat', she replied, 'and secondly it was just like Snow White and the Seven Dwarfs'. I quickly realised that what I took for granted – the obsession with Burberry, with designer labels, with Scotch, with Mappin & Webb and with English golf courses – were all things unappreciated by those beyond the walls of our Gresham Street building. As we left, we bumped into Mike, the Japanese travel agent, so went through all the rituals of introduction again. 'Do you know every Japanese person in London?' my sister asked.

A very big thing was looming as we approached the summer months and that thing was a massive cocktail party to be thrown by New Japan Securities at the very exclusive venue, The Inn on the Park. This was partly to demonstrate that it might not be the biggest of the Japan securities houses in The City, but was very serious about growth, and was also being thrown so as to entertain every important client and every prospective client that the firm wished to impress.

The organisation of this event was massive. It took weeks and weeks to compile lists of all invitees, issue invitations (in English and Japanese), collate responses, follow up with those who hadn't sent back an RSVP, check which employees should attend, book flights and hotels for the real big-wigs in Tokyo, who would be arriving just for the event and sort out dress codes, canapé preferences, the cocktails to be served and much, much more.

The tension mounted as the weeks passed by and it was very soon time for another visit to Mappin & Webb, but this time with the intention of buying something very special, such as crystal, as 'visitors from Japan' would not get any more important than those on their way. This included the head of the Tokyo operation. As wives were also flying in, jewellery also had to be bought – involving a whole new look at the product line in my most-frequented retail outlet.

The impending visit of the Tokyo board sent Mr M into a frenzy with the dusters and the polish. Everything in the office was falling under his scrutiny and that included my desk. My work area was rather large, with a long desk at the front and then a range of cabinets behind me. I had inherited two rather ugly and dull Japanese pot dolls, which looked rather like squashed pumpkins and which had never held a shred of appeal to me. In his whirling dervish state, Mr M was carrying out an in-depth visual inspection of my desk – the first thing visitors from Japan would see when entering the office – and espied the two dolls, which he had probably never given a second thought to.

'These are not good dolls', he declared in an authoritative tone. 'We go to Mitsukoshi. Call chauffeur'.

I duly summoned the chauffeur with great glee. Being taken on a shopping expedition was not the usual run-of-the-mill afternoon and Mitsukoshi would be a real treat with someone else's money to spend. For those unaware of it, it is a superb Japanese department store in St James's, with first class product lines, exquisite furnishings and other luxury items.

There seemed to be no time like the present now that this shopping idea was in Mr M's head, so he and I piled into the limousine and drove to St James's, being dropped right outside Mitsukoshi by the chauffeur. Once inside the shop, Mr M seemed content to let me go wild with the credit card and we compiled a little basket full of items to spruce up the reception area. Then, almost simultaneously, our eyes alighted on a range of stunning Japanese dolls, not of the dull, squashed pumpkin variety, but about 18 inches tall, housed in a mahogany and glass cabinet and wearing full kimono and obi. They were truly exquisite and eye-catching and we were both equally convinced that one of these was just what my desk needed, despite a price tag of around £250 each.

But therein lay the rub. There were two different dolls from which to choose, one dressed in a blue kimono and one in a red and pink kimono.

My heart sank, but to my amazement, Mr M said, 'Which one is best?' At this point, the only thing running through my head was the blue good/pink bad conversation, which we had on a regular basis. I was reeling slightly from the fact that the blue doll wasn't already sitting on the till, but given the fact that the fate of the two dolls seemed to be in my hands, I played devil's advocate, as well as being true to myself, and told him that the doll in the pink and red kimono was much more beautiful and attractive to the eye than the blue one.

I was literally awaiting the usual outburst about pink clothing, but didn't get it. As if I had put some sort of spell on him, Mr M picked up my preferred doll and started walking to the till with it. I could feel a smug smirk breaking out over my face and believed that this was the ultimate triumph in our long-standing battle of the colours. I had won all hands down and my beautiful doll was being wrapped even as these victorious thoughts were racing through my head. I was so pleased with Mr M that I could have kissed him.

We carefully carried our breathtaking, and now wrapped, item to the car, which had been circulating outside. While I surely had a self-satisfied air, the same seemed true of Mr M. I had fully expected it to be a case of the chauffeur having to get his foot down and get us back to the office, but Mr M leaned forward and ordered, 'Find us good place for afternoon tea'. Within minutes, we were again piling out of the limo and into a very refined Piccadilly teahouse, where we dwelled for quite some time as tea and cakes were ordered, as if to put the seal on a most successful shopping trip.

When we did eventually arrive back at the office, we unwrapped the doll and I created the ideal place for her behind my desk. She looked truly perfect and Mr M buzzed up and down and up and down, continuously eyeing his new purchase with great pride. The pumpkin dolls were instantly despatched to some pottery heaven in the sky, which only admitted the ugliest of visages!

My contentment knew no bounds, the doll being a symbolic icon of my views on fashion and colour – views that had now made Mr M nail different shades to his mast and fly them high. I had fully expected him to suddenly change his mind and send us all whizzing back to Mitsukoshi, but that hadn't happened. The doll was in situ and it appeared that this was now her glorious new home, as she prepared to welcome the most prestigious of 'visitors from Japan'.

The following morning, I had just stepped through the main door and had hardly taken my coat off, most definitely not getting as far as the fax roll, when Mr M came flying up to my desk. His eyes alighted on the doll and a smile broke out across his face. It then seemed as though he had to rein in the true pleasure he was feeling in viewing his purchase, to bow to the law of the land. He adopted a deadly serious face, bending over the desk towards me to say, with great emphasis, 'Jane'. He paused and I held my breath wondering if the hallowed 'san' was finally to be attached to my name! He continued, 'If visitors from Japan say to you, 'Is this geisha doll?' you must say, 'No, this is lady of very fine repute'.

This instruction was delivered in such a matter-of-fact, order-like way that I almost burst out laughing instantaneously, but bit my lip, straightened my face and looked him in the eye. I had to think really fast to prevent my precious doll being whisked away, never to be seen again. I answered, with equal gravity in my voice, 'Of course she is a lady of very fine repute. If she were not, you and I would not have bought her and Mitsukoshi would not sell her'.

He beamed at me in total joy. 'Quite so, quite so', he said, 'You and I would not have bought her. Mitsukoshi would not sell her'. My victory was sealed!

The Inn on the Park event seemed to arrive really quickly after that and, to repay Mr M for his big U-turn on colour in relation to the Geisha doll, I decided, in turn, to sort out a dress that would be a real pleaser for him. I am sure this was all part and parcel of our long-running colour saga, which was undoubtedly one big mind game, but now that I was pretty sure I had won that for time immemorial, I didn't mind making concessions one little bit.

I found a beautiful dress for the occasion, drop-waisted, made of patterned silk material and a mauve-blue in tone. Mr M had not asked me once about the colour of my dress, but as I arrived late that afternoon at the Inn on the Park, I could see immediate joy and delight when he saw the hue I had chosen. I am sure I detected a look in his eye that showed he knew exactly what I had done in conceding on this issue on this occasion and his appreciation was visibly apparent. Within around half-an-hour he had come over to whisper, 'This is beautiful dress', in my ear and I will always treasure the official photo that showed myself looking radiant and still basking in my earlier victory and him looking on like a proud parent who has finally brought their truculent and obstinate daughter into line!

It's really not just in marriage that it's a case of give-and-take, you know! Without any need of relationship counselling, we had sorted this situation out in our own high-powered mind game sort of way and found common ground, giving in at the important moments so that we both enjoyed a win-win situation. Despite this entente cordiale, however, not all of us bowed to the demands of Japanese culture on the night!

That may well have been because, by now, it had been decreed that there would be two after-parties – one for Japanese staff and one for English staff, in two different London venues. Japanese staff would to go on to a Japanese restaurant and English staff to a very fashionable fish restaurant of the time (just perfect for me with my ever-growing intolerance to fish!) I had already nearly collapsed on the way home from one of the work's parties for 'visitors from Japan', having not ordered the buffet myself that day and foolishly taken one small bite of something disguising itself as a ham sandwich, when it was actually salmon. I had enjoyed the most painful Tube journey back to Tufnell Park, as I started to feel sicker and sicker, but had at least managed to stagger through the door before being violently ill. Little surprise, therefore, that I resolved to eat virtually nothing on this occasion.

The cocktail party went swimmingly and we all then started to leave at around 9pm, just one problem emerging as the two groups stood in Park Lane trying to hail taxis. The issue was that nobody had told my latest arrival from Japan, who had been testing out his English on me for weeks, that we weren't all going to the same restaurant. As the news broke, I became aware of this painful wail, ironically in English, which comprised the words, 'I want to go to restaurant with Jane-san' being screeched in a manner worthy of a banshee or a two-year-old toddler. As I looked at the Japanese group, my little muggy weather friend was trying to make a break for it, but was being restrained by his colleagues. The English group were just looking terribly amused by it all and muttering things like, 'Well this is what happens when you have f***ing ridiculous rules'.

I was just looking over at my friend sympathetically, in the hope that this would calm him down, but I just seemed to make matters worse. He suddenly broke out into fake tears, which was all terribly embarrassing. I scuttled into a taxi quickly and left the Japanese group to it, not even shouting 'muggy weather isn't it' out of the window as a parting shot!

By now, however, it was going to take more than mind game victories and the attachment of 'san' to my name to keep me at New Japan Securities. Much as I liked colleagues, appreciated the inflated salary and relished the lunch vouchers, I now had real experience in the world of work and a burning ambition to start making my mark in a role that would count. I began to apply for jobs as we headed into the summer.

The trouble was that I still didn't know what I wanted to do, so just applied for jobs that sounded quite good, whenever I spotted something. The ball had started rolling even before heading to London, as I had sat a civil service entrance exam and had ticked the box stating that my first choice would be a job in the diplomatic service, largely because I wanted to see the world and felt that working in the diplomatic service capacity would allow me to do that in a sort of 'protected' way, sheltered by the embassy, wherever I worked, and presumably given somewhere decent to live. The exam had happened so many months before, that I was amazed when I was invited to an interview for a position and even more amazed to find that this would be at the Foreign Office itself.

I was terribly excited about this, to the extent that my Kiwi flatmate offered to drive me down to the St James's Park area, rather than having me catch the Tube. This was the latest in a series of strange things he'd done, progressing from just asking barmen to give me as many maraschino cherries as possible with my Martini, to seemingly being more thoughtful. I accepted the lift and travelled in his Honda Civic for the first time as his only passenger. For some reason, I will always remember Simple Minds' 'Don't You Forget About Me' being on the radio as he drove me down there.

I can remember knocking on the front door and being ushered into a beautiful entrance that smacked of colonial life and absolutely everything I expected the diplomatic service to be. I was totally entranced by it all and drank in every aspect of the ambience before being called for my interview. I was quizzed extensively and asked why I wanted to work for the Foreign Office. I answered passionately and with informed reasoning, talking about my studies in Indian history and my other historical study of colonial history and expansionism. I thought everything was going really well, but then the interview took a turn for the worse. The interviewer began suggesting that I was far too social a person to work in the diplomatic service and that I would miss interacting with lots of people and would not appreciate having just a few colleagues around me. I was devastated by this, as I really didn't feel this way and was passionate about working in the diplomatic service. It was as if my dream was slipping away as I sat there in that magnificently furnished room, with its quintessential London feel with colonial twists. Everything was falling out of my grasp and no matter how much I put up a case against the interviewer's viewpoint, I knew I had lost the battle.

I left there like a zombie and knowing there was only one thing I wanted to do. I crossed over the road and headed into St James's Park – in my view the most beautiful of all London parks – plonked myself down on the first relatively private bench I found and just burst into tears. I wept absolute buckets – more probably than I've shed after any interview or pitch since – and spent a good hour in that state before deciding to head back home. My dream of working abroad nose-dived that day and never really materialised again.

With the door of the Foreign Office now very much closed on me, I had to start thinking more broadly about what I could do to escape life as a PA, albeit a well-paid one. I began to avidly scour 'The Guardian' on its media day, in the hope that something would leap out of the page at me.

One day it did. It was an advert for a job in a career about which I knew nothing – public relations – and it was with an international freight forwarding company called MSAS (McGregor Sea and Air Services). I applied for the job and was invited to an interview at the head office in Bracknell. At this point, I must consider myself to have been truly lucky.

Had the format of the interview not played into my hands, I might never have become a PR person. As it was, the bulk of what I had to do was based around a writing test, with various pieces needing to be written in the space of about 2 hours. I completed all tasks feeling quite confident. That confidence proved well placed and I was offered the job.

The news was not greeted particularly well at the office. Mr A seemed to get the blame for blocking any prospective internal career move for me and Mr M just seemed terribly upset. My leaving do was arranged for the pub that the English staff regularly hung out in, which was virtually just across the road in Gresham Street. I never expected any Japanese staff to attend. A few did – my 'muggy weather isn't it' friend from the fax machine (my other friend had been sent somewhere else by this point) and, to everyone's profound amazement, Mr M, who was not renowned for his attendance at leaving do's for 'English ladies and gentlemen'! I was so touched by this, because I knew that it was a true sign of respect for someone of a nationality that he found hard to fathom. We even posed for a picture together, which I will always treasure, particularly as I was wearing my favourite pink dress! I knew I was saying goodbye to a true mind games' adversary. But, although I knew I would miss our daily banter very dearly, it was time to move on … the weather in The City had finally proven just a little muggy for me!

Chapter Four
FREIGHT, PHONETICS & A FROND

Getting my new job came at a weird phase in my life in London. At roughly the same time, I was due to head on holiday to Majorca with my friend around the corner, my trips round to her house avoiding Edam-cheese man having become much more successful since the adoption of the umbrella strategy. Unfortunately, what had set off as a great holiday idea amongst two single friends turned into vacation disaster, when she suddenly found a new man in her life.

The first I got wind of this was when I was summoned round to her flat to be 'vetted' by the afore-mentioned boyfriend – a bearded photographer, who had been through a tug-of-war divorce custody battle over the dog. When I discovered the reason for the summons, I was livid and got the distinct impression that his agenda was to get the holiday cancelled, as I felt I had been deemed 'unsuitable'. Nevertheless, foolishly, we went ahead with it, spending a miserable time in El Arenal amid an 18-30s type holidaying mentality that didn't exactly suit the needs of a fluent Spanish speaker with bearded, divorced photographer waiting for her back home or an executive secretary pining for her teriyaki chicken.

I did, however, find a new love interest in Majorca – a master baker from Bristol. I returned from holiday to think this would make my kudos in the house in Tufnell Park rise, but only found frowns of disapproval, especially in certain quarters. When I then announced that I had a new job and would now have to commute to Bracknell every day from Waterloo, the frown-lines seemed to deepen.

That's exactly what I had to do for a while, once again frequenting Waterloo Station, with which I had become so familiar during my research days at the India Office. I would catch the early train every morning, travelling through leafy boroughs and romantic sounding places like Virginia Water en route to Berkshire, to arrive at the office by 9am, using a strategy to get me through this, which was to eat one half of a Twix bar as my breakfast while on the train and then the other half when I arrived.

As it turned out, my new boss had plans set up for me. I was to spend the first week of my time at HQ in Bracknell, then go to the UK head office in Sunbury for a week. Next, I was to move on to Glasgow office for part of the third week and then on to Bradford, where the road haulage head office was based during the fourth week. I was then to make a trip to the sea freight division in Liverpool during the fifth.

The HQ in Bracknell was pretty much situated in the middle of a concrete jungle just off the ring road. Bracknell very much suffered from having been one of the 'new towns' set up to alleviate the housing shortages during World War II. Its town centre was pure concrete – something that was all the rage in the 1960s, but not very attractive twenty-something years later. The biggest thrill to be had at lunchtime was that of walking to a newsagent's, located in the middle of the concrete jungle of a shopping centre, to buy a can of Coke.

The office itself was open plan and very modern and occupied about 20 staff on our floor and three directors on another. Along with my boss, our secretary and our marketing director, I formed the fourth part of the entire marketing department, not just for the whole of the UK, but for around 61 overseas offices around the world as well.

My role was a dual one. For half of my time, I was to handle all media relations work both at home and abroad on behalf of the air, sea and road freight divisions of the company: for the other half, I was to be the writer and editor of the worldwide staff glossy magazine, TopCat, and the UK staff newsletter. The name TopCat came from the cheetah logo that the company had – a logo formed in red and black, as I would one day form my own PR agency's logo.

My induction tour around the UK was obviously intended to bring me up to speed very quickly with all elements of the operation, so that I could quickly perform both sides to my job. Having just got to know the people in Bracknell, where I was the youngest member of staff, I then had to get out and about and quickly put names to faces elsewhere, while making loads of notes and gaining an understanding of what the world of freight forwarding was all about.

My first stop was the UK headquarters of the airfreight division in Sunbury – ideally located close to Heathrow, its freight terminals and its bonded warehouses. I was set up with appointments across the operation, starting with the director, who I rather liked, thanks to his very posh mannerisms and the fact that he had a home in Henley, which I found terribly glamorous. I spent whole afternoons in departments such as sales and entire mornings with the head of customer services, while also being shipped out to other appointments, including one with a Heathrow-based manager, where I have to say I struggled to understand a single word he said, due to his very heavy Indian accent.

Having spent a week in Sunbury, I was then off to Glasgow, doing things like visiting the operation at Prestwick Airport and becoming familiar, for the first time, with the 'Glasgow's Smiles Better' slogan and smiley face. People were very hospitable and I was taken for a night out in the centre of Glasgow, being told how much it had improved and been cleaned up from 'the old days'. I'm pretty sure we didn't have 'Taggart' back then, or I might have felt slightly less safe and convinced about this statement, but I had a very jolly time anyway. For something to do with me, the sales manager also drove me around Edinburgh one day, to show me the sights!

My notebook was becoming very full and I was certainly meeting a lot of people – something that continued when I reached Bradford and met the sales manager there, but before that, there was more with which to fill my pad. To get up to Bradford, I had to travel by rail from King's Cross and so had an early morning start from one of my least favourite stations (bearing in mind that Platform 9 ¾ didn't exist then!). There was some sort of mayhem occurring as I arrived on the departure platform and I stood behind a man, who was swearing and moaning at length about British Rail workers and their lack of organisational abilities, to put it mildly. He was basically ranting to himself, as I wasn't engaged in any conversation with him at this point, but then he must have realised someone was behind him and so swung round. To my astonishment, this person in front of me transpired to be no other than a leader of one of the big trade unions. Before I could consider how my flabber had never been so gasted, given the total lack of any brothers-in-arms mentality or solidarity with fellow workers, as evidenced in his slating of the British Rail staff, he had started running up the platform. He was not heading to second class, with mere mortals like myself who were sitting with the proletariat, but to first class, at the front of the train!

Luckily, despite this disappointing encounter, I really liked the road haulage story, even though it was very gritty and not maybe as glamorous as airfreight. I enjoyed learning about 'curtains', how freight could be hijacked and pinched on the road and all about tachometers, as it all made perfect sense to me, but then again, I had benefited from the 'being in a truck' experience after my A1 accident!

I was, of course, living in hotels throughout this time and getting used to that strange scenario of a businesswoman on her own staying in a half-decent hotel. It was completely different from my overnights in those basic hotels in London, in which I had to eat a cold can of ravioli with a fork. Luckily, Bradford and Glasgow had both saved me from the ignominy of being a woman eating along in the hotel restaurant, though I would get plenty of practice of this in years to come. All in all, I liked my stay in Bradford, but then again it was where I had been introduced to the hottest curry on the planet, so maybe I felt semi-rooted there.

The same sense of satisfaction was not derived from my trip to Liverpool. At this time in my life, I had a black, woman's briefcase that was fairly trendy, but a briefcase all the same and that's what I was carrying when I arrived at the taxi rank at Liverpool Lime Street railway station. I jumped in a cab and asked to go to the MSAS sea freight office.

A bespectacled, ageing Liverpudlian driver totally ignored what I had said and barked in a most guttural fashion, 'So you want to go to Bearch-khern'edd?' I replied that I didn't want to go to Birkenhead, but to the MSAS office, which was on the waterfront. At that, I received a barrage of abuse, punctuated with four-letter words and the phrase, 'I ****-ing knew it when I saw your ****ing briefcase".

Although slightly shocked at this, as chatting to London cabbies had become one of my favourite pastimes (and is to this day, as I find them a mine of information, enormous fun and hugely helpful), I sat back in my seat and decided to ignore it.

My journey then proceeded with emergency stop braking, at every possible point en route to my destination, this resulting (bearing in mind that there were no seatbelts fitted at the time) with me flying around the back of the bomber, landing on the floor and crashing into the sides of the taxi. I knew this was all being done deliberately and was now absolutely fuming. For the first and only time in my life, jotted down the cab's number so that I could report the driver.

I still remember the triumphant look on his face when he dropped me off (far from where I needed to be, but I didn't care by then). I was black and blue and in no mood to be messed with. 'A tip would be nice', he said sarcastically. I just turned away, getting another barrage of abuse and almost gave him a good tip! I was just so disappointed that a city that was subjected to so much stereotypical criticism produced someone, who completely conformed to type. From that day, I have been disappointed in anyone who lives up to the way they are typecast in society and in the media.

After this month-long adventure around the UK, I returned to Bracknell and, at weekends, started to look for my first property. This started with a viewing of an 'apartment' in Datchet near Windsor, which transpired to be a veritable shoebox – a one room abode with a bed that pulled out of the wall, so the lounge and kitchen, by day, literally became the bedroom by night. The price of the apartment was absolutely extortionate and I didn't think there would be the perk of Liz inviting me over to the castle of a weekend, so had to think again.

I didn't actually see that many other places before arriving in Faygate Way in Lower Earley, then one of the biggest housing estates in Europe, located on the outskirts of Reading. Number 18 was a one-bedroom house, with a smallish lounge and kitchen downstairs and a few square metres of garden, grassed and just about large enough to get away with having a shed within its bounds. It was, however, perfect for one single person. I viewed this and had an offer accepted on it on the same day, which was July 13th – a date I cannot forget, as it had a real significance that year, being the day on which Live Aid took place. By September, I was ready to move in.

I arrived back in Tufnell Park that evening and explained to everyone that I had bought a house and would need to give notice on my room. This was met with glum faces. I too was going to miss living in Brecknock Road, but probably less so since my friend had found her photographer. I guessed my flatmates were also going to miss me, as I had most recently become the girl they sent down to the off-licence, as the owner wanted to take me out and gave me a discount in an attempt to woo me! This, the Aussie encounters and the Peruvian interludes were soon to be no more.

My Kiwi flatmate had been acting strangely for a few months, as I have said, which left me totally unprepared for the day that I moved out. We had a pay telephone at the bottom of the stairs, just outside the kitchen and, as I came down with some of my last bits and pieces, he backed me up against the phone and said, 'So maybe I could come down and mow your lawn?' I must have looked at him as if he had come from another planet.

'What are you talking about?' I asked, in a state of confusion.

'Surely you remember that night I told you that I used to be a lion tamer!' he continued. By now, baffled had turned to bewildered.

'What, the night you got me about 10 maraschino cherries on one stick?' I answered.

'Yiss', he said, in his broadest New Zealand accent. I still looked non-plussed, so he continued to explain. 'That was one of my best chat-up lines'.

'Well it must have been lost in translation', I responded.

I think it was when he said, 'You must have known' that my heart sank. Not knowing, or perhaps not ever thinking anyone that gorgeous would be interested in me, was to prove to be one of my big failures in my personal life.

I did seriously consider the lawn-mowing offer, but I had now got my master baker in Bristol in tow and was very loyal. The moment had passed and Tufnell Park had not delivered my Thomas Magnum looka-like in time. It was time to move on.

And so I did, settling myself into my little house and making the acquaintance of my next door neighbour immediately, by asking him to help build my bed, which had just been delivered. He dutifully obliged, though I'm not sure his wife was too pleased when she returned from work! Although small, Faygate Way really suited me down to the ground, with an under stairs area to house my pretty massive record collection, as acquired mainly at Cambridge market over the years, and a decent-sized kitchen. After the tiny room I had lived in during my time in London and the small college rooms before that, this house was positively palatial – and all mine!

My mother gave me some strange advice at this point, which was to be able to pay the mortgage by learning to sew my own clothes, something she could do brilliantly, but in the same way that she'd never passed her swimming talents on to me (she could have swum at the Olympics if she'd not been unexpectedly pipped in a race by a certain somewhat unknown Anita Lonsbrough), she'd kept her seamstress skills to herself.

I signed up to dressmaking classes and lasted about four weeks, until it reminded me too much of office practice class to continue. Somehow, I still managed to pay the mortgage! My weekdays were mainly spent on my own at home, while my weekends were largely spent with my master baker down in Bristol, as he played rugby every autumn and winter weekend for Frampton Cotterell RUFC's second team. I became quite adept at retrieving the ball at these matches, given that I was usually the only spectator, and our holiday romance began to blossom into something more serious. There were, however, the strains of a long-distance relationship.

I didn't spend too many nights sitting in on my own, however, and would have undoubtedly had someone popping round continuously had I not knocked it on the head very quickly, in my own inimitable fashion. The person concerned was the son of my Nan's neighbour in Poulton-le-Fylde and my family and his thought it a great idea that I 'get to know him', as he lived only about half-a-mile away from my new house. Consequently, having never met him before in my life, I was invited round to his abode.

I'm not too sure that I have ever seen a place of residence doing more to communicate that it was a bachelor pad, devoid of female touches and taste. Now I have never been a fan of the colour green, particularly as I was always told by my Nan that it was unlucky and then broke my arm when playing tig in the playground at Claremont Junior School in Blackpool, while wearing an emerald green dress. Since then, I've rarely worn it, but maybe this experience with this man is partly responsible for bringing on a traumatised state when I see it!

As I was offered a seat in his lounge, I became aware of green all around me – wall-to-wall green and not just one shade of it. Oh no, he had gone to enormous lengths to show his passion for the colour green, by painting his plastered walls with about seven different shades of it, ranging in deepness of green from the skirting board to the ceiling, where it reached a pale lime colour, having started its life at the bottom of the wall as a deep conifer. Now, as this guy was in IT and not a graphic designer, who could have claimed an attachment to his pantone chart, the only explanation I could possibly give to this system of décor was some sort of psychotic episode! There was simply no getting over this green hurdle on my part.

That was at the back of my mind when he came round to help me fit up a coaxial cable – which, believe me, once again was not a euphemism. He arrived in a white silk shirt, unbuttoned almost to the waist, his best black trousers and far too much male grooming for my liking for a man who was sorting out a TV issue. Given these circumstances, what else was a girl to do but to invent some reason to send him into the loft, knowing that the loft entrance was rather mucky and there was no loft ladder, so he would have to hoist and swing himself into there, rather ruining his dapper image. It worked a treat, with the wannabe Romeo emerging with the look of a chimney sweep from belly button to neck. Not surprisingly, I never heard from him again! Perhaps he considered me a rogue elephantessa!

As it was, I certainly wasn't bored. My duties as editor of the UK staff newsletter kicked off in a big way and it became necessary to traverse the country, interviewing employees at offices all over the place, to gather stories for publication, whether that was about business successes, or personal interests and triumphs. In the course of flitting from office to office, poor old Sophie, who had done such sterling work in keeping me alive on the A1, started to feel the strain and was constantly breaking down in inconvenient places like Luton or Nottingham, making my time away from home even longer!

At times, that was no bad thing, especially when the 'alarming incident of the shaggy rug' reared its head. Still having a great affection for Habitat in Tottenham Court Road, I had headed up there one Saturday and fallen for a shaggy cream rug that I thought would look perfect on my lounge floor. I bought it and carted it all the way back to Reading Station on the train, which was a little difficult, as I had to sit with it between myself and a rather well-to-do lady, who was wearing what was obviously a real fur coat.

Having bought the rug, it was my wont to sit on it, on the floor, when making my regular phone calls to my master baker and it was during the course of one of these conversations that I became aware of things leaping out of it. To my horror, after further inspection, I realised that it was infested with fleas so, in a panic, took it to the kitchen sink and drowned it. Having then dried it out, I treated it with some rapidly bought cat flea powder, before drowning it again a few days later. That seemed to do the trick. To this day, however, I will be ridden with guilt wondering if I infested the posh lady's fur coat with fleas. However, I do occasionally debate, when feeling rather less generous, whether her coat infested my rug!

At the start of November, my travelling became more expansive, with a trip to the Jersey office! I was much looking forward to some autumnal sunshine, but arrived to find the runway thick in snow! I spent three nights on the island, but luckily found a really brilliant girl from Corby working in the Jersey office, who was a bit of a kindred spirit. While not learning about the Jersey operation by day, we were out in the bars buying very cheap tipples, or in the shops buying duty-free items to take back with me!

When not cavorting around the country, running into aggressive taxi drivers and breaking down, I was very much occupied with the other parts of my job, starting with the worldwide magazine. Gathering stories for that was rather trickier, with calls to interview members of staff in offices such as Philadelphia or Hong Kong having to be timed according to the time zone and taking into account language barriers. With 61 offices to choose from worldwide, there was always something going on, so I was never short of material and the TopCat magazine carried larger features on the whole, which could contain a variety of photos and other graphics to fill the space.

There was a dual use to some of the stories, such as the tale of how we shipped a cat to Philadelphia and how we managed to air freight a whole marble sculpture out to one of the Arab states. These stories were also used in the freight press, such as International Freight Forwarder (IFW), becoming press releases that typically had an interesting edge to them.

Dealing with the freight forwarding press at a pretty intimate level was very much part and parcel of the job, this entailing a lot of liaison with the Society of Air Cargo Correspondents (SACC), as well as various one-to-one media briefings with key features writers. Some were far friendlier than others. I well recall going to see one editor, a formidable lady, who cut me dead mid-conversation and asked me what I considered I was going to do for MSAS that would make the difference. To be honest, still in my early twenties, this made me draw breath and ponder, but having done that, I had to ask myself the same question!

I did manage to use my organisational skills and knowledge of London restaurants, however, in organising a splendid SACC Christmas event in the exquisite French restaurant, Au Jardin Des Gourmets, in Greek Street, which in a way was a gesture of thanks – or maybe not – to one of the editors. My dubious feelings in relation to this revolved around an invitation I had received to a 'Beaujolais Nouveau' event being organised by IFW magazine, in some London backwater's trendiest wine bar. In accepting the invitation, I don't think I had any idea how rough 'Beaujolais Nouveau' could be, so unwittingly threw myself into the event, having my glass filled a couple of times by the IFW chap who had invited me.

Now, of course, when you live in London, worries about driving home don't tend to crop up, as all you do is hop on board the Tube, try your best to look sober in front of fellow passengers and save your staggering until you've passed the final barrier. On this occasion, however, I had foolishly accepted an invitation extended by the Sunbury sales department to go to an Indian buffet event out near Heathrow that evening – with a view to covering the do for the UK newsletter.

I'm sure that I hadn't actually drunk that much Beaujolais, as it really wasn't very palatable, but the effect of it certainly made its presence known. I started to feel extremely dizzy as I left the bar and my head started to bang, as if some joiner was hammering away in it. I sort of struggled on to the Tube and immediately began to feel extremely sick – great news given that I had to travel quite a way before reaching Heathrow. I resolved, there and then, that Beaujolais Nouveau would never again pass my lips as long as I lived and I have stuck to that resolution ever since!

As I was attending the evening event, I had a hotel room booked, but when I finally arrived at the Tube station, I was in no state to walk the short distance to my overnight accommodation. I almost begged a taxi driver to take me there, explaining the state of my head, and in the end he agreed – in exchange for a mighty tip.

I had about an hour to try to regain my senses, so shoved masses of water down my neck, feeling that I truly wanted to die, while trying to change clothes, do my make-up and groan at the same time. Amazingly, however, I suddenly got a second wind and some other effect of the Beaujolais kicked in, which seemed to make me life and soul of the party. I can remember circulating around the restaurant, avidly trying to get a story that wasn't actually there, as it all just seemed like one big knees-up. Despite this, I was having tremendous fun mixing Indian food with my stomach full of Beaujolais and I can only put what happened next down to this lethal combination. It was at this point that Heathrow-based Mr P cornered me and persuaded me that I really ought to run a feature on his team. In my heady state, I agreed!

Now, I did briefly mention earlier that the first time I met this man, I hadn't understood a word he had said and just smiled and nodded in what I thought were the right places. Having now agreed to do an entire feature on him, I realised that I was going to have to really fine-tune my ear and concentrate incredibly hard on what he said, if I was to get my story down on paper. This thought was worrying me for the weeks leading up to the interview – weeks punctuated only by the arrival of a new UK chief executive, Mike Hauck.

The dreaded day came and I dutifully headed up towards Heathrow. I stepped through the door absolutely determined not to look stupid by getting no information down and equally committed to not having to keep asking Mr P to repeat what he had said. This seemed to work a treat, proving that you can really train your ear to listen to what someone is saying, no matter how strange their accent – or so I thought.

The interview went swimmingly and I got the gist of nearly every-thing he told me, before proceeding to chat to other members of the team. I was feeling exceedingly pleased with myself and thought it had all been plain sailing, not at all living up to my worst fears. But what's that phrase … pride goes before a fall …

Suddenly, out of the blue, Mr P suggested that we should go and get some lunch and I really didn't know how to wriggle out of it. It was very hard to put an age on him, but I guess he might have been in his 40s, if I was being generous, or maybe a little older. As someone in her 20s, he seemed a lot older to me. He was a rather squat man, I seem to recall, but very pleasant in his own way and obviously keen to be courteous.

We piled into his car and started to drive – not just round the block to some local eatery, but quite some way into the heart of a residential area. We eventually arrived at an Indian restaurant and, when we entered, I am pretty sure it wasn't open, but my companion rattled something off in whatever language he spoke and someone disappeared to the kitchen. I was already experiencing a feeling of déjà vu – in an empty restaurant, at lunchtime, with an Indian man. I was getting very nervy.

Plates of Indian food arrived at the table, though I hadn't ordered a thing. 'Have some chicken tikka', Mr P kept urging, almost forcing down the spicy dishes down me. Just as had been the case when the sitar play-er had been serenading me at another encounter with an Indian man, I started to feel decidedly shaky and ill. There was just something too attentive and over-the-top about this meal and there I was, stranded in this suburb, unable to get up and leave and being bought food I didn't really want.

I made some excuse at really not being that hungry and a sign of deep discontent swept across Mr P's brow. I could tell I had offended him, by not polishing off the massive plate of chicken tikka. He clapped his hands and the 'cook' disappeared to the kitchen once again. Mr P handed me the key to his car and told me to go and wait in it, while he attended to some business. Relief swept over me and I hurriedly rushed out, got in and waited.

When he finally appeared, he was carrying an entire Indian takeaway that he had had prepared for me. My stomach began to churn again. He presented it to me on my lap and just got a little too close, invading my personal space. Butterflies were racing in my stomach and flying out of the window with them went my focus on concentrating on what he was saying and any hope of understanding his accent.

He shunted his seat back a little and adopted a relaxed pose at the steering wheel, not looking at the road ahead or preparing to drive off. Instead, he was looking straight into my eyes and that's when my worst fears were realised.

'What do you tink of my cock?' he asked, still leaning back in his relaxed pose. I didn't dare let my eyes wander to his crotch to try to answer the question.

'Sorry', I bleated out, hoping against hope that I had misheard.

'What do you tink of my cock?' he demanded, this time more insistently. This time I couldn't help but cast my eyes downwards, hearing the urgency in his voice.

I must have been as white as a sheet by now, trapped in his car, pretty sure the doors were locked, with a two-foot square takeaway bag full of tikka chicken weighing me down, with this obviously being the bartering tool provided to make me answer this very personal question. I was dreading him starting to unzip.

'Why won't you tell me what you tink of my cock?' he asked again, this time a little more kindly.

I knew I had to answer the question, but my mind was void of anything to say. I wimped out. 'I don't know what to say', I bleated, by now blushing a deep shade of red and feeling totally embarrassed. 'Could you just repeat the question for me one more time?'

By now, I thought that my only hope of extricating myself from an answer was to offend him, by claiming that I couldn't now understand his accent. My dearest wish was that he would just give up the line of questioning and drive off.

'It is very simple', he snapped. 'What do you tink of my cock?' My heart sank, but this time he was continuing. 'I want to know what you tink of my cock'. Again my spirits nose-dived. He carried on, as I was shutting my eyes and desperately thinking what I could say. An insistent voice then clarified everything.

'What to you tink of my cock, my cock … you know, my cock, Mike Hauck, new director?'

I must have exhaled more heavily than I have ever done in my life, when I finally got what he had actually been saying and not what I thought to be the case. A wave of total embarrassment then engulfed me, because I was sure that, by now, he must have realised what I had thought he had been saying in his strange accent, rather than what I now knew he was asking. A voice was running through my head saying, 'He must really think you've got a filthy mind', and I was even thinking that of myself at this point, wondering how my powers of comprehension had slipped from an A-grade level at the office, to an F-minus now. I put it down to the pressure of the one-to-one lunch in a deserted, closed-to-all-others suburban Indian eatery.

I now decided the only possible tactic to adopt was to try to play it incredibly cool, as if it was just a blonde thing to be so dim. 'Well', I said, really casually and leaning back in my seat, 'I don't really know him, so can't really comment. He seems OK to me'. I stopped, wondering if I'd got away with it.

I somehow got the impression that this wasn't the answer that he wanted and that I had disappointed him greatly by not divulging any insider gossip gleaned at head office. He huffed a bit and finally made a move to start the car. I breathed another sigh of relief. I thought I'd pulled it off. As the car drove off, I stared out of the window, hoping that no other confusing questions would be asked.

When he dropped me off back at the station, I have to say that I legged it with my chicken tikka, having decided there was absolutely no point trying to refuse to take it and that speed of exit out of this situation was of the essence. He made a move for a cheek kiss, but I was already out of the door, making a resolution to never return to his department for any other stories in the future!

That wasn't, however, the end of this story. Just after Christmas, I had to visit an MSAS office, to write an article on their function within the MSAS set-up. When I made contact, to arrange the visit, it transpired that one of the managers I had met previously had now transferred there. He offered to pick me up in a pub car park and drive me over to his office.

This was a long journey and we chatted and laughed all the way there, not to mention all the way back, building up a really fabulous rapport. On that day, a real chemistry emerged and this person was never far from my thoughts, particularly as he would arrive on my doorstep and say that he was just passing by – rather strange, as it was at least a 50-mile round trip from where he lived!

We became amazing friends, but I still had my relationship with the master baker in Bristol, so nothing could happen. Despite this, he would urge me to break that off and give in to the chemistry. Tempting though that was, I didn't do it and ironically got another job offer, in Bristol, in the midst of all the contemplation on 'what to do'.

There's a song by Joan Armatrading that always reminds me of this time, when he would just turn up on the doorstep and want to chat to me for hours and hours and then drive home again. It's called 'The Weakness in Me' and it just summed up how I felt and how torn I was between doing the right thing and the wrong thing and not knowing which way round these two things were.

One night, as my new job was fast approaching, he drove me out to Cobham and was more or less insistent that I give up the Bristol job offer. He'd actually gone to the length of getting a friend of his in marketing to offer me a job, so that I would stay. I told him I was committed to the job in Bristol, so had to take it up. He jumped out of the car and came back with a piece of pampas grass, saying it was a frond indeed for a friend in need. I kept that frond for over 20 years.

Given how close we were and how we would laugh and chat, I relayed the Mr P story to him one day and he absolutely roared with laughter, appreciating how hard-to-understand this man was and how my misconception could so easily have occurred. After that, at another meeting, he said the story had been told, by Mike Hauck himself, at a top managers' meeting, Mike had apparently heard of the tale, as it circulated, and found it hilarious. I couldn't believe it had been shared!! Whether Mr P ever knew, goodness knows!

MSAS had been a great first job in PR, with my boss teaching me a lot about writing for the media, sending me on training courses, letting me have free rein with my writing for the newsletters and offering good guidance. However, living in Lower Earley was dull and it made sense for me to go for a better-paid job in Bristol, or so I thought. I earned less at MSAS than I had earned at New Japan Securities and didn't get any lunch vouchers! I would also save money on the travel between home and Bristol.

That Christmas, my house in Lower Earley had completely flooded, while I had been at home back in Thornton Cleveleys. Severe cold had caused havoc with burst pipes on the housing estate, with all houses of similar design having experienced bursts. As I hadn't been there, water had been pouring into the house for a few days, until my neighbours somehow noticed something (I suspect it was the noise of gushing water!) and rang me.

The house was a total scene of devastation when I arrived back, with the carpet under a few inches of water, all my records damp, with covers destroyed, lots of my books ruined and the walls damp and peeling. Having a flood in a one-up-one-down house is no laughing matter.

All the carpets had to be ripped up and tons of stuff thrown out. I was distraught, but was determined to stay there, even though the loss adjuster offered me hotel accommodation, as he felt it too great a health risk for me to live in the property for several weeks. As it happened, he was right and I went down with a terrible chest infection.

The upside to all of this was that my house had to be completely redecorated and re-carpeted, just before I was ready to sell it to move to Bristol.

Try as he might, my devotee didn't persuade me to pull out of my move to Bristol. I needed to be in North Bristol, to be near to Frampton Cotterell and managed to find a beautifully decorated, Georgian-style, though modern, house in Yate. My new job was to be in a role of Assistant Public Relations Officer at the South Western Electricity Board, based at its head office in Colston Square in Bristol, in a peculiarly shaped building just down from the law courts and right in the city centre. From Yate, it would take me about 20 minutes to reach the city centre, where I could park in a public car park about 10 minutes from the building and alongside the river.

I am not sure I was ever that excited by this job, other than for the fact that it meant I could move to a place where I had some ties and earn a pretty decent salary – much more than that on offer at MSAS. Additionally, as long as I didn't leave within 2 years, I would have my removal expenses paid, plus a sum of money for the purchase of furnishing and white goods for my new home. All in all, it seemed like a pretty good deal.

I knew that my friend was devastated and, if the truth be told, a portion of my heart went with him. Until I could move into my new home, I had to spend some time living in a hotel just off the motorway into Bristol and it was there that I received a letter from him. Although all we had ever done was talk and laugh and laugh and talk, it read, 'For want of something better to do, I have taken someone out'. I cried for hours on receipt of this letter – the sort of communication you just don't receive these days, but one that made me think I had made a terrible mistake. A man had gone to the lengths of getting a friend to offer me a job and I had rejected him. I had felt it time to move on, to do the right thing, but it was to be one of the greatest regrets of my life. All I was left with was my frond.

Chapter Five
ECCENTRICS, ENIGMAS &
EMERGENCIES

I started my job at the South Western Electricity Board, colloquially known as 'SWEB' in March and continued to live in the north Bristol hotel for a while, until the house purchase went through. The PR department at SWEB was under the charge of a former BBC editor called Michael Harman, who had been in charge of such names as Kate Adie, Michael Burke and Sue Lawley during his prestigious career. However, what impressed me more was the fact that he had been the man at the microphone for a truly iconic moment in history – the day The Beatles returned from their triumphant USA tour.

The PR department was located on the first floor of a multi-storeyed building. The ground floor contained the reception area, but also the SWEB shop, where electrical appliances of all sorts were on sale. It was here where I spent some of my removal allowance, making the most of my staff discount to buy some new white goods. I quickly wished that I hadn't been so tempted to do so.

There was also a basement to this vast, corridor-riddled building, but that was where the 'car pool' was housed. If you wanted to travel anywhere at SWEB, you had to book out a pool car, all of which were Vauxhalls and all of which I hated. It also made it pretty awkward when you had to juggle a pool car and your own car in the course of a day. By now Sophie had had to be sold, as she simply couldn't cope with long journeys any more – a sad parting after the way she'd somehow managed to save my life. I was now on to a black Fiat, which I also loved, but which would never be my little Sophie.

When I first started, the PR department comprised Michael and a chap called Peter. Michael worked at the desk behind me, although my desk was set at an angle, so he was able to watch everything I did. I faced Peter, at an equally strange angle. The fourth member of the team, Katie, was on maternity leave.

We were located in a long thin room, which we also shared with some members of the legal team, Jill and David, who were responsible for SWEB estates' work. This was down to the fact that the PR department came under the control of the Secretary & Solicitor's department, which had an overall head and a deputy head. This in itself was a big PR challenge!

The patch that we covered was vast, stretching from north Bristol right down to Land's End, covering the counties of Avon, Somerset, Devon and Cornwall. Each of these counties had regional offices and control rooms and there were smaller operational offices scattered around and then all of the SWEB commercial shops. This was a lot for a small PR department to control, particularly when Peter was actually a trained journalist only employed to write, design and edit SWEB News, the main communications vehicle for the entire SWEB employee and pensioner empire.

We didn't have any administrative or secretarial staff as such. Computers weren't really in use at the time, so we had to draft all work by hand and take documents to the typing pool, where around 15 women shared the workload of the head office staff that didn't have personal secretaries. The head of the typing pool was a really formidable lady, whom I quickly realised was not to be pushed or messed with. The done thing was to smile sweetly and deliver your file of work to the in tray, just hoping that it might be tackled reasonably quickly. If you tried to push things through any quicker, you were doomed to fail and be pushed back in the queue, waiting for your file to be returned for hours or even days!

My very first day at SWEB introduced me to something that was to become almost second nature – the world of the emergency. Microwaves were fairly new on the market at the time, so relatively few people had one and just hours into the job, I managed to answer the phone to someone who had blown up their microwave by trying to boil an egg in it!

Such calls were commonplace, with a disaster never far away, or waiting to happen and loss of electricity supplies almost inevitable during the course of a working day.

The reason that I wasn't that excited about the job was that I knew it would probably be quite dull even before I started. This was because all customer complaints were directed into the PR department and my role was to log each one, send an enquiry to the manager or department concerned, elicit an answer and then draft a response to the customer who had complained. While this would probably have suited some people to a tee, it was all very methodical and administrative for me, but I was prepared to grin and bear it for the sake of the move, or so I thought.

Given the number of complaints piling in from across the vast region all the time, some justified and many not, my trips to the typing pool were constant. If I wasn't there, I was taking the drafted response to the Secretary & Solicitor's secretary, or sitting in his office, or that of his deputy, listening to an explanation as to why we couldn't say this or that, on legal grounds.

We would also receive complaints submitted by MPs on behalf of their constituents, which was a little bit more exciting, if a letter from Paddy Ashdown or Dawn Primarolo came in, as that then required different treatment within the 'system'.

In between all of this excitement, there were the interludes provided by my nuclear protesters – pretty much the same bunch of people who would write every quarter to attempt to pay their electricity bill to the sum of the total, minus 10 per cent – the amount they said was generated by nuclear power. Every quarter, I would have to write to them to explain that, if they didn't pay their bill in full, they would be at risk of disconnection. Luckily, it was never my name on the bottom of the letter! Some would even draw me pretty pictures in crayon, to help express their views, but somehow even the most psychedelic designs could not prevent me realising that my job was very dull indeed and, thanks to the payment of my removal expenses, I had signed up to at least two years of it!

In many ways, it was as if I had taken a step back, leaving the excitement of my jaunts around the UK to be stuck, on most days, in the

Colston Avenue offices writing letters. It was actually a much less glamorous version of my life as an Executive Secretary.

There were some stand out cases that I dealt with on a regular basis, such as that of a farmer, who would not accept any correspondence from SWEB, as he had a long-running dispute with the Board over rights of way over his land. Other than that, it was typically something to do with disconnection, or a moan about a faulty appliance, or a whinge about service.

We also handled constant complaints by telephone, which involved all manner of things. There was the regular caller, who was convinced his wife was having an affair with an appliance repairman and wanted him removed from his job. There was also the very strange case of the exploding light bulbs in Somerset, which even eventually came to the attention of Roger Cook and his TV programme.

Calls about loss of power were to be expected and the greatest 'joy' surrounding this was that the three of us were on call on a rota basis at night and at weekends and could be contacted at any time of night or day by a member of the press, or by one of the regional controllers, if they needed to alert us to a loss of power on their patch. This could be at 1pm on a Saturday, or 3am in the morning on a weekday, the latter entailing a bit groping around the bedside table for a bit of paper and a pen and necessitating a quick switch from dopy and drowsy mode, to bright-eyed, bushy-tailed and super-efficient mode! Sometimes even focusing on which control room was on the line, at that time of day, was a challenge in itself, particularly when the caller was always on-the-ball and lively, being well into their shift, while I was emerging from under the duvet and trying to slap myself around the face to get my brain in gear.

Days were very long when answering all of this correspondence and had it not been for the joviality of Peter, I think my working life would have been unbearable. There was also the benefit of being on flexi-time for the first time in my working career, so I would typically arrive and clock in early and, if things really got too bad, leave as soon as possible.

My early days in post were marked by two particularly interesting interactions with other staff. A few weeks after my arrival, I started to get internal phone calls from a chap called M, who sounded absolutely gorgeous on the phone and was always very flirty. Every time I tried to quiz Peter about who M was, he would just laugh and say, 'I'll expect you'll meet him some time'.

My second regular caller didn't work at head office at all, but at the Severnside operations office in Bristol. He was called David, had the broadest Bristol accent you could possibly imagine and was constantly pestering me for help with a marketing course he was taking. I would get a call at least once a fortnight and then have to send him information to help him out, always being as much amused by his amazing accent and turns of phrase, as I had been the previous time he'd called me. It took me some time to meet David, but my encounter with M was a lot quicker.

In my head, M was a six-foot Adonis with rippling muscles and a physique to match his sexy voice. We didn't have the luxury of being able to google someone, or look them up on their Facebook page, so you had to judge your instincts alone. As they say now on a popular talent show, 'It was all about the voice!' In this instance, however, it just went to prove that you should never be lured into a false sense of security by someone's tone. I do think my fantasies about M had been encouraged by Peter, however, as he had never once contradicted me or set me straight on what M was really like. I had to discover that for myself.

After weeks of flirty phone calls, the actual 'meet' occurred when I had been forced to go up one floor to get coffees from the machine on the floor above, as ours was broken. I had just managed to get three cups of coffee into my wooden holder, when a very short, bearded man approached me. He obviously knew who I was, but I hadn't a clue, or the slightest inkling who he was.

'Hello, we've talked many times, but now it's time to put faces to voices', he said in a very clichéd way, trying to be all husky and sexy. 'I expect you've guessed, but I'm M'. At this point, I almost dropped the coffee holder in shock. Nobody could have differed more from the vision I had in my head of them than this man. I was also now trapped up against the coffee machine and had to make small talk with him for a good five minutes, before making an excuse about coffee going cold and hot-footing it back down the stairs.

'You took your time', said Peter, only to then burst into hysterical laughter when I told him why and how immensely disappointed I was. He sported a cheeky grin all day, chuckling to himself now again and I suddenly realised that Peter was my new Dougie. I think I took the only action possible at that point and threw my drink coaster at him!

By now, a nagging voice in my head was telling me that I had been too quick to move and that maybe I should have considered taking the marketing job that my friend had fixed up for me. With this thought constantly controlling my mind, there was little wonder that I became quite ill, things being made worse by my suddenly being advised that I would have to man the SWEB stand at the three county shows that spring and summer.

This was the first time that I realised that on-maternity-leave Katie's job would always be mine when it suited SWEB. I had no option whatsoever to agree, leading to me having to pack up a massive stand and cart it off to all three shows, driving to each one and staying over at two of the three.

The three shows I had to attend, and at which I had to host a stand that show visitors had not the slightest interest in, continuously, all day, on my own and without any back-up, were the Devon County Show in Exeter, the Bath & West County Show in Shepton Mallet and the Royal Cornwall Show in Wadebridge. All were for the farming community and quite honestly visitors were only interested in the scrumpy tents, animals in the parade ring, competitions, farming equipment, food and crafts and meeting up with farming neighbours. The words 'visit the SWEB stand' were nowhere to be found on the must-do list!

My first county show experience was at Exeter, which I didn't mind too much, despite the fact that the ground underfoot was decidedly soft and I had fears that my car might get stuck in the mud. Despite this, it was easy enough to get into the showground, was reasonably busy and frequented by fairly pleasant people.

The second county show at Shepton Mallet was a nightmare. I queued in a tail of traffic, which stretched right back to the outskirts of south Bristol, crawling along to the showground where luckily someone else had said they would erect the stand prior to my arrival. Despite all this traffic, I hardly saw a soul in the tent in which I was cooped up all day, was bored out of my skull and in need of other things to do. These days, I guess someone would just sit on a laptop all day playing computer games: if only I'd had this luxury!

The last county show was just draining. It took me hours to get down to Cornwall and, because of the distance, I had to book myself into a B&B in Padstow – now a buzzing place thanks to Rick Stein, but then a sleepy fishing village. It was all very awkward being on my own in the B&B and I encountered language issues. While my Japanese men may have been hard-to-understand at times, at least they did make an attempt to speak English. Here in Cornwall, people didn't seem to bother and it was as if I'd stumbled into an alien world!

A stand fitter tried desperately hard to have a conversation with me about what seemed to be some pressing matter with regard to the stand – or maybe just about his sandwich filling for that day – because, in all honesty, I didn't have a clue about a single word he uttered! I just nodded my head where I thought head nodding was appropriate and wrinkled my brow if I thought there was an issue. We finished the conversation and I was none the wiser.

I left the Cornwall show breathing a huge sigh of relief that at least this was all over for another year, resolving that if I had to do it again, I would employ new 'survivor' strategies.

I was beginning to appreciate that the West Country accent was an art form of its very own. I had noticed that colleagues would add an 'l' to the end of certain words ending in a vowel, so Madonna became 'Madonnal' and video became 'videol'. I quickly picked up on the fact that the way to greet everyone, every single time you saw them, was to utter the obligatory, 'All royte' (alright to you and me) and, if you disbelieved something, to say a phrase along the lines of 'Oh, ee nevver did, did-ee?' lifting one's voice at the end of the sentence as high as possible. As I now know, having studied Italian for so long, Italians call this 'tone of voice'. I think in Bristol, it's probably something else.

The upshot was that, within three months, I had developed a real West Country 'twang' that is still with me now. Whenever I go back to the area, I can slip back into it like a shot and find myself back in the groove of talking like a 'Wurzel', according to people from the north!

By the time I had done six months in this job, I knew that I desperately hated it, to the point of being decidedly miserable every time I thought about work. Being under the thumb of the two legal heads was just impossible, not because they necessarily disapproved of activity, but because of their own relationship. As they disliked each other intensely, it was completely impossible to be in favour with both of them at the same time, as I was warned in my first week. If one of them decided to praise you for something, you could be sure that you would be in the doghouse with the other within a day or two. It was like treading on eggshells, so the best course of action was actually to keep both of them absolutely neutral in regard to your work and thus create no great reaction from the other. This was pretty difficult, as I got the impression that both of them wanted to curry favour and get you 'on side' versus the other.

The mind games, the boredom with my letter writing, which was more customer service than PR, and other things in my life were making me completely depressed. Life with a master baker wasn't that great when they got up at about 3am every morning to go off and tackle their buns! Being really ill didn't help, as I would literally be crashed out on the sofa every evening, hardly able to move until my treatment kicked in. All of this led to my decision to end my relationship with the greatest doughnut maker I've ever known.

This proved to have its repercussions. I had just become a singleton once more when I got new next door neighbours – a young couple who rapidly became the neighbours from hell. Every night they would bring back about 20 friends, who would be drinking, playing music at full volume until 2am at the earliest and then starting up cars, motorbikes and vans outside. No matter how much I tried to stop this happening, it was to no avail. Within a short space of time, I could take no more and put the house on the market.

At around this point in time, my friend in London decided that he would come down to see me. I took a day off work and waited patiently, but he didn't arrive. In the end, I rang his office and was told that he had gone to another office. I was devastated and annoyed at having wasted a day off. Naturally, I did what any self-respecting girl would do and decided to head into town and shop. Shopping certainly helped take my mind off the fact that I had been stood up and I didn't return until around 5pm, at which point I found a note through the door, which said he'd arrived about two hours late, but found that I wasn't in and had waited a couple of hours and then decided to head back. If only we'd had mobiles back then!

This just made the whole situation ten times worse. In the end, we decided to try to put things right by meeting up in London. This time I was late and found him slouched against a lamp-post looking really fed up. It was more or less concluded that unless I gave up my job, there was no future. Financially, I couldn't do that, which made him seem even more fed up with me. A month or two later, I received a letter to say he'd got married abroad after a whirlwind romance.

Now all alone in Bristol, I had to do something to survive my 'sentence' at SWEB, which is how I saw it. The duration of that sentence was the length of time that had to pass before I was no longer obliged to pay back my removal expenses. I knew that the months and the passage of time would be unbearable unless I did something about it, so I had to be pro-active. To fill every working minute of my day, I decided to volunteer to do not just my job, but Katie's job as well, taking on board all the promotion of the commercial department's activities, for no extra pay. Some variety in my working day would be my reward.

The commercial department looked after the retail functions of SWEB, in terms of managing all of the shops, their launches and re-fits, as well as the creation of point-of-sale and promotional materials. They also handled the exhibition side of things, primarily the catering shows at which SWEB's offer for hoteliers, restaurateurs, pubs and leisure complexes could be showcased. They would then assist with placing adverts for certain schemes that were carried out by SWEB, as well as handling generic advertising for the Board.

There were about five members of the commercial department, but then all the managers from the engineering and commercial side, who fed into them, whether they were responsible for lighting projects, heating and ventilation, catering or electrical safety. Projects handled by this part of the company were varied, exciting in comparison to what I did day-to-day and more likely to require creative writing skills. Little wonder then that I put myself forward, even though M was technically part of this department!

Perhaps I wouldn't have made as forceful an entrée into this world as I did, were it not for a man called David Lock. David and I hit it off straight away. He was probably in his 50s at the time, but was very lively, passionate about his catering projects and full of beans. When he latched on to the fact that I wanted to help him, there was no stopping his almost childlike enthusiasm. He would literally burst through the door of our part of the open plan office and be bubbling with excitement at something or other, while my boss Michael frowned over the frames of his spectacles at this shattering of the holy peace within his well-run and sober PR department, in which one could get away with chuckling, but not engage in outright laughter!

David's visits to my desk were so frequent that it started to spawn other visits to see me from other managers, who had got wind of the fact that here was a girl who wanted to help. The more visitors we had trooping through the door, the more Michael got tetchy, much to Peter's amusement. For my part, I lapped it up, realising that this was all standing me in very good stead for a possible exit from the mundane world of complaints answering and an entrance into a far more 'electric' role, should Katie decide not to return from maternity leave.

As the visits increased, so did the sight of people having fun at work for poor Michael, who wasn't used to such inter-departmental liaison. In his usual terse way, rather than be angry about it, he chose to employ sarcasm, declaring one day, 'I should have a revolving chair situated next to your desk, Jane, given the number of male visitors who come to see you in the course of a day'. As there were probably only two or three women employed on the whole of the floor that comprised the commercial department, most of these being PAs, his point about male visitors, made in the way that it was, was slightly barbed, but this was something I became very used to. When he really used to wish to emphasise the point he would mutter, 'Like bees around a honeypot' and tut loudly!

Despite this dislike of the status quo being disrupted, there was little Michael could do to stop me, as the commercial department really did need help. Mr Lock had catering shows all over the place coming up, including one at a place called Saunton Sands and a big one in Bristol. He needed editorials written about particular types of electrical equipment used in commercial kitchens, with technology such as 'bake-off' ovens just coming into use. He also needed case studies of particular restaurants written up for use with other prospective customers and if there's one thing that goes hand in glove with case studies, it's usually out-of-office visits.

He and I spent many an hour on the road, whizzing up and down the M5 to visit customers, who had a story to tell about electricity in their catering business. At times, this would entail calling at his house in South Bristol, where I soon got to know his wife, who was a brilliant dressmaker and seamstress and who would invariably be surrounded by bits of materials and yards of cotton whenever we called, this continuing to take up her attention as David reeled around the room like a dervish looking for whatever document he needed.

I truly enjoyed every minute of working with Mr Lock, who I found hugely entertaining and kind. Things do happen for a reason and I believe that my decision to volunteer to help him paved the way to the forging of one of the most valuable friendships of my life – that with the other David – the one who had been ringing me up for marketing advice for months and who I had dismissed as a bit of a bumpkin with his broad, accentuated Bristol accent and the continuous lifting lilt in his voice! As he has been a firm friend for well over 20 years now, I'm allowed to say that!

Mr Lock had asked me to call in at the stand at the Bristol catering show and, as I dutifully did this, a tall, tanned, dark-haired guy approached me and asked if he could help. I introduced myself and he did likewise and I could have fainted with shock. It was completely the reverse of the M experience and there was no turning back after that. Once we'd realised how well we got on face to face, we would meet up for lunch in a city centre pub from time to time, with the Maltese Falcon, as I christened him, picking me up and whizzing me across the river to a little hostelry. It was just pure friendship, he having a girlfriend and I now having found a graphic designer who worked at SWEB as a new boyfriend. We just talked and laughed and laughed and talked and we've been doing that ever since, decades later.

All of this made life with the customer complaints letters much more bearable. In between writing to the crayon crowd and bolshy farmers, I was dealing with exciting things such as the lighting up of the two towers on Falmouth harbour, heading out quite literally into the field to see pylons either being built or dismantled with TV crews in tow (invariably in the pouring rain) and writing case studies about all sorts of businesses using electricity.

The Taunton shop had to be re-launched and the commercial department had booked chef Keith Floyd, who lived in Bristol, to officially open it with a cooking demonstration and cutting of the ribbon. I was asked to handle the PR for this, with Michael raising his eyebrows and saying he'd 'heard all about Keith Floyd'. He'd probably heard right, as it was the most flamboyant, wine-filled shop opening you could imagine, with Keith cooking some sort of fish dish and continuously saying 'gas' instead of 'electricity' as he sloshed wine here and there and kept the crowd in raptures with his antics!

Days out in the field became great fun, because it typically meant that I travelled to jobs with the SWEB photographer, Jim, who was a very entertaining travelling partner and prone to getting us lost up all sorts of lanes, or taking detours, to suddenly have us arrive at some little pub or café in a backwater, where some kind person would serve us cider or cake! We would spend hours travelling around what seemed like half of the southwest before heading back, as

Jim found countless errands to do en route!

Of course, the complaints still kept coming in with one of the most bizarre telephone complaints handled by myself. I had learned by now that the first five minutes of a telephone complaint were spent letting the customer get it off their chest so, as the caller rambled on about a foreign body in his tonic water, I didn't really bat an eyelid, thinking that this was all leading up to some electrical disaster as some spillage occurred, or a fly got electrocuted. But nothing further developed and the diatribe ended with, 'So what are you going to do about it?'

A puzzled look must have developed on my brow at that point.

'Sorry, Sir, do about what?' I asked in a totally baffled way.

'About the foreign body in my tonic water', of course, he replied.

By this point, the conversation and the sight of my furrowed brow had caught Peter's attention. He was all ears. 'Well, unfortunately we can't control what's in your tonic water, Sir', I answered, as Peter chortled away. By now, I was thinking that this was obviously yet another eccentric, who was just ringing up for something to do with his day.

'Can't control it, can't control it!' said the caller, 'Well that's a terrible thing for a company like yours to say. You're supplying thousands of bottles of tonic water. Who's to say there aren't more flies in them?'

Somehow, at this point, the penny dropped with me and I got the thread of what was going on. 'Sorry, Sir, can I just ask who it is that you think you have called?' I asked, as Peter continued to stare at me.

'Well, Schweppes, of course', he shouted. 'Who do you think I'm calling?' The complaint quickly diffused, when I explained to him that he was actually calling SWEB!

Other incidents were not as easily resolved and left a lasting impression on me. Most of these involved electrocutions – such as the lady who had been ironing in her garden on a summer's day and had some form of faulty wiring and the son who had been mowing the lawn before his parents' return from holiday and cut through the cable. Every time I mow the lawn I think about that incident and the terrible tragedy of it all. I always use a circuit breaker, for this very reason. Back then, circuit breakers were not that common, which was a tragedy. Whenever a fatality occurred, a little bit of me died inside with the person who had lost their life.

When I sold my house in Yate, I moved to a Victorian terraced house in Shirehampton, which I fell in love with. It had real character, big rooms with high ceilings, a charming patio area at the back and, once I'd bought it, a Victorian fire surround, into which specially bought tiles were slotted. It backed on to allotments and beyond those to a quaint little train line that hardly generated any noise at all, with just a few local trains trundling up and down it each day. A few streets away from the front door lay the River Avon.

Getting to work was a breeze now, straight down the main road that ran parallel to the river and into the city centre within 10 minutes. As it happened, Peter's mother lived in Shirehampton and I would bump into him in the village centre, when he was out getting provisions in for her. It was a happy place to live, particularly after all my troubles with my former neighbours.

However, finding this residence had not been plain sailing and actually resulted in a visit to the doctor for a tetanus jab – not your normal post-viewing situation! I had discovered that the Maltese Falcon lived in a pretty nice house in Knowle, so I thought that looking at a property there might be a good idea. I soon realised there were two distinct sides to Knowle!

From the outside, everything looked fine, apart from the fact that there seemed to be a lot of chains on gates, spikes on walls and even barbed wire in evidence in the lane behind, where I had to park. The owner, an elderly man, with impaired hearing, opened the door and started to show me around. As the last point on the tour, he took me into the kitchen. He had his back to the kitchen door and, on account of being deaf, didn't hear what happened next. A humungous Rottweiler somehow managed to shift the bolts on the back door and came pounding through it, leapt straight at me and sunk its teeth into my arm before the owner had even realised it was there, on account of his deafness.

In fairness, he got it off me quite quickly, but I was in total shock. The owner was very apologetic and even said that he hoped it hadn't put me off buying the house! When I got home and told other people, I was advised to go straight to the surgery, where a tetanus jab was duly administered. Surprisingly, I didn't move to Knowle!

Having thrown myself into every aspect of Katie's job at work, I became absolutely livid when she decided not to return and I was told that I could not apply for her job, as I already had my own role. This infuriated me. SWEB was very happy to have me doing that job plus my own when it suited them, but pedantic about the rules and regulations and not willing to budge.

The day of the candidates' interviews was just awful, as I had to sit and hear about all interviewees. It had, however, been decreed that I could carry on with the catering PR, but the new candidate would handle new projects like the sponsorship of the Bath Jazz Festival.

Michael returned from the interviews looking particularly pleased with himself and announcing that they had found a fantastic woman for the job. He knew this was riling me, but on and on he went. In the end, I just turned round and said, 'We'll see'.

As it transpired, wiser words were never spoken. Within a week, this woman had managed to get almost every department's back up. Her writing skills were non-existent, she had few interpersonal strengths and absolutely no tact. She would talk about the most inappropriate things at the most inappropriate time and most certainly fell foul of the doyenne of the typing pool.

Within about six weeks, she had received her first official warning. Within around 4 months she was fired completely. Michael made some reference to me probably feeling pleased with myself for being right about a new candidate not working out. He was right!

While she had been a complete whirlwind and bull in a china shop, another storm was brewing for the SWEB PR department and it was a natural phenomenon. That was the year that the 'great storm' struck (those of you who are Vicar of Dibley fans will remember the 'great storm episode, which I guess was based on ours!) Some would say it was down to weatherman Michael Fish, but I think it a little unfair to blame him for the totally unprepared state in which we found ourselves.

As the October storm whipped through the southwest, we lost power supplies to a substantial proportion of our network, particularly south of Bristol, with power taking nearly a week to restore in our area, before our power crews were shipped off to the southeast to help them out. The office was put into overdrive, with the three of us constantly on the phone or fax machine getting reports on each loss of power, in each individual town and village, from the regional control rooms, before writing that up as the latest status quo on that particular place and then ringing back all the journalists that had enquired about their town or village's loss of supply.

At the same time, we issued hourly bulletins to all media in the

southwest, ensuring that every status was updated before doing this. As
the phones were red hot, we had to commandeer helpers from the legal
department, just to try to keep up. It was the biggest crisis anyone could
imagine and if you think you would like to know what crisis PR is like on
this scale, think again. It certainly drove home how vast the SWEB territory was and how many communities and media we served.

As each power supply was re-established, we all breathed a sigh of
relief, knowing that things could only get better. Eventually it did, but it
was a sharp learning curve in how to cope under the most severe pressure imaginable.

I split up with my graphic designer boyfriend and headed towards
Christmas that year on my own. Michael seemed to revel in my single
status, uttering the words, 'Things have come to a pretty pass if Jane
doesn't have anyone to take to a party'. He was probably right and I
did completely the wrong thing about it, hooking up with an accountant
from SWEB about 7 years older than myself, but attitudinally about 30
years older than me, stuck in bachelor ways and an epoch that I could
not comprehend, as it was rooted in the historic past, not the present or
future. Within just a few months of knowing each other, we booked a
holiday in Portugal in January and got engaged there. The wedding date
was set for September.

Throughout this time, I was still firm friends with the Maltese Falcon,
who had once been on a training course with my new man and had found
it highly amusing that an accountant had had to get into role as 'Luigi',
an Italian waiter. I don't think he could ever really understand how I
had managed to become involved with 'Luigi', though he never actually
told me to wise up and realise that he was never going to be the one. He
too changed partner, moving on to an older woman with two children,
which I always found quite endearing, as he embraced the role of father
figure with great gusto.

Our friendship was based on so much fun and I ribbed the MF un-
ceasingly having been asked to go through some old editions of SWEB
News and found stories about him from when he was 18. He had been a
shining star in his early days and one article talked about the great things
expected of this young genius! Another talked of his footballing prowess

and another about his studies. My personal favourite, however, was a story about a pancake race he had participated in, which ran under the heading of, 'Well tossed, David'. I've never let him forget that one!

One of the advantages of working at SWEB was the proximity of the head office to Bristol city centre, which you could reach in minutes, passing by the law courts that sat behind SWEB. A few streets on there was a tanning shop, where I started to go in my lunchtime, but which I had to cease to frequent due to technical and personal disasters! The first of these involved being trapped like the meat in a sandwich by the top and bottom of the tanning bed, which operated by means of a button that lowered or raised the top half. On one particular day, when I pushed the button to bring the top half down, it jammed and wouldn't stop pressing in to me. In the end, I had to physically wrestle with the top half to keep it off me while I tried to squeeze out from under it and roll on to the floor. Hulk Hogan had nothing on me!

The second unfortunate incident involved walking out of the place, having got dressed, with my skirt tucked inside my knickers. I managed to return right through the city centre in this mode, only being informed about my wardrobe malfunction when I arrived back in SWEB reception. I could have died of embarrassment thinking about how many sniggers and how much finger pointing I must have caused!

I suppose certain things that happen in a city always make you think, 'that could have been me', particularly when people at work keep coming up to you and saying, 'You're blonde: it could have been you'. Such was the mood that surrounded the abduction of Shirley Banks in Bristol, after she had been out late night shopping in Bristol city centre. Everyone was addicted to news on the case at the time and then, when an arrest was made, the plot thickened, with supposed links to the Suzy Lamplugh abduction. Whether these were fictitious or had any ounce of truth in them we will probably never know.

Another shocking incident occurred to Jill, the legal assistant. Driving home after a night out in town, she took a short cut through the St Paul's district of Bristol and was forced off the road by a black BMW, which had been cruising alongside her for several minutes round the one-way city centre road. She got out to complain and a gang surrounded her, with demands for money being made. A police car drove past and had a brick thrown at it, but failed to stop to assist. She then burst into tears and luckily the gang decided she had nothing to hand over to them and let her go. I never took a short cut through there after that.

Perhaps, however, that was because I was aware that our repairs team would not go into St Paul's alone without back up and always had to take extra precautions and means of communication, if they had to venture in to what had become pretty much a no-go area at the time.

It wasn't the only part of Bristol to suffer this fate, as I was to discover, when yet another part of the now vacant job that had once been Katie's was given to me to fulfil. I absolutely hated every minute of this particular mission, which started with me having to take a gigantic exhibition stand and panels from school to school on a weekly basis. The kit was far too big for one person to manage on their own and yet no assistance was ever forthcoming at either end. I would have to lug this monstrosity around schools single handed, before then trying to put it up or dismantle it.

One of the worst parts of this was, however, down to geography and my knowledge of Bristol. This was long before the days of sat nav or even AA route planners, so all I had to guide me from school to school would be mumbled instructions from Michael, which never made any sense at all, and an A-Z of Bristol, which it was impossible to read when driving.

Without fail, whenever I had to cross the river I would get hopelessly lost, much to Peter's amusement, when I returned with my tales of the unexpected! On one of these occasions, I really did leave myself vulnerable and should have known better, after both the Shirley Banks and Suzy Lamplugh abductions. I had pulled over to speak to a man on the pavement to my left, speaking to him through the window as I leaned over from my side of the car and asked him for directions. All seemed normal at first, as he told me to where I needed to head. I thanked him and was ready to pull off when he suddenly came back to the car, having walked on a little way and flung open the passenger door. I was absolutely petrified, not knowing whether he was attempting to get into the car, or trying to pinch my handbag on the floor on the passenger side. Perhaps he saw the look of terror in my eyes and changed his mind, as he just mumbled something about the door not being properly shut and then closed it. There had been absolutely nothing wrong with the way the door was shut. I sped off as fast as I could, but then cursed the weekly school exhibition mission even more than usual after this close shave with who knows what.

Things then got worse, as Michael volunteered my services to various schools. My mission was to go in and talk to them about electricity, particularly with regard to the dangers of playing around with electricity. I bet they could hardly wait for me to arrive! I knew things were going to be particularly bad before I even set off for one of these visits, which was to a school in a deprived area of south Bristol called Hartcliffe. Michael, who never used to bat an eyelid about sending me out on the school run, was particularly flustered that morning, though, as it transpired, he was more worried about the SWEB pool car than me.

'Make sure before you try to drive away from the school that the car still has four wheels and isn't on bricks', he warned. I think it was his way of inspiring confidence in me ahead of my talk!

This was without a doubt one of the hardest talks I have ever had to give and I don't really like giving presentations to big groups at the best of times. The children were a fairly wild and unruly bunch, but I somehow managed to ignore what was going on. I just wanted to get the whole thing over with and could well have done without the teacher asking the class if they had any questions. Up went a hand. 'Can I take you on a date and shag you?' said one boy.

His embarrassed looking teacher reprimanded him. 'For goodness sake don't be so rude', he said. 'Now I want a question about electricity and nothing else'. Up went another hand. I looked over at this second boy with trepidation.

'Yes', I said, nervously.

'How do I fiddle the meter to get free electricity?' asked the very eager-to-learn pupil! I left praying the wheels were still on the car.

As I entered my second year of assisting Mr Lock with his catering, I had the bright idea of setting up a catering newsletter, which could be distributed through a publication called SW Caterer. David loved this idea and so did I, as it entailed lots of trips out with him, to venues such as a riverside restaurant in Taunton, so that I could do my research and write up stories.

At about the same time, Peter dropped a bombshell and announced that he was leaving SWEB to set up his own business. This, of course, just left Michael and I to manage the entire PR operation. Somehow, although I'd never been officially appointed to Katie's role but was doing it and was still doing the full customer complaint answering role, I found myself also having to become editor of SWEB News for three months, until a replacement could be found.

I don't really know how I managed this, but I did love being the editor as it took me back to my MSAS days and sometimes even my student days on 'Stop Press'. What I did insist upon, which has stood me in really good stead throughout my career, was training in the art of layout and sub-editing, as the SWEB News editor needed to not only write the entire weighty publication, but produce a to-scale layout for the printer, putting all text into a column-based, paper layout, using an Ems ruler as one's best friend, and scaling all photos to fit the design. Headings and sub-headings also needed to be planned on the page, with all of this being done on paper, as there were no computerised design tools to assist this process. This was design layout the old-fashioned way, based on sound rules that I like to think have given me a really good eye for page design and layout ever since.

Ironically, my training was booked in with Peter and I used to trot off to his house to have my lessons in his back bedroom. He was a great teacher and I learned so much from him. To this day, I still have the notebook that I took to those lessons.

Ironically, this little bit of heaven in my working life coincided with the last three months of my prison sentence at SWEB, as I had now passed the date when repayment of expenses was no longer necessary. I truly felt a new lease of life at this point, doing things I enjoyed, but knowing that the SWEB News role would not last longer than three months. With this in mind, backed by the fact that I didn't think it healthy to work in the same place as my future husband, I started looking for a job. Another incident had also confirmed my decision to leave as soon as I could.

This incident occurred on a Saturday, when I was on-duty according to the emergency call rota. A control room alerted me to the fact that one of their engineers had suffered 80% burns when attending to a sub-station. He had opened the door and been engulfed in a ball of fire, seemingly caused by a build-up of methane gas. He had been taken to the severe burns unit at Derriford Hospital.

I was really distraught by this story and naturally had to handle all press once I'd had my briefing. I really didn't expect people at work to be so matter-of-fact about this tragedy, when I relayed the details on Monday, but they were. It made me realise that I was in totally the wrong job.

The fact that I was forced to suffer the fate of, yet again, manning the stand at all of the County Shows probably didn't help, particularly as I was this time standing next to a cow in a pen and under a looped video called 'Underfloor Heating for Pigs'! I admit that I did what any self-respecting girl would do under such circumstances, making friends with the cow owner, asking him to keep an eye on the stand for 15 minutes and downing a swift half of scrumpy in the beer tent when it got to 4pm! That was my survival strategy for year 2!

Within a very short space of time of starting to look for an alternative job, I had been offered a position as PR Manager at British Gas Southwestern, based in Keynsham, between Bristol and Bath. I left SWEB in June and had a glorious leaving do in a pub down in the harbour, with few regrets about leaving other than having to say goodbye to David Lock. I had well and truly served my sentence and at times it had been a long stretch.

While all this was going on, I was planning for my September wedding and dreading every minute of it. This was all down to a set of circumstances that had made the whole thing a nightmare waiting to happen. When I had first met my fiancé, his mother and father were both alive, but before I'd even had chance to meet his father, he suddenly passed away. This now changed the whole relationship between mother and the bachelor son, who had been on his own for so many years. Suddenly, I was a real thorn in her side, as she clearly wanted her son to move back to live with her and get a job in Devon.

Whenever we went down to see her, it was truly painful and full of every mother-in-law nightmare that you can imagine. I will never know whether she did it deliberately, but if I was sitting on the sofa, she would shuffle over and wallop her rather large frame down on the other end of it with such force that I would be popped up into the air. I learned to grip and hope for the best. On the whole, I found it more attractive to stay in the bedroom as much as possible.

As the wedding approached, things got far worse, to the extent that she expected us to spend our honeymoon at her house in twin beds! I promptly found the first available option and booked a villa in France.

I didn't have a hen party of any kind, probably because I know that would have just caused more trouble, so my family and his all (very unwisely) decided to go out to dinner the night before. I can remember going home, sinking my head into my hands and crying for hours, with my sister urging me to call the whole thing off and leave him at the altar. I was tempted.

It was all such a great shame, as I'd picked a beautiful church south of Bristol and out in the country, had done my utmost to convince the vicar that he should marry us, though we weren't from his parish by any stretch of the imagination. I also had a beautiful dress, not to mention a fabulous Italian going-away dress that reminded me of one that I'd had when I was five, which was always known as my 'harvest festival dress'. Admittedly the original HFD didn't have a plunging and cleavage-revealing neckline! There certainly wasn't much love to be harvested as we departed for our city centre hotel in Clifton.

I think the night prior to the wedding and events on the wedding day itself were the nails in the coffin of my marriage that I never managed to extract with the forgiveness pliers. Even if I didn't know it for sure on the day – ironically the day that World War 2 broke out with Chamberlain declaring war on Germany – it was time to move on, emotionally and geographically. I'd let another rogue elephant rampage through my best-laid plans!

Chapter Six

JUMPIN' JANE FLASH, IT WAS A GAS, GAS AND ALAS

I can unashamedly say that I loved absolutely every single minute of being a British Gas girl. From the moment I joined the company, I was its devotee, to the extent that I even began to envy the turquoise and blue dresses worn by the shop staff and bought a dress in identical colours, with a pattern that could have passed for the gas flames in the right light! Gone was my desire to wear pink and red at this time – I was suddenly a true blue with BG running through my veins.

I think this was partly because it immediately felt like freedom. Gone were the days of having to walk down dark and gloomy corridors to have to knock on a thick, oak door before being summoned into their office by one of the SWEB engineering directors. That honestly smacked of something out of Dickens and I'd stand there, with a draft press release or letter quivering in my hand, like Oliver Twist in front of the Beadle, expecting the director to roar, 'Approval! You want approval girl!'

There was an end to the near silence in the office that Michael had insisted upon and I quickly learned that, on the whole, I had joined a quite unruly bunch, which I loved. There was openness, communication, fun, laughter and god damn it privatisation!! Oh yes, Sid had been well and truly told and there was no longer the sombre air of a nationalised organisation stifling life out of every member of personnel in the building. Unfortunately, SWEB had not yet had its shroud of state-regulated sobriety lifted, but I suspected that my husband rather liked that.

I was very lucky in joining the PR department at the same time as a new secretary, Wendy, who became my best buddy and partner in crime.

Wendy was a bit younger than me, which I don't think met with the approval of my husband, but I'm good with younger people. Wendy and I got on like a house on fire, whether I was coming out with all the obvious puns when she was dating a carpet fitter, who'd just left a girlfriend who had shown her grief by shaving her eyebrows off, or grabbing some retail therapy with her in the high street.

The department was much bigger than SWEB's. It included Michael, ex-BA and the overall PR head, Tony, my direct boss, Wendy and myself, Don Veale, the editor of Sou'wester (the staff magazine), Christine the head of internal communications and video productions and others.

Wendy and I quickly discovered that Don was the heart and soul of the office, a joker, prone to clown around at every possible opportunity, a smooth-talker when he wanted to get something from his regional correspondents and an absolute hoot when he delivered a straight-faced piece of comedy genius.

Don was just Don – a big, bearded comedian, who could chip in with a funny answer to anything with fantastic comic timing and a deadpan face. He also put a twist on phrases, coming out with classics such as, 'Let's get the road on the show' and 'No use spilling over cried milk'. He would spin us many a yarn, being given away only by the twinkle in his eye when he was winding us up, but what I particularly loved about Don was his pinboard! Behind his desk he would pin up pictures that he had been sent that month and attach speech bubbles coming out of the mouths of those depicted. Some of these just used to make us cry with laughter and if that wasn't enough, some of his telephone conversations had us in stitches, particularly when he was trying to smooth talk one of his lady 'correspondents' around the southwest.

Don was just a loveable rogue and he managed to persuade Wendy and I to do all sorts of daft things in return for milk in our coffee, or borrowing his stapler. He thought himself a bit of a ladies man, but he was just like a cuddly bear.

Don quickly commandeered my services for writing a regular double-page feature in Sou'wester, as well as other smaller news items when necessary and also decreed that I should join him when proofing each edition – a task that involved a trip to Yeovil to see the designer and printer, Robin and Gordon. I wasn't going to argue.

Tony, in the meantime, quickly inducted me in the ways of handling press calls at British Gas SW, with set forms being ready for use to log journalists' questions and the answers given. These then sat on file, so that anyone could quickly see the dialogue that had taken place. My days of answering customer complaints were, however, well and truly behind me, as we did what a press office actually should do and dealt with the press! We even had an emergency drill, which would have to swing into operation if we suddenly received a call from head office, which contained certain code words. That was something I dreaded, but found quite exciting all the same!

Tony was an interesting character. He didn't say very much, but had lots of facial expressions behind his beard and moustache, which meant that he didn't really have to. What was really exciting about him was the fact that he was a balloon pilot and flew the British Gas balloon around the southwest. Now anybody who knows Bristol will know that it is the spiritual home of ballooning in the UK, with the Balloon Fiesta being an absolutely fantastic event taking place each August. I had already visited the Fiesta and laid back in the grass, listening to the strains of Peter Gabriel, while watching balloons float overhead and off to create photographic heaven as they sailed above the Clifton Suspension Bridge or across Bedminster Down. Now, here I was working for an expert balloonist, who was already planning the first ever Balloon Glow in Bristol – an idea picked up in Arizona, I think. In a balloon glow, each balloon lights up its burner to create a sequence of light that runs around a park like a domino effect. I was well and truly hooked by this dream.

Christine, on the other hand, was also absorbing. She was dating a man around 20 years younger than herself, which led Don to make jokes nearly every day, such as, 'Christine's late in because she's dropping her boyfriend off for his paper round!' Much as I laughed at Don's witticisms, I admired Christine, as she didn't give a damn what people thought and I think she and her boyfriend were really happy together. I envied her in a way, for turning conventionality on its head and, I suppose, being a cougar way ahead of her time. She would toss her permed brown locks and command attention just by being in the room and I found her intriguing, especially when she did unexpected things like revealing she had bought her young boyfriend a shirt in the charity shop during her lunch hour (something that left Don raising eyebrows behind her back, but something that I found so open and such a statement, telling everyone that she really didn't care about anyone else's view).

Christine originated from Manchester, so we had that northern bond and she had a deep, husky voice acquired from smoking far too many cigarettes, but then it was an office where smokers ruled the roost and we non-smokers just had to accept it.

I think in my own mind I looked at Christine and her independent, strong-willed nature, talent for creativity and account direction – even control over Don – and sub-consciously decided that I wanted to be like her one day. I would like to think that a little bit of her rubbed off on me and taught me to do what you want to do, rather than what people want you to do, as you only get one chance at this life.

Michael concerned himself mainly with highbrow policy and he and Tony didn't have much to say to each other. Someone told me that Tony had wanted the job to which Michael was appointed, so there was always going to be friction. It took me a few weeks to discover that the same applied to my position.

In a small team, a square peg soon stands out from its round hole and that was the case with another member of staff. Worse than that, this person also harboured a simmering resentment, as they had wanted my job. The fact that I had been given it was no real fault of mine, but I was made to suffer for it. The resentment soon manifested itself in actions such as 'forgetting' to pass on phone messages relating to press calls, or handling them without any authority to do so, or worst of all diverting mail to their desk rather than mine, using an accomplice.

If you have ever worked in a situation where this is going on, you may understand the frustration that it causes when someone is constantly trying to undermine you to suit their own purposes. Although there had been frustrations in London and at SWEB, there was never any office politics to deal with like this and I found it debilitating at first. Luckily, I quickly latched on to what was happening, so stayed on the ball, keeping my eyes and ears open for any sort of subterfuge going on. However, I am sure that, if looks could kill, I would have been dying at least 10 times a day.

I am sure it was a real irritation to this foe to find that I took to the job like a duck to water. I'm certain that my role as a contributor to Sou'wester got their hackles up even more and I'm pretty sure that they thought I would crack under the pressure of coping with it all. I didn't.

Don, being as laid back as he was, only really got riled with my adversary when they stuck their nose into editorial matters and there was one notable afternoon on which this happened. It started with a challenging of Don on his use of hyphens with the word at the centre of this debate being 'nose wheel'. 'Was it hyphenated, or wasn't it?' was the big issue raised that day, to the extent that it became worthy of a debate at Prime Minister's Question Time. For some reason, known only to themselves, my adversary choose to deliver an opinionated lecture on the use of hyphens, which not one person in the room cared about, but which went on for about 30 minutes. It was the most pedantic conversation anyone could imagine and Don was fuming about two minutes into the debate, but held his end up well.

At the conclusion of this ridiculous conversation, however, I think Don just threw in the towel and decided to let the person place their hyphens where the hell they liked. To this day, I have no idea whether 'nose wheel' is hyphenated or not, but I don't believe my life has been deprived by this lack of knowledge!

Not surprisingly, getting out of the office was an absolute joy. I loved the writing brief that I had been given by Don, as it involved me assuming the role of a 'mole', who went around investigating what different departments in British Gas Southwestern got up to. This suited my natural Mata Hari instincts down to a tee and I went out on the road with engineers, members of the forensic team, who cleaned up gas holder sites, those responsible for 'pigging exercises' (inspecting the inside of pipelines for leaks and faults), gas fitters, pipe layers and controllers of the whole gas system, sometimes even by night if it meant getting a 'scoop'!

I was then allowed to write entertaining copy, which brought each aspect to life for the reader once my powers of detection had been at work, so that all could understand what different divisions of British Gas

Southwestern did on a daily basis. Don always seemed appreciative, but it was when Christine would read it and give me great praise that I felt really elated.

Another chance to escape would come when Don and I had to go down to Yeovil for our day's proofing. That was great fun, with Don being really entertaining company in the car. There was also always a pub lunch provided by our hosts and a fairly relaxed time spent gazing at colours, pictures, fonts and words on the proof sheets and sorting out any widows and orphans – words left dangling at the top or bottom of columns to those not in the know.

For all the benefits of using computers for design, I still believe that the best designers are those who have had this sort of experience, had to physically lay out a page according to the old rules of typesetting and sketched their vision for a page before doing anything else. In the years that have followed my design experience, I have often looked at a page, seen it looks all wrong, sketched out my vision and asked the designer to try to do it like that. Invariably, it has looked much better when they have done this, rather than just letting a computer set the boundaries of what it thinks acceptable. Not all innovation is good.

The British Gas Southwestern 'patch' was even bigger than SWEB's, stretching all the way from Pershore in Worcestershire down to Cornwall and even taking in parts of Wiltshire. This again meant having to deal with lots of control rooms and being on call at weekends and in the evenings, to deal with press enquiries about suspected gas leaks and explosions. In many cases, the explosions were down to bottled gas, rather than natural gas, but we got calls all the same, on the assumption that it was our fault.

My arrival in the British Gas Southwestern office came after a major incident in a Gloucestershire village, which had seen a house demolished through a gas explosion and had apparently led to Tony having to be on site all through the course of the night. I was told about this at length, as I was given a pair of massive and ridiculously heavy rubber boots and a special yellow, high visibility safety coat, which I would have to don if such an incident occurred again. I quickly learned the term 'pinch point', as it was heavy traffic at a pinch point that was thought to have caused the pipes to break under the road surface in the village.

All sorts of new words entered my vocabulary within a very short space of time, as I advised press or my readers about polyethylene pipe (the yellow ones) or learned about bullets – not the ones fired by James Bond, but those that stored vast amounts of gas and which were much more efficient and less obtrusive versions of gas holders.

I just revelled in explaining to people how gas holders would be tall during the night and then start to lower as people woke up and started to draw gas for cooking and heating. I loved revealing how the smell that everyone associates with natural gas is actually manufactured and put into it for safety reasons and I delighted in having a hooter of such delicate persuasion that it could have been a 'trained nose'. Yes, believe it or not, British Gas had trained noses, which were particularly good at detecting the whiff of gas on the wind – I like to think that I'm red hot at that and always have a vision of Steve Martin in the film 'Roxanne' as I say this! As I said, I was just a British Gas girl through and through and the company's biggest fan.

One of my first immersions in the world of gas safety came when covering what I have always considered one of the best events I've ever seen in my career – the annual gas safety contest that BGSW ran. Gas safety crews from across the region would compete against each other by tackling various challenges, some of which involved actors and extras, who would be creating hazards or needing to be rescued. Some of it was done against the clock, while other bits were just down to skills and technique. It was just a brilliant day out and something really fun to write about and I must have enjoyed it so much that I wrote an article that ended up winning a British Association of Industrial Editors (BAIE) award – accolades given to those working in internal communications.

I also managed to get out of the office by accompanying Tony on various jaunts, with trips to places like Torquay and Newquay being very pleasant days out. Unfortunately, however, I must confess that travelling with Tony had a very strange effect on me, which I have never encountered since. He had a very comfortable Mercedes with lovely wooden dashboard and leather seats and I could only travel a few miles in his company before falling asleep. I have never quite worked out whether this was down to the comfort of the car, or the fact that he didn't say much and was quite taciturn, but I used to be very embarrassed every time I woke up, praying that I hadn't been dribbling down my chin halfway down the M5!

I loved being in Keynsham. There was a nail bar I could frequent across the road, a library just around the corner, some decent pubs nearby and different, independent shops. It was a bit of a drive from Shirehampton, but at least I wasn't parking halfway across the city centre and having to walk for 10 minutes in the driving rain. I also had a British Gas company car now, so gone were the days of having to hire out a pool car and lug exhibition materials around. Mine wasn't a hatchback and my job role was rather more exciting now.

As I began to settle in, I started to hanker after my catering PR again, so had the bright idea of selling a similar idea to that which I had had at SWEB to the British Gas SW manager in charge of catering sales. This was a man called John Williams, who not many people seemed to take to in the way that I did. I found him a great laugh and sometimes he could read me like a book, which I appreciated, as not many people can. He liked the idea of setting up a catering newsletter and so another catering publication was born and off I went again, visiting restaurants, hotels and all sorts of hospitality businesses that used gas.

I also did some of this roving on behalf of Sou'wester, whether that meant being dispatched to cover a story about a tile manufacturer in Marlborough, or an ancient church that needed to heat the poor souls in the pews with the warmth of natural gas. It was all great fun and I met people from all walks of life.

My wedding came along two months after joining British Gas SW and I sensed that the office felt all was not wonderful in the marital home when I returned. I can hardly have been glowing when describing my honeymoon, given that the most dramatic thing that happened was that I fell asleep on the beach, ended up with a red raw back and then, while having to leave it exposed to heal, ended up with a million mosquito bites! To be honest, the whole thing was dull, spent wandering around the Dordogne debating the ethics of buying foie gras and yearning to be elsewhere.

So returning to work was quite a relief and I was really able to throw myself into the catering side of things. A pretty significant event came along just at this very moment, this being the 'Catering Student of the Year' contest sponsored by British Gas. At this early stage, we just had a regional heat to sort out, which John and his team had set up and which I had to promote. Around eight keen catering students, of both genders, competed for the prize, cooking a three-course meal that they hoped would woo the judges.

The winning student of this heat was a very shy and timid girl, who John and I thought was an excellent chef, but maybe too introverted to go on and succeed at the national level, where the prize on offer was employment in the kitchens of the Roux Brothers. We decided that only time would tell.

Being in Keynsham had other great advantages for me, but I suppose that depends on how you look at it. The Maltese Falcon was now working in Bath, so was much closer at hand and he devised two delightful lunch-time excursion options – one to an idyllic pub in Combe Hay, which was absolutely blissful, but goodness knows how we managed it in our lunch hour – and the other just down by the canal, just outside of Keynsham. I grew to love that pub, as we could also walk along the towpath, or just sit and talk in the beer garden. Wendy and I would also head down there at times, for a good old moan and escape from the office, while if we got dragged off by Don, it was to a much more traditional pub in the high street, where he was virtually part of the furniture.

Trips out with the Maltese Falcon soon led to trouble at home. Jealousy started to rage and no matter how many times I explained that I had been friends with him long before I started seeing my husband, there was a big black cloud whenever his name was mentioned. I grew to re-sent this, as we were simply great mates, him really being like the brother I'd never had and he never calling me by my name, but addressing me as 'Sibs', as he said my witticisms reminded him of Sybil Ruscoe, who was at that time on the Radio 1 Breakfast Show.

Christmas came and I was presented with the most awful green vel-vet, tasselled lampshade for a standard lamp, as my Christmas present from my mother-in-law. I didn't even own a standard lamp! I'm 100 per cent certain that she bought it deliberately, knowing I would hate it, as nothing about it said 'me'. I consigned it to the loft.

Then my mother won a trip to New Zealand for four and she offered to take my husband and I. I had the most fabulous time in New Zealand, largely without any assistance or input from my other half. I simply fell into the New Zealand way of life, recalling my days in Tufnell Park with my Kiwi flatmates and realising that life back at home wasn't now that great.

I adored Auckland and desperately wanted to live there, while for me the Bay of Islands was just heavenly. I could picture myself learning to sail and taking to the Auckland waters the minute the clock struck five and then heading off for weekend picnics on Waiheke Island, where life seemed to have stopped in a freeze-frame in the 1950s. I was at my happiest at the prow of a boat, having the waves splash over me as we headed out to open waters and loved the relaxed BYO mood of the restaurants. I'm pretty sure my husband felt none of this. That, I think, is what happens when you marry an older man, who's already much older than his years.

We returned and I got back into the routine of work, but then had to head off to London with John for the final of the catering student of the year. I actually went up there earlier, as cooking was taking place at the Kensington Tara nearly all day, in various cook offs and heats. I was innocently sitting by myself, in a pretty empty room, containing relatively few observers, when someone joined me – a guy about my age, in a cream raincoat, which I came to view as his trademark. He sat in the row in front of me and then turned round and started to come out with all sorts of comical remarks about the massacre of chicken that was taking place before my very eyes. He said he worked for another British Gas area and was pretty bored so had decided to descend on me. I think the words were. 'When you come to these events you have to look around the room to find your own amusement and I looked at you and thought you could be that amusement today'. I rather liked that and have remembered his philosophy ever since, whenever I've had to attend events that have not been that enthralling.

He (who I shall call P) stayed there chatting to me throughout the morning, the afternoon and then right up to 5pm, when I had to leave him there and explain that I had to go and get changed, as some colleagues and myself were taking our regional winner out to dinner in advance of the grand final the following day. I didn't think I'd ever see him again.

I duly went and got dolled up, checked that John had arrived and went to meet him in the bar. As I said, somehow or other, John could read my mind better than almost anyone. 'Why are you looking so happy?' he asked, almost the minute I sat down. I blagged my way through that, saying I didn't know what he was talking about, but he wouldn't give up. Every half hour or so, throughout the drinks and then the meal, he kept saying things like, 'I'm looking in those big blue eyes of yours and they're sparkling tonight', or 'You just look so radiant tonight'. All I could think was that I probably looked pretty damned miserable most of the time, if this was the case.

This went on and on, even when we had retired back to the hotel bar after the meal, with me vehemently denying that I'd done anything out of the ordinary and he saying there was definitely an aura about me.

I kept my end of this up right until the moment when we had decided to leave the bar and head to the lifts. The lift doors opened and a group of guys stepped out. I saw a cream raincoat and I think I turned scarlet as twinkling eyes eyed me up and down and said, 'Fancy seeing you here', in a truly seductive voice that has never changed over the years. I muttered something and stepped into the lift with John, saying absolutely nothing. He, on the other hand was already grinning like a naughty schoolboy and chuckling.

'So that's what it was' he said smugly. 'I knew I was right'.

The next day was all terribly exciting, as it was the grand final, being staged in the totally divine Café Royal on Regent's Street, with all its decadent furnishings, gold leaf embellishments and echoes of past glories. The room was absolutely packed and we were seated according to a strict seating plan. Try as I might, I couldn't help wondering where the raincoat-wearing P might be seated.

We'd all chatted to our contestant the night before and had received monosyllabic responses for the most part. I think we were all secretly praying that she wouldn't win the top prize, as none of us could imagine her uprooting from the southwest and moving to London to take on the high pressured role. She was somewhere tucked away at this stage, having completed her final cookery challenges and we had to get right through lunch before the result would be known. As coffee was served, we were all on tenterhooks, knowing what a great coup a win would be for the southwest region, despite our concerns.

Albert Roux eventually took to the stage and began to announce the results. We waited with baited breath, focusing on our coffee cup or a chandelier and then almost collapsed with joy when he declared that the winner was representing the southwest. I looked triumphantly at a man in a grey suit to see if he would acknowledge that I'd been right when telling him that our contestant would win. He looked back and started to clap very slowly. My superior assessment of catering students had been noted!

Things were just a flurry after that, as we went to congratulate our winner and tried to assess whether she was bold enough to take the prize. She surprised us all. She had grown in stature in just the 10 minutes since she been announced as the winner and had found some inner steel. It was like conversing with a different person and she had no doubt whatsoever that she was taking up her prize. I got back to my seat just as someone was walking past.

'I'll call you', he said. John was approaching the table and just smiled like a naughty schoolboy again.

Back in Bristol, there were other distractions to keep us entertained. Michael had been offered a post in the London head office and a replacement was being shipped in – a man called Bill. I don't think I ever really got chance to establish much of a rapport with him, but he was supposedly a very trusted, safe pair of hands. What he did bring to the party, which was very much appreciated by all three ladies in the office, was a French boy called Nicolas, aged about 19, extremely dashing and handsome and with an accent to die for. Within minutes of meeting him, Christine, Wendy and myself were all lapsing into our own version of Franglais, as we tried to make him feel 'welcome'. The men largely just humoured us with this, while someone just wore their usual air of disapproval.

I'm pretty sure that it was Christine, who, after all, had a boyfriend of around the same age as Nicolas, who came up with a challenge for us ladies, which was basically to see who could take him out and about the most, during his time on work placement. She was definitely in the driving seat for this one, having some filming to do with her video crew. I wasn't too badly off, as I had one of my site visits to a case study to make. Poor Wendy had to devise stratagems to take him to lunch and show him the high street!

I have to say that Nicolas certainly put some colour into our pre-summer days as we all invented reasons to take him out, just to win the challenge. None of us were ever entirely sure whether he grasped what was going on with all this female attention, but if he did, he certainly played along with it. He was staying at Bill's house, being a son of a friend of the family, so I think Christine managed to convince Bill that we all felt sorry for him and wanted to make sure he got the most out of his experience in England. I'm pretty sure Christine won this contest, but we all had a lot of fun with it.

My husband and I, as a last attempt to find some common ground, booked a holiday in the Dominican Republic and caused another up-roar with his mother. A 'bad turn' then developed and I had truly had enough. We went through with the holiday and it was even more of a non-event than our honeymoon – in fact, events turned out even worse than the sunburn and mosquito bites.

This started when we arrived to find ourselves in an absolute dump of a hotel that was filthy, had armed guards on the door and none of the facilities we'd been promised. The whole group kicked off so much that we were immediately transferred to the Victoria Resort – a gated resort of luxury hotels, but very much life on a compound. Though I like exploring places and drinking in the culture, I didn't mind too much, as I could lie on a sunbed and pretend to be asleep rather than talking, with the sounds of Julio Iglesias washing over me like a wave of Spanish seduction.

For some unknown reason, I decided I wanted to go pony trekking, which I think was probably done to get away for the day, but the person I wanted to get away from came with me. Having been told I had a really calm horse, it turned into a demon and instead of staying with the pack, as I had been assured it would, took it upon itself to charge to the front as we were climbing a mountain, terrifying the living daylights out of me. My inability to walk was in evidence even before the return trip, as I emerged from a dip in the mountain pool and felt every muscle aching.

The other trip out of the compound was unique and one that I will never forget. We'd toured different places and had then been dropped off at the bottom of what I suppose would have passed as a town's high street. We were told we could shop here and return to the bus after an hour. Not surprisingly, I wasn't near my husband when pandemonium broke out and people started to scream and run frantically dashing around me in all directions. I was a little bit rooted to the spot at first, as I saw a man waving a pistol around and starting to shoot into the air. I can remember thinking that it was like a scene from a Wild West movie and wondering if there was some filming going on. As I was bundled into the inside of a shop, carried along by the momentum of about 80 people, I realised this was all for real.

The shop I was pushed into was a material and haberdashery shop and it became very evident that what was going on was a regular oc-currence, as everyone except me knew the drill. Almost instantaneously, everyone had dived under the trestle tables on which material was cut and the shop staff had taken roll after roll of material and piled it all up against the glass windows, to seemingly prevent bullets from coming through into the shop. I actually stood marvelling at this ingenuity for a while, until some stranger took pity on this naïve little English girl, grabbed my leg and pulled me under a table to squat with all the others.

We stayed under there for about 20 minutes and then finally the shop staff began to stir, moving the rolls of material and tentatively peeking outside. It seemed that the danger had now moved on, or been removed, so within seconds everyone just came out from under the tables and trooped out again. I was left with the impression that they all probably added an extra 20 minutes on to their predicted shopping time to al-low for this eventuality. It was bizarre, as I heard nobody chattering or panicking at all once we were inside the shop: it just seemed to be part of a safety drill!

Of course, by this time, I had no idea where my husband was, but I did find him again, loitering in the high street having been pushed into another shop. 'That was interesting', he said. I just nodded.

Just before we were due to fly home, I became violently ill, with memories of Sri Lanka and the sanatorium flooding back. I wasn't the only one. Other members of our party started to drop like flies, one by one, and I was actually lucky, as I had got over my issues before the flight home. The really unlucky ones were those who started being sick on the plane – not just a handful either, but a good 30 or 40. Things had got so bad by the time that we touched down, that men came on board to de-fumigate the plane and we all had to be seen by medical officers. It appeared that infected water, fruit or eggs on the breakfast buffet were on the shortlist for being the culprit.

After yet another horrendous holiday, I told my husband that I thought we should go for a trial separation and he moved out, while I went off to stay with my sister for a weekend. She was very keen to urge me not to try again. I didn't actually take much encouraging.

A big decision was brewing now in my head. I was desperate to get out of Bristol because the marriage thing was all too messy and I was too close at hand for odd visits and drive-bys. This coincided with the return of Michael from London, just for a short visit, but one that was long enough to plant a seed in my head. Michael informed me that the British Gas HQ press office in London was a member down, due to a terrible accident that had befallen a girl called Gillian, who had been mowed down when crossing Tottenham Court Road and had had to have her leg amputated. This meant that she was on long-term sick leave and there was a secondment up for grabs.

I just absolutely jumped at this opportunity, as if it was manna from heaven. I could not only escape Bristol for a while – an estimated 9 months – but also gain fantastic experience in the national press office. Just to put the icing on the cake, Michael said there would also be a place for Wendy as his secretary.

I was overjoyed by this news and didn't need asking twice. Wendy was less convinced, but I took her up to London one weekend, to show her the office and a little bit of London. I thought she was really keen at that point and was elated. Tony was not on the same happiness cloud. He had always maintained that the head office press office did very little and didn't exactly see eye to eye with Michael, so it was never going to be an option that impressed him.

But despite this opposition, things moved remarkably quickly. I was called to the Chief Executive's office and he talked to me about the move and within days it was all agreed, thanks to the Chief Executive regarding it as a real opportunity for my career development. Michael had obviously oiled the wheels and I was told that British Gas in London would start searching for a flat for me. In the meantime, I could live in hotels and have all my expenses paid. Wendy, on the other hand, decided she wanted to stay in Bristol with her mother, with whom she lived. I was going to have to go it alone.

While in the Chief Executive's office, I got wind of another move on the cards – for British Gas SW to employ a struggling Bath RFC player who needed a better income in order to keep on playing. His name was Jeremy Guscott and he was destined to join the PR department, after a stint touring the region making appearances at various shops.

Tony wasn't the only one knocked for six by my decision. When I told the Maltese Falcon, he looked a little crestfallen and muttered something about London being a lonely place. In response, I asked him if he would be a key holder and look after my burglar alarm, if it went off. I thought this a worthy duty to bestow on him, befitting of his important place in my life! He took this on board, in a rather downbeat way, as I thought it really funny. He insisted that he take me to lunch and to the station on the day of my departure. I agreed, as he obviously hadn't been impressed by the duty I had bestowed!

The big day came and my suitcase was packed, I was a little nervous, but also very relieved to be getting out of Bristol for a while: the MF, on the other hand, was behaving very oddly, even by his standards. First of all, I'd built up in my head this idea that a pub lunch would be in the offing, but he drove into the city centre and parked up. When I asked where we were going, he answered, 'MacDonald's'. Now, in all the time I'd known him, we had never ever been to a burger bar or fast food chain for lunch, but I just accepted it and got on with it, thinking he'd finally lost the plot.

The next bizarre thing came when we arrived at Temple Meads Station. I must have travelled much lighter in those days than I do now, as he whipped my suitcase out of my hands and started walking with it perched on his head right through the station.

'Why are you doing that?' I hissed, quite embarrassed at him attracting so much attention, as literally everyone we passed was sniggering.

'Now, now Sibs, don't you fret about it', he answered in his broad Bristol accent, still marching along with my case balanced on top of his barnet.

We didn't wait that long on the platform and, as the train pulled up, I prepared to say goodbye. He wouldn't let me, insisting that he get on the train with me and take me to my seat. It all seemed very gallant of him, so I didn't put up a fuss. I was seated opposite a pensioner, so the MF did his best to shuffle my case next to his belongings. The guard put out a call for all non-travelling passengers to leave the train.

What happened next was just a total surprise. I was expecting a peck on the cheek, which I got, but at the same time, I also had this letter thrust into my hand. 'What's this?' I asked. He didn't answer and just got off the train, waving to me from the platform as we pulled out of Temple Meads.

The pensioner was now looking at me quizzically. I opened the envelope under the table, so that he couldn't see, to find a note on Winnie the Pooh paper. What I read just made tears start to roll down my cheeks, which I tried to disguise so that the pensioner wouldn't notice. I couldn't concentrate on anything other than the note in front of me and my mind was a complete mess. I realised that Swindon station would be coming up and I debated for about 10 miles whether to get off the train and catch one back to Bristol, or stay on the train to London. The voice of conscience was telling me that people had made arrangements for me to work in London and I couldn't let them down. My heart was telling me to get off the train. Swindon Station was fast approaching and one of these two forces had to win. In the end, I resisted the temptation to stand up and grab my case. I just couldn't let people down and be unprofessional.

So it was, that I stayed on the train and arrived in Paddington, as intended, but with no bear hug to look forward to, as I would have had if I had returned to Temple Meads. To this day, this has been one of my greatest regrets, as I will never know what might have been. However, within weeks I was having far too much fun to really think about it.

Chapter Seven
PASSPORT TO PIMLICO

My arrival in London was timed to perfection, it being mid-November just as party season was getting underway. Maybe that was what made it easier to stay rooted in London than running back to Bristol, or perhaps I just thought that the only way forward was to throw myself into everything, so that I didn't feel lonely and give in to weakness.

My first night was spent in a horrible hotel near Victoria, where I suffered the huge indignity the next morning of being unable to get the lid off my little mini jam pot at breakfast. Three waiters stood and watched me struggle with it, gripping tightly, screwing up my face and resorting to the serviette-round-the-lid technique, but still it wouldn't budge and neither would they. After the embarrassment of having looked like a woman who was pushing a baby out, I felt I couldn't spend more than a few days in this hotel.

My new office was located at Rivermill House, right on the Vauxhall Bridge and what instantly struck me about it was the way that you were dramatically blown into the revolving doors as you arrived, thanks to the force of the wind off the Thames. As I stepped foot in the press office, what I couldn't take my eyes off was the panoramic view of the river, with all the barges and tug boats, pleasure craft and smaller vessels sailing up and down and going about whatever trade they had. The office had huge windows, so you could easily watch the traffic on the river numerous times in a day. I think this is why Canaletto's painting of 'The River Thames with St Paul's Cathedral on Lord Mayor's Day' holds such fascination for me.

I didn't have high expectations of the press office given the negativity that Tony had exuded, but Michael welcomed me, so at least there was one friendly face to help me settle in. The press office occupied quite a massive area and was split into the PR and media side and then lobbying, as well as having its own photographic team and numerous secretaries, who it transpired were all temps.

Michael took me to the desk that had been occupied by the girl I was standing in for, which felt a little weird, as if I was stepping into someone else's shoes. I wondered how my new colleagues would take that. It was a desk directly sandwiched between two of the temps. The first was Michael's PA and I'm pretty sure she spent the first hour I was there moaning about him continuously. On the other side was a lady called Angela, who I found quite intimidating at first. She was quite loud and very London and spoke at about 100mph in her Cockney sparrow twang, making it quite difficult for me to understand what she was saying.

Opposite me was the first of the Scots, a girl called Nancy and just up from her an elderly, rotund and grey-haired Scot called Drew. Two other senior press officers sat at the head of the office. Sandy was yet another Scot, while Mike just happened to be flying the flag for St George. We also had a temp called Maria, who originally came from Jamaica, Felolina – a proud Maori from New Zealand, Sandra from England and our boss Fred and his secretary Julia.

Of course, I arrived and didn't have anything to do, which led to Angela talking to me incessantly, quizzing me about my background, why I was in London, what I was going to do and lots more. To be honest, half the time she was talking another language and I didn't have a clue what she was going on about. I remember one particular part of this when she was saying, 'Oh, 'e's a right old spic, inn-ee', before moving on from that mystery and launching into tales of The Arsenal, Frank Warren and the Krays and life in Islington, which she clearly thought was the centre of the universe.

I must have glazed over and asked some dumb question or other, because what I got as a reply was, 'E're darlin', wot planet are you from?' I resolved to learn everything there was to know about Islington and Frankie Warren from that point on.

Despite this start, which was actually all really jovial, I absolutely adored Angela. She was so full of life and bubbly and yet so fiery when someone riled her and quick to defend anyone she thought under attack. Seeing her whizzing around the office like a wasp, trying to get her timesheet signed, so that she could get to the temp agency before it shut, was a sight worth its weight in gold and accompanied by lots of noise and banter, especially if someone queried 20 minutes here or there!

Nancy was just the opposite, very quiet, pensive and super-dedicated to her role, which largely involved the commercial department in Holborn. She was very kind to me on my first day, though made her loyalty to her injured colleague very clear.

It was probably Drew who first took me under his wing, treating me a little bit like a daughter and coming over for a chat, just probably to check that I was alright and settling in. He was a typical Scot in terms of his sense of humour and comic timing and always had a twinkle in the eye and a funny sentence to drop into every conversation, as he twirled his spectacles around between his fingers while talking. Drew would always be the one to ask me if I would like to go to the local pub at lunchtime and thanks to this, he taught me all about the Dare family – the people you can't recall from Adam, but know deep down that you should, so rather than uttering their name, you just say, 'Hello Dare'. I loved that bit of knowledge!

Mike was terribly quiet all the time I was there and used to deal with very techy matters like running cars on chicken poo, while Sandy was busy dealing with big projects – especially the Calcutta Cup sponsorship, as tickets were involved and nobody else was going to get their hands on them while this Braveheart was around.

Fred and Julia were tucked away in their own little office, while Eugene and Sandra were also outside of the main open plan office area and down the corridor.

One of my very first missions was to go to the British Gas half-year results announcement at the Queen Elizabeth II Conference Centre, in the shadow of Big Ben and Westminster Abbey, and help man the reception desk, signing in the top City journalists and analysts and distributing the financial reports.

Shortly after that, I had to go the Kensington Roof Gardens, where a launch of British Gas's sponsorship of the National Youth Jazz Orchestra was being held. Again, I was signing people in and all sorts of celebrities appeared – Polly James and Nerys Hughes who had starred in The Liver Birds, Paul Jones (star of stage musicals and former lead singer of 60s band Manfred Mann) eminent musicians and, to cap it all, Hughie Green. I signed him in realising exactly who he was, though of course, at the time, it was not widely known that he was Paula Yates's biological father. Had I known that, it would have been another link to Bob Geldof, which I have uncannily had several times in my life.

There was nothing like the frequency of press calls that I had been used to in the regional office, because everyone was dealing with more 'important' matters than gas leaks and explosions, in a sense. What we did get a raft of calls about were TV advertisements. The first of these was a British Gas advert that featured a baby swimming underwater and which was reminiscent of the Nirvana 'Nevermind' album cover. Seemingly, this advert upset the sensitivities of a whole heap of people, who thought British Gas was drowning infants!

The second advert wasn't even a British Gas advert, but everyone thought it was. It was actually advertising real fires and was a British Coal advert featuring a dog, a cat and a mouse all sitting together in front of a fire. People loved this advert so much, they wanted to know how British Gas had made it. The short answer was that we hadn't!

I was given a few odds and ends to do in the office at first, like writing press releases and helping Nancy with a few things, but gradually as they got to know what I had done in the past, they latched on to the fact that catering PR was a big passion of mine. On hearing this, Drew informed me that he had to work on the British Gas Chef of the Year sponsorship, but said that it sounded like something I could really get my teeth into, which I subsequently did. Added to that, Drew dropped another little gem into the mix – the British Gas School Cook of the Year contest, which also needed promotion.

I threw myself into these things with great gusto. Both were to coincide with big exhibitions at Olympia and were not too far away in the calendar. It was also suggested that I get myself down to yet another British

Gas office, in Tottenham Court Road. I put an appointment in the diary.

The backdrop to all of this was life living out of a suitcase and in a hotel. Having ditched the hotel in Victoria after the strange case of the mini jam jars, I decided to opt for the Kensington Tara just off Kensington High Street and the Kensington Close Hotel, moving between the two according to which could accommodate me. This shuffling between hotels in Kensington went on for about two months, which meant lots of time to check out every shop in Kensington High Street and every item on the menu of both hotels.

The worst thing about it was the boredom of being in a hotel room on your own, so I bought loads of music and played it on a mini sound system, to keep my spirits up. As it happened, life was a social whirlwind when I first arrived in London, with everyone wanting to take me out to show me around. I would go to a shopping centre with Nancy in Queens Park, ring up my friend Michael (who was probably grateful he wasn't having to blow up a bed for me every night again), meet up with Kevin (who I had partially forgiven for the May Ball nightmare) and take up every opportunity for free tickets that British Gas could muster, whether that meant going to a piano recital just off Oxford Street with Nancy, or volunteering to help supervise the British Gas management on a corporate night out in Covent Garden. This really meant checking they all got off the coach and got back on it, so the rest of the time it was just a heap of fun.

At the time I was living in the Kensington Tara, which was the hotel I preferred of the two, there was a 24-hour armed guard positioned outside Penguin Books, which I had to walk past to enter the cul-de-sac in which the Tara was located. This was all down to the furore and death threat issued after the publication of Salman Rushdie's 'Satanic Verses'. In some ways, on dark winter nights, this was a relief and felt like added security if I came 'home' late: in others, it was quite scary, with lots of 'what ifs' entering my head as I walked past.

The only real issue I ever had in the hotel came quite early on. I had been back to Bristol and returned on the Sunday night, heading down shortly afterwards to have dinner in the restaurant. As usual, I had taken a book to read, which I had discovered to be the best tactic, as it prevented the staff from being over-attentive. There was a man on another table diagonally opposite me and although whenever I looked up he seemed to be looking at me, I didn't think too much of it.

It all kicked off, however, when I asked for the bill. The waiter brought it to me and at that moment, the man leapt out of his seat making a move to grab the bill off of the waiter's plate. 'I'm getting that', he declared in a JR-like American accent. The waiter looked taken aback and I must have looked mortified.

'No, you're not', I retorted, reaching out to get the bill myself.

'Hell, yeah, I insist,' the man drawled, again making a move to wrestle it out of the now mummified waiter's hand.

'No, you are not', I stated firmly. 'I'm quite capable of getting my own bill thank you and really don't want you to pay for my meal'. I made a lunge for it and finally managed to get a hold of the bone of contention, much I think to the waiter's relief, as he no longer had to make the decision as to who to give it to.

At this, the man turned quite nasty and menacing. A crowd of waiting on staff had started to gather, although the restaurant itself was thankfully quiet and no other diners seemed to have yet latched on to this contretemps.

'Well, honey, do what the hell ya want', the man shouted. 'I was just thinkin' ya mighta wanadda bit of company and it might ha bin nice to share a bottle of sum-thing together'.

I looked at him in disgust, which seemed to make things even worse, but I'm not very good at disguising the way I feel when people really get to me! 'No thank you', I said curtly and tried to indicate to the waiter that we should move away to the payment desk. I escaped to the sound of snorting and swearing coming from the American's table.

Word must really have travelled fast, because by now I was becoming known as a dining 'regular', so I can imagine they'd all had a good old chinwag about it in the kitchen. The next time I went down to dinner, they were around me in a flash and leading me to a booth table, which was tucked away and screened off. From that moment on, this became Jane's booth and, without fail, I was shown to it.

In the end, I didn't even really need to order my meal, because the staff knew exactly what I wanted and could pretty much order it for me. After just two months, I was part of the furniture. If I didn't go in for dinner one night, it was immediately commented on the next night with some phrase, delivered in a lilting Irish voice, such as, 'Ah, we missed you last night Miss, so we did'. I would then have to explain what I had been up to and where I had eaten. By the time my sojourn in the hotel ended, I felt that I had acquired a whole load of Irish brothers and sisters!

My other 'night out' option was P, who would drive up from Surrey, still sporting his raincoat and take me out for dinner or drinks. We pretty much frequented all the restaurants in Kensington High Street during these months.

As Christmas approached, I was hardly at the hotel at all. There were so many functions and different parties going on that life was a real blast. By now, I had met another division of the PR team, who were also housed in Tottenham Court Road. Here, there were two women who handled all of the event management and corporate hospitality events and two guys – C and J, who did video productions and lots of other stuff. I found the pair of them a hoot, particularly C, who I just clicked with straight away and found hilarious. He was quite a bit older than me, but he was tremendously droll and just one look at him used to set me off giggling.

Our PR department Christmas night out was in the 'Slug and Lettuce' near Victoria and, somehow I found myself opposite J and next to C, who I was really just getting to know. I had a black top and skirt on with a silver design printed on to it, which I had first bought for my engagement party. I had always been particularly fond of it. As the evening proceeded, it became more and more unruly, with drink being downed at an alarming rate by everyone in the department. While trying to hand yet another glass of red wine across the table, J suddenly jolted forward sending the entire glass of red wine down my skirt. While I was still debating how perturbed I was by this, C picked up a full bottle of white wine and poured the entire contents over the red wine stain. 'That'll get it out', he said, without batting an eyelid!

I was now absolutely soddened, desperately trying to mop up some of the liquid with serviettes and fanning my skirt out as a punkah wallah might fan a rather heat-weary memsaab. C was just rolling around in hysterics, setting J off, who I think was slightly more concerned, while I was rapidly losing the desire to care any more. When I felt it safe to stand up without it looking like my waters had broken, I got myself to the ladies and spent about 20 minutes drying out under the hand-dryer.

Given that I had only just met C, this was quite an induction – in fact, maybe it was his version of a Hell's Angels initiation ceremony, to welcome me into the wider PR department. Anyway, it certainly resulted in fast bonding, quicker than one could say super-glue, and we became great mates.

'We could keep you apart and let you loose into a room of people from different doors', said Nancy one day, 'but within minutes you would be together again, because you would have found everyone else in the room too boring'. I rather liked that, as it was probably very true. We just had a great chemistry and the same sense of humour.

I suppose what I loved about C was the inner child that did naughty things and tried to rebel. One great instance of that came after another night out in town. We'd already arrived in the Tube station and I was travelling to Pimlico on the Victoria line – the only one travelling in that direction. 'Right, I'm off south', I said.

Before I could say my goodbyes, C had chipped in with, 'Yes, so am I'.

At this point, Nancy grabbed him by the arm forcefully and said, 'Oh, no you're not, you're going north back to where you live'. As I waved goodnight, she was still clutching on to him and taking him in the other direction. I laughed all the way down the line.

Now, the reason I was going down to Pimlico that night was because after all those weeks of living in Kensington hotels, I was suddenly given my long-awaited company flat, which I had been promised when I arrived in London. I had expected something reasonably decent, but not fabulous, so was absolutely dumbfounded when I was told that I was to have a flat in the same complex as my boss Michael, right across the road from the office, in the security-gated (yes it was that plush!) Bessborough Gardens.

I could not believe the flat when I was taken to view it. It was absolutely gorgeous, though not massive, with a small lounge, one bedroom, kitchenette and bathroom. Everything was beautifully decorated and furnished and the lounge had glass doors, which led on to a balcony that overlooked the central garden of the complex below. Every visitor had to go through security control and an intercom allowed me to buzz up visitors to my first floor abode. It was just a haven of cream and white and just a two-minute walk from work, across the central garden, through a gate and across the main road.

The complex had an underground car park, so for the first time since I had arrived in London I could use my car. Sainsbury's was a short drive across Vauxhall Bridge and I soon mastered the route. I was now, once again, free to drive to wherever I wished in London, which didn't scare me in the slightest.

I shared a landing with another resident, who I got to meet a short time after moving into Bessborough Gardens, when he came to ask if he could borrow some dinner plates for a meal he was cooking. He explained that he was a stockbroker, so I trusted him with plates that weren't mine anyway. The day after his party, I arrived home to find my plates outside my door and two Ferrero Rocher chocolates on the top. I reported on this 'find' to Angela, telling her that I thought he was my version of the smoothie from the Gold Blend adverts. Angela promptly broadcast the story to the whole office and 'Gold Blend' was christened – in fact, I'm not sure I ever knew what his real name was.

To celebrate my leaving the hotel and moving into this palatial pad, I was told that I should hold a party for the entire PR department – both Rivermill House and Tottenham Court Road. I agreed and spent an entire day preparing food for it, knowing that they would all bring a bottle. I had decided to invite my neighbour, realising it would probably be a noisy 'do', but never expected him to come. Quite a few people had arrived before the bell went and Angela went to open the door. From inside the lounge, I could hear a conversation taking place, but then, at a high decibel level that probably meant she could be heard by those arriving at Pimlico Tube station, I heard Angela bellowing as she laughed, something she was remarkably good at, 'Oh, so you're Gold Blend; come in darling'.

On hearing this, with a particular emphasis on the 'you're', as if he was the central point of every conversation I had with her, I just wanted to crawl under the sofa wondering what on earth his reaction would be and feeling pretty sure that it was the end of my Ferrero Rocher chocolate gifts! When he entered the room, I just smiled a hopeful smile and then made some comment about Angela being barking mad, but a great hoot and not having a clue how she'd dreamed up this latest jest! I'm sure he didn't believe a word I was saying, but he looked bemused and stayed for one drink!

Everyone else stayed for considerably more tipples, which was absolutely what I would have anticipated after my Slug and Lettuce experience. But somehow, in the middle of all the hilarity, I became aware that there was something going on outside on the balcony, the doors having been opened to cool the room down. When I enquired what it was, I was told that this young guy, who'd I never met before, but who seemed to be doing something at Tottenham Court Road, was attempting to traverse his way across from the balcony and into my bedroom window, which someone had been and opened, totally ignoring the huge gap between the two and the sheer drop on to the paving below!

I was absolutely horrified, imagining some awful disaster at any minute, so rushed to my bedroom to find him coming through the window. At that point, I wondered if it had all stemmed from tales of Ferrero Rocher and Gold Blend and this was a re-enactment of the exploits of the Milk Tray Man! How on earth the security guards didn't spot all this going on was beyond me, but I was so relieved to see him back in the flat, and not splattered on the ground below, that I didn't care about much else at that point.

The party went on into the wee small hours, with C, predictably, being the last to leave. I think I then just closed the door and collapsed!

Having my plush new pad so close to work actually made me one minute late for work nearly every morning, as I would sit with my cereal and think that I had bags of time to make a move. Sometimes, Angela and some of the other girls would come back and eat their lunch there, so we really all used it as a home from home. Pimlico Tube station was about three minutes away out of the main security gate, so I couldn't have been happier with my wonderful new, all-paid-for abode and I also rather liked Pimlico, once I got to know it. The Tate was just a short walk away and there was a delightful little boutique that sold Fenn Wright Manson clothes at bargain prices. I have a black jacket that I bought there that I am still wearing today, as the quality was sublime.

The time was fast approaching for both the Chef of the Year finals and the finals of the School Cook of the Year, both of which were to be centred around Olympia's Hotelympia exhibition. This was January, so I had to really crack on with the PR, which didn't seem to have been rolling out as it should have done several months before. One of the things I really had to get my head around was the way in which the Royal Rota operated for press photographers, as the fantastic news was bestowed on me that Princess Diana would be presenting the prize to the winning School Cook of the Year.

For those of you who don't know what the Royal Rota is, it is a group of up to 20 photographers who are allocated places to be at a Royal engagement. They then supply their pictures to media around the world. The size and composition of the Royal Rota has to be agreed with Buckingham Palace or the Royal press office, so I had to ensure that all arrangements were in place for the key media representatives.

As for Chef of the Year, Drew and I had to attend the cookery finals, which were held in a hotel, though I don't recall where. What I do remember is Drew being particularly devilish and playful that day, winding me up about all sorts of things. One of the chefs in contention was one named Idris Caldora, who I started to chat to and found very interesting. When our conversation eventually ended, Drew came over and said, in his broad Scottish accent, 'Christ almighty; you had that poor man pinned up against the wall and he couldn't escape from you!' He was making a big jovial song and dance about this and the winding up continued all day.

We travelled back on the Tube together, packed like sardines with the people in our carriage, as it was by now rush hour. I had to get off the train first, so started to make my move to the doors as we approached the station and said goodbye to Drew. I couldn't actually get very far, as there was no room in which to manoeuvre and just as the train was slowing down to stop at the platform, Drew grabbed me, kissed me and said in the loudest voice he could muster, 'Thank you so much for today darling: It's been wonderful ... if only I didn't have to go home to the wife'. The heads of everyone in the carriage turned to look at me in disgust, with Drew just chortling merrily to himself, as I got off the train as fast as humanly possible to escape the shame! As the train pulled out, I looked up to see every face in that carriage still staring and a rotund Scot waving goodbye in a very self-satisfied manner!

The result of this cook-off was to be announced at Hotelympia and then the winner was to be taken to dinner in Brian Turner's restaurant in Knightsbridge. Meanwhile, the School Cook of the Year was to be crowned in the cookery demonstration area at Olympia. While waiting for this to take place, I was to hang around the British Gas stand. My plans for the evening were to go out to dinner with P, who was coming up from Surrey to visit the show in his catering capacity and who had not yet had a tour of my wonderful flat.

I was terribly excited at the prospect of meeting Princess Diana and bought myself a suit in a classical Diana style – red with a black velvet lapel. I really loved that suit from the moment I bought it, so hoped it would be suitable for the occasion. When she arrived to present the prize, I was struck by how much she seemed to emanate kindness and genuine interest in the people she was talking to. I was lined up with the media in the Royal Rota and never expected her to say anything to me, but she worked her way down the line of photographers, all busily snapping away and ended up in front of me. I curtsied and she stopped and, to my amazement, but delight, said, 'That is a really lovely suit that you are wearing'. I was completely made up!

I had agreed to meet P on the British Gas stand at about 4pm, but by 3pm a gale was raging through London and, although we were in Olympia, we could all hear how bad it sounded. After about 20 minutes of this wind swirling around in the glass-topped building, a near fatal occurrence brought the seriousness of the situation to everyone's attention. Shafts of glass started to fall down from the roof on to the British Gas stand, leaving everyone completely alarmed and leading to security being informed. Glass continued to fall and the wind continued to howl. Everyone on the British Gas stand was told to leave the vicinity at once.

I was now in a real mess, as I had no idea where P was (remember that mobiles were massive bulky devices in their infancy at this point, so nobody had one). I went up to the area where Princess Diana had been, thinking that P might have realised that the stand was a no-go area and gone to where he logically would assume I would be. I spoke to an exhibition supervisor at the desk there, but P hadn't been there.

The next thing I knew there was a tannoy announcement advising everyone in the exhibition hall to evacuate the building immediately, as the whole roof was unstable in the wind. This started a stampede of wildebeest, all heading to the Tube station in an attempt to get away from Olympia as fast as possible. Now anyone that knows Olympia will realise that it is located on a spur that shoots off from the District line, so trains are few and far between. It was almost impossible to stand on the platform, due to the number of panicking people trying to get on a train to escape and pandemonium had broken out, as people realised just how diabolical the weather was. I scoured the platform in the vain hope of seeing P, but there was just no way of knowing where he might be and I got pushed on to a train.

I got as far as Earl's Court and it was just bedlam, with no real possibility of changing on to a train that would take me to Victoria. I left the Tube station and hailed a black cab, as pieces of paper swirled around my head in the horrific wind. At least I felt safer in the taxi. The driver was really kind and did his best to get through traffic that was just at a standstill, as it was as if the whole of central London had realised that it needed to get out and get home before matters got worse. We crawled along and he thrice turned the meter back, in good Dick Whittington style, as we had knocked up a bill of about £30 each time. In the end, he turned to me, on the Gloucester Road and told me that I would be better off walking and trying to get to Victoria on foot.

I got out and it was truly frightening. Scaffolding was collapsing, pieces of wood were being ripped up and thrown around, I was nearly hit by masonry and, to cap it all, I didn't know where I was going!

I have no idea how I managed it, and it took me about 2 hours, but I made it back to Bessborough Gardens eventually. The answerphone was flashing and there was a message from P saying that he'd tried to find me and knew I'd spoken to the security guard. The message said that he was leaving Olympia.

About a half hour later, I received another call. This time, thankfully, P said that he was in a phone box near Pimlico Tube station, but didn't know where I lived. I hotfooted it out of the flat to find him and there he was, standing in the booth for safety and wearing his famous cream raincoat. Suffice to say, we didn't chance going out to dinner.

Having now assisted Drew with his projects, I was able to devote more time to other aspects of the job that I had been given to do. The first of these involved Nancy, who was organising British Gas's stand at the Ideal Home Show. I was drafted in to help her with that, writing some press materials and then attending on the day, as we had a royal visitor coming to the stand and it would be a case of all hands on deck, as so was chef Raymond Blanc. Raymond was just really starting out as, I suppose, one of the first 'celebrity' chefs of an era that, as I already knew, included Keith Floyd. My task, on the day, was to 'look after' him, as he signed copies of his book.

Raymond arrived at the stand and charmed everyone, of course, but then proceeded to tell us that he had a live TV slot booked, in which he would knock something up on toast. This wasn't part of the original plan, so I was despatched to shepherd him to the TV shoot and then get him back on the British Gas stand as quickly as humanly possible, so that he could be there for the arrival of the royal visitor.

I wouldn't say 'shepherding' was the right verb to use for this logistical exercise: it was more like playing kiss-chase without any of the fun of kissing. In what one could say was a typically French way, Raymond left it until the very last minute to head off to his TV appearance and then set off with all the pace of Red Rum towards the Earl's Court escalators, giving me little warning of his intention to flee the stand. Caught unawares, I was then trying to play catch up as he darted between startled show visitors and I ran after him, as if I wished to make a citizen's arrest. Up the escalators he ran, taking about three steps at a time, while I struggled behind teetering on my heels.

By this point in my life, I had a bit of a phobia about escalators anyway. A criminal called the 'acid attacker' had been frequenting Tube stations and spraying acid on the legs of people on escalators, so I was always a little bit fearful when riding up, but worse than that, just a few weeks before, an impatient commuter had gone up the outside of those calmly riding up the escalator, caught the hooked end of his umbrella on my skirt and whipped it over my head as he carried on climbing the stairs. I was mortified! As these thoughts flooded my head, Raymond was disappearing into the distance like a little dot in chef's whites.

By the time I caught him up, he had already dashed into the cooking arena and was fishing out pots and pans ready for his live cookery slot. He was a maestro at work at this point, showing his ability to multi-task and get everything on the boil at once – or so I thought. He'd put two slices of bread on the grill, as he worked on something else and suddenly this horrendous smell of burning emerged. In a panic, Raymond rushed back to the grill to find he'd made that most student-like of culinary mistakes – cremating the toast! He looked slightly embarrassed, but made some joke about it to deflect attention. The TV cameras captured it all.

He came out of the cookery demonstration area and was ready to chat to the crew, but looking at my watch, I could see that time was running out for him to get back to the stand for an important slot there, so I had to do a bit of interrupting throat clearing and attract his attention. Luckily he got the hint, looked at his watch, muttered something like 'Zut alors' and off we went again, heading down the Melling Road, back down the escalators, past the grandstand and onwards to the British Gas stand, where we arrived just in the nick of time for him to get in situ for the arrival of royalty.

After that, he was charm personified, signing copies of his book for all and sundry and chatting to everyone about his venue 'Le Manoir aux Quat' Saisons', which was much lesser known at the time than it is now. I decided to buy a book and asked him to sign it, so he wrote a little message in it for me and drew a funny little drawing of a chef's hat. From there, it was all plain sailing until we bid him adieu, but my legs didn't half ache when I got back to the flat that night.

I had become pretty friendly with Nancy at this point, as she had always been so kind to me, taking me to the shopping centre near Queen's Park, introducing me to her two gay flatmates (one of whom would always save me if I was being chatted up by someone I didn't like) and accompanying me on occasions when we were given free sponsors tickets to some event or other.

The big news in theatre land at this time was that Jerry Hall, then still the other half of Mick Jagger, was going to play the role of Chérie in the William Inge play 'Bus Stop' – a part played in the film of the same name by Marilyn Monroe. This was a new departure for Jerry Hall and her first major acting job. For some reason, I desperately wanted to go to the opening night, so bought two tickets and invited Nancy.

The play was on at the Lyric Theatre in Shaftesbury Avenue and it was said by some commentators that Jerry Hall's legs were about half as long as Piccadilly! Nancy and I arrived at the theatre and had to climb the steps avoiding a heap of paparazzi, who were just clicking at anything that moved, including us. We had only just stepped inside the doors when a girl swooped down on us and asked if we would mind if we were upgraded to VIP seats. I think we were quite flattered by this, assuming that we must have looked like ladies of a certain status in life, so we had no hesitation in trading in our tickets for the better ones.

With all the flapping around outside and the sudden ticket swap, I hadn't really had chance to look around the foyer, but Nancy left me for a minute or two and as I stood there on my own, my eyes descended on P, the man who had tried to woo me with his Dire Straits and U2 verses at Cambridge. I couldn't believe it!

Naturally, I went straight over to say hello to him, which was just as Nancy arrived behind me. He looked at me strangely, avoiding eye contact and more or less staring straight past me and didn't utter a single word. I tried again, reminding him of who I was, though he would have needed to be an idiot not to recognise me after all the effort he'd put in to his love missives! Again, I just got a blank stare and a mumble, but nothing more. This was when I realised that a woman, who I had thought was just standing there waiting for someone else, was actually with him for the evening and that he was deliberately trying not to acknowledge that he knew me.

As this realisation dawned, I withdrew, feeling like a complete idiot and, for some reason, walking backwards, in slow motion, as if retreating from a lion that I had unexpectedly encountered in the bush. I was still staring at him, as he looked down at his feet, until I drew parallel with Nancy again.

'Did you make a mistake and thought you knew him?' she asked.

'No', I said, now beginning to feel my blood boil, 'I do know him, but he's pretending that I don't.'

'That's awful', she said.

'Yes', I agreed, still fuming. That was the last I ever saw of P so my abiding memory of him is as a man who couldn't tell his girlfriend or acquaintance that we went to university together!

Luckily, a bell tinkled just after that and Nancy and I proceeded up some stairs to the VIP area, leaving P to presumably make his way to the cheap seats! We studied our tickets and found ourselves in the second row of the VIP area in the circle. As we sat down, Nancy whispered in an excited Scottish accent, 'Oh, my God, look who's sitting in front of us'. There, directly in front was Mick Jagger, sitting with the actor Ben Kingsley. We were transfixed by the back of their heads!

Jerry's Texan drawl certainly suited the mood of the diner in which the play is set and her rendition of 'That Old Black Magic' was poor, but apparently she was playing it that way. Her legs were certainly very long, but what I couldn't take my eyes off was her hair, masses of it, which I don't think had ever came across to me before when I'd seen her on screen. When she took her curtain call and bowed, her hair virtually touched the floor and then flew back over her head just to tumble down again when she gave her next bow. Mick looked suitably proud and Ben very supportive!

As we left the theatre, we were full of the thrill of sitting behind one of the country's biggest rock stars and Mahatma Gandhi – not many girls can say that! I was slightly less thrilled by the behaviour of a man upon whom I had once bestowed an Ugly Mug!

The rest of my time at British Gas HQ was spent on very interesting stuff indeed. Fred, the head of the press office, called me in one day and suggested that I, 'trot down the corridor and down the stairs', to visit a division called Social Policy, which needed PR support for their sponsorship programme. I duly went down the stairs and was amazed by what I discovered – a small department handling some of the most significant sponsorships in the country, all of which needed to be maximised through PR.

The months that followed this discovery were very busy indeed, whether I was liaising with the chap responsible for English Schools Basketball, or heading to the Natural History Museum for a meeting about the British Gas Wildlife Photographer of the Year Competition. There were numerous environmental sponsorships to handle and some really unique ones.

One of these stemmed from a new wave of British Gas branding, which was all built around the letters BG. I'm sure this stood for 'Bloody Galling' as far as the press office staff were concerned, but we were all encouraged to use the BG theme as much as possible. Hence, when a group of schoolchildren asked British Gas to fund a bus trip to Berlin, to help East Berliners integrate with the West, I christened the initiative 'Bussing Goodwill'.

The 'Bussing Goodwill' project involved liaising with the bus operator over branding across the body of the vehicle, arranging branded merchandise for the kids, sorting out some video footage of the children setting off and organising a national press call, which had to be held on a Sunday. A venue for the photo call and bus's departure had to be sourced and this ended up being at County Hall, on the banks of the Thames, close to where the London Eye is now located.

I sold in the story to various editors and managed to get ITN News interested in coming along to do some interviews with the kids and film the children setting off. The day set for this was a Sunday and the weather gods were anything but kind. I was being picked up by a photographer called Grant from Monitor – a company British Gas used a lot – and from the moment I stepped out of the door, to the moment I got back in, it bucketed down. Grant and I spent hours in the car park at County Hall, as the film crew got seemingly every angle, from down from the luggage racks, to up from under the wheel arches, while we got a complete drenching, save for the precious five minutes, when I was taken on board the coach with the kids to do a quick interview.

All of this resulted in several minutes' coverage on ITN that night, with my left arm quite prominent on camera throughout! When Grant dropped me back home again, all I wanted to do was warm up in the bath – and they say PR is glamorous!

The other really interesting sponsorship was that of the English National Opera's tour of Russia – the first ever tour of the Soviet Union by a major foreign opera company. I was summoned to Fred's office and asked to attend a public announcement about this momentous occasion, which included an address by Douglas Hurd, as this tour was as political as it was artistic. The room was packed with press and the news that a truly English institution was due to venture beyond the Iron Curtain and almost march its sopranos into Red Square seemed to surprise many. This briefing was just the starting point of my involvement. Now it had been announced, I had to maximise this sponsorship.

Nobody was under any illusions as to why British Gas was sponsoring this arts tour. Russia had rich natural gas reserves and, even then, British Gas knew that we would be running out of gas within decades. This sponsorship was an approach – an entente cordiale to be extended to the most powerful people in Russia so that British Gas could start a dialogue about the gas reserves and a supply chain from them.

To this end, wooing the Russian media was a must and this was still the USSR, not the Russia we know today. It was a country in which TASS was all-powerful as the country's main news agency and disseminator of information. Getting TASS to sit down with British Gas would be a real coup.

I started to think about how we could maximise this sponsorship and as ideas emerged, I gathered a crack team around me – Angela and a new temp in the office, S. By this point, Angela had fully inducted me into the ways of Islington, having arranged a few nights out for the girls at a cocktail bar she had a particular fondness for. I, on the other hand, had tried to induct S into the world of cricket.

S was very different from the other temps, as she spoke as if she had been born with a silver spoon in her mouth and lacked both the earthiness of Angela and the laid-back air of Michael's secretary. She was really quite prim and proper and a bit of a fish out of water when she arrived. I felt rather sorry for her, so tried to take her under my wing a bit, which is when the invitation to the cricket was extended.

Now cricket is something that has always been a passion of mine, in fact one of my real ambitions is to go on tour with the Barmy Army. At this point, however, I had only been on tour in South Wales for a day, but did know quite a lot about it. Whenever I had been shipped off to my grandparents in Chesterfield as a child, I used to watch cricket with my granddad, as he was older than my grandma and retired while she was still at work. I had also had cricket-mad friends, spent days at Lords with my flatmates, while living in Tufnell Park, and even spent at day watching New Zealand v Pakistan at Eden Park in Auckland, just so I could see Imran Khan.

While living in Bristol, I had supported Lancashire whenever they played Somerset or Gloucestershire and had devoured Graeme (Foxy) Fowler's book from cover to cover. Now, living so close to The Oval – just a few stops away from my flat in Pimlico – it would have been a crying shame not to go and watch cricket in the shadow of the gas towers.

I hadn't really intended inviting S to go with me, but she'd got wind of it somehow and hinted that she might like to come. I caved in and invited her. This greatly amused Angela, who didn't know how I would cope with the new recruit for a whole day. Even I was worried.

On the day, I got there nice and early, so that I could watch practice in the nets. The teams were warming up and I was virtually sitting in the stand on my own, which prompted Alec Stewart to come over and say hello, which I found very sweet and polite. I was just dressed in shorts and a T-shirt, ready to soak up some sunshine: I wasn't expecting S to turn up dressed for Henley-on-Thames.

As she approached me in the stand, I couldn't believe my eyes. She was dressed in the finest white blouse and skirt, brandishing a very posh picnic basket, which put my carrier bags to shame and, to cap it all, wearing a string of pearls! I didn't like to mention that she was a little overdressed, but I could see people nudging each other as she smoothed her skirt and sat down.

S was no more clued up about the rules of cricket than she was on dress etiquette for the public stands at a county cricket match. I spent a long time trying to explain the rules to her, while she reached into her picnic basket and withdrew all sorts of delicatessen delights, which must have cost her a fortune. I felt truly mortified for her when a batsman hit the ball for six and it came flying our way. I swerved and ducked and S just sat there as it landed on top of her grapes, which sprayed juice all over her skirt. I think she maybe then appreciated why it's wiser to dress down at a county cricket club game.

My crack team were to help me with my chosen strategy – well the second part of it, at least. The first part was highly visual and required the services of an up-and-coming photographer called Stewart Bernstein. The plan was to make the most of our access to the prima donna in the opera that was to be taken to Russia, which was that which should not be named – Verdi's Macbeth. This was an American opera singer, making the tour of Russia perhaps even more significant, and she was willing to be taken out on location for a press photograph.

Something truly dramatic was needed and the idea that emerged was to take Lady Macbeth to a British Gas site, where she could sing from the top of a gas holder. I had to do quite a lot of ringing around to find the perfect site, both in terms of her location and the positioning of gas holders. After a fair few conversations, the Fulham site was selected.

Myself and Stewart set off for the shoot, with a taxi arranged for Lady Macbeth. There were half a dozen British Gas workers on site when we got there, all wearing their hard hats and keen for us to do the same. While we donned one, it was absolutely essential that Lady Macbeth did not. I don't recall Shakespeare mentioning such an accessory in his murderous play and we were going for the highly dramatic shot, not a hugely comical one!

When Lady Macbeth turned up, the workers could hardly believe their eyes. She was wearing a long, flowing black gown, a long black wig, the most dramatic stage make-up and a chilling expression. To say she looked every inch a manipulative murder beholden to witchcraft and skullduggery would be an understatement.

She was extremely obliging and eager to please and didn't bat an eyelid when we suggested that she climb the metal steps up the side of the gas holder. Once she was positioned at the top, Stewart began snapping away, framing her dark silhouette against the skyline, as the camera lens looked up from ground level.

Stewart then wanted to get another shot – that of Lady Macbeth singing from on high to one of the hard-hatted gas employees down below. There were no shortage of takers, but one guy, probably the most senior, pushed himself forward and played his part in this photographic exercise.

The resulting photos were simply breathtaking and the aim was to now get these placed with the arts editors – particularly those on The Guardian and The Independent. I wrote short but message-filled captions for the photos, encapsulating exactly what the story was about and British Gas's involvement. Given the gas holder setting, it made little sense for an editor to try and cut the sponsor's name out of the story and so we were hopeful that the sponsorship would receive great arts page promotion.

This proved to be the case, with the dramatic pictures appearing large on the arts pages of both of the key target publications. This was such a massive success that Fred instantly came to my desk to praise my work. I was extremely proud of this PR exercise and the results that it had generated.

The second part of the strategy revolved around a launch in a Russian restaurant. There were several from which to choose, so carrying out a recky was imperative and I and my crack team set about our business with great energy, visiting various Russian restaurants, the most famous of which was Borscht 'n' Tears in Knightsbridge.

For some reason, we didn't get that much assistance from whoever met us at the bastion of Russian cuisine at the time, finding that the owners at another Russian restaurant, just off Baker Street, were much more obliging. We opted to have our launch there, liking the room size, trusting the owner to devise a suitable Russian menu for the event and ticking the box for Russian entertainment.

What then remained was to write a press pack, get it translated into Russian and then get invitations out to all key Russian media. Thankfully, all key Russian media responded in the affirmative, including the mighty TASS, who asked to send the head of the London bureau and his wife.

Myself, S and Angela ensured that everything was in place on the day of launch, working out seating plans, when Lady Macbeth should enter the room, drafting question and answer briefings and ensuring that the research I had conducted had been assimilated by the British Gas management attending on the day.

All went extremely smoothly, with our Russian guests seemingly appreciating our efforts to entertain them and enable them to take up the option of an in-depth interview with a British Gas chief at a later date. I sat opposite the TASS bureau chief and tried to make him feel at home. Valuable relationships were forged that day by the time the Russian media representatives departed and the British Gas management followed hot on their heels.

This really just left myself, S and Angela, waiting on staff and the band of Russian gypsies who had been playing and dancing their traditional dance 'the kalinka' during the course of the event. We were all huddled together when one of the musicians came over to me and said, completely out of the blue, 'Would you like me to give you a gypsy kiss?' I was just fathoming out what to say, which took a good 30 seconds, by which point he must have thought that I wasn't going to answer and had gone back to the rest of the group.

Angela was totally bemused by this and said to me in her typically loud London voice, 'What's a gypsy kiss then darlin'. Wish you'd found out!' I shrugged my shoulders, totally unprepared for what was coming next. The prim and proper S, sitting on the other side of me, assumed a very learned expression on her face, as if in deep thought. She then leaned across me so that both myself and Angela could hear her, without the gypsy band listening in. She adopted an even more serious look.

'I think I know what a gipsy kiss is', she whispered, in her terribly posh, plummy voice, but with an earnest tone that we could not ignore. Angela raised her eyebrows in expectation. I looked S in the eye, expectantly. S continued, undaunted. 'I think it's one of those', she paused for a couple of seconds, maybe for dramatic effect, though I think it was more a question of steeling herself, and then started up again. 'Well, you know', she whispered in an even quieter voice, '… one of those … those … those … down below kisses'.

My mouth must have fallen open at this point, while Angela, never one to stay quiet, broke out into the most uncontrollable, loud laughter I have ever heard. She was rolling around on her chair, as if she was about to fall off at any moment and had become the centre of attention, as all staff and musicians turned their eyes on her. Within seconds, tears were rolling down her face, which set me off into hysterical giggles too, leaving S just sitting there clueless as to what we were laughing at.

I think all of this concluded with Angela saying, 'Oh S, you're just priceless darlin' and saying to me, 'Didn't you want a down below kiss then?' This just set the pair of us off even more, as S got into a slight huff, still not knowing what the hilarity was about, or what she had said that was so amusing.

As everyone else had left at this point, I never expected to hear any more about this hilarious offering from the charmingly naïve S. All the management were delighted with the event and the relationships it would forge and I was called to Fred's office to receive some praise and to review a sheet of thumbnail photographs taken on the day. We started to pick some out, when he pointed to one of myself, Angela and S. 'Jane, should this one have a caption, do you think?' My brow creased in puzzlement. 'Well', he continued, 'I just thought it should have a caption that reads, 'I think it's one of those down below kisses'. At this I just cracked out laughing, while wondering how on earth Fred had heard about S's classic statement. The source was never identified, but I have a copy of that photo and every time I look at it I just burst into laughter!

I absolutely loved my time at British Gas HQ and the people I worked with too, but all good things come to an end and this experience ended far too abruptly. The woman who I was filling in for was brave and resilient and overcame all the adversity that life had thrown at her far faster than expected and British Gas was then thrown into a frenzy, adapting the office and making numerous arrangements to make her re-entry into her working life as easy as possible. I wouldn't have expected any less of them.

They tried to keep me, but British Gas Southwestern demanded my return. I had neither the spirit nor the inclination to go back to Bristol. The Maltese Falcon had broken up with his girlfriend and found another, there were too many bad memories of my marriage and I had lived it up far too much in London. British Gas HQ said they would try to create a temporary job for me in HR, until they could move me back into PR, but they needed time. By this point, I had started seeing the deputy pub manager from the local pub now and again. He could get his own pub to run, if I joined him. It seemed a working marriage of convenience. Though it was a massive wrench, it was time for me to move on.

Chapter Eight
PUB PURGATORY

There are some mistakes in life that you make for good reasons and I think that opting to work in a pub, as the 'landlady, and earning the minimum wage was one of those. I longed to be back at British Gas and hoped they would manage to sort the personnel wrangles out. Little did I know that events would take over and completely turn my life upside down.

True to their word, the brewery gave my 'other half' a pub to run – a newly acquired establishment that was completely run down and in major need of a facelift despite being in one of the most fashionable streets in Chelsea – Flood Street. It was an old-fashioned pub, with kitchens that were filthy and tales of a landlord, who had completely neglected his duties echoing from every wall. The wallpaper was peeling off the walls in the upstairs accommodation, springs poked through mattresses, furniture was broken: it was a tip.

Professional cleaners were brought in to sort out the kitchen, but little was done to address the other issues. I sort of stumbled along through these early days like a zombie, feeling a huge sense of loss at no longer being part of the BG press office and hoping that something would turn up. In reality, despite my title, I was no more than the cook and the barmaid.

It has to be said that I threw myself into the cooking. I compiled some really great recipes – though, in reality, I had no choice. People needed feeding and I was their only option. I quickly learned how to create three main dishes for the hotplate by 12.00 on the dot, set myself up for the sandwich and jacket potato rush, get the fryers ready for the chips and prepare for all the washing up. I tried to convince myself that this was good, that this was what life had been like in my Nan's hotel, that this was just a temporary blip.

It's so true that you don't know what people are like until you live with them and that was certainly the case. Certain personality traits and habits displayed by my new man had been well hidden from me. It was true that the pressure was well and truly on him, with the brewery judging his every move, so I made some allowances. I had a Aussie barman called Dean who I could turn to when I needed a sensitive ear and some of the British Gas girls would come and see me from time to time. In reality though, I think it was the locals who kept me going.

Although the Cooper's Arms was just a few minutes walk from the King's Road, it sat on the border between the fashionable, toffs' Chelsea and the real Chelsea, on the nearby council estate. Its clientele reflected this divide, with everyone from architects and office workers to a man who was once a stunt actor in the movies, gradually filtering back through the door, when they heard the previous landlord had left. Certain people who gave us their custom will always have a place in my heart for the way they treated me, but more importantly, for the way they ignored what happened to me.

This trauma started after I had been told that my secondment had to end, due to the return of my role's former occupant. I first noticed clumps of hair coming out when I washed it, but didn't think too much of it, but this continued and continued, with more hair falling out by the day when I reached Chelsea. My long, blonde locks were soon stumps of hair poking out of my scalp, with the hair loss totally disproportionate across my scalp. I suppose the sensible thing would have been to shave it all off and buy a wig, but I couldn't bear it and secretly hoped some miracle would happen and I would wake up and all would be back to normal.

There wasn't one single occasion that anyone in the pub mentioned this to me, not the customers, not the brewery, not even my other half. I wished that someone would, as I felt desperate and alone. In my own head, it was clear to me that everyone thought I was having chemotherapy, so nobody dared upset me. The only person who ever broached the subject at all was Angela and she tried to buck me up by saying that she had lost a lot of hair when she had been pregnant. Without Angela and my Nan, who would tell me on the telephone that she had suffered from sudden hair loss too, I don't know what I would have done.

What this did to me was to make me completely withdraw from social contact. I would literally hide upstairs in the kitchen as much as possible, only scurrying to the hotplate if I absolutely had to. I would beg not to have to man the bar and would volunteer to do the banking, getting out into the wider world of the King's Road rather than having to see people face to face: people who might ask, query, probe and upset.

Getting out on to the King's Road had it own perils as, at the time, a hair salon was actively promoting itself, by continuously leafleting in the high street. Every time I went to the bank I would be given a leaflet offering me a hair offer of some sort or other. I cringed every time the leaflet went into my hand and a little bit more of me died inside. A woman's hair is supposed to be her crowning glory. All I now had were a few clumps here and there. Until this has happened to you, you have no idea how hard and soul-destroying it is. It is the worst pain imaginable and one that I truly hope I will never experience again. Finding the inner strength to stand up and walk down that street and say, without verbalising it, 'Take me as I am, and, by the way, I might have no hair, but I am wearing a Benetton jumper', was excruciatingly hard.

When I looked in the mirror, all I saw was a gaunt, semi-bald person looking back at me: a person I didn't recognise at all, a phantom that had appeared overnight to take over my body. I came to note the pitying looks. I cried alone upstairs for hours, wondering how this nightmare had started. I did nothing about pushing for another job at British Gas, as all I wanted to do was hide away in shame.

I had left British Gas in the summer and I went with my new boyfriend to Tunisia in the October. I think this was a turning point, as what happened there made me realise that I had to do something other than hoping that things would just get better. This realisation came to me in a Berber village where they had filmed a Star Wars movie. We had pulled in there for lunch and were taken to meet some of the villagers. An elderly Berber woman took one look at me and pointed her wizened finger at my hair, laughing and commenting in her own tongue about it. Amazingly, I didn't cry, though I did wince a little. I just accepted that she was being honest and truthful and doing what nobody back in London had dared to do. Her frankness was my turning point.

In fact, the village then also gave me the first real laughter I had enjoyed for an age. Perhaps laughter is the best medicine after all and maybe that was another factor that helped me turn the corner. We had gone to the Berber village on a tour bus that comprised passengers of all nationalities. During our lunch stop, we were told that a toilet block was at our disposal, so before boarding the bus again, I headed into the building.

Inside, I found around four metal cubicles that appeared to be normal toilets, but before I could head into one, a Danish woman from the tour bus emerged from the cubicle at the end of the room. She headed towards me, wearing a strange expression and an ambassadorial air, as if she had been given the duty of explaining the toilet situation to me. She moved her face close to mine and declared eagerly, in a lilting Danish voice I had only previously heard in a 'Two Ronnies' sketch, 'Eet waz kwite haard, but I managed eet in zee end'.

I stopped in my tracks, wondering what on earth she was talking about and whether she too had suffered alopecia. She saw the bemusement on my face, so led me into the cubicle she had been in. "Eet iz because eet iz in zee corner", she said, pointing to what, to me, was clearly a shower hole, though the shower attachment was nowhere to be seen. 'I had to, how you say, squat', she explained further.

I stared in amazement at what she was showing me, as she left me to it and headed back to the bus. 'This can't be right', I thought, wondering how logistically she had even managed to pee in the hole given its position tight in the corner of the metal cubicle. I tried to contemplate directing pee into this hole and was sure I wouldn't manage it. Instead, I made my way back down the line of doors, questioning what on earth was inside those. As I opened each door, I discovered perfectly normal toilets in every single one. My Danish friend has seemingly made the assumption that she was in an underdeveloped country and that squatting to pee in a shower hole was what went on here. I just couldn't stop laughing, even when back on the bus. Every time I looked at her, I imagined her squatting and that just started me off all over again – it was a truly welcome tonic.

As I have said, this holiday was a turning point for me. I returned for a weekend in Bristol shortly afterwards, to check the house was fine for winter and went back to my former hairdresser. To say she was horrified when she saw me was putting it mildly, but she did what the doctor had been unable to do and actually helped me. She gave me some special scalp treatments that encouraged hair growth and gradually these started to work, with patches of baby hair beginning to appear. It was just like growing up all over again.

Once the hair started to re-grow, there seemed to be no stopping it. It was actually quite thick and healthy and I think the fact that I had now just accepted my lot in the pub helped. I had given up on the British Gas dream and the lack of fretting about what might happen seemed to allow my body to heal, whatever misfortune had befallen it.

I started to frequent the bar area more and I got a new playmate in the kitchen – a girl called Erica. At face value, Erica and I were like chalk and cheese. She was a bit of a girl, to put it mildly, and would date almost anyone in the pub who asked her out, regardless of age, looks, or personal hygiene levels, but how we used to laugh in the kitchen. The most hilarious time of all was when one of the regulars, someone who had been very high up in the Royal Navy, decided that he wanted us to handle the catering for a party that he wanted to throw for his Royal Navy association. He had asked for a pretty advanced buffet and I had started to prep things a few hours before Erica arrived. By the time she got there, we had virtually no space left in the kitchen, very few bowls or pans to use (as we had virtually none to start with) and almost no time left to throw the rest of it together.

Erica decided the only way forward was for us to open a bottle of wine, which we did. This seemed to do the trick and somehow, using absolutely and surface and piece of equipment we could find, we got the whole thing together, knocking up everything from sausage rolls to guacamole, despite being in hysterics for most of the time we were working on it.

The party went down a storm, to the extent that I was presented with a beautifully decorated old-fashioned flagon with stopper, which was full of Navy Rum. I have no idea whether there was any value to this, but it was of immense value to Erica and I, as it proved that out of total adversity there really does come triumph.

That was not the only triumph to be scored at this pub. Once my hair had started to grow back, I had become much more involved in the more strategic running of the pub, being actually able to face meetings with the area manager, who kept saying that my other half could get his own pub, if he proved he could make a success of this one. The figures were getting better with each passing week, so in my own head, I saw light at the end of the tunnel: he could have his pub and I could perhaps get another job in PR.

The thing that set me alight was a 'Wines From Spain' promotion, which was being run across all of the brewery's pubs in London and the South East. The winning pub landlord would win a trip to Spain, while runners up would receive a crate full of Spanish wine. I had my eyes well and truly on the prize and threw myself into this with great gusto.

For once, I could use my promotional skills and I went to town. I created all kinds of magic in red and yellow, which spruced up the tatty pub no end, created special Spanish dishes to put on as menu specials, highlighted Spanish wines that could be sampled, ran Spanish events and so much more. I knew that we could never sell the volume of wine that one of the big brewery pubs would shift, but thought that perhaps our promotional efforts would score highly in other aspects of the voting, particularly when the judges came round in person. So it proved. Our tiny little run-down pub gained a runners-up accolade. I was so proud, particularly as some of the diners told me my Spanish pork olives dish was absolutely divine!

All sorts of people drifted through our door. One day it was John Hurt just having a quiet drink at the bar: another day it was Wayne Sleep pirouetting around a chair. I would see celebrities on the King's Road quite often: Jane Asher in Waitrose, George Best coming out of a bar and, very regularly, Bob Geldof and Paula Yates, who only lived around the corner. Sometimes, from the kitchen window I could see Paula pushing a pram up towards the King's Road. Strangely, the Geldofs were again having an association with my life.

However, our most regular 'celebrity' started coming in very soon after we had taken over, always wearing sunglasses, whatever the weather. She had an entourage, which included a friend called 'The Major' and a live-in nurse named Greta, as the mysterious customer was not in the best of health. We soon discovered, that our regular visitor was Lady Redgrave, mother to Vanessa, Lynn and Corin and widow of Sir Michael Redgrave. In her acting career, she was known as Rachel Kempson. She was part of one of the most famous British acting dynasties of all time.

We never knew exactly what mood she would be in when joining us – sometimes upbeat, sometimes down, always heavily reliant on her companions and very rarely saying anything to us, largely communicating through Greta. I liked Greta a lot and she told me that life had been hard at times for Lady Redgrave. We did what we could to please her when she came in and served her food quite regularly, but I never imagined that I would be asked to serve her a Christmas meal on Boxing Day. This sent me into a panic really, as it was such a huge commitment and I didn't want to mess it up, but I was asked to do it by Greta and did what I could to make it special. In her way, I think Lady Redgrave appreciated it and I even got a 'that was very nice' when I cleared the plates. That was a massive relief.

Although I thought she might quite like her outings to the pub, I had no idea how loyal she would be when bad news struck. Despite all our efforts, the full support of the regulars, the awful living quarters we had endured and our success in the Spanish promotion, the brewery decided to lease the pub out and not make my other half the landlord. This was a massive kick in the teeth and I was devastated. When Greta heard that we would be leaving, she told Lady Redgrave, who put up the most enormous fuss. She actually said that she would contact Vanessa and organise a petition, which just blew me away as I envisaged the placards waving and some sort of siege with Vanessa chained to the front door barring anyone from entering! I knew it wouldn't actually happen, but just the fact that she felt so strongly about it was enough. When we did leave, she gave me a gift of a signed book, which I still have in my possession. That meant the world to me.

Some of the regulars, who had been so kind to me during my hair loss, were also massively supportive. I had become very close to a couple from the Peabody Trust Council Estate and we went to a sort of farewell party at one of their houses. They gave me an engraved glass, which read, 'You have to kiss a lot of frogs before you find your prince'. Truer words there could not be.

We were tossed out into the world of 'relief managers' like flotsam and jetsam floating on the tide, never knowing where we would be sent next. I absolutely hated every minute of this existence, it holding virtually no pleasure whatsoever. Wherever we went, we were simply stand-ins and the staff always thought they could get away with things that they wouldn't have dared try with their full-time bosses. One of the best places was actually another pub in Chelsea, close to the football ground, where our former regulars all turned up during our two-week stint. The landlady had left a lot of food for us to use to keep her menu going – it would just have been helpful if she'd explained that the lentil soup, which we had thought a vegetarian option, actually had bacon in it!

When we went to another pub in Kingston-upon-Thames, Drew turned up with his wife and I had a great time reliving days in the British Gas press office and wishing I was working there, rather than in this life of drudgery.

We were shipped out to Chislehurst for three weeks, not to act as relief managers, but to pick up the skills of running a restaurant and extremely busy bar. This was one of the worst of the experiences for me, despite it being a really nice pub. I was shoved into the restaurant on Mother's Day, when tables were heaving, a woman was wailing as she'd lost a diamond from her ring and pandemonium reigned. I was allocated the task, at one point, of serving desserts from the hostess trolley and try as I might, I couldn't cut one of them. At that point, the Spanish front-of-house manager came running over saying, 'What you need is the Black & Decker!' – at least that made me laugh.

I desperately wanted to leave this world and get back into PR, but I was semi-stuck by this point, being part of the management programme at the brewery. I was told to wear plunging necklines and short skirts and totally resented being pushed into wearing what wasn't of my choice.

Things were never worse than when, in the middle of January, we were told to go and stay in a brewery-owned house in Wandsworth and await instructions. The house had no heating that worked and was absolutely freezing, to the extent that we had to switch the kitchen gas rings on to try to get some warmth that would make it habitable.

All I wanted to do by this point was get back to Bristol, to my nice house in Shirehampton. My opportunity came when we were given two weeks off. The next place to which we were ordered to go had a bit of a reputation. I refused point-blank to go and sent my other half off on his own. I had suffered more than enough of this appalling itinerant life, could see no real prospects of any permanent position being offered to my boyfriend and thought that he might as well go back to being a deputy somewhere, ideally without me.

Fortunately or unfortunately, whichever way you look at it, a job advert leapt out at him in one of the trade papers. Things happen for a reason and although what occurred next was awful in so many ways, there are aspects that I would not change for the world. This period in my life almost destroyed me, but it also made me complete. Without it, life would have been very different.

The job was for a manager's position in a country pub in north Somerset, about 15 miles south of what you might term Bristol itself. The pub was extremely well furnished and kept, had a sports bar, a main bar, a massive family room and also a big garden. It was in the middle of nowhere, but had a huge flat covering most of the downstairs lounge areas. After experiences with no heating in Wandsworth and troublesome staff elsewhere, it seemed like heaven. Appearances can, however, be deceptive.

We went along for an interview and somehow got the job. The flat was painted throughout, as the departing landlord and landlady were heavy smokers and the walls were completely stained with nicotine. They were moving on to their 'dream' pub in another part of Bristol, which was their choice entirely. We were to take up the reins just before the August Bank Holiday weekend.

And so we did. As you can imagine, this was a bit of a shock to the system, with so much to learn and so little time in which to do it before one of the busiest days, if not the busiest, of the year. The pub heaved on the Friday and Saturday and then Sunday lunchtime. We thought there might have been some respite then, but the Sunday night was also pretty busy. At the start of it though, I did find some time to sit in the sportsman's bar and start to study menus, planning what I might want to put on or change.

I'd situated myself here deliberately, as it was very much a locals' area with skittles, dominos and other traditional pub games. It was very rustic in this part of the pub, with the main lounge being much more modern. That's probably why I took such note of what happened that night.

While in the course of studying my menus, a group of youths wandered in and the sound of voices made me look up. Although I'd only lived there for a few days, I knew instantly that they weren't local. They were in designer bomber jackets and trainers, with four boys and one girl in the group. I love people watching and there was one I couldn't take my eyes off, as he stuck out like a sore thumb, wearing a green baseball cap and being remarkable for what I would call Scandinavian blonde curls and piercing eyes. The moment I looked at him, I saw the racing driver Niki Lauda looking back at me. I tried not to stare, but in the smallish sportsman's bar could not fail to overhear the conversation.

They were asking the member of staff serving them where they could find the nearest petrol station, as they were out of fuel. If I'd had a clue, I would have probably told them, but I hadn't the foggiest, so just kept looking at the menus. They got their drinks and moved away out of the sportsman's bar. I thought they'd probably realised that other parts of the pub were more suitable for them, though I didn't watch where they went.

The pub was again really busy, with lots of families coming in to eat, plus regulars and others just passing by. When it came to closing, my other half decided, for whatever reason, that he wanted to get to grips with the books and count up the takings, making all the entries in the relevant accounts systems. As all of this was new, it took him hours. It got to 1am and I was beginning to fall asleep, so I left him to it. He must have continued working on the figures way after 2am.

Having finally got to bed, I was awakened by the phone in the bedroom ringing. I sat up, though my other half did not stir. It was dark and I stumbled out of bed to pick up the phone. I only half realised who it was – one of our cleaners, who we had been told was a little bit simple and not terribly coherent. I'd not even met him at this point. His voice was full of panic and he was rambling madly. 'Missus, Missus, I'm not coming in, I've got to tell you Missus. There was a man by the back door and I ran away Missus'. As I have said, we'd been warned that he was as good as gold, but not altogether right, so I wasn't sure what to make of any of this. I woke my boyfriend up and told him what had happened.

Our bedroom was the furthest room along a long corridor that ran the width of the pub. To reach the door leading down the stairs into the sportsman's bar entailed walking past three other bedrooms and the lounge, with every floorboard along this route squeaking in this old building with its creaky timbers. We didn't do anything to be quiet as we couldn't make head nor tail of the cleaner's story.

At the bottom of the stairs leading out of the flat was a thick wooden door that had to be opened outwards into the sportsman's bar. To the left of the door was the start of the long corridor that led to the kitchen and back door, if you took another left, or to the back of the pub and the family room if you continued straight. Access to the back of both bars was via this corridor, though both were closed off with gates. The cigarette machines were also along the corridor.

My other half opened the door into the sportsman's bar and I followed, taking one step out. I signalled to him that someone was rustling something behind the bar. We both assumed the cleaner had now come into the pub and was back behind the counter, where we couldn't see him. I'd taken a step out into the centre of the bar. My other half started to walk up the corridor to find the employee.

As long as I live, I will never forget what happened next. As my boyfriend walked down the pub, a sub-human growl shattered the silence, unlike any noise I have ever heard a person make. It made me freeze on the spot, as if my blood had been instantaneously chilled. I couldn't move and felt mummified, even though by now I was watching a man pounding his fists into my boyfriend's body, having pinned him to the ground. I watched as he then started kicking him ferociously in the ribs and then started to aim for his head. I can remember thinking that I was watching him die.

At that point, something stirred within me, which was completely stupid, as until that moment the sub-human beast hadn't known I was there. I didn't know what I was doing at all, but something just took me over. Had I been thinking with any logic, I would have picked up the bar stool that was right in front of me for defence, but I wasn't thinking rationally for one minute. I'd seen the man's face lit up by the torch my boyfriend had been carrying. It was 'Niki Lauda', still wearing his green baseball cap and green designer bomber jacket. He stared back at me, startled by me screaming, probably louder than I've ever shouted before, 'I know you; you were in here earlier on'.

Why I chose to shout that, heaven only knows. Maybe my voice just blurted out the information that my mind had just processed, as the logical thing would have been to shout 'stop' or 'get out'. I think, having alerted him to my presence, I actually started to feel something – a fear that I had been too paralysed to feel until that point. He was just a few yards away and I had nothing in my hands to defend myself. He could easily just have attacked me too, but for some reason, he ran the other way into the darkness.

I turned, ran to the stairs and shut the door, putting the bolt on to it. I then ran as fast as I could the length of the flat, back to the phone in the bedroom in a blind panic. I picked up the receiver and dialled 999. A voice asked me which service I wanted and I said police. I thought I was getting somewhere, but then just burst into tears. The operator asked me for my telephone number and I didn't know it. 'I don't know; I don't know, I've just moved in', I wept, 'and I think my boyfriend could be dead'. I hadn't seen him move after the kick to the head and I didn't really have a clue what was now going on downstairs. The choice had been to go to him, or to summon help and I'd chosen the second option. The operator kept asking me for information and I must just have babbled randomly, making little sense. All I could tell them was the name of the pub. I was told help could be some time – we were in the middle of nowhere, after all.

I don't think I was entirely sure that help was on its way when I made my way back down the stairs. I didn't have a clue what was going on behind the solid wooden door and I knew that to get out I would have to open it outwards, with the possibility that the man was standing there ready to attack me too. I tried to listen for noise, but could hear nothing. I remember just saying, 'Are you alive, or are you dead?' What answer I thought I would get if it were the latter, goodness knows.

I heard a groan, but wasn't sure who it was. I called out again and heard his voice, but still had no idea if he was on his own or with someone standing over him or making him talk. I was shaking like a leaf, but couldn't just leave him there. Tentatively, I opened the door, scared stiff of who might be behind it, but deciding that I would have to risk it, as he might need help. I stepped out and thankfully just found him, attempting to get to his feet, looking groggy, but at least appearing to be alone.

I looked around the dark interior of the pub, wondering if someone was lurking in the shadows, but suddenly realised that something had changed, or maybe it hadn't and I just hadn't noticed it before. The front door of the pub was now wide open. I panicked at this, wondering what was going on and hurried my boyfriend behind our door and on to the stairs, slamming it shut behind us and securing the bolt. He looked as white as a sheet & said he thought his ribs were broken. Having seen the kicking he'd had, I thought that might be the least of his worries.

I think the stress of it all, coupled with a sudden feeling of safety then took over. I'm not sure how we knew that the police had finally arrived, though it must have been a good 45 minutes to an hour before they did, if not longer. I presume we heard voices and realised we could open the door. It was by now heading towards dawn and we were sat down in the bar and asked to give statements. I can remember saying over and over again that I would recognise the Niki Lauda guy anywhere, in any street, in any shop, in any mall. I was asked to give my description of him so that a police artist could draw up a photo-fit. That was easy. I could describe him to the last detail. Around this point, our female cleaner arrived, having heard there was trouble. It was she who discovered the pile of human excrement in the corner of the bar. This it transpired was a 'calling card' that he or they had left at various pubs in the valley, as was the turning off of freezers. Nobody had ever seen the culprit(s) before though. It suddenly dawned on me that this meant I was the only person that could identify the green baseball-capped assailant and this was why so much time was being taken over my photo-fit description. That suddenly placed a huge burden on my shoulders.

Throughout the interviews, I felt that there was something bigger going on here that we weren't being told about. I just detected signals between officers and odd comments that seemed strange given the ferociousness of the attack. I didn't understand why there wasn't more urgency to try to find them. Maybe it was just the police way.

In the midst of all the bedlam, with people now running all round the pub making cups of tea, bringing me several brandies now the interviews were over, cleaning up the excrement and taking photos, several things came to light. Firstly, the assailant had managed to get in to the pub through a window in the family room, which it seems he had probably opened while in the pub during the evening. Perhaps the group had been casing the joint the moment they walked in. The window only opened very slightly though, so to get in was quite a skill.

Secondly, they had, at some point opened the front door and it was felt there were at least two of them, as the cleaner had now been interviewed. It was discovered that they had also tried to steal our car, but his arrival had probably prevented that and our appearance in the bar had come too soon for the theft to be completed. As I knew, they'd claimed they had no petrol. Perhaps they had no car either at that point, so planned on stealing ours and potentially having to buy petrol if it was empty, probably figuring that rural garages wouldn't have cameras.

One really significant thing was that they'd got away with nothing. There was no money in the tills and although they'd smashed all the cigarette machines, they'd run off leaving a holdall full of cigarettes and another with the money in.

Finally, it came to light that one of our customers had actually picked them up and driven them to the south of Bristol, as he was a printer and worked a really early shift. He'd found two of them hitchhiking on the road and had let them jump in. From my point of view, at least that meant there was another witness who had seen them. Of that I was truly grateful.

The three of us (though what use my boyfriend was heaven only knows) were asked to go to review photos of various criminals down at the central police station in Bristol. I scoured the books we were given, but there was nothing even close to the man I'd seen. I felt really flat and despondent after this episode, as I'd really hoped we'd identify at least the aggressor, if not the accomplice.

Shortly after this, we were approached, via the police, to film a re-enactment of the night's events for the local version of Crimewatch. The Bristol Evening Post also sent a reporter to take stills photos of how the acting panned out. I refused to take part in it, primarily because I was still too traumatised by the whole thing. My boyfriend played himself, even though I probably had a better recollection of everything than he did and they brought in an actor/volunteer, who couldn't have looked less like the 'Niki Lauda' figure if he'd tried! To be honest, I found the whole thing a farce.

The next thing to happen was that my boyfriend received a 'reward' of vouchers from the machines company – for having 'saved' their money from being stolen.

The most important thing that happened from my point of view was that I made the flat like Fort Knox, with triple bolts and padlocks and all manner of things to stop anyone getting from the bar into the flat. But, more importantly, I got a fluffy baby.

I spotted an advert for Golden Retriever puppies and we drove all the way over to Trowbridge in Wiltshire to view the litter. I'd done some research and had found that you should pick the puppy that makes themselves known to you by approaching you at the time. I already had my eye on a very blonde Golden Retriever pup, but then he came and pooped right in front of me. From that moment, I knew he was my baby and that's how he stayed until the day he died.

We couldn't collect him immediately, but said we would wait until the time that he could be released by the owners, who lived on a farm. He was Kennel Club registered, but we had no idea what his Kennel Club name was. In my head, I had already named him and his name was Troy, after the character Sergeant Troy in Thomas Hardy's 'Far From The

Madding Crowd'. It seemed so apt for a puppy from Hardy's 'Wessex'. I'm not sure my boyfriend had a clue what I was talking about, but he went along with it anyway. Ironically, when we checked his Kennel Club registration, his Kennel Club name was 'Royal Troika' – some would say this was another example of my renowned spooky insights.

Over the years, my darling dog and I went through different changes of name, he becoming Troy Bear to me, or more commonly, TB. Whatever he was called, he was always my dog, my soulmate and I the one he came to when all the furore of the day had settled down and it was time for him to jump into my lap and rest his head on my shoulder.

When he did eventually come to live with us, the first thing the pub regulars said was that he looked like me and that dog owners always choose a dog that looked like themselves. For me, that just strengthened the bond.

Without TB, I would have gone insane during those months after the burglary. Both staff and regulars started to play up, staff just because that's what pub staff often do, as I knew, and customers because the former landlord and landlady had kept trade sweet by having lock-ins most nights of the week. The pub's owner had told my boyfriend, in no uncertain terms, that this was not to continue, but the regulars took it out on him and not the owner.

Similarly, trouble with the kitchen staff began when the previous owners found they hated their new pub and started angling to come back, undermining us through some staff. We soon also discovered that living in a tiny village was no joke and that fabrications spread like wild fire.

Luckily, we had two loyal part-time barmen – N and G, without whom I would have ended up in an asylum, partly through what the staff and 'regulars' did and partly through the behaviour of my boyfriend.

There was never much happiness in this place, my only real joy being when we would close up and N, G and I – and sometimes my boyfriend – would spend hours playing on the quiz machine.

I loved that delay – the playing of the quiz machine, the cleaning up of the bar, the taking Troy outside for the last time, because it prevented going to sleep. From the moment the burglary had taken place, I had one thought in my mind and that was arson. We were in a building in which all of the windows at the front were shuttered, continental style, so once upstairs, I couldn't see out. I knew how long it had taken the police to get there on the night of the burglary and all I could think about was how long it would take a fire crew to get down to us. I saw it as the easiest way to get rid of us and I couldn't get it out of my mind.

We were now approaching November – dark winter nights and darkness falling by four in the afternoon – the very time when I would be preparing dishes for the next day's service, or cleaning up after lunchtime. The kitchen had one side bordering on to the car park, which was all glass, so I felt like I was in a goldfish bowl and couldn't see out into the darkness to see who was watching. Come 3pm, my boyfriend was always asleep upstairs; all the staff had gone home and I was all alone in the kitchen.

To say I was terrified during these awful hours was an understatement. As my boyfriend was always out of it, upstairs, I also had to take Troy out. We had built a little paddock for him, surrounded by wire, so that he could run around as a pup. In those early days, he would bite my toes and fingers with his little sharp teeth and chase around frenetically until I managed to pick him up. Then, he would sit on my knee for hours inside, like a baby on my lap and snuggle up into my chest.

All of this paranoia in my head was there even before it started. 'It' started on one of my fear-filled afternoons in the kitchen, when I was all alone downstairs and the sky outside was too dark for me to see out into the car park. The phone in the kitchen rang and I answered it, expecting it to be a table booking or enquiry. Instead, I got a voice that said, 'You've got my mate, but you haven't got me. I'm coming after you'. I threw the receiver down in terror and ran upstairs to tell my boyfriend. Though I was petrified, it was clear he didn't understand why. In some ways, it is easier to be the victim than the onlooker.

The death threat phone calls then came in regularly, always after the pub had closed after lunchtime and when I was alone in the kitchen. I felt that someone was out in the car park watching me and I was terrified. I hated having to take Troy out into that darkness, but had no option. The police were told of these calls, but seemed to do nothing about it. I asked whether they had 'got' one of the perpetrators, but again got no real answer. Once more, I felt this was all part of a bigger plan to get these people for something else.

My boyfriend thought I was mad and, considering that he'd been the one attacked, was very relaxed about it all. I still had my nightmares about an arson attack. They were all about to get a whole lot worse.

For once the phone hadn't rung to threaten me. I'd cleaned up in the kitchen and had gone up to the flat. The TV was on and my boyfriend was asleep in front of it, as usual. Troy wanted to go out, so I took him outside and then we came back in. He was off his lead and ran upstairs happily. I sat down and realised Byker Grove was on. I started to watch it, but within 10 minutes Troy was bombing down the stairs out of the flat. I couldn't believe it, as he'd only just come in. I got to my feet, which is when I heard the commotion that made my blood run cold once more.

I could hear pots and pans flying around the kitchen and a man's voice shouting, 'Get off me you little shit, see how you like that'. There was a crash and my panic dissipated as my mother's protective instincts took over. I ran down the stairs, shouting to my boyfriend at the same time. He began to stir, but I was halfway down the stairs calling Troy's name with all my might and heading to the kitchen to protect him, when he came bombing back up the stairs and running straight past me. I thought of nothing but our mutual protection and continued my journey down the stairs, heading towards the potential danger, which must have been just around the corner. I slammed the door shut and applied all those bolts that I'd had fitted.

'Call the police', I yelled. I ran to find Troy, but couldn't. He wasn't in the bedroom, where I'd expected to find him and I had to search every room. Eventually, I heard him whimpering under a bed in one of the spare rooms. When I peered under, he was shaking and making pitiful noises. Tears fell down my face. 'Come on out, baby', I kept urging, but he was scared rigid. I took me three hours to get him to come out.

The police did come and an inspection of the back door took place. Someone had broken into it using a screwdriver or chisel, as there were marks in the wood. It didn't make sense that they would break in at that time to steal any takings, as the tills were always back upstairs. It seemed that the threat to us had been enacted and only Troy had prevented it from being worse than it was.

From that point on, Troy and I were truly inseparable. I cuddled him for hours that night and the wayward puppy suddenly grew up and part of that growing up was to never leave my side. Whether he just didn't like my boyfriend, or grew not to like men after this attack, who knows, but he never wanted to go out for a walk with anyone but me and would play up terribly if he had to. In a very short space of time, it was he and I against the world and against anyone who crossed us. I had my baby, or so I thought.

They say that there are watershed moments in life, after which there is no going back. My boyfriend was drinking and that was taking its toll on me and some of my favourite possessions. But this wasn't the straw that broke the camel's back of my relationship with him. That came in November when he decided to take himself off to an Aston Villa match in Birmingham one Saturday. This meant that I, recipient of death threats, the only one who'd know anything about the subsequent break in and the one who was terrified at the best of times living in this pub, was asked to close up alone on the Saturday lunchtime, stay in the pub alone all afternoon and then open up again at 7pm, alone. As the pub was so massive, this meant having to close one door at a time after punters had left, potentially leaving the opportunity for someone to get in by another door and hide away, as I went to lock another.

These thoughts ran through my head after his announcement of his intention to go to this match. He wasn't even a great Aston Villa supporter and I doubt whether he'd seen a match in 10 years. To decide to do this, knowing what the implications were for me, at the worst possible time and at the height of my fears, was something that I found truly unforgiveable.

No matter how much I begged for him not to leave me to do this, he wouldn't listen. He did nothing to ameliorate the situation, so I then implored our female cleaner, to come in at 7pm with her keys and knock on my door, so that I knew that it was safe to come downstairs. I made plans for Troy and I to hole ourselves up in the bedroom, so that we had about three bolted doors between ourselves and the bar. I even brought the kettle into the bedroom, so that I could make a drink without going downstairs. I planned to take Troy out just before we closed and then pray that his bladder hung on until after 7pm.

The pub wasn't that busy that Saturday, which made it worse. The last punters were the in-laws of football goalkeeper, Bruce Grobbelaar and they were in the main lounge. That meant that I needed to lock the main door, the kitchen door, the French window doors of the lounge and then the back door, close to the family room. That was the one I was absolutely dreading and I cannot describe the fear I felt as I walked down that long corridor to the back of the pub and then locked the door, wondering if someone was already hiding somewhere, under a table, or behind the bar. I literally ran to the door of the flat where Troy was already waiting. I slammed the bolts on the bottom door on, shaking like a leaf and burst into tears. I swept Troy up in my arms and said a silent prayer into his fur, begging him to not want to go out again.

He must have picked up on my need, or else been too comfortable curled up with his Mum on the bed as we begged the hours to tick by until the time when the cleaner called us to say she was in the pub. I was paralysed with fear laying up there and clung on to Troy for dear life, to keep him still and content. Amazingly, it worked, but during those hours of terror, the resentment about the unnecessary trip to Villa Park grew and grew, until it became planted like a seed in my heart that could never be tweezered out, no matter how much time passed.

The cleaner was true to her word and did exactly what she had promised, so I opened up the bar at 7pm and the wanderer returned by 10pm, clearly worse the wear for drink and trying to cajole and laugh off his misdemeanour. I had no time for anything he had to say.

In my own head, I was ready to move out by the time Christmas came. By then, however, I had just discovered some significant news. In a totally unplanned move, I was pregnant. I couldn't believe this. I had been to the doctor for a test, as just opening a fridge door in the morning made me terribly sick. The thought was that maybe this was down to the upset and the stress. I was told they would ring me if my test was positive. No call ever came, so I dismissed the very notion as nonsense.

However, I continued being horrendously sick every day and then I got knee pain and N jokingly said that knee pain was a sure sign of pregnancy, even though he knew nothing about my test. In the end, I rang the doctors, explained nobody had ever rung me and asked them to check the test. I discovered I was three months pregnant.

I was summoned to the village surgery and think that may have been my downfall as news of my pregnancy seemed to go around the village. We spent Christmas in the pub, working like Trojans, despite my feeling terrible. A form of release was sitting at the bar with N and G on New Year's Eve all taking our parts in our rendition of Bohemian Rhapsody. In the first week of January, my boyfriend was dismissed because the stock takes were down. I had little idea what had happened here, but I certainly had a gut feel, from some strange questions I received, as to what might have sparked this. We were told to pack our things and be out by 11am that day. We had two hours.

I was totally distraught. Nobody asked where we were going to go. We had possessions that needed to be packed up, with all our clothes and belongings being in the flat. We were told removal men would sort that out. I was so upset, that an older lady who worked in the pub took us home to her house, Troy included, to stay there for a few nights. She and a German barmaid were the only comfort I received at this traumatic time. Without them, I could either have collapsed completely, or done something I would have regretted for the rest of my life.

Luckily, I still had my house in Shirehampton, so when our things had been packed up by the removal company and delivered there, we were able to return. We had had no opportunity to say goodbye to anyone. It had all been arranged that the previous, landlord and landlady would be moving back in. It was a fait accompli.

Once I had got over the initial shock, not least of which was how we were going to live with no income, I began to feel a huge sense of relief. My days of pub purgatory were finally at an end and I would never have to pull a pint, clean out a microwave, face death threats or knock up a menu again. Freedom was mine. It was time to move on.

Chapter 9

TRANSITION

I was extremely happy to be back in Shirehampton, even if we were both jobless and hardly in the best of relationships. I had been to hell and back since leaving British Gas and this was my chance to start to build a new life, albeit with a baby on the way in June. Our possessions arrived, badly wrapped, clothes just shoved into bags any old how and with no knowing what might have been left behind. At least I was home, surrounded by my own furniture, my Victorian fireplace and with my lovely big Victorian bedroom to relax in.

Making ends meet was traumatic. I began a course in how to start and run your own business, which I enjoyed, mainly because it got me out of the house and allowed me to focus on being a potential wedding planner. I sold my British Gas shares to try to raise some money. My boyfriend made little or no effort to get a job for months and I would sit in what I called the 'middle room', between kitchen and lounge, opening bills that arrived in the post and crying my eyes out into Troy's fur as he sat on my knee, while up above someone was still enjoying their slumbers, seemingly happy to let me take all the strain. How my baby survived all this, goodness knows.

My German friend was lovely and came to see me bringing with her some old baby items that she no longer needed. I was, however, absolutely terrified of giving birth and knowing her did nothing to allay my fears, as she had nearly died during her delivery. I started going to antenatal classes and I had to suffer a load of really right-on women in my group. They all insisted that they wished to give birth naturally, with no painkillers whatsoever. When the nurse who took the class asked me, I openly said quite categorically that I wanted every painkiller going.

The sudden move from Somerset had completely messed up plans for the birth. I was originally down to give birth in a south Bristol hospital, but now I had to have my notes transferred to the main Bristol Maternity Hospital in Clifton. We hadn't had time to buy any items for the birth while in the pub, thanks to not having been rung with confirmation of pregnancy, so everything had to be bought on a shoestring budget, thanks to having no income. We also had a major battle regarding Council Tax and I spent three hours standing up in a queue at the Council Tax offices trying to sort out what we did and didn't owe, while heavily pregnant.

I only had two maternity dresses in total – a navy blue and white spotted one made of cotton, which was fine for the late spring and a sleeveless summer dress which I wore in the last few weeks. Luckily, I really didn't show at all until I was five-and-a-half months pregnant and even then I only had a tiny bump. The women on my business course were amazed when I said I was expecting. The upside of this was that I got away with wearing normal baggier tops and jumpers, plus leggings and didn't have to go out spending on maternity clothes.

In the last few months of my pregnancy, I had another stroke of luck. I wrote to Leedex, the PR agency that had done some work for British Gas South Western, while I was there. I asked if they had any freelance work that I could do and I got a positive reply – a commission to write some articles related to gas safety. That gave me a real purpose again. It felt as if I had got my identity back – as a PR person, rather than a skivvy and kitchen maid. I worked like a Trojan on the first batch of articles and then was asked to write a few more. I was truly grateful to Leedex and always will be.

In the midst of all this, it was decided that we ought to get married before the baby was born. I don't even recall a proposal. Similarly, I cannot remember the date that we married – all I know is that it was one of the last days in April. What I do remember is my father talking to me in the bedroom before I went downstairs, on the day of my wedding and asking me if I really wanted to do this. I took the easy way out and said yes, so we drove to Bristol Registry Office for a completely forgettable ceremony at which there were probably no more than ten people present.

This small little group of people then made their way to a hotel right by Clifton Suspension Bridge, which was the best part about the day, as there was a nice view. I then went home and put the kettle on, taking off my wedding dress – a cream and black Mothercare creation – which I don't count in my total number of maternity dresses, as I only ever wore it the once.

Even then, I felt it was Troy and I against the world. He had still not developed a relationship with my husband and would defend me to the hilt. I think my husband resented him greatly and would moan about him constantly if he took him for a walk. One day I saw him pulling on the lead so hard it made me want to hit him. After that, I tried to do the walking myself.

My love for my darling dog knew no bounds and, no matter what, I could never be mad with him. I had managed to save enough money from the sale of the shares to decorate the back bedroom and make it babyfied. It had wallpaper with pink, blue and yellow elephants, which was just lovely and then I managed to buy some material that was yellow with a little teddy bear motif, so that I could make some curtains.

This was a task being taken on by a woman who had cut short her dressmaking classes in Reading and who had few sewing skills at all, save what she had done at school, but I was determined to make these curtains and make them well. I got a book and followed the instructions to the letter, washing the material first, to ensure that any shrinkage was accounted for and then setting to work to do the hard bits. I lovingly hand-stitched the hem and the ruffle and was so proud of my handi-work, as it looked sublime. I was just finishing the last curtain off one day, with the material draped across my knee, when my husband let Troy in from the yard. He did his usual thing and made a dart for my lap, but couldn't quite manoeuvre all the material between him and me. Instead, I got some delightful muddy paw-prints all over my curtains. Somehow, I couldn't be cross with him even then and thankfully it all washed out and no more shrinkage occurred!

As the birth approached, I was dreading it more and more. We had made several visits to the Maternity Hospital by this time and had realised what a nightmare it was. Situating a maternity hospital at the top of probably the steepest hill in Bristol wasn't the brightest thing to do, though someone had tried to compensate by situating benches every few hundred yards up the steep climb. Parking was virtually impossible and when we had a 'trial run' it raised more issues than it solved.

As June approached it was hot and sticky and my legs were really painful and swollen. I had stocked up on raspberry tea and other things to try to induce the birth and had bought a TENS machine for when contractions started and I needed pain relief. In this grumpy, swollen state, I received a phone call one day, which in one way gladdened my heart, but in another made me feel hopelessly trapped. Out of the blue, someone who I had worked with at SWEB rang up to explain that his marriage had broken down and he had been apart from his wife for a while now. He asked whether I would like to go out on a date, revealing that he had always secretly had a thing for me.

I was absolutely amazed by this, because I wouldn't have suspected this in a million years and I began analysing things and wondering why I'd never noticed anything in his behaviour to suggest this. He carried on with his tale and then awaited a response. I vividly remember saying, 'I'm really sorry, but I'm eight months pregnant!' That was a romance killer!

The last few weeks really dragged, but suddenly at around 10am one morning I felt different. I started to get contractions while ironing and they strengthened within a relatively short space of time. At around 11.30 am I received a call from Leedex, asking if I would do some more writing. I had to say, 'Sorry, I can't today, I'm in labour, but I can maybe do it in a day or two'. Such was life and my commitment to work!

By teatime, despite the TENS machine, I was in agony and we set off for the hospital. They took a quick look and sent me home again, telling me to eat something. I did and promptly threw up everywhere. All I could was take to the bed and lay down scrunched up, thinking that childbirth was every bit as bad as I had imagined – exactly like all the Wild West films in which some woman would be screaming blue murder in a closed off room, while the men folk fiddled with their gun and waited for the moustached doctor to emerge demanding hot water and towels.

As might have been expected, I got no comfort from my husband, but my real hero leapt to my rescue. As I lay on the bed moaning and in excruciating pain, Troy came and joined me and laid by my side, allowing me to hang on to him as the contractions struck. He licked my face as if worried and concerned and lay his head on my swollen stomach. This was something he'd done for months and I suspected that he could probably hear the baby, or sensed it.

It turned 1am and I could take no more. We rang the hospital and they told me to go back. I got into a maternity ward for inspection and the first words that greeted me from the nurse were, 'I was supposed to go off duty hours ago and now I'm stuck here'. She proceeded to slam paperwork and other items around the desk in the room, making it quite clear that I was nothing but a hindrance to her.

I explained that I wanted every painkiller they could give me and she scoffed. 'You're nowhere near due', she said nastily. I just kept rolling my eyes at my husband who said nothing. The pain was unbearable and all I could think was that if this was hours off the birth, I would never survive it, just as my friend nearly hadn't. In the end, the nurse deigned to get a more senior colleague. She agreed that I should have an epidural, but informed me that this could take 45 minutes, as an anaesthetist would have to be called. She didn't seem happy with the midwife, so I suspected that she should have booked an epidural before this stage.

'I think the baby's coming', I said to my grumpy midwife.

'Of course it isn't', she snapped.

'But I've got a terrible pain now as if it's arriving', I explained.

'Well, I suggest you go to the toilet', she barked. I got up and did as she said, but something felt wrong.

'Could you just check again?' I asked, in fear of getting my head bitten off. She begrudgingly came over to the bed. She looked a little chastened for once.

'Baby's on the way', she declared. 'It's decided it can't wait any longer and is trying to push out. We need to correct this'.

'I need some painkillers', I stressed.

'No time for that now', she barked. 'Here, have some gas and air'.

There was a flurry of activity as another nurse arrived and I wondered what on earth was going on to correct whatever was happening. I recalled that it was meant to be the person in labour that bit off everyone's head in childbirth, not the midwife, but just took in some gas and air and tried to do whatever I was asked. After a lot of breathing and pushing, out popped the baby, delivered without any painkillers, but not through choice, believe me. I had a baby son.

'What are you calling him?' snapped the midwife.

'Scott James', I replied, in homage to F Scott Fitzgerald and Scott Baio (of Bugsy Malone and Happy Days fame) and James for my grandad's sake, as all males on that side of the family had James as their middle name. In fact, let's play down the F Scott Fitzgerald thing. I'm pretty sure my pin-up Scott Baio was the main reason my son is called Scott! I think it was the Latin looks, winning smile and cheeky expression – I know I certainly wasn't alone in thinking him my dream man.

I was transferred to a ward and told to get some sleep, this now being 3.40am. A strange thing happened when they put my 8lb baby son next to him, as I looked at his face and thought that he looked exactly like P from Surrey. I knew that it wasn't possible for my son to be his son, but it was uncanny. I could almost see my son wearing a cream raincoat and being rescued from a phone box in a violent storm one day!

At this point, I knew I was supposed to do the mummy thing, pampering myself a bit while baby slept and then learning all the stuff like nappy changing and breast-feeding. To be honest, that scared me to death. If I was going to be useless at it all, as I was pretty sure I would be, at least I wanted to be useless with nobody watching and judging me.

I started chatting to another young Mum and we decided we would go and get some breakfast. I just felt relieved that the trauma was all over and I felt really light and burden-free. I didn't want to take to my bed to recover and spend days learning what to do. I had far more important things on my mind. It was June 10 and the European Football Championships were starting that night, with an England match coming up the next day. I had to get home!

I waited for doctors and nurses and all the rigmarole that you have to go through when having a baby. I could see that other new mums were more than content to be in hospital for a few days, but it wasn't for me and never will be. I just wanted to be at home. Thankfully, I got my wish and went home mid afternoon.

I was really worried about how Troy would react to the new arrival, having read lots of books that talked about how to handle the jealousy of a dog. I needn't have worried a bit. I put Scott down in his baby carrier next to Troy, to let him smell him. He then just lay down snuggled up next to the carrier, as if guarding him. Maybe it was because he'd been listening to him inside me for months, or probably just because he was the most loving dog I could ever have wished for. From that moment on, he would wait until I had put Scott to bed and then take his turn by snuggling up with me on the sofa. Everything was perfect.

That idea of perfection lasted about five days. At that point, my idyll of motherhood was blown apart by the colic. The relatives had been and gone and there was no sign of angst at that point, but all that changed dramatically. It started with just continuous crying and screaming and no matter what I did, what position I held my son in, what I did to soothe, it continued and continued and continued.

We consulted our health visitor and she diagnosed the colic and recommended Infocol. That helped a little, but on it went, for hours and hours each day and I felt helpless, whether I was out with the pram and getting black looks from passers-by, or in a supermarket. I was told that it would last almost exactly three months and then just miraculously end. I marked up the three months on the fridge door and crossed each day off, one by one. Sure enough, at almost exactly the right date, the crying stopped.

My husband had his life all planned out. I would go back to work and he would stay at home. By this point, I was tired of the lack of effort on his part to get a job and more or less pushed him towards an interview at a motor accessories business, as his life before the pub game had been spent as a mechanic. Somehow, he got the job.

My days were then spent trying to get both my boys around. This was made ridiculously hard after Mona, the health visitor, diagnosed that I had a very intelligent baby, who didn't want to lay down in his pram, or just lay on a playmat, but wanted to kick the hell out of dangling items above him and watch everything going on. He was fascinated by Troy and Troy by him. His first word wasn't Mummy or Mamma, but 'Og'. His desire to watch 'Og' meant that I had to carry him in his baby carrier in one hand and cope with Troy on his lead with the other. We would head off to the shops in this mode, or to the vets, where there awaited the truly difficult manoeuvre of negotiating door handles, just as your dog spotted other canines and went tearing off towards them, while you were still trying to get yourself and your baby through the door! I must have built up some incredible muscle strength.

Being so far away from both families wasn't proving practical and so I started to look for jobs in the northwest, for the first time ever. The only time I had ever worked in the northwest, apart from my Christmas postal round and my pub work, was as a Saturday girl at first BHS and then TopShop. I had hated both, but then I don't think shop work was for me. I applied for the first job I saw, as a PR Manager at Swinton Insurance, went for an interview pre-Christmas and was told to start in January. I moved back with Scott and Troy to live at my parents' house and never returned to Bristol again. In the meantime, my husband stayed at the house.

During these early months of the move, I had my work cut out. Troy delighted in being able to roam a garden three-quarters of an acre in size, but more importantly, with fences, hedges and ditches that were easy to negotiate to get on to the farm land all around. He had been born on a farm and I think he must have remembered what it felt like. There were times when he couldn't be found at all and I would be out at midnight, with my torch, scouring the hedgerows and calling his name for ages. My mother used to remind me that I had a baby in the house that needed looking after, not realising that my second baby was missing. Eventually he would come back, filthy and needing me to give him a thorough washing before I went to bed.

At other times, I would see him about six fields away and he would play me up, waiting until I got near to him and then dancing around me so that I couldn't catch him and get him on to his lead. I would crawl through cowpats and over barbed wire to try to get to him, ending up as filthy as he was, before getting very cross with him. At this point, he would realise the game was up and would follow me back to the house, keeping about half a field behind me. When he got into my parents' orchard, he would often start to limp, letting me pick him up and carry him the rest of the way. As soon as we got back, he was as right as rain!

I soon got into the swing of this change of lifestyle and it was nice to be spoilt for once, with meals cooked for me and someone else to look after Scott once in a while. My two boys and I were pretty happy together and I felt free. Although I had a husband sitting in Bristol, it didn't feel like it. If I rang him, he often wasn't out at the house and many a night I didn't even bother to ring. I had already realised that it was time to move on.

Chapter 10
THE MANCUNIAN WAY

My new job was based in a building in Great Marlborough Street, which I always thought of as a Tardis, as it was deceptively large once you got inside, with hidden floors and facets. It housed all HQ functions for the insurance broker, which at this point had 750 branches around the country, which all required some managing! It also housed a large administration unit handling particular aspects of the business and being more of a call centre in character.

My job comprised two elements: handling public relations activities to support all products sold by Swinton, as well as branch initiatives and being the writer and editor of the Swinton staff magazine, which circulated to all branches and also to parts of the Royal Sun Alliance Group, who had bought into Swinton.

As my husband had still got the car down in Bristol, I had to commute to Manchester on the train, which meant a ridiculously early start in the morning, not just for me, but also for my poor father, who insisted on taking me to the station and picking me up at night. The first of these might have sounded the worst, especially on the freezing cold winter mornings of January when I started my job, but actually it was the latter that caused the most trauma. Mobile phones were still not widely available and I would regularly be stuck on a train that had decided to pack up at Bolton, or await a new engine at Preston, and be completely helpless and unable to advise my father where I was. I would be greeted by a very grumpy parent, who had sat in a cold car for an hour and who didn't want to hear that there was absolutely nothing I could have done about it.

I caught an early train from Poulton to Preston and then would spend 20 minutes or so awaiting the Manchester Airport train, which would take me to Oxford Road Station. I would then have to bomb out of the station, up the main road, walking away from the Palace Theatre, until I reached the railway arch spanning the Cocotoo Italian restaurant. It was then a quick dash down Great Marlborough Street and into work.

My direct boss was a dynamic, go-getting Scot called Gill Shaw and all these years later, we are still in touch. Gill was a human dynamo, particularly when it came to branding, which was her passion. Above her was a lady called June Price, who was equally as committed a career woman, but in a very different way to Gill. Between them, they taught me an awful lot.

My desk was part of an island of interlocking desks that comprised the marketing department, while Gill was just a short hop away behind a screen. At the 'head' of the island sat the advertising manager, a sound chap called Paul Gomersall. He was just above a low level screen from me. Next to him sat Annie, the Direct Marketing Manager and there was Jo, a marketing assistant. Directly opposite me was Rex the point of sale manager, while a little further down sat the advertising assistants Graham and Charlie. Our secretarial support, who did our typing for us, comprised Gillian, Carmella and an older lady, while June had her own secretary.

It had been 21 months since I had last worked in an office and I found it really difficult to re-adapt, not in terms of the working environment as such, but in terms of the fluorescent tubes in the lighting. At first, though I never told anyone, it drove me absolutely mad and made me feel physically ill. It took me weeks to get used to it, even though I had spent all my working life, bar the last few years, in an office and never noticed it at all.

It took a little time to suss everyone out and they all had their own ways. Once everyone realised that I had a good sense of humour (probably once I'd got over my fluorescent tube phobia) they all started to have some banter with me. Paul's favourite trick – and one that I loved – would be to sit on his wheeled chair and drive it towards me, pretending to be in a wheelchair and saying he was the TV detective Ironside! His other great trick was to go to the vending machine and buy snacks, coming back to his desk, to ask me if I wanted to get my hands on one of his cheesy Nik-Naks.

Rex and I, became great pals. He was the most unusual point-of-sale manager I have ever met, as he was colour blind, so if the design company brought him some artwork to look over, I would have to tell him what colour it was! Rex would look over our little dividing wall and say, 'Don't bat your eyes at me', when I wanted some favour or other, which made me do it even more.

Charlie and Graham just teased and tormented me all day long, with various members of staff presenting them with lots of ammunition with which to do so. What I found really sweet about them was, however, that although they ribbed me endlessly, when it came to cricket season, they did ask me whether I wanted to go to Old Trafford with them.

Gillian was our nearest thing to a celeb, as she had been Howard Donald's fiancée and ballroom dancing partner for many years. They had split when Take That had just started to make it big, due to the pressures of having crowds of girls pursuing him wherever he went. One of our greatest thrills as a department was the day that Howard rang her to say that he was at a party with Lulu, having just recorded 'Relight My Fire' with her.

Carmella was a true Italian lady, with quite a fiery personality and, in many ways, characteristics very similar to Angela's in London. However, her fire paled into insignificance with that of the older lady, who was a devout Christian and who, I am sure, thought we were all doomed for hell and damnation, particularly as she told us that about two times a week!

I would say that what characterised my life at Swinton, more than any other job, was the number of meetings that we had. We would seem to spend half our day in different strategy meetings, without then having much time left to do any implementing. This made life extremely difficult, especially as I had such a tight monthly deadline for the production of the Orbit magazine.

Gill decided that we had enough money in the budget to take on a PR consultancy to handle some sort of project, so we put out a brief to a couple of agencies. One, which had been pushing for the account for a while, turned round and said that it was totally impossible to promote the product without having a new product launch to focus on. I found this frankly ridiculous, as they didn't show one iota of creativity or willingness to work with what we already had. In the end, it was decided that I would promote the product, but that we would take on a London agency, Lawson Dodd, to help with some projects, such as a Swinton Young Driver of the Year competition, to be staged at Oulton Park.

I liked Belinda at Lawson Dodd a lot, as she was quite down to earth for a London PR agent and also had a lovely Soho office that it was fun to visit. Apart from these visits, it took me a while to get out and visit other parts of the Swinton empire, though when I did, it was enormous fun, particularly when I did a whistle stop tour of the London branches.

Working at Swinton was difficult, if you considered things in terms of staff morale. Direct Line had been in business for a fair few years, but was only just beginning to bite into Swinton's customer base, as the annoying red telephone with its 'cut out the middleman' message drove thousands of insurance seekers to pick up the phone and ring for a quote, rather than walking into a Swinton branch. The outer wall closest to our marketing island mapped the customer case count on a big chart and every Monday the line dipped, showing less business than ever coming through the branch doors. Without a direct arm, there was little response. As Direct Line head Peter Wood had predicted, the traditional insurance companies were like juggernauts, which could not change course quickly and react to the competitive threat.

Morale wasn't helped in any way by the friction between the marketing department and the sales section, who shared the same floor. A lot of antagonism seemed to come our way, as these mainly ex-branch personnel objected to this bunch of graduates posing as marketeers. At times, it was as much as they could do to add us to the list of sandwiches being ordered in at lunch. Only one of their mass broke rank – a solid chap called Ian, who became a really good friend to me when I needed one.

Ian had a difficult relationship of his own and it was he who delivered words of wisdom to me that have stayed with me all my life. Ian's philosophy was that all any of us can expect in life is 'a little bit of sunshine to fall on us now and again'. How very true that is and how difficult it is when that sunshine disappears. Ian and I got on famously. We were both avid Man Utd fans and suffered the same mood swings according to whether the Red Devils had won or lost.

I quickly realised that working in the north was very different from being in the south. Walking out with a male colleague at lunchtime immediately started tongues wagging, even if it was as innocent as Rex and myself going to The Lass O'Gowrie. Exiting the building meant walking through the goldfish bowl that was reception, which was where a lot of rumours began. Even talking to someone by the photocopier was tantamount to having an affair. On this basis, the arrival of a new, brash sales department employee from Portsmouth was bound to set tongues wagging.

This new cocksure employee was at first a source of amusement to me. His name had circus connotations, so on the many occasions that he would visit my desk during the course of a day, the men with whom I worked would burst out into the da-da-dadda-dadda-da-da-da-da circus tune as he returned to his desk (I believe it's called Entry of the Gladiators). I would just blush madly and say that I didn't know why they were making such a song and dance about things. Secretly, I was enjoying the flirting that was coming my way – something that had been sadly lacking in my life for a long time.

Carmella would just roll her eyes and say, 'You need a good Italian man'. I never knew whether she had anyone in mind, but her first advice was usually followed by, 'If you were being sick over the toilet, that one wouldn't lift a finger to help you'. This was certainly not as romantic as the vision of the good Italian man!

By May, my house in Bristol had been sold and this meant the return of my husband. It also coincided with me moving out of my parents' house and into my own home. I found it unbearable. After months of it being myself, Scott and Troy, we were again a very strained four, within which two of us had nothing to say to each other. Someone had to go before matters got any worse, so although I knew it would be extremely difficult to cope, if not nigh on impossible, I had to call time on the relationship that never really was in the first place. I went to France and learned the art of crying behind sunglasses while pretending to sunbathe in the garden. I call this the St-Jean-de-Monts method.

I returned to hell on earth. In my absence, Gill had created a spreadsheet for all marketing budget and projects, with each of us having our own individual sheet. Unfortunately, as I had been away, she had created mine as the first one, so as a bit of test sheet. Although I had never used Lotus, I couldn't get anywhere with it and spent every night trying to make it work – and failing. I was literally reduced to tears by it, both at home, where it was the last thing I needed, and at work too, where Ian found me crying at a computer one day. The dratted spreadsheet was taking away the very little sleep that I managed to get anyway.

The others hadn't got to the stage of using their spreadsheets fully, but Gill had filled in some figures on mine, so I was more 'advanced' down the route of suicidal frustration. In the end, I just couldn't take it any more. Someone suggested that I call the IT help desk, which I didn't even know existed. I was the luckiest girl on earth to find a guy called Va on duty.

Va was patience personified. I took my spreadsheet down to him and he started to explain to me how it should work. At this point, some glaring errors in Gill's coding came to light and he corrected those. I began to feel sane again.

Unfortunately, the whole thing was riddled with errors. Every day, I would have to wait until Va was on duty and either go to see him with my dreaded spreadsheet, or ask him to come and see me. Swinton being Swinton another rumour circulated thanks to the amount of time we had to spend together. Charlie and Graham took great delight in devising a new little 'jingle' that went, 'Ooh, aah, I.T. Va!' It didn't help one little bit that he was actually very good looking.

The upshot of all these many hours spent with I.T. Va was that a mini miracle happened. Having been the unrivalled dunce of the spreadsheet, I became the expert, as I had literally been through every fault in its creation and now knew how to rectify it. Rex would start to curse about some error in his spreadsheet and I would urge him to check a certain formula: his glasses would nearly fall off his face. Paul would be heard munching his cheesy Nik-Naks more loudly than usual and utter some exclamation, at which point I would say, 'Well have you tried this, Paul?' Va must have been an exceptional teacher.

I met some interesting people while at Swinton. One was a racer of Cosworths at Oulton Park and he became the hub around which our Swinton Young Driver of the Year contest revolved. I placed this with 'Auto Express' as an exclusive competition and the entries rolled in. In the meantime, I went down to Oulton Park and was treated to a twirl around the circuit by one of the racing drivers, who delighted in pointing out the speed dial as we rounded one of the bends at 100mph. I wasn't scared – perhaps my own experience on the A1 had hardened me to dangerous motoring moments – and I felt quite exhilarated when we ended the drive.

The day itself was wonderful. We had about 10 finalists there, Gill was in her element as she was a real Formula 1 fan and lived in Cheshire where she could be near to the thrill of the circuit and even the organisers (myself, Gill and Lawson Dodd) had the chance to challenge ourselves to some of the elements. My particular favourite was the skidpan, at which I excelled.

There might not have been that much laughter at Swinton once you set aside the banter in the department, but the trick to that is to unwittingly seek it out yourself. To be honest, I'm not sure that any of us were that enamoured when we were told that Swinton was going to be taking part in a brand new concept – the Manchester Business Games. Our involvement was to sponsor a go-karting event, at an old mill near Oldham that had diversified and set up an inside circuit. Gill was in her element with this and, when it came to the event, delighted in trying to ram everyone and push them into the tyre wall. Only Gill and I went to this event and this seemed to be the format of these Games ... myself + a different companion at events taking place during this fortnight of business frolicking.

The most exciting part for me – or so I thought – was meeting Sir Bobby Charlton, who was setting up a scheme to help young players cope with all the elements of life that surround football. I found his humility truly touching – the fact that he shook our hands and said, 'Hello, my name is Bobby Charlton', was just inspiring. I was accompanied by

Paul that day.

It was Paul and I who also went to the opening event of the Manchester Business Games, staged in the Yang Sing restaurant – a real star on the Manchester restaurant map. Working at Swinton, if you went out for a proper lunch, you typically went to either the Yang Sing, or Cocotoo under the railway arch, or to a little Thai restaurant in Princess Street. Each had their attractions. I used to love going to the Yang Sing on a Monday, which was when the Chinese community descended on the place to sort out their financial affairs and their socialising. Cocotoo in Whitworth Street was remarkable for its re-creation of the ceiling of the Sistine Chapel on its railway arch-shaped roof and because we all liked watching the accountant at work on his little till, totting up the figures – something that always reminded us of the 'Bookkeeper' in 'The Untouchables.' The Thai was remarkable for its jasmine rice, which stuck to the chopsticks with just the right consistency, and then its lunchtime offers. It was a favourite haunt when I went out with Jo.

Paul and I arrived at the Yang Sing not quite sure what to expect, but grateful to discover that a sumptuous Chinese buffet had been laid on. It was all a very relaxed affair – a kind of company-meet-company get-together for all the sponsors. Paul was quick to grab a plate and then even quicker to point out to me that a photographer that he'd encountered was very keen to get my number. I chose to ignore him!

The one thing stopping Paul and I from getting near to the buffet table, despite all the diving under armpits and quick tackling of the ankles, were a group of over-enthusiastic men in emerald green jackets. One could have easily assumed that they were Irish patriots, if being very stereotypical, but one would have been wrong. As it turned out, these strange men carrying the most enormous, retro video cameras that you've ever seen in your life, which could have easily knocked you unconscious while doing the armpit manoeuvre, or have taken your eye out as you reached for a spring roll, were the 'Russian Business All-Stars" and hailed from Kiev.

They were the keenest filmmakers you could imagine, being up the nostril or skirt before you knew it and filming everything that moved, even the noodles! Paul couldn't stop chortling about their antics, though if you'd seen the original 'Man with Big Glasses' adverts that Swinton was thinking of reviving, he didn't have that much to laugh about. In fact, I'm sure one of them would have been perfect as the 'Man with Big Glasses mark 2'.

We eventually beat a retreat from this lunchtime shindig, with Paul still chortling about the Russian All-Stars all the way back to Great Marlborough Street. He had room to laugh: I, on the other hand, had to go to the closing ceremony of the Manchester Business Games, to be held in the Yang Sing again.

I virtually pleaded with everyone in the department to come with me, with Ian, who had to go down to Wales, as he usually did at weekends, and with anyone else who would listen. The only one who both listened and agreed to go with me was the print manager, Mark Dodd, with whom I did have quite a laugh. He used to frequently offer his thoughts on what hairstyle would suit me, though I'm not quite sure why. He had just started dating someone, but said he would be OK to accompany me as long as he left about 10pm. That seemed fine to me.

As it was an evening do, I stayed over in the Palace Hotel, having been in negotiations with the marketing manager in recent times about an 'Orbit' offer and been given a good rate for the night as a result. I shimmied along to the Yang Sing at the appointed hour, trying to tuck something under my arm for fear of being seen and ridiculed. The item in question was Swinton's prize for the charity raffle, which was to be held on the night after the dinner had been served. To my deep mortification it was the most glamorous thing the marketing store cupboard could muster and the Swinton budget stretch to – a Swinton golf umbrella.

When I arrived at the Yang Sing, I hurriedly shuffled it on to the stage, mumbling to some administrator what it was and which organisation it was from and found my seat. Mark and I shared a table with about eight others, including a couple of employees from Addleshaw's solicitors, who set a debate going as to whether Roy Keane was a good buy for Man Utd.

As is the wont with these events, things overran terribly. It got to 10pm and we'd only just had dessert. I had been dug in the ribs twenty times over, as Mark, clearly briefed by Paul, kept pointing out that I seemed to be attracting the attention of the Russian All-Stars. I told him to shut up and eat his food. It was just a pity that they'd felt the need to again turn up in their emerald blazers, but perhaps they'd travelled light on the road from Kiev.

I did my best to keep Mark there as long as possible, as we hadn't, of course, yet had the highlight of the night, the charity auction! I was virtually pulling the sleeve off his jacket as he stood up to go, just as they were announcing the first prize – a trip to Thailand. 'Do you really have to go now?' I hissed at him, trying to hook my leg around his ankles to keep him in his seat.

'She's waiting for me', he replied.

'But how am I going to survive the indignity of the golf umbrella?' I hissed again.

'Nobody will associate you with it', he said, laughing to himself. With little more ado, he gave me a kiss on the cheek and abandoned me.

What neither of us had realised in all the flapping around and sleeve grabbing was that Sir Bobby Charlton was not only presenting the prizes to the lucky raffle winners, but also inviting a representative of the do-nating company to head up to the stage to help hand it over. As the full magnitude of this struck me, I wanted to die a slow death, desperately hoping someone had shoved a cyanide tablet into my drink, as would have been the case in some Agatha Christie plot, but this Murder By Embarrassment was still unravelling.

I prayed that the trip to Thailand had been a one-off, but out the priz-es rolled: short breaks here and TVs and video players there. Computers and meals at plush restaurants followed and then, as undoubtedly the booby prize of the evening, the amazing, not-to-be-missed and much-coveted Swinton golf umbrella in all its bright orange, blue and white glory!

I felt physically sick as I stood up on very wobbly knees in response to Sir Bobby announcing, 'And now we have Jane Hunt, from Swinton Insurance, who will be …' At that point I would have liked to pour water on his microphone so the indignity of it all was never discovered, but no, the words 'golf umbrella' were actually uttered. I could feel eyes burning holes into me as I walked past several tables and could almost swear I could hear the words 'tight gits' being murmured amidst the clinking of wine glasses and the lighting up of cigarettes.

Sir Bobby gave me a comforting smile as he picked up the umbrella and let me share a hold of it. I must have been beetroot in the face by this point and quickly shoved it into the hands of the lucky winner, who more than graciously decided to give me a kiss. Foolish man!

As this was, quite naturally, the last prize of the night, people started to mingle as soon as I'd revealed the full extent of Swinton's generosity, so I suddenly found myself cut off at the pass, en route back to my table, by two green-blazered men. One was a tall, blonde and reasonably handsome man in a good light and he appeared to be poking a shorter, dark-haired man in the ribs. I took a step to the left to try to get round them and then two to the right, but found myself faced with Kiev's equivalent of the Berlin Wall. No woman, and certainly not I, was getting past.

The shorter of the two men looked beseechingly into my eyes and then up at his taller counterpart. 'I am interpreter for Russian All-Stars', he explained. I sort of nodded some sort of appreciation of this, given the telltale, giveaway sign of the emerald jacket. He continued. 'My friend, here (he pointed upwards at this point), wishes me to tell you that he thinks you are the most charming person in the room'. I cannot stress how much emphasis was put on to the word 'charming', which was pronounced to about twice its normal length, to emphasise how charming I was, I would imagine.

I felt like saying, 'Yeah, right, you just feel sorry for me because I've suffered the huge embarrassment of having to take a golf umbrella out of the hands of Sir Bobby Charlton and present it to the unluckiest person at this event', but kept schtum, as I was pretty sure the interpreter wouldn't get it. If there was one thing I didn't want, it was pity!

But I didn't even get a chance to respond, as a bag was forcefully thrust into my hands, as the blonde man smiled at me expectantly. The shorter man, who was doing the shoving didn't take the pressure off the bag, so there was no giving it back. 'For this reason', he said earnestly, 'My friend wants to give you a special gift from the Russian All-Stars'. I have to say that, at this point, the words 'I bet he does' were not far from my lips and thoughts of fending him off as I made my way back to the Palace Hotel were beginning to emerge.

'Right', I said, looking down at the bag for the first time. 'Thank you', I continued, hoping that this was the gift he wanted to give me and nothing more, as by this time I had remembered the enormous video cameras and could see myself starring in some sort of Russian porn film costing 10 roubles a viewing.

'I will show you what we have here', said the interpreter, as if he were Q talking to Mr Bond, clearly thinking that, if he really sold the contents to me enough, extolling their virtues in all their glory, his friend might be in with a shout. 'Here, vee have wonderful pictures of Kiev', he exclaimed. Now I did remember the sort of concertina little book of photos with popper stud fastening that he pulled out of the bag and then unravelled before my eyes, as my Dad had once done a grand tour of Europe with my Nan, after his father had died, and I recalled photo books of Naples and Sorrento and Tangiers. I hadn't seen anything like it for a few decades, however, with its very 1960s black and white photos of a very communist looking Kiev.

'Lovely', I said, lying through my teeth as the blonde guy simpered, seemingly believing I was pleased with it. Out came another item in which they obviously took great delight – a very colourful – and I mean very colourful – silk scarf. Then, just when it couldn't get any better, out came a Russian Cossack doll in full traditional costume with crazy hair and a droopy moustache. He reminded me of someone, but I wasn't sure whether it was Rod Hull or Catweazel. It was clear to me that the doll was the date clincher and that I should have been wowed by it, but instead I was just standing there puzzling over its features.

'My friend gives you ziz gift from the depths of his heart', said the interpreter.

'Yes', I thought to myself, 'I've already got that'. It was obvious that I was meant to throw my arms around him with gratitude and collapse against his beating chest, but instead I just took the bag, said a polite thank you and left them both there dumbfounded, wondering where their strategy had gone wrong.

Having nobody to now act as my chaperone and with eyes burning into the back of my head, I grabbed my things from the table and beat a hasty retreat back to the Palace Hotel, where I pretty quickly jumped into bed exhausted by the trials and tribulations of the night. Now at this stage in its history, the Palace Hotel was notorious for its fire alarms and even when we had been on training courses there, the damn thing had gone off and disrupted everything. I had just snuggled down nicely for the night when off it went. I couldn't believe it and tried to ignore it, but on and on it went. I think the word 'shit' might have passed over my lips, as I realised I hadn't got time to get dressed. The lucky part was that I had a long black nightie on; the unlucky part was that I had borrowed my mother's coat that day (I have no recollection as to why) but this pink anorak was what I had to sling on top of my night attire.

To be honest, I was so sleepy that I really thought that everyone would be in the same boat, as it was way past midnight by this point. Off I trooped down the corridor, following the signs to the fire exit and wondering where all the other guests were. I headed down the fire exit steps, still thinking it was slightly odd that nobody was already down there, when to my horror I realised that a fire exit door had opened up from a function room and hundreds of people in black tie and ball gowns were flooding out to fill the vacant space into which I had now landed, in my long black nightie, bare feet and my mother's coat, being completely devoid of make-up and presentable hair. If presenting the golf umbrella had been bad, this was 100 times worse and I half wished I'd taken the Russian All Star back to my room, as he could at least have shielded me. I stood there, cowering on the stairs, thinking 'Perhaps nobody's noticed'. I think they call that a moment of sheer delusion!

I stood there, shivering in embarrassment, for a good 15 minutes, while the hotel decided the alarm was yet again a false one and then I scarpered up the stairs as fast as I could, desperate to get back to my room and put an end to this appalling evening of shame.

Work on Monday was interesting. I made the mistake of pummelling Mark for abandoning me to the mercy of the Russian All Stars, which just made him guffaw loudly in front of the whole department, who then heard the whole sorry tale. Paul was beside himself with laughter, having experienced my suitors himself, so it took ages to live down. Surprisingly though, I still have the Russian doll, which I get out now and again when I need a laugh. Not so sure I have the wonderful pictures of Kiev, but if I did, I'd sell them to the Ukraine tourist board!

That Christmas, the marketing department and sales department decided to join forces for their Christmas party – in Blackpool. I wasn't at all in the party mood and not even wanting to put up a Christmas tree. Only the big boss, June and I represented the marketing department, which was quite easy for me, given that I only had a few miles to go to get to The Hilton, Blackpool. Everyone else was staying over.

Unfortunately, this evening all went pear-shaped at about three in the morning too. We had retired to the upstairs bar of the hotel, which was for residents only, but I got in. This was probably the one and only time that I really spoke to the manager of the sales division at a personal level and it was a damn good job that I did, as I suddenly found myself stalked by this crazy man, who just wouldn't leave me alone. He just kept pestering me, no matter how much I tried to politely push him away. My male companions only came to the rescue when the man offered his final chat-up line, which actually left them in stitches, 'You don't know what you're missing; I've just picked up my redundancy packet'.

June gave me a real talking to about feeling down that night and so I went home and put up the Christmas tree the next day. I was now starting to get used to being single parent, which was just as well, as another 20 years of it – and counting – lay ahead!

There was a new and interesting twist or two awaiting me after Christmas. The first change was the arrival of a new security guard, appointed because of fear of bomb threats allegedly. His name was M and he wore a very smart uniform and really looked the part, right down to the 'Love' and 'Hate' tattooed on his fingers. He would stand in reception each morning, so there was no way to avoid bumping into him. At other times of day he would loiter in other parts of the building. For some reason, M took it upon himself to put me under his personal protection.

M sensed that certain potential suitors in the building were not right for me and went out of his way to point this out to me every morning, accompanying me a few more paces than was necessary from reception to my desk. 'He's taken a real shine to you', declared Carmella one day, in her cockney accent, making me wonder if she considered him the sort of man who would look after me when I had my head down the toilet throwing up. He certainly wasn't a 'good Italian man', but maybe she'd given up on that one.

As Valentine's Day approached, I was seriously dreading what might happen – and it did. There, awaiting me in my in-tray was a card – semi-romantic, I suppose, depending upon whether you call, 'I would crawl over broken glass all the way to Blackpool to have my way with you', the verbal offerings of Cupid. It was me that wanted to crawl – right out of the department, to hide in the store cupboard for half-an-hour until the laughter abated.

If I did venture out with anyone, even dear old Rex, black looks were a certainty, but now, with the benefit of hindsight, maybe M had got it spot on. Had I listened to what he was saying, I could have been spared later heartache. In his black and white world of love and hate, I think he really had the soul of a philosopher.

I somehow managed to 'ignore' the card, but walking past him in reception each day was very hard. I had something new to keep me oc-cupied, however – as a direct result of the falling case count chart on our office wall. To try to stem the tide of lost business, the Chief Executive decided that a change committee had to be set up and I was told that I was to be seconded on to the communications committee headed up by him. There were some really high-powered directors on there and the only person I really knew was a guy from the personnel department called Richard Boardman.

We had to set about really trying to communicate the big changes that would have to be implemented as the branch network and staffing structures were whittled down, to cope with the rise and rise of Direct Line. A major focus for this would be the branch managers' conference, of which I would probably never have had the delight, were it not for being part of this committee.

All the different working groups were working on their own agen-das for change, so my role was to really provide the right messages to employees, using Orbit and other communications vehicles. I enjoyed working the Chief Executive, Glyn Jones, particularly when he suggested that the agenda for one morning should revolve around Manchester United's quest for the title! He was my kind of guy.

One of the most difficult times of working life happened during this period. We were all advised that there would be compulsory redundancies and that the people who were selected would be tapped on the shoulder and asked to go with a manager to discuss their futures. In an open plan office, this was absolutely awful, as you could see people being approached, watch their faces turn to an ashen colour and, in many cases, detect the tears. Nobody knew whether they were safe and I dreaded the tap, or seeing any of the marketing team asked to leave. The worst part was when a really nice chap, who worked in an ancillary role to what we and sales did, was approached and emerged from behind his divider screen looking absolutely devastated. I just started to cry.

Feeling motivated to start writing about the need for change was pretty hard after that, but it had to be done and I wrote an edition of Orbit that elicited huge amounts of praise from directors at Royal Sun Alliance. I then contributed to some of the materials used at the branch managers' conference, which was an away trip to Birmingham, with an overnight stay thrown in, for hundreds of Swinton managers.

I had been warned that this descended into chaos by the time the evening came around and that proved to be the case. I didn't know the majority of people there, as they were branch employees, so I had few faces to chat to. By a great stroke of luck, I then ran into Tony, a branch manager I had visited on my recent Croydon trip. He introduced me to some of his friends and before we knew it we were jiving to a Dirty Dancing medley, doing the mashed potato and twist like they had gone out of fashion!

The great thing about the Swinton top management was that they were all party animals at heart, so as I looked around the floor, I could see several of them twirling each other around and getting into the spirit, the wine and the beer!

I am not quite sure how this happened, but it came to the time to do the obligatory conga and Tony grabbed my waist, pushed me forward and said, 'let's go'. Before I knew it, I was leading a massive line of people round the dance floor, round the back of the staging and out of the door! I can vividly remember lots of cabling and wiring round the back of the stage, which I neatly avoided with my own version of Riverdance. What the rest of the line behind me did, goodness knows!

When the night broke up, I was more than a little giddy. I went back to my room, where I ignored several knocks on the door. I'd been warned about the branch managers' conference!

Although I still quite enjoyed my job at Swinton, as Yoda might say, 'Much uncertainty there was'. As all of this began – and probably around the time of the spreadsheet episode – I had applied for a job at a PR consultancy in south Manchester and had been unsuccessful, but had been told that my details would be held on file. I never expected to hear any more of it, but then I received a phone call, asking me if I would meet up, as I would be perfect for a new account that was coming on board. I agreed and went to meet the managing director after work one day. I was offered the position of Account Director for Privilege Insurance – a high risk motor insurance company that had not even been launched, but which was the baby of RBS chief executive, Peter Wood, who had just received a multi-million pound bonus from RBS and struck a deal whereby they would part fund this new venture.

I was a little torn as to what to do, as I had never worked on the consultancy side and Cheadle was a lot further than Manchester city centre. My other issue was that my husband had taken our car, leaving me paying off the finance agreement on it. Taking the Cheadle job would mean buying a car and driving there every day. My potential suitor (the most undesirable man in the building in M's eyes) suggested that we go for a drink after work and discuss it. Usual haunts were 'The Cornerhouse' or 'The Garratt', but on this occasion we went to 'The Peveril of the Peak'. I made up my mind that night that I would take the job.

It was really hard to hand in my notice. I had to present it to June, the marketing director, and she seemed really disheartened by it. I tried to explain that I had to think about job security and she at least appeared to accept that. On that basis, the deed was done.

Some of the details of my leaving do are quite hazy, but I can recall Charlie sitting opposite me in a Greek restaurant, where about 20 of us had decided to go for a Greek buffet. We then moved on to various pubs and nightclubs, at which point M, who had insisted on coming to the event, managed to track us down. I can vividly recall being on the dance floor in some basement dive, with M standing guard over by the side of the room, saying that he didn't feel comfortable being in this club and it was essential that he 'keep his back to the wall'!

As for any other details of the night, it was all a blur. It was the weekend before Easter and I had a new beginning to look forward to right after it. It was time to move on.

Chapter 11
HITTING THE MARK

My new job was something completely different for me – a role in a PR consultancy, where suddenly I had clients to nurture and assist. Some people spend their PR careers never crossing over to the agency side once they have worked in house and vice versa. If anyone is contemplating moving from one to the other, I would advise them to look at their skills set and assess whether they have the capacity to work on either side of the fence, or stay in the comfort zone that suits them as individuals. I have certainly seen some people who cannot make the transition during their career and I guess that I wondered, for a time, whether I was one of those people.

The agency I moved to was very small comprising, at the time, just me and the owner of the consultancy, who had moved up from London. She definitely brought more than a touch of London with her, claiming that she never felt dressed unless she was wearing Armani and thinking that people in the north were far less beautiful than those in the south.

It was a bit strange that this small consultancy had been chosen to launch Privilege Insurance, but that wasn't my first concern. Within my first week, I was thrown into a pitch for business, for the Manchester Paralympic Games, or an early version of the Games, as I can't remember its exact title. The pitch happened within just days of my starting and was scheduled for a 6pm slot at a Manchester hospital. I had advised a little on the proposal, but now had to suddenly present someone else's thoughts as, in reality, there was little I could do to have an impact on the overall pitch. All I could do was turn up and play my part.

We left the office really early, just to make sure we arrived in time.

When we got there, we were in situ before the agency that had the 5pm slot. We got news that they were running slightly late, so without any compunction, my boss told the committee that we were ready to pitch and would go in first. She virtually pushed her way into the room without waiting for an agreement on this and suddenly we were pitching, even though the other agency was only running something like 10 minutes late. This, I came to realise, was very much the order of things at my new employer's. Maybe it was part of the dog eat dog world of London, but it didn't quite sit well in the heart of Manchester.

We presented the plans, which didn't seem to go down a storm and exited the room – my first experience of the awkward moment, when you've presented to a potential client, ended the question and answer session that follows and then have to pack up all of your stuff, with the people in the room staring at you and urging you to leave as quickly as possible as your slot is over. If clients knew how awfully embarrassing this point of the agenda is, I am sure they would amend their thinking and take a break themselves, rather than sitting rooted to their seat and staring you out. That's my word of advice to anyone inviting an agency to pitch.

Conversely, it would be nice if you were given time to set up before presenting, rather than again being hurried and having to engage in conversation, while sorting out your paperwork, computer or portfolio flip presenter.

On this particular occasion, as we exited the room, we came face to face with the agency who should have had our slot. My new boss apologised, rather insincerely, for having jumped in, underlining the point rather emphatically that we had been there and they had not. Their MD just nodded, but was clearly not amused and saw it as an underhand tactic. Underhand or opportunistic, take your pick, but it didn't do us any good, as we did not win the pitch.

Although I had been appointed to mastermind the Privilege Insurance launch, that was some way off, scheduled for the autumn of that year. When I started in April, I mainly worked on the Mountain Breeze account, promoting a range of ionisers, air purification systems and aromatherapy units. One of the first tasks on this account was to organise a photo shoot at a photography studio called Tyger Tyger in Manchester. From the moment I stepped through the door, I loved everything about Tyger Tyger – the ambience, the laid-back feel to everything, the attention to detail in dressing each shot and taking the best possible picture with exactly the right lighting and staging. Fresh flowers were brought in from a nearby florist, to make each shot perfect; little gusts of wind were created to make a voile curtain blow, as if being wafted by the Mountain Breeze unit; bathroom products were exquisitely laid out around the aromatherapy product.

What I also loved about Tyger Tyger was 'Blue' – an adorable, three-legged Husky who had run out of the studio as a pup and been run down in the road, losing a leg. While not as adorable as my Troy, he was a lovely dog and devoted to his owner, Frank, who ran Tyger Tyger with Phil, with whom I had some affinity as his parents lived in Kirkham, not too far away from me.

I greatly enjoyed my first photo shoot there, really trying to be creative and contribute as much as possible to the final product shot. My trips to Tyger Tyger were to be like oases in an otherwise very stressful life at times.

I had to quickly start promoting the Mountain Breeze products as aids for those with hayfever, as we were already in April and hayfever season was just around the corner. Other themes had to be employed for longer lead-time press, particularly women's magazines and to that end, I established a user-panel among leading health and women's interest titles. Each member of the panel would be given an F-400 product to test, to assess how it purified the air, made life easier for asthmatics and hayfever sufferers and also promoted a more alert mental attitude. In an age when smoking within offices was still commonplace, the F-400 gained much appreciation.

I also dipped in and out of a pizza account. Meetings at the pizza company were fun, because invariably some pizza or other was brought out for elevenses. Through my time on this account, I met someone who would later become my own client when I set up my own agency – proving how small a world it can be.

My other slightly 'quirky' client at this time was a doggy car seatbelt manufacturer. The doggy car seatbelt prevented one's canine friend being thrown forwards with the force of a baby elephant under braking conditions. The harness kept a dog securely in situ on the back seat, preventing damage to both them and their fellow passengers. To help promote this, we had a cute picture of a Terrier strapped into his harness and this enabled the story, complete with its well-researched facts and figures about injury, to go down a storm, securing many slots in consumer magazines, as well as national dailies and regionals.

In the lead-up to the Privilege launch there were a few changes in the office. The first one is that we recruited a new assistant, called Nina, who was a bright young thing pretty much straight from University, who was offered an absolute pittance of a salary to work at the agency. Desperate for experience, she accepted.

There was also much research to be done for the launch and I spent numerous hours in the Manchester Central Library, where I could use micro-fiche records to access national newspaper articles about the difficulties faced by high risk drivers when it came to finding affordable motor insurance. This enabled me to build up a good knowledge of the issues encountered by young drivers, those with high performance vehicles, those with certain medical conditions and particular occupations and those with driving convictions.

Furthermore, it also allowed me to establish which journalists had shown an interest in the subject matter and were, therefore, likely to be receptive to stories about a new motor insurance provider that was actively trying to make life easier for those in niche segments of the motor insurance market, who could not afford to pay for their motor policies.

A full strategy document for the launch was put together, this revolving around a national press conference in London at which Peter Wood and Privilege's chief executive, Ian Chippendale, would both be present. I researched various venues for the launch, finally deciding on the Brewery in Chiswell Street, EC1. It was agreed that we would make a film for the launch, interviewing various people about the need for a high-risk motor insurance provider, including Ian Chippendale. I hired a video production company and set up to film Ian Chippendale in a park close to Privilege's head office in Leeds.

This was a September's day in Leeds, so the weather was still decent enough to allow us to film outdoors and we were able to bring in lots of different interviewees, who could talk about the problems they faced in getting insurance. I'm not quite sure how it happened, but I became the interviewer, putting the questions to each person for them to answer while the cameras rolled on beside me.

All of this was going swimmingly until a female tramp suddenly emerged from the bushes and started taking a great interest in what we were doing. She was clearly high on something or other, but rather pitiful. She kept shouting out to the group of us who were making the film and interrupting some of the questioning. The filmmaker went on undeterred, working around the comments that were being directed at us.

All of this was manageable until we came to the final interview, which was myself pitching questions to Ian Chippendale. For some reason, at this point, the presumably homeless lady walked right up to the group and seemed to be taking more of an interest than ever. Maybe this was down to a pinstripe-suited man being interviewed rather than a jeans-wearing student, who knows, but she was well and truly within the melee as I began to put the questions.

I had literally just started the interview when she came and stood right next to me and rested her head on my shoulder. Off-putting as this was, I took the view that at least she was now being quiet and seemingly very attentive. On that basis, I didn't flinch or push her away, but just carried on conducting the interview with her head on my shoulder. I could see Ian Chippendale wondering how on earth I was managing, but somehow I did and, even more surprisingly, given that he was watching this scene, he managed to answer the questions without fluffing any. Very quickly, it was, as they say, 'a wrap'.

As I finished asking the questions, the woman extricated herself from my right shoulder and shuffled around a bit, obviously losing interest now there was nothing going on. Ian Chippendale just said, 'You did really well there'. I felt quite proud of how calmly I'd taken it all.

The lead up to launch was full of visits to Leeds, parking in one of the worst underground car parks I've ever encountered in the Privilege basement, where huge yellow concrete pillars seemed out to get you at every turn. Gradually, a telesales team was recruited and started to settle in, so that a soft launch of all the operations could be managed. My main contact was the head of marketing, Jim Wallace, and together we started to pull together all that we needed in terms of press materials for launch.

Working partly from my own knowledge of the financial services media and partly from the research that I had done to discover who had written about the subject matter previously, I drew up a media invitation list. To this, I then had to add motoring writers, who would be just as important to Privilege as the money media, though a tougher nut to crack, as given a choice between test-driving the latest Porsche, or writing about insurance, I think we all knew which they would prefer to do!

The third main target audience was that of the insurance trade press, which had to be fed the right messages about Privilege and what it stood for.

To get as much ammunition together as possible, I took myself off to the Association of British Insurers' office in London, where it was possible to access statistics held in their library. Ironically, the ABI's office is in Gresham Street, where I had worked for New Japan Securities, so I knew exactly how to get there!

Research conducted at the Home Office was a little more problematic, the system there being very much like that I had once encountered at the India Office – waiting hours for a publication to be brought out of the vaults and then having to plough through it as fast as possible. The atmosphere was always very strange in that library, but the material I unearthed was very useful.

The day of launch soon came upon us, with full press pack and a lengthy Q&A briefing document written. I'd even gone to the trouble of arranging a trial Q&A session, with some journalists who fired questions at the team, so that they could assess if any awkward questions might come up.

We had rooms booked in the Tower Thistle, which has become a regular hotel haunt of mine over the years. We had a dress rehearsal booked for the evening before and then the main press launch was taking place the following day. Our group consisted of ourselves, the video producer who was looking after all the audio-visual needs of the day and the Privilege management, as well as the advertising agent for Privilege, Ken Gosling.

Anyone from the Manchester advertising scene from the 1970s and 80s will probably have known and loved Ken. He was a larger-than-life character, who I found to be a truly kind man beneath his continuous humour and wit. He has sadly left this life now, but he was a constant source of strength to me when working on the account and afterwards, when I occasionally met him to discuss possible work projects. He was also extremely encouraging to me, when I established my own consultancy.

The press launch went off like a dream, with some very influential media from both broadsheets and tabloids arriving to quiz the Privilege team and some of the main national picture desks too. The venue was a perfect choice and I felt extremely proud to have pulled all of this together. Nina had been a great help, but unfortunately wasn't allowed to join the rest of us in the hotel bar after we'd all had dinner together – a source of constant amusement to both she and I, as she now runs her own consultancy in Manchester. As we were all heading to the bar, we were just passing the lift when its doors opened. In a flash, our boss pushed Nina into the lift and said she thought it was time she went up to her room. I will always recall the look on Nina's face as the lift doors closed and she was whizzed up many floors! The drinking in the bar went on for hours, much to Nina's non-amusement the next day! She felt like a little child who wasn't allowed to party with the adults!

The months after launch were extremely busy. The mission was to move the focus away from Peter Wood and to raise Ian Chippendale's profile as the chief executive. To this end, I placed interviews with him in all manner of publications, including the News of the World, who ran a full-page profile of him.

We did so much during this campaign – quotes comparisons for young drivers, market traders, Jaguar enthusiasts, those with different medical conditions and offences and all combinations of these. We placed case studies, sought out sponsorships and, above all, held media one-to-one briefings, at which I introduced Privilege to various personal finance editors and motoring journalists, so that we could then sell in story angles to different national titles.

Not all of these media briefings were as easy as others. One of these occasions came when I was due to meet a doyenne of personal finance writing, who I had never met before, but who I had heard was a character to be somewhat feared. We had arranged to meet with the Privilege management, but something happened on the day and, just before she was due to arrive at the restaurant that I'd booked, I discovered that they couldn't be there and I was going to have to go solo and pilot the briefing myself. I had a feeling this wouldn't go down that well, so sat in some trepidation awaiting her arrival.

She was a little late, which was nothing unusual for journalists. However, this meant that she immediately spotted that we were now just two in number and nobody else was at the table. I instantly explained what had occurred and apologised profusely for it, but it went down like a lead balloon. She snatched the menu out of the hands of the waiter and held it in front of her face for about 15 minutes, not uttering a word. The stony silence was unbearable, so I attempted to break it, starting an explanation of what Privilege stood for, which I knew off by heart. She lowered her menu, fixed me with a stare that could have turned me to a pillar of salt and said, 'With all due respect my dear, PR people really don't know what they are talking about and cannot represent their clients effectively'. I felt the floor give way beneath me, but was determined not to fall through the whole. I plucked up courage to continue my spiel.

At first, it appeared to me that she wasn't listening to a word I said, but I was saved by the arrival of the starter. Between that and the main course, I gave still more information and by now was actually receiving some form of communication coming the other way. I dropped a few little facts and figures in while we were enjoying the main course and then upped the ante between that and dessert. By now, she seemed almost engaged and was asking questions and, more importantly, getting informed answers to her questions. It came to coffee and she lowered her spectacles, fixed me with another stare and said, in a most grandiose fashion, 'My dear, I take it all back. You are indeed a very good PR person'. To me, this felt like manna from heaven. Somehow, I had prevented a walkout, an early exit and a slating.

Another media luncheon was also very problematic, but for very different reasons. We had by now had quite a few functions for a wide variety of editors, one of these being a group function at which I sat next to the highly entertaining George Fowler, motoring editor of the Daily Star, who, on finding that I came from Lancashire, regaled me with tales of his visit to haunted Salmesbury Hall. On this basis, when it came to hosting a media lunch with one particular editor, I thought nothing of it and was happy to go solo, particularly after my successful experience with the doyenne.

I typically booked all venues for media lunches and what venues they were – The Ivy, San Lorenzo, Café des Amis in Covent Garden, Rules, a Polish restaurant in Kensington, the Marco Pierre White restaurant at Canary Wharf and a particularly memorable Middle Eastern restaurant that I once went to, again solo, with personal finance writer, Tony Levene. On this occasion, however, I didn't book the restaurant, as the journalist insisted on doing that, which I did think a little strange, but didn't argue about it.

When I arrived at the restaurant, which I think was an Italian somewhere near Waterloo, I couldn't actually find the journalist. I eventually, to my horror, found him nestled at an intimate table for two in a very dark corner where the only illumination was by flickering candle, presumably to add to the air of romance. My reaction wasn't helped any by the fact that virtually the first words he uttered were, 'Now isn't this romantic', which was followed by a long, deep look into my eyes. I could feel panic hitting me in the stomach with all the force of a Joe Calzaghe punch.

It quickly became evident that this chap – by this point probably in his late 50s or 60s even, only had one idea in mind and that was to woo. Things became increasingly uncomfortable throughout the meal, leaving me squirming in my seat and desperately wondering how on earth I was going to extricate myself from the situation without offending him outright, or displeasing him so much that he wouldn't write about the client. I went through hand stroking as I tried to cut my bread roll, a little footsie under the table and innuendo packed language. I am sure I have never eaten a meal as fast in my life, feeling that I had been stitched up like a kipper good and proper.

Throughout all of this, what I couldn't take my eyes off was his amazing moustache, partly because by focusing on that I didn't have to look him in the eye. I've never been one for a tache and this particular one repelled me more than most. I was developing a phobia of it the more I sat looking at it.

Having rushed my food, I made some excuse about having to get off, but I was virtually pinned in the corner. On the basis that nobody keeps baby in the corner, I made a bit of a dash for it, as he had insisted on paying and I thought that if I got a head start on him, I might be able to make my escape before anything dire happened.

As bad fortune would have it, although I'd walked a little way up the street, I couldn't hail a cab for love nor money and I could by then see him emerging from the restaurant and crossing the road towards me. My heart was pounding in sheer panic as the tache approached, but hope was in a sight as a bomber approached with its 'For Hire' sign lit up. I jumped into the road to stop it, but my wooer was now upon me. I had one arm on the door handle and one leg ready to lift into the cab when he swung me round and did what I dreaded most. In total abhorrence I jumped into the taxi, slammed the door shut and told the driver to put his foot down. The tickling of the tache stayed with me for hours.

I stayed in London that night and arrived back at the office mid-morning the following day. In my shocked, post-tache trauma, I had rung Nina from London and told her about my dreadful ordeal, getting no sympathy whatsoever and just a lot of laughter. As I walked from my car, I looked up to the top floor of the building to see Nina hanging out of the window laughing again. 'He's already rung the office asking for you', she yelled, so that half of Cheadle could hire. 'Shit', I muttered under my breath. Funnily enough, though various invitations to meet up again were extended, I never took them up!

One of my favourite meetings of all time was with Ian Miller, who was a deputy to John Husband on the Daily Mirror personal finance desk. From the moment I met Ian, I just adored his very dry sense of humour and his wit. In fact, at our first meeting, we were just rolling around with laughter at watching a fake beggar touting for pennies in the street below, before hopping on a flash motorbike and scarpering.

Ian would regale me with his tales of life in the empire of Robert Maxwell – this being before the Mirror moved out to Canary Wharf and in its Holborn days. Ian told me this story about Maxwell hating smoking within his building and so was more than irate when he got into a lift with a man with a lit fag in his hand. He instantly asked the man what his annual salary was, whipped out his cheque book, wrote him a fat cheque for a couple of years pay and told him to leave the building and never come back. The chap accepted it willingly as he was just delivering something and didn't work at the Mirror anyway. I do hope Ian's story was true! If not, he was a very clever raconteur.

Ian and I kept in touch for years and he would frequently invite me to visit his family in St Ives in Cambridgeshire. We always sent each other Christmas cards, but I haven't had one for a few years and fear the worst, as his last card said he had been ill. I hope I am wrong and he has just forgotten me.

My other great buddies were Mr Prestridge and Mr Day, with whom I spent many a happy lunchtime and evening, sampling red wine by the magnum, engaging in all sorts of banter and eating at some great places, with and without clients in tow. They will both always have a very special place in my heart, but I suspect they both know that. They are also part of a very select group of people, who have been treated to the sight of my high leg kicking, as learned in the Winifred Clarkson School of Dance. I did, however, show some restraint when summoned to the Ritz piano bar by the dynamic duo, way past midnight. The pianist never achieved the right sort of rhythm for a high leg kick!

Back in Leeds, there were new developments at Privilege with the arrival of a new marketing manager to work under Jim. This was one John Grimbaldeston and, if someone had told me what part he would play in my life then, I wouldn't have believed it. Eighteen years later, we are still great buddies, having had various epochs together. Then, he was just a bright chap from near Skipton who instantly impressed me by telling me that I wasn't, 'all tits and teeth like most PR women'. A straight-talking Yorkshireman if ever I've known one.

Shortly after his arrival, the very keen Grimbaldeston decided to give me a special case study that he had unearthed in the Privilege database

– the strange case of what I quickly dubbed a 'prang prone pensioner' thanks to having had numerous prangs in his car even since being a Privilege customer. Grimbles decided to dispatch me to Blackburn to track down this man and create a story around him, which I dutifully did.

On arrival at his house, he seemed normal enough and was very happy to give me chapter and verse about his many accidents, scrapes and near misses. I wrote it all down very diligently and then turned to the photographer I had booked and asked him to take a photo of this customer with his car. At that point, the photographer decided to get all arty and suggested that it would be much better if he took the car down the street a bit, as it was on a hill and it would give a good camera angle looking up towards it. The Privilege customer said he didn't mind and would get his car out of the garage.

Well, to say I have never seen a worse bit of driving is not quite true, as my friend Michael (of the blow-up bed fame) once gave me a very scary experience in the underground car park at Euston and did once drive all the way to Catford from Southwark with a completely flat tyre, despite me sitting in the back and saying to him 'Don't you think there might be something wrong with the car, Michael?' Undoubtedly, however, it wasn't the best and the prang prone pensioner only just managed to avoid a parked car, as I closed my eyes and hoped for the best. My prayers must have been answered, as he managed to avoid the crunch, enabling him to proceed down the hill towards the photographer, who was very bravely standing in the road!

This is where it all went a bit Pete Tong, as the photographer, in his arty mode, decided that the PPP needed to reverse a little back up the hill, which he promptly did, hitting the lamp-post. Before my very eyes, I had seen why he deserved Warhol's '15 seconds of fame' and why he had so deservedly earned the title I had bestowed upon him!

Another bright idea that Grimbles stumbled upon resulted in he, his wife and myself spending a weekend in London together, during which time, he taught me a valuable PR skill that has stayed with me for life. Grimbles had realised that the winner of a very flash sports car, (which had been given away by a TV game show) would have real trouble getting any insurance cover for it, given their age, so had leapt in and offered to insure it for free – a prize worth several thousand pounds. The winner had to agree to attend a national press photo call for Privilege in exchange.

Once this deal was struck, I had to find a venue at which we could site the car and the customer, so carried out some research. I wanted an iconic venue and discovered that it was possible to hire Trafalgar Square and get the necessary permissions. I booked hotel rooms close by and the winner was invited to attend the photo shoot with their magnificent new wheels.

The photo call was being staged on the old Sunday-for-Monday basis, which meant inviting photographers on a Sunday, so that the story could run on a Monday – a traditionally quieter day for the media, which enhances the chances of the story being used. John, his wife and I went out to dinner together the night before and I vividly recall Grimbles describing the SAS at Blackburn Rovers as if they were Greek gods. For the uninitiated, this was Shearer and Sutton, who helped Rovers win a Premier League title that season and who were clearly revered deities in the Grimbaldeston home!

After a lovely evening out, John and I met up in reception the following morning and walked into Trafalgar Square. The whereabouts of the sports car winner were unknown for quite some time, so the pair of us were on tenterhooks wondering what on earth had happened. Eventually, after much watch action and pacing up and down, the sight of a bright red sports car gladdened our mince pies and we could at least calm the waiting photographers down.

As the insurer's representatives, John and I went to try to converse with the winner, who clearly couldn't have cared less who we were. They were more concerned with posing for the cameras and wallowing in the limelight and as we walked away, we could hear sentences like: 'Do you want my top on or off?' which did slightly alarm us, as it had not been intended to be a glamour shoot!

This posturing went on for ages and nothing we tried to say received the slightest bit of attention. It was then, on that bright spring morning, in the shadow of Nelson's Column, that Grimbles turned to me and uttered the words, 'Smile through gritted teeth'. I have made this an art form over the course of many years and it has served me very well!

Another interesting thing that happened to me at this time related to a dinner date with an associate, who was based in London. The evening was going swimmingly and all very romantic, until I leant over the table and accidentally dangled my hair in the candle in an attempt to grab a kiss. There was a perceptible fizz as the flame travelled up a section of hair measuring around 1cm across, reducing it from a length of about six inches to three! I discovered at this point that this man, who I had through a possible love interest, had total mastery of the understatement. 'Gosh, that could have been serious', he declared in a laconic fashion. I rolled my eyes, thinking 'tell me about it'. For months, one side of my hair wasn't in sync with the other!

A truly noteworthy episode then occurred on the M61, when I was travelling back from work one night in summer. My husband, as I have said, took the car that we had and left me paying the finance agreement off, despite having no transport. In the first few months after our separation, it was possible to track him down now and again and for about six months I received a small amount of money to help raise our child. That soon petered out, with no money being forthcoming and a declaration being issued that the car was no longer on the road. Imagine my surprise, therefore, when I found myself travelling down the motorway following the car that was no longer on the road – which was only surpassed when I realised that it was my husband's father who was driving it. I have never before felt such an urge to ram a car off the road from behind

Life at the agency was not all fun and games, however much it may sound it. There were some very difficult things to deal with – and I don't just mean after our move to the attic, when previous occupants of that space told us of the squirrels which could reputedly find their way into the store cupboard! The strain of it all got to me, to the extent that I began to find a 19-year-old goth, who liked to hang out in graveyards, strangely attractive in the right light. I then knew it was time to move on.

Chapter 12

KANCHELSKIS, KORMAS & KICKING OFF

What Jane did next wasn't what she wanted to do, by any means. I had lodged my CV with the lovely Jonathan Hirst at Network Marketing, who I recognised as being a really professional recruitment consultant, who actually cared about placing the candidate with the right organisation for them, rather than just bringing in the recruitment fee.

Jonathan quickly found me an opportunity with a sales promotion agency on Trafford Park. They had said that they wanted to find an in-house PR consultant, who could help raise their profile, but also handle PR for their high profile clients, effectively running integrated campaigns combining a couple of below-the-line disciplines.

I went to my interview there and absolutely hit it off with the MD in a big way, achieving an instant chemistry and really feeling that this was absolutely the job that I wanted. I've always believed in going with one's gut feel and I was absolutely walking on air when I came out of my interview. Feedback from Jonathan was just as positive, saying that I'd wowed the MD and he just needed to discuss things with his board. In my own mind, I was already sizing up my desk and thinking how nice and close it would be to the Old Trafford cricket ground.

In the meantime, however, Jonathan had lined up another interview, this one being in an agency located on an industrial estate in Leeds. They wanted an account director to work across several accounts, but there was no definite role outlined at the interview. Again, I met the MD, but I didn't get any of the chemistry that I had reaped in Trafford Park. I went through the motions of the interview and then left feeling pretty flat and certainly not inspired to work in this environment.

For some reason or other, I was with my sister and we went to try to get something to eat. We decided to ask someone if there was a decent restaurant around. The woman who answered my question very much reminded me of the man who drives the pony and trap when the Railway Children first arrive at their hovel in Yorkshire, having left their plush London home. She looked at me dolefully and in a long, drawn out Yorkshire accent said, 'You won't find anything like that: not on the Dewsbury Road'. From that point on, the Dewsbury Road was life's equivalent of Colditz to me – full of deprivations, barbed wire and kommandants trying to monitor your every move.

I didn't pay too much attention to this Leeds interview, being absolutely desperate to work for the sales promotion agency, where I felt I would be really appreciated and have a true challenge to tackle. Day after day, I waited for news of an offer, but Jonathan kept telling me that the MD hadn't yet been able to get Board approval to create the post. Typically, the Leeds agency made an offer almost immediately and was pressing for an answer. After about four days, Jonathan said I would have to decide whether to accept this or not and indicated that he had heard that it could be some time before the post at the sales promotion agency could be created. On that basis, with a heavy heart and somewhat begrudgingly, I agreed to take the Leeds job, with the hope that the other one might then come through and whip me away.

When I look back, this must have been sheer madness. I would leave my house at 6am and arrive at about 8am in Leeds. I wouldn't then return until about 7.30-8pm at night. In winter, I never saw my house in daylight, other than at weekends. My son was by now four years old and it was really hard doing that commute five days a week and, as it was to turn out, frequently working weekends as well. However, I suppose, as a single mum, you do whatever it takes to bring the money in. It was only when I stopped making the journey that I realised that it had almost killed me.

I was, on the plus side, given a company car – one that was totally impractical for a woman with a four-year-old child and a Golden Retriever

– a white Rover cabriolet! As it happened, it was also a death threat, frequently being lifted up by the strong winds blowing across the M62 as the motorway dropped down to Rochdale. It was also inclined to spin on the motorway too – or maybe that was just my driving. It certainly had a lot of thrust!

This was not, however, a plus for my new employer and if I had been less than enthusiastic about joining this agency it was to get worse. On my first day, the MD started asking me how I'd found the journey from Blackburn, at which point I corrected him and said Blackpool. He went a paler shade of grey and said he hadn't realised it was that far and paying for the petrol would kill him. He tried to present this in a jokey way, but I could tell it was an issue.

I absolutely hated my first week in this job. I was introduced to the Queen Bee of the office, who had worked there from when there had been just herself and the boss running the ship. She was really barbed in all of her comments to me that day, saying that the boss had mentioned that I could maybe support her on the Green Flag account. She mentioned this with a look on her face that I instantly recognised as being the face of a woman who didn't want me anywhere near her account.

I was stuck on a desk in the open plan area of the office, which I didn't mind, but it was obvious that nobody had decided what my role should be. Consequently, I was initially told to help a part-time, freelance member of staff who was working with a work placement student on plans for the launch of the Royal Armouries Museum in Leeds. I was given a few press releases to write and tasked with interesting some children's press in a site visit, which I promptly achieved by fixing up a Young Telegraph press trip.

Within just a few days, I longed to just pick up the phone to the sales promotion guy and just beg him to take me on. In the end, I didn't phone, but I wrote a letter virtually begging him to do just that. It met with the same response about how impressed he had been with me, but how he couldn't persuade the board to sanction the additional expenditure. I was totally gutted.

Luckily, towards the end of the first week, someone told me not to let the Queen Bee get me down. They said she was like this with everyone that she felt threatened by and I wasn't to take it personally. These pearls of wisdom were all that brought me back to work the following Monday.

If the truth be told, working on the Royal Armouries account was a bit of a hot potato. There was real opposition to the idea of moving the collection out of the Tower of London and up to Leeds and that was from within the Royal Armouries itself! Following the habit of a lifetime, I set off to London to conduct some research, having been given special permission to look at documents held within the Tower of London. It was a somewhat eerie experience and I half expected Anne Boleyn to leap out, or Sir Walter Raleigh to appear from behind the door. Nevertheless, I could grasp why the traditionalists would not want the collection of arms, costumes and other pieces to sail off to a brand new building slapped up in the middle of Leeds.

One of my missions was to organise a Royal Armouries roadshow, which meant contacting shopping centres within a drive-time distance of Leeds and assessing whether we could set up a video wall (which had to be hired) and information desk, as well as leafleting shoppers. Around 12 venues were selected, from Meadowhall to the Hounds Hill Shopping Centre in Blackpool, where I subsequently had the pleasure of manning the stand for a full Saturday and then the equally dubious pleasure of having to retrieve my client's jacket from the Savoy Hotel, where he had left it during his stay!

The grand unveiling of the Royal Armouries collection was accompanied by evening fireworks and the arrival of media and tourism officers, who had been offered a facility visit. I only mention this fact, because the spookiest thing happened many years later, which relates to this evening. I vaguely remember talking to two tourism officers from Taunton, while out in the cold watching the fireworks, but that's about it. We then toured the museum as a group, viewing collections and admiring the facilities.

By the time all this was taking place, a new role (or two) had been found for me. I was to become second in command on the Green Flag Motor Assistance account, which I half dreaded given the reaction I had so far received in relation to this move. The more exciting news for me was that the agency had won the Danka account and had been appointed to maximise Danka's sponsorship of Everton FC. This was on the back of having got into football sponsorship through Green Flag's sponsorship of the England football team (as they were already Green Flag's product agency) and then having won the Cellnet sponsorship of Middlesbrough FC. Additionally, they were in negotiations with Vauxhall over the maximisation of the car manufacturer's sponsorship of Euro '96 and just about to get involved with Packard-Bell and Leeds United.

Although a lifelong Manchester United fan, I was absolutely overjoyed when asked to become the Danka account director. It made perfect sense, given that I lived that side of the Pennines, but more importantly, it was a way to cure my broken heart – a breakage that had started when walking up the High Street, while in my last job, and spotting a newspaper A-board sign that read, 'Kanchelskis to leave United'. Tears welled up in my eyes that day, but strange things happen and having thought I'd lost my hero forever, here I was being offered an opportunity to get closer to him than I had ever imagined possible. Naturally, I agreed to run the account.

My mission, now that I had chosen to accept it, was to meet the two representatives that I would deal with in the marketing department at Everton and then get myself down to the training ground, to organise various initiatives involving the players. Kanchelskis was by now one of the star names of the team that had won the FA Cup in the previous May. Duncan Ferguson had just been released from Barlinnie, following his internment for violent conduct, and was deeply suspicious of the media, to the point that any photo calls or interviews were impossible. Other players in the team at the time were Dave Watson (Captain), Andy Hinchcliffe, Graham Stuart (Diamond Geezer), David Unsworth, Gary Ablett, Daniel Amokachi and Anders Limpar.

My first encounter with any of the Everton hierarchy was at an event being organised in the club shop, where the club had put together three famous Everton number 9s – Bob Latchford, the manager Joe Royle and Dave Hickson – and was having them photographed as if sitting in the dressing room. There was a melee of press there, including the chap from BBC Radio Merseyside, who also ran the Radio Everton broadcast service. Neville Southall was also around and I will never forget the scathing way in which he was described by some of the assembled media. I instantly made a mental note that he wouldn't be one to ask to do photo calls!

Anyone wanting to succeed on the sponsor's behalf needed an 'oppo' – a good photographer to take with them to the pre-arranged photo shoots. It was suggested to me, by the team in Leeds, that I should try the son of famous Daily Star football photographer, John Dawes. They believed he was a young photographer trying to make the same sort of mark that his father had made. As a result, I made contact with someone whose name always amused me – Jack Dawes.

To me, Jack will always be Jack-the-lad and I will always hold him in the deepest affection, though I haven't seen him for years now. We spent many a long hour, sitting in his car in the rain, waiting for training to finish or a player to appear, running across the training pitch in pursuit of some player or another, trying to sweet-talk our way into some area or other where we wanted to do a shot and often ending up in the pub having lunch. Although Jack was a real lad, he was so patient and help-ful. I can never remember him being grumpy about anything – other than when I was replaced one day by one of my colleagues! He did then rant for a good 15 minutes. I was very lucky in my choice of 'oppo'.

The other great thing about Jack was that he was an avid Man Utd fan too, so was equally in love with Andrei Kanchelskis in his own way. We had a lot to talk about, as a result of this, during those hours of twid-dling our thumbs and, even better, a lot to laugh about.

At first, dealing with the club proved very problematic. There were issues on all sides. Firstly, the club were not at all used to having a spon-sor who wanted to maximise their sponsorship. As nobody in the coun-try would have ever guessed that Danka was an American photocopier and fax company, just having the name on the shirt was not satisfactory. I also quickly came to realise that those who work for football clubs get a certain aura about them, a feeling of importance and of rank. These traits were never more evident than in an indomitable lady with whom I had to 'liaise'. They were further accentuated by the fact that I worked for an agency whose name began with a silent 'P', but this woman would spit out the 'P' as a letter in its own right with real venom, before pronounc-ing the rest of the name. As I never used the 'P', I am pretty sure she did this deliberately, to wind us all up.

The most classic example of her attitude towards us came when I wanted to get some shirts signed by the players, so that we could use them as prizes in consumer competitions. At Middlesbrough, this was a two-minute conversation with the commercial department. In my case, it took more like 20 minutes. I had rung up the 'P' spitter and asked very politely if it would be possible to have 20 signed shirts for Danka's use. The response was, in a thick Scouse accent, 'No, you can't do that'. I asked why this was and she said that shirts were only signed at certain times. I think she was a little taken aback when I said that this was fine and that I could wait until the next time that shirts were signed. This caught her a little on the hop and I could feel a 'P' waiting to be spat out.

'Well, that's no use either', she said, suddenly changing tack.

'Why's that?' I asked.

'Well you can't just ask for shirts to be signed. Someone has to take them to the training ground', she replied. I explained that I was quite happy to pick up some shirts and take them there, if this was an issue.

She climbed to higher ground to fend off my attack. 'Well, you can't just turn up and get shirts signed without permission', she said, in a haughty tone. I began to lose the will to live at this point, getting a long explanation of why permission had to be granted and everyone would want shirts if that were not the case etc. etc. I explained that Danka, as the sponsor, had a right to signed items in their contract, so were not asking for anything that wasn't already agreed.

After a good five minutes spent on the ins and outs of getting shirts signed and all the protocols and red tape, I was by now losing patience. I cut to the chase. 'So', I said, 'If I need to get permission, who do I need to get it from?' In this way, I had made it impossible for her to say 'no'. I required a definite answer, but I certainly wasn't prepared for the one I got.

'Me', she said triumphantly. At that point, I felt like banging my head on the desk, but it wouldn't have been the 'P' word I was spitting out! She'd had me going round the houses for this entire conversation knowing all along that all she had to do was agree. At that point, I resolved to use the back door routes to what I wanted to achieve at the club: I just needed to find them.

The starting point for this was the Everton training ground at Bellefield, where Jack and I had access and technically had permission to take photography of the players. Technically having this authority and actually having it are, however, very different things. The main barrier to this was Joe Royle's secretary, who definitely took her role as his buffer extremely seriously. I will always recall the way she bristled when first approached, how she would arch her back and then say, 'I will have to ask Mr Royle', in a certain tone. She was fearsome and I knew I would really have to go to charm school to win her around, as it felt as if I was running the gauntlet in 'Gladiators' and coming up against some big springy buffer and he-woman that was bouncing me backwards, to the point from which I had started.

I had several re-buffs like this and still hadn't discovered how to crack this nut, but there was a bit of progress when I was told that players had been 'informed' that I wanted to do photo-calls with them. I am pretty sure that this was because the player that I wanted to do something with was Andrei Kanchelskis and, to anyone who didn't know better, he didn't speak much English. I think there was a calculated guess going on that I wouldn't get anywhere anyway.

Now in recent years, there has been much made on YouTube of how ridiculous Steve McClaren and Joey Barton have appeared when giving interviews in which they sound like they're talking Dutch-English or Franglais, mixing up their natural accent with some sort of native pigeon-speak. Well, I have to confess that I've done exactly the same, but luckily never been taped!

Coming face to face with my hero Kanchelskis was like being a child in a sweetshop and it was really difficult to concentrate, so perhaps that's the reason I started to talk pigeon-Russian, or probably more like swooning gibberish. I can't actually remember what I asked him to do first, but I'm pretty sure it went along the lines of, 'Andrei, we do nice photo?' That started to be my most popular photo chat-up line, much to Jack's amusement as he hovered on my shoulder.

From day one with Andrei, I knew that mind games were going on. Without fail, he would turn up his nose when I suggested something and take about three paces, to see if I would chase after him and beg him to do whatever I wanted. He would then half turn around, which told me that the game was afoot. However, I had instantly identified the game plan, so didn't chase after him. This meant that the half turn would become a full turn and he would back down and say, in the most irresistible way, 'OK, we do photo'.

I think there may have been some eyelash batting and an attempt to put on big blue puppy dog eyes somewhere in the mix, but had never thought that this had worked, until one day much later on in this relationship.

I think the fact that I had managed to get a photo with Andrei was met with some amazement in the Bellefield office and perhaps, also, a modicum of respect. Having achieved photo one, there was now a clear path ahead with regard to how to tackle these things and I think some players, particularly Graham Stuart, latched on to the fact that Danka wanted to have some exposure from its sponsorship.

The Danka label was another issue, however. As the sponsor, they had little involvement with the club, with their head being an Arsenal fan. The Danka people hardly ever went to Goodison Park. Consequently, as I was continuously pushing the Danka name, I became known around the place as 'the woman from Danka', even though I was actually the woman from an agency in Leeds!

Another route in to the inner echelons proved to be Radio Everton, perhaps because I had met the producer during the famous number 9s shoot in the club shop. I was frequently at the club early on a match day and Radio Everton started broadcasting at around lunchtime, so naturally was a little short of material. That was probably why I was interviewed on there nearly every time there was a home match! I would be dragged into the studio and often just asked to describe my week. I would sit there and answer the questions, but always have in mind that line from 'The Three Amigos' … 'they're really starved for entertainment around here!'

Nevertheless, this was all very useful, as the Radio Everton recording studio was located just off the tunnel and so in the very heart of the club – where there was opportunity to 'go on manoeuvres'. Getting into the Park Suite with sponsors' passes was also extremely useful on match day, but I found a new 'in' mid-week too. The guy who manned reception developed a love of telling me about various issues in his rat-infested flat! This meant he would often let me in, after I'd chatted to him for a while, so this again proved a real plus point.

I think all the chatting to him was responsible for another strange linguistic trait that I developed. Apparently, the moment I crossed the Liverpool border, I started to talk in broad scouse, whether that was to a taxi driver, a newsagent, or the guy on reception.

As we headed towards Christmas, I was making in-roads and I managed to get a really good photo of Kanchelskis and Limpar decked in Christmas tinsel. Jack and I waited ages that day to get this shot, but it was once again proving that we were getting somewhere. We headed to a pub a short drive away to have lunch and warm up.

Over the Christmas period, I had to go to a match at Leeds United, with Jason, the person with whom I now shared an office. Jason was the son of a former Leeds player, so was well connected at the club, particularly in the boardroom, where we headed at half-time, for wonderful pies and a delicious spread, which was apparently one of the most renowned in the league! I met Norman Hunter in there that day, as well as former Liverpool legend Tommy Smith, but the most notable part of the day took place before the match. Jason pointed out Jack's father John, so I went to introduce myself. When I said who I was, John responded with the words, 'Oh, so you're the lovely Jane; Jack never stops talking about you'. I could hear Jason guffawing and I'm sure I blushed a bit, but I was actually really chuffed. I am sure Jack would have died a death if he'd known!

By this point, I had started to build up a rapport with Joe Royle's secretary. We had taken Christmas gifts for the players and she had hinted that it would be nice to be included. When I made sure that she was, some bridges were most definitely built. I could almost see the ice-maiden melting before me, especially when her daughters also received a little something. Suddenly, I had access to Joe Royle, who will always be one of my favourite people in life thanks to the total generosity of spirit that he showed to me.

All of these factors converged together after Christmas in a truly adrenaline-filled day that will long live in my memory. I had discovered that it was Andrei's birthday on January 23 and had arranged with the club that I could present a birthday cake to him on the day. I had found a baker in Leeds to make a big blue, iced cake and had hired a translation service to give us the correct lettering for the phrase 'Happy Birthday, Andrei' in Ukrainian. Everything was going according to plan and I loaded the cake into my car on the day and started to drive to Bellefield. Sky TV had said they would be there to film the presentation, so all was hunky dory. All, that was, except for a voice in my head.

This voice was really battering at my brain, as I approached Switch Island on the approach into Liverpool. I'd had this vision of Andrei and his cake running through my head, based totally on the experiences I had had with him over the last few months. The little voice speaking to brain was saying, 'I reckon Andrei doesn't like cake'. This little voice got louder and louder, until my brain responded by saying, 'No, you're right, but he does like vodka'. At that moment, I hung a sharp left and shot into ASDA, as if under the influence of some strange external force.

I ran into the supermarket, found the alcohol aisle and headed straight for the vodka section. I chose a massive bottle of vodka, not having a clue which of the brands he would prefer, but reckoning that size would matter. I hurriedly purchased it, ran back to the car and drove to Bellefield.

From the moment I pulled into the car park past the security guard, I sensed there was something different going on. The whole place had a strange air about it and this feeling became stronger as I walked up the stairs to the first floor, where Joe's secretary sat on reception and where Joe's office was located. The corridor was completely packed with what I can only describe as Bond villains – fairly sinister looking men, for the main part, all of whom were described as 'agents', but one can only speculate as to what kind.

It quickly became apparent that these tall, muscular men were all Russian – this being the only tongue audible in the place that day. The players were all out on the training pitch and Joe's secretary wasn't even visible behind her glass screen thanks to all the bodies in the way.

Carrying a big blue cake hardly made me conspicuous. Jack hadn't arrived and, on reaching the top of the stairs, I immediately locked eyes with a tall, blonde guy, who paid great attention to both me and the cake. I managed to push my way through the melee and took my cake down to the end of the corridor. The blonde guy followed me.

'What eez dis', he asked in his broad Russian accent. I explained that it was a birthday cake for Andrei. 'Is this correct', I asked, pointing at the wording.

'I no know', said the Russian guy, lifting his shoulders in a laconic manner. 'I am Russian: no speak Ukraine'. I wondered how hard it could be to fathom a guess, but didn't fancy an argument with this chap. 'What you do here', he asked, at which point I realised the cake was only an icebreaker. I tried to explain, but it was far too complicated and pretty pointless. I reciprocated by asking what he was doing here.

He responded by telling me that he was an agent for a Russian player, who was in talks to sign for Everton. I looked around and wondered how many agents one player needed, but didn't like to speculate. This guy seemed pretty high up the pecking order! He then started to say that he wanted the cake and that he was far more important than Andrei. Again, I didn't beg to differ, but told him that the cake was for a birthday and it wasn't his birthday! At that, he did what I would dub the 'Andrei shrug' and walked back down the corridor. It was quite a relief to get rid of him and, at that point, Jack arrived.

I shared my master plan with Jack, revealing the vodka in the carrier bag. I'm not sure he was convinced by it, but he did share my view that Andrei might not like cake. I was becoming more depressed about my chance of success by the minute. While feeling rather downhearted, I heard the unmistakable sound of players' boots on the stairs and realised they were now coming back in for lunch. Eight or nine players trooped past me before I spotted Andrei. I quickly grabbed my cake and went to head him off at the pass, otherwise known as the top of the stairs.

I beamed at him and spouted out, in my truncated pigeon English. 'Happy Birthday Andrei. We eff cake for you. We get nice photo with you and cake?' I thrust my sweet offering forward towards him, being ever the eternal optimist.

A totally unimpressed look crossed his face. He stared down at my lovely blue offering, looked back up again, wrinkled up his nose and said, 'I no like cake. Uhh cake. Me like caviar, no cake'. He started to turn his back on the offensive item, but I was too quick for him. Like grease lightning, I delved into my carrier bag, pulled out the vodka and said, 'Vell, Andrei; you like vodka?'

His face totally transformed, after just one glance of the translucent potato stuff! He positively radiated happiness as he grabbed the massive bottle from me and proceeded to swing it round his head like a cowboy preparing to lasso a cow. He was half-crazed by this point and shouting out, at the top of his voice, 'I love vodka: Andrei love vodka'. All I could do was beam back. Even better, he then grabbed the offensive cake off me and said, 'We do nice photo with cake. Come on; let's go!'

Jack and I hurriedly followed him down the stairs, as this now totally enthused Russian took to the field, with SKY News now also in tow. 'Where you wanna do photo?' he asked happily, giving Jack the opportunity to get in and start snapping. The resulting picture was just tremendous, featuring one overjoyed Russian, seemingly wowed by his cake and with not a sign of the vodka bottle he had just put down. Every time I look at that picture, I have a secret grin to myself.

Having done the photo, Andrei was in a sharing mood. 'Come on, let's go!' he ordered again, leading us back into the building and into the player's canteen. He plonked his cake in the middle and gave some sort of order to share it out, 'But no share vodka', he said, again whooping and swinging it round his head. Gary Ablett was right by the canteen door. He called me over. 'It's my birthday too', he said, 'Do I get a cake?'

'No it's not', I replied. 'I've checked all the birthdays!'

SKY Sports filmed this entire episode and it resulted in fantastic footage on that day's news. I just about appeared on that, lurking by the canteen door, while an ecstatic Andrei continued to whirl around the room like a dervish. I had had a truly successful and inspired day!

Things were well and truly on the up after this, with photo calls arranged continuously with various players. We took players polo shirts with the Danka logo embroidered on collar and chest, for branding

222

purposes, when on camera, and these started to be worn when needed. Joe's secretary was by now like a best friend and totally obliging when I wanted to see Joe.

Shortly after the day on which all the Russians had been hanging around, Joe asked me whether I fancied a cuppa, so I naturally said yes. I was so glad I had, as he told me the whole sorry tale of this near signing and how the Russian footballer had pretended for days that he couldn't speak English, to the extent that Joe had been making biting on apple gestures when trying to ask him if he wanted a bit of fruit! Apparently, after days of this demeaning behaviour, when it came down to the nitty gritty of the contract talks, Joe had discovered that the guy spoke very good English and had just been stringing him along. I think he was pretty happy that he hadn't signed him!

Around this time, I came out of Joe's office one day to find Andy Hinchcliffe keen to get in. 'Have you finished with the gaffer now?' he asked, as I emerged. I nodded and wondered what it might be that Andy wanted.

This followed a reserve match, at which I had been present, as it was against Man Utd. It was probably one of the most embarrassing moments of my life, as a penalty shoot out contest had been arranged prior to the start of the match, but nobody was prepared to take a kick for Man Utd and I was asked to do it. Admittedly, I did get a hug from Fred the Red, but that by no means compensated for the fact that I had made a total prat of myself.

The evening moved on and the game started, but then, unfortunately, a duck stopped play and decided to park itself in the Everton net. Various feeble attempts to shift it were made, by which point it had waddled out on to the pitch, but it was still interfering with play. In the end, Andy Hinchcliffe went up and put his boot behind it (fairly gently) and it flew off to the rapturous applause of the crowd.

When next at Bellefield, I started to hear rumours that Andy was extremely worried, as he had received a letter on headed paper from an organisation called something like 'The Duck Preservation Society'. The letter slated him for his actions and said that an investigation was being launched. Andy took this at face value, but it was actually a letter put together by his teammates. I don't think he had yet discovered this when being so keen to see Joe!

Easter brought another great episode with Andrei. I had arrived at Bellefield with hand-decorated Easter eggs for each player's children, which carried an iced Danka logo. We had organised who needed what, but had to try to catch each player as they left the building that day. Various eggs had already been distributed and had been well received when Andrei appeared. I remember my pigeon Anglo-Russian being particularly evident that day, the subject matter being quite tricky.

Andrei was on his way to his car and nodding at me in acknowledgement, when I stopped him with the words, 'Andrei, you no eff Ees-tar eggs'.

A puzzled luck crossed his brow. 'What eez Ees-tar eggs?' he asked.

'Easter eggs; chocolate for cheeldren', I explained.

He looked around at another player, turned back to me and said,

'Ah, Ees-tar eggs', looking absolutely delighted. His obvious joy made me happy too.

'Yes', I said enthusiastically, pushing two eggs into his arms. A sudden crestfallen look swept over his face as he moved away, allowing me, for the first time to see what the player he had looked at was holding. It wasn't a chocolate egg, but a very swish and, no doubt, very expensive leather wash bag. I felt Andrei's pain!

I had really worked on my rapport, not just with Andrei, but with several other players too, so when a colleague from Leeds had to deputise for me one day, I was a little miffed at the thought of someone muscling in on my patch. I needn't have worried one bit. This young Scotsman, who had thought it would be a 'piece of ****' in his words, to get a photo, failed miserably. The report was that the Everton players were very apathetic, wouldn't co-operate and made everything as hard as humanly possible. He never wanted to go there again. I have to say that I did have a secret smile that day, thinking that for all his cockiness and bravado what he hadn't learned the art of was pigeon English and lots of flirting! When I next did a photo call, I seem to remember having a lot of putty in my hands!

By now, I had other photo call options. Graham Stuart had continued to do a sterling job, but now Dave Watson was getting involved, as was David Unsworth. This made things a lot easier, as the pressure was off Andrei and Graham. I cannot recall why we did this, but Jack and I took a big plate of German salami sausages down one day, as a prop for a photo. Graham Stuart did the shot, to the accompaniment of the rest of the squad standing on the balcony watching and jeering. Jack and I then drove to the club shop and couldn't bear the smell of the sausages any longer. I have to admit that we found the nearest bin and dumped them!

I had really worked on my 'ins' into the club and a new one had emerged. This had been brought about initially when someone from the club had asked whether my agency might support the Everton Girls Under 13s team, who were really very good and often picking up trophies, but who needed kit and a sponsor to fund that. Two season tickets were on offer in exchange and I got agreement for this, with my agency paying a fairly small amount and getting its logo on the girls' kit.

This opened up an introduction to the club's education officer, Ken Heaton – another person whose praises I can only sing, particularly as one of his favourite phrases was, 'What charm school did you go to?' I rather liked that. Ken and I started working together as much as possible, with a view to producing various items, including a Danka education pack for schools. Through Ken, I reached still more previously inaccessible parts of the club and found new ways of promoting Danka, through the community route.

I was still regularly attending match days on behalf of Danka, with the match versus Chelsea being particularly memorable. I had arranged a competition with Teletext, which a delightful grandfather won, bringing his grandson with him for a meal in the hospitality suite and seats in the Park End stand, where I was to sit with them.

I had spent quite a bit of time with Radio Everton that day and was keen to hang around the tunnel, as we had permission to take the winner down there and let him get whatever autographs he could grab. When Ruud Gullit agreed to sign an autograph for the winner, I couldn't resist asking for one for myself, which he kindly agreed to do. I was swooning to the point of almost fainting, but somehow composed myself. At one point, just prior to the match, I was having to walk up the tunnel with a big cardboard prop, just as John Collins came running down the tunnel from the other end and collided with me midway. As the cardboard hit him, all I could think about was impending news of a pre-match injury to Collins, but thankfully he laughed it off and carried on jogging!

The Chelsea fans, as usual, were particularly vociferous. The trouble was, that the ones being particularly loud were sitting in the Park Stand rather than the away section and were jumping up and down to the extreme annoyance of thousands of Everton fans. I began to speculate how this could have happened, when I was told that these were Danka employees, sitting in Danka allocated seats. Before I could do anything about it, they were ejected!

My prize winner really enjoyed the match, or rather, Ruud Gullit's complete mastery on the ball. I heard him say to his grandson, 'Look how he lets the ball do the work; that's sheer class, that is'. I could only agree, as he splayed it left and right. This is probably why the Chelsea fans were to be triumphantly heard singing that old classic, '10 men: we only needed 10 men', come the final whistle, having had a man sent off, but having had the impact of six in Mr Gullit alone.

Another memorable match was the Derby match v Liverpool. Danka had allowed us to do all sorts of things with this match, with competitions, merchandise giveaways, entertainment and, above all, thousands of blue plastic clowns noses branded with the Danka logo. To distribute all of these things, I had the help of a couple of the Leeds personnel and this time all of us had to do the Radio Everton interview! I think this was the day that I was asked how I came up with all my great ideas and replied as wittily as possible that a bottle of gin usually helped!

I was hanging around the tunnel area with my blue noses, when Andy Gray came along with the SKY crew. He foolishly asked me what I'd got in my hand, so I immediately shoved a blue nose on to his hooter, much to his amusement. 'I'll wear this all day now', he declared, 'Just to show I'm not biased in any way.' I would expect nothing less of a former Toffees player!

To add to the fervour, I also made sure that all the guys in the press box got a blue nose to wear, as well as equipping the ball boys, kids around the perimeter and others who might be caught on camera. It all worked marvellously on the TV coverage that resulted, even though Everton lost the match in a most disappointing fashion.

Back at base, I suddenly found myself the first one to realise that a crime had been perpetrated. This related to the theft of sportswear – which was held in various locations around the office. I was actually the first to detect that a crime had been committed, as I had ordered my Everton polo shirts in specific sizes for each player. When I came to put them into marked bundles to give to each player, I realised that certain sizes weren't in the box. I checked with the supplier and they said they had definitely been delivered.

This led Jason to go and check his stock of Cellnet England rugby shirts and even more of those seemed to be missing. An office-wide enquiry was launched, but nobody seemed to know anything about it. Some of the boys were out on the Dewsbury Road grabbing some lunch one day, in the midst of the enquiry, when they spotted a young, rough looking guy coming out of the bookies wearing a Cellnet England rugby shirt. As the type of shirt he was wearing was only available to England players, the lads immediately realised that this was one of the shirts in our missing stock. However, they didn't fancy their chances in tackling him!

The spotlight shifted on to the office cleaner and this resulted in the police going to question her. When they investigated her property, they found all sorts of missing items from our stocks, which might never have been noticed had it not been for my Everton polo shirts!

One exciting thing that happened was the arrival of the World Cup in the office and not just the World Cup, but also all of football's biggest trophies. Being allowed to divert them from their route had had to be carefully negotiated with football authorities, with lots of red tape to go through, but they all arrived in the office and we all had our picture taken with them. I never, in a million years, thought that I would ever be holding the World Cup.

I had a really good little pal in the office – Paul – who was only an office junior, but one that I had bags of time for and loads of respect. He was such a helpful, kind lad and we got on really well. As a Mac user, I needed lots of help with PC operation and Paul would always help me to sort issues out, laughing at me quite a lot as he did so, but that was all part and parcel of why we got on so well.

Paul, a few others and I would head out to a pub near a railway track, where a Thomas the Tank engine appeared at times. What I found fascinating about the menu here was the fact that you could order omelette baguettes – something I had never heard of in my life! Paul would occasionally have one and I could never really get my head round it at all. Bacon and fried egg sandwiches, bought on the Dewsbury Road, were something I did treat myself to now and again. Pork pie and mushy peas was a Yorkshire dish I could never relish!

By now, I had become the outright account director of the Green Flag account and quickly found that I had a real supporter there, much to the amazement of my boss, who I think, in his mind, had sent me into the lion's den when he suggested that I set up a media one-to-one lunch in London for the Green Flag Chief Executive, Yuseph. I set up the lunch at a fabulous restaurant called 'The Bleeding Heart' with a journalist called Matthew Vincent, the Moneywise editor at that point in time. I was walking on eggshells at first, having been told that Yuseph was fiery, but I actually found him delightful. I just spoke to him in the way that I would anyone else and we got on like a house on fire, having a very long lunch in the restaurant, partly due to the typical late start and partly because it just seemed a good thing to do. I really enjoyed myself and travelled back on the train thinking it had all gone pretty well.

In the office the next day, the boss was on tenterhooks wanting to know if I'd managed to cope! I told him I didn't know why he was so worried about it and that all had been fine. I think his paranoia stemmed from the fact that he'd had the hairdryer treatment from Yuseph on many an occasion, though I've no idea why. Mid-morning, he came into my office with an amazed look and grin on his face. 'I don't know what on earth you did to Yuseph yesterday, but I'm not sure I've ever heard him sound so happy', he said, beaming broadly. 'It's tremendous. He's really impressed with you', he added! I was absolutely buzzing.

From that point on, Yuseph and I did a number of media one-to-one briefings with personal finance editors together, each one as enjoyable as the last. I also invited other journalists to meet him at Wembley on Green Flag nights there, as we had the hospitality suites at our disposal and it was a perfect opportunity to entertain. I vividly recall my boss laughing at me wearing my old Uni scarf one night – until Yuseph intervened and stuck up for me.

I also got on extremely well with the head of Green Flag home assistance, Patrick. The home rescue product had never really had PR support, but I saw a load of potential in it and wanted to link it to home disasters, such as being unable to cook the turkey on Christmas Day because of a home emergency. I found some fantastic case studies and had lots of success with the product, generating widespread national financial headlines for the first time. I then started to host media briefings with Patrick, having the same sort of success at those I was staging with Yuseph.

The third jewel in my Green Flag crown was the head of a company called UK Insurance, which had office space in the Green Flag HQ in Pudsey. Again, I was sent along to establish a rapport with the head of this insurance company.

Once again, I fared really well. I love eccentric, memorable characters and, to me, this person fitted into this bracket, with his bright red braces that he didn't even bother to hide. He reminded me a lot of some of the Bond dealers at New Japan Securities, so just took it all in my stride and convinced him that I could do a really good job for the wedding insurance product that he underwrote – Wedding Plan.

Media exposure was also pretty much virgin territory for Wedding Plan, but I diligently researched the product, came up with a strong angle for Valentine's Day and generated a lot of national coverage for the wedding insurance product, as well as highlighting the need for wedding insurance. This formula has since been followed by many other wedding insurance suppliers, but I would like to think that I was the trailblazer.

The company that actually marketed the product was based in Norwich and they were so impressed that they asked to meet up. I flew in a tiny aircraft from Manchester to Norwich and found, on arrival, that my ears were all fuzzy and hadn't popped at all following the flight. This lasted all day, so everything I heard was muffled and I suspect I was shouting at people all day!

As time went on, I became a director of the agency, as did the Queen Bee, who I came to understand a lot more. She pointed out a few things to me about the way that things worked in this place, which suddenly made great sense.

The Green Flag account became a very different kettle of fish when Yuseph left quite suddenly and there was also a change of PR manager. I put to them the idea of a Green Flag Challenge, which would operate within the world of sport and highlight achievements that were the 'fastest' within particular sports, to highlight that Green Flag could rescue a motorist quicker than either the AA or the RAC.

I meticulously researched the options and decided to try to reward the fastest 50 scored in the county cricket season, the fastest goal scored during the season, the fastest try and then something within the world of athletics. I wrote to the FA, the ECB and the RFU and then myself and a fairly junior member of staff called Julie, who had been assigned to help on this project, drove down to Birmingham for a meeting with what is now UK Athletics.

All of our proposals were accepted, with the athletics chiefs suggesting that their award be given to the most improved young athlete.

Having agreed all of the awards and the rules applying to them, I set about creating a national media launch for this initiative, which entailed finding a venue in London. That wasn't as easy as it seems, given the size of room needed, a good location and the need to have a venue that would be a draw in its own right. Although I considered several, the one I had my heart set on was the Bombay Brasserie in SW7 – and that was even before I had visited.

A facility visit was, of course, necessary, so I packed myself off to London to view a venue that even then attracted the glitterati, captains of industry and political animals thanks to serving not Anglicised Indian food, but authentic fare from the Bombay (now Mumbai) area. This was clear to me when I arrived, overhearing that tables in the restaurant were booked up for weeks if not months ahead. A board also apologised for the fact that there was a waiting list for the Bombay Brasserie cookbook. I just hoped that there was still availability for the hire of the new conservatory, which is where I wished to hold the event.

The manager was absolutely charming and I regaled him with tales of my PhD research into the history of India. I suppose I must have struck him as someone who was genuinely interested in his country and its cuisine, because to my amazement, he went to a little ornately carved chest, unlocked it and handed me one of the coveted Bombay Brasserie cookbooks as a gift. I have treasured it ever since.

To my great happiness, it was agreed that Green Flag would hire the venue, so I now needed to ensure that an absolutely fabulous invitation be designed. I found a very talented Yorkshire designer and briefed them to create an invitation that would unfold like a snake from a snake charmer's basket. The resulting invitation was absolutely stunning and totally unlike anything else that a journalist would receive in their in-tray.

A variety of media were invited – across sports desks, financial desks, motoring and consumer magazines. The response was tremendous and the acceptances came rolling in. It seemed as if the draw of the venue and the beautiful, quirky invitation had worked a treat.

The evening itself ran beautifully, with some of my favourite financial editors turning up, sports writers like Des Kelly and Harry Harris arriving and top Green Flag managers in attendance. The food was divine and everyone had a great time.

This would a good entrée to a summer of great sport in which we experienced the euphoria that was Euro '96, in all of its 'Three Lions On A Shirt' glory! For me, the lead-up to Euro 96 resulted in one of the most painful, yet pleasurable days of my career – and all at the hands of Messrs McManaman, Fowler and Redknapp.

I knew something was up when I got a call at home on the Sunday evening from my office-sharing buddy Jason. It just started all too full of butter-her-up chat and my guard was instantly up. When I heard that he was ringing because he wanted me to do a Green Flag Team England photo call, I knew there was more to this than met the eye. The pretence was that they wanted to launch the new Euro '96 training kit by getting the three Liverpool players to wear it so that we could get publicity shots and, as I was that side of the Pennines, it made sense for me to do this. Jason swore to me that all three had been briefed on this and that I was to go to the Liverpool training ground, find the kit in the office and then ask for Robbie Fowler, who knew exactly what was needed.

I was highly dubious about this. Normally, Jason jealously guarded the right to handle such photo shoots, which made me suspicious. Nevertheless, I agreed to do it, having little choice in the matter.

I drove to Melrose at the time I had been told to arrive and got past the security gate with little bother. I sought out the office and there was a package there for me. Things seemed to be going swimmingly. I then asked for Robbie Fowler. This is where it went pear-shaped. I was told that Robbie Fowler wasn't around, though there wasn't much explanation as to why. A bit of phoning around took place, but not with much gusto, and I was told to go and sit in the canteen. That was really quite interesting, as I ended up sharing a table with Stan Collymore, Ian Rush and John Scales, but not a sign of any of the three musketeers I had been sent to find!

As I looked out of the canteen window, I suddenly saw Steve McManaman walking towards me, so I dived out and stopped him in his tracks. I explained to him that apparently Robbie Fowler knew exactly what was needed and had been briefed. McManaman just sort of shrugged his shoulders and said he didn't know where Robbie Fowler was. Feeling next to useless at this point, my heart suddenly leapt with joy at the appearance of Robbie Fowler from around the corner. I rushed over to him and started explaining that I believed he'd been briefed on the shoot for the new England training kit. He too just looked blank and muttered something, but there was no real indication that he knew anything. He did at least ask what I wanted him to do, so I asked him to try to get the other two to the shoot.

At this point, the photographer turned up and I couldn't help wishing that I'd got Jack with me, as he would have been an enormous support – a feeling that intensified as events unfolded. Eventually, after the typical 'hanging around' that went hand in hand with being at training, Robbie Fowler and Steve McManaman came over. It was apparent that they were deliberately winding Jamie Redknapp up, by coming to do the shoot while he was still training. They grabbed some of the kit as Redknapp shouted over, but they just laughed and ignored him. They looked pretty gleeful about this whole thing at that point, though that enthusiasm soon waned.

The photographer requested a number of different poses and each one was met with a lot of larking around and backchat. While Jack would have just sorted it out, the photographer I was with didn't really take command and the whole thing was descending into a bit of a farce, which is when I thought 'enough is enough' and decided to sort it out myself. McManaman had been asked to kneel down for one shot, which was met with, 'I can't kneel, my knees are too bad' and a grin that instantly conveyed that this was another lame excuse.

'That's a shame', I said, 'I'll have to point that out to Terry Venables. Not sure he'll want you in the squad if they're that bad'.

McManaman looked at me, must have seen a steely look in my eye, laughed and said 'Good point'. After this, he started to behave a bit better, but suddenly decided he had to go for his 'suit fitting'.

Now anyone who knows about this period in Liverpool FC's history will instantly remember that this set of players were known as the 'Spice Boys'. Well, it transpired that these two Spice Boys were both off to have a fitting for their infamous white Wembley suits, designed by Paul Smith. McManaman appeared to have an earlier appointment, so off he shot, leaving us with Fowler alone. Now things got really tough as the excuse we kept getting was, 'You didn't make my mate do that, so I'm not doing it'. I did begin to add 'and footballers' to that famous epithet of 'Never work with animals and children', but tried to keep counting to 10.

After a few more shots, with me trying to appease and encourage, to little avail, he'd had enough and I told the photographer to leave it, as it was like pulling teeth and Robbie was clearly itching to get himself into a white suit too. I had definitely lost the will to live, but my faith in human nature was about to be restored, by one Jamie Redknapp. He'd stayed out at training much longer than the others but suddenly came bounding over and in his cute Cockney accent said, 'Oh, 'ave I missed out then?' He looked so eager to please that I grabbed a training coat.

'No, not at all', I said, 'we really want you in the shots'. He looked delighted and even more eager to please.

'Where d'ya want me then?, he asked. 'Shall I stand by the goalpost, or over 'ere .. or I could do this maybe?'. Never a keener model will I ever encounter. I couldn't believe how obliging he was being after what we'd been through with the other two. Basically, anything we wanted, the lovely lad did, bless him. We finished the shoot and Jamie turned to me and said, 'Are you alright to wait until I've 'ad a shower and bring this kit back to you?' How could any girl refuse that request!

Sure enough, after I had hung around outside the shower block like a groupie, he emerged in a brown chequered tank top looking very easy on the eye indeed and handed me the training coat he'd been wearing! Just clutching it was enough!

The one good thing about this whole stressful experience was that the shots got fantastic exposure in the nationals – though if anyone had known what it had taken to get them, they'd have given me an OBE! You can rest assured that when I next got back to the office with Jason, I shut the office door and had a few choice words for him – much to his amusement!

As Euro '96 approached, Green Flag was given a ticket allocation and I had seats allocated for a match at Old Trafford, so invited two journalists from the Everton reporting ranks, one of whom was a very young chap editing the Evertonian.

Unfortunately, an evening that had been really wonderful turned into a nightmare. The poor Evertonian writer had only just passed his driving test and had to drive home to Liverpool. He had banked on his colleague helping him, but he had gone AWOL back at the hotel to which we'd retired for drinks. I was left talking to the young journalist, who by this point was in an absolute panic. We sat in the lounge reception area for ages, praying that he would return.

In the end, there was nothing else for it but to seek him out. I eventually found him and insisted that he go back to his colleague and help him get home. He still didn't reappear for a while, leaving me having to head out into the car park to try to give advice on how to use the car's headlights.

I went on holiday to Spain shortly after this, returning to the really exciting news that Everton were about to sign Gary Speed. I'd always quite liked Gary Speed as a player, but with him being at Leeds, hadn't paid that much attention to him. It was only when I met him that I realised what a lovely person he was. However, his signing proved a really challenging day for me.

Just before I'd gone away on holiday, Joe had given me a kiss on the cheek when I was standing by a string of reporters on the ground floor of Bellefield. As I had learned at Swinton, the northern way of viewing innocent kisses on the cheek is very different from that in the south, but I hadn't given it a second thought.

This, however, had given someone enough ammunition to try to pepper me with gunshot. They, for whatever reason, decided to try to do this at the Gary Speed signing.

I had enough problems as it was. Still in my Spanish mode, I had turned up in a turquoise batik dress and Jack kept chirping on and on about how much this dress (and my tan) suited me. While trying to deflect this, I had in mind the fact that my account manager had kindly told me, just before setting off from Leeds that a rumour had spread that there was something going on between Joe and I. I instantly recognised why this had happened, and whose agenda this was, but that didn't make it any easier, despite it being nonsense.

When I entered the news conference, all of the assembled media were already seated and I stood at the back with some TV and press photographers and club personnel. What happened next couldn't have gone worse for me.

Into the room came Joe and Gary Speed and they took their place at the main table. Joe settled down into his seat, looked up, presumably caught a glimpse of a kingfisher blue dress and said, in front of all of the press, 'Hello, sweetheart, how are you?' I felt the eyes of Liverpool turn on me, as the poor man stumbled into a trap that he didn't even realise he'd strayed in to.

I smiled and said, 'Fine thanks, Joe', knowing that he knew I'd been away on holiday, but I could see the elbow digging going on. The person who'd set me up looked really triumphant.

When the conference broke up, I had some shirts that I had already planned for Gary to sign, so I didn't have to get permission from my friend in the commercial department. He was absolutely lovely as he signed them and nothing was too much trouble. It was then a case of going outside for the official signing shots, at which point Jack started up again about my tan and my dress. By that point, I just felt the safest thing to do was to get out of Goodison and collapse somewhere in a stressed-out heap.

Visits to Goodison were few and far between after that, due to the sponsorship changing hands, much to my distress, as I really missed Joe and the gang. Luckily, we had another encounter in the Green Flag hospitality suite at Wembley, where he suddenly walked in with the SKY crew and I just got a huge hug, which was absolutely lovely. It sort of amazed the bunch of personal finance journalists that I was talking to at the time, buy hey, you've got to grab your affection where you can!

The Green Flag account was still very interesting, particularly when Jason and I were invited to join some of the fleet management guys on a sailing day out of Southampton. About eight of us were privileged enough to be taken on board one of the yachts that was about to compete in the BT Global Challenge and literally taught a few of the ropes of crewing a yacht. It was a gloriously sunny day and Jason and I had such a laugh. I still have this vision of him trying to wind a rope around and just collapsing in a fit of giggles. I would like to think that I was more competent than him, as a crew member let me steer the yacht out of Southampton harbour, as we headed towards the Isle of Wight! I don't think I even came near to crashing into anything and kept my cool as Jason clicked away with the camera to capture this moment of female supremacy. Come to think of it, I think I was the only woman on the trip!

There was another fantastic day out with Green Flag still to come though, which I have to say makes other corporate events seem really dull. This was the finals day of a footie tournament for Green Flag associates and those who had made it through to this stage got to play on the Wembley pitch, much to their delight, as you can imagine. I've never seen a bunch of men look happier with their lot in life and it was just magnificently staged, with the teams coming out of the tunnel and then standing to sing the national anthem. All the supporters in the stands joined in, to add to the atmosphere and it was just such fun, from first to last. It has to rank as one of my favourite days ever, partly from the pleasure I derived from seeing these proud men revelling in their moment in the spotlight.

What was not such a great night was an England Under 21s international v Poland played at Molineux. My Green Flag assistant and I were asked to promote this match for the FA, which was a great little project to work on. We did all the comps, radio promo and community type stuff and went down to the team hotel to meet up with the FA press officer. Nicky Butt was playing snooker and asked me if I wanted a game, but I looked at the length of my skirt and decided against it! We met Peter Taylor and he and some of the players gave a press interview, before we watched them board the team bus, blowing kisses to us as they pulled out of the car park! Nothing like the confidence of youth!

All of this was great, but unfortunately, we didn't have a crystal ball. The ground had filled up really nicely and we were heading towards kick-off when suddenly there was this massive security alert and everyone within the ground was ordered to evacuate it as fast as possible. I looked at my assistant and neither of us could fathom what was going on, but knew it wasn't good.

Our 'evacuation' consisted of being taken to a hospitality bar, behind a flimsy bit of glass, which would hardly have protected us had the security alert been real. It was actually a bomb scare, with an unidentified object having been found in a bin. The bomb disposal unit had been called, but still we all sat there, with the FA officials. One hour passed, then another, with quite a few bottles of wine having been cracked open. We couldn't conceive that the match was going to go ahead at such a late hour, but I guess the other team had flown in and the match had to be played. By the time it kicked off at 10pm, I'm not sure any of us could really focus on the ball at all and the ground was pretty empty, as it was well past the bedtime of all the kids who'd been given tickets in the family stand. It was awful for the players, but somehow the game was played and ended with a few hundred people there to witness the result.

The offending 'article' transpired to be someone's sandwiches which their mum had probably made them and which didn't have a filling to tickle their fancy. The sarnie army had truly scuppered our best-laid plans good and proper!

The next thing to occupy me was a financial services account, for which I pitched with my boss and another girl who had joined the office. The account was for Yorkshire Bank, which had had a product called the Flexible Payment Mortgage for around three years, but had never really promoted its benefits, which were rooted in daily interest accreditation.

We won the account and I started writing a PR plan for the launch of the mortgage (effectively a re-launch, but as the product had not had general exposure, nobody was really any the wiser). The strategy was built around using a shock figure relating to the amount of money being overpaid on mortgages in this country and as this was felt to be just a fraction of the true figure, I suggested something truly ambitious – the creation of a massive ice sculpture that would have the figure carved into it.

For this to work, I knew we had to have a London photo call and so I went back over some of the research I had conducted for the Privilege sports car shoot in Trafalgar Square and came up with an option on the banks of the Thames. I hired a respected national photographer and is-sued a press call notice, which was picked up by many, including SKY News.

I had suggested that consumer research be commissioned and had written questions that would produce strong news angles, which could be tailored in 10 different parts of the country. I spent hours writing the various press releases and making sure that they would all hit the mark.

To maximise the impact, I had sold in an exclusive to my good friend and journalist (then at the Express), Steven Day. I briefed him on the story and made sure that his story could appear in print prior to others getting their hands on it. It was to appear in the Wednesday edition of the paper and I finalised all the details with him the day before, ensuring that he got the iceberg picture sent over before others had it.

On the day of the launch, the photo call was staged fairly early and then a press briefing session was arranged in a London venue with func-tion room. A radio interview with consumer programme 'You and Yours' was set up for that day and went out live.

This combination of activity had an absolutely phenomenal impact. Within half-an-hour of the 'You and Yours' programme going out, a queue had formed from out of the bank door and up the street from the Cheapside branch of Yorkshire Bank. The same sort of impact was soon to be experienced at branches across the country, as consumers flocked to get details of what was being called the 'Aussie Mortgage'.

Yorkshire Bank reported incredible results from this campaign. Unfortunately, I can say no more and am only to state that I was responsible for 'part 1' of this campaign, for legal reasons. The whole campaign went on to win a CIPR Sword of Excellence for my previous employer.

For me, the biggest recognition of the success of 'part 1' of this campaign came from the fact that within weeks of launch the RBS, with whom I banked, suddenly slapped point of sale all over their branches which said, 'We also have the Aussie Mortgage!' To me that speaks volumes.

The final days of my life at this agency were joyous on the one part and plain miserable on the other. With the arrival of the Britannia/Stoke City sponsorship as a PR account, it was essential to open an office near Manchester, to service the account, so I was asked to find one. I came across a really nice office in Altrincham, which was initially in the downstairs part of a suite of serviced offices not far from the famous Juniper restaurant. I moved in and immediately met a really nice chap called Mark, who had the office next door. What was more intriguing to me, however, was my neighbour on the other side, Dez, a young black guy with very long dreadlocks and a really interesting lifestyle.

On further investigation – quite ironic under the circumstances – I discovered that Dezy, as he liked to be known, was a private detective. He mainly worked at night, but on those occasions when he was around, he would suddenly get a call and absolutely fly out the door like a bat out of hell. When I finally made it into his inner sanctum, he showed me all his gadgets – cameras hidden in ties and other strange places, recording devices and some undercover techniques. I was wowed by it and he obviously knew that, as he sent me the most graphic birthday card I've ever received in my life!

I had to recruit someone to work on the Stoke City sponsorship with me and I took on a really kind-hearted guy called P, who had done a lot of fundraising-type activity and wanted to work in sport. He was a very able chap, but one who had had a hard life, being brought up by his Nan, who he adored, rather than his mother. He and I got on very well, even if he wasn't a true rapport person. I discovered that when he got bad news about his Nan's health and I reached out to touch his hands in support and he leapt back and almost fell off his seat!

He wasn't by any means the typical, personable PR professional, but he was bright, clever and able. Unfortunately, however, he never gelled with the client and they asked for someone else to replace him. I recruited two new people – Laura, fresh from an MA at Manchester Met and Michele who had some PR experience. Both of them were really lovely girls, but P was never the same again.

Both of the girls started to work on the Stoke City account with me and there was some instant planning to do with that. There was a new manager announcement planned by the club in the lead-up to the opening and their PR department really hyped up the forthcoming news, leading all Stoke City fans to believe that this was a really big name who was coming to manage the club – a fatal error. There was even talk of this being Joe Royle, which would have been fantastic. When the news broke however, it was someone nobody had really heard of – Chic Bates.

When I met Chic, I realised what a lovely guy he was and felt sorry for him that the wave of expectancy was really now reverberating and generating negativity with regard to his appointment. He was very supportive of everything we were trying to do and happy to get the players to help as much as possible.

Unfortunately, this led to someone having the bright idea that Laura and myself should present the PR plan to the whole team squad, in the team bar, after a training session. Neither of us wanted to do this in the slightest, this being one of the most embarrassing things imaginable. We were practically the only women in the room and I'm sure everyone can imagine what the players were like – boys will be boys after all.

Laura and I somehow got through the presentation, which was taking place on a small plinth, but one with quite a deep drop when wearing a tight, shortish skirt and heels. As I started to step down off the plinth, one of the players suddenly shouted out in a voice that everyone in the room could hear, 'Beautiful'. I must have turned scarlet in embarrassment! Chic made some sort of kind speech to say that everyone would be behind it and that, thankfully, brought this episode to an end!

In these early days of the Stoke City account we attended match nights at the old Victoria ground in the centre of Stoke, as the Britannia Stadium wasn't much more than a building site at the time. We'd made a few contacts there and Laura and I went to an evening match at the stadium, which then resulted in us getting an invitation to a night out in a very trendy bar in Newcastle-under-Lyme. That was quite an evening.

The main thrust of everything we were doing at this stage was that of putting a strategy together for the launch of the Britannia Stadium, at its new location on the ring road. There was a drip feed of press material needed as we approached launch, but we also needed a big bang on the day itself.

Instrumental to this was the creation of a Stoke City mascot. I discussed this with my mother and together we came up with the idea of Potamus – a hippopotamus who would reference the fact that Stoke City's nickname is 'The Potters'. The idea went down a storm and a rather cute design for Potamus was drawn up. To this day, you can still see Potamus walking around the Stoke City stadium – my lasting legacy to the Premier League side, which hadn't yet earned promotion in my day.

Another element of the opening was the entertainment. We decided that, to get the crowd going, we would find a Tom Jones impersonator, who could arrive in a pink Cadillac, have knickers thrown at him by women in the crowd, drive round the perimeter and then take centre stage to lead everyone in a rousing rendition of the Stoke City fans' song 'Delilah'.

We managed to find a guy who had been on the TV programme 'Stars in their Eyes' and who was perfect for the role we wanted him to play. He was more than happy to do what we wanted, so that element was in place.

The next part was really a club-organised element, with the idea being that Stoke City FC and Blackpool FC legend, Sir Stanley Matthews, would kick a ball into the net in front of the kop end and this would set off a series of fireworks. Other smaller elements were added in.

The lead up to this opening was busy on all fronts. We all went out tenpin bowling with some staff from Stoke City and player Graham Kavanagh, who was extremely helpful, whenever we had to ask for appearances for PR stories. The night out seemed to help a bit with the bonding, though it did rather seem that my male employee was siding with me and letting the girls bowl for the other side.

In the lead up to the opening, Laura and I, Michelle, Mark from the office next door, a few other people and some of the Stoke City guys decided we would have a night out in Manchester to celebrate my birthday. This was one of the most disastrous nights of my life, which started badly and deteriorated as the night went on. To start with, we managed to lose Michelle and Mark from the word go, all departing in different cars and not really knowing where we were all heading. A little later into the night (by midnight-ish), Laura and I became separated from the others and she decided to take me to this bar she knew.

By this point, I really wasn't enjoying anything and Laura, by her own admission on the Monday after this nightmare night, was totally out of it. I decided I had to try to get her home and then head back to the hotel that I was staying in, which was in Altrincham. I knew Laura lived in Stockport, but I had to try to sober her up enough to give me the address. There was a cab waiting right outside the bar, so I bundled her in the back and got in with her.

I can remember thinking that we were driving miles and miles, but Laura was in no condition to tell me whether we were going round in circles or not. Eventually, we arrived in Stockport and she managed to confirm that she was at her house. I got her out and then got back in the taxi, in the back seat.

This is when I started to get really worried, as it was obvious to me that we were driving in a completely different direction from the way that I knew how to get from Stockport to Altrincham. Unfortunately, as Laura left the cab, I had started to silently cry, thinking how awful my birthday had been and the driver noticed tears rolling down my face. He told me that someone like me shouldn't be crying and started telling me all about his life in Rusholme and how his cousin had been arrested for murder! By now, I wasn't crying, but really panicking, thinking that I was really not in a good place.

I queried if we were going in the right direction and he assured me that we were. We couldn't possibly have been, as we drove for ages. Eventually, I recognised a part of Altrincham and before too much longer, we pulled up at my hotel. I couldn't see anyone sitting in reception and that made me really nervous, particularly when the driver suddenly locked the taxi's doors.

'What are you doing?' I asked in a panic.

'Take me into the hotel with you', he demanded. I knew that if I rejected this outright, there would be trouble.

'I can't', I said, 'There will be someone just beyond the reception doors and they will notice'.

'I want to spend the night with you', he insisted. 'It's your birthday and you are unhappy'. I just didn't know what to do now. All I could think was that I was going to be driven away and killed somewhere and Laura wouldn't remember a thing about the driver or the taxi.

I insisted again that I had to get out and was really tired. 'Then give me your number' he said, 'and promise that you'll come out with me'. It was amazing how sober I felt at this point and what danger can do to get you into a really clear mental state. Thinking remarkably quickly, I gave him the office fax number. He unlocked the doors. I got out and tried to calmly walk to the hotel entrance door. I managed to get in, and then, when out of sight, ran like hell to my room.

On the Monday morning, I told the girls the whole sorry tale and Laura was devastated. As I had suspected, she wouldn't have remembered a single detail – she could hardly remember how she got home at all. The fax machine must have rung at least 300 times that day, from 9am to 5pm solid!

Luckily, I went on holiday in mid August, with the last day of my holiday being the day before the official opening, which had been set for August 30th. All plans were in place and the girls just issued things when pre-determined. I had to drive back from Kent on my own, in order to get to the Saturday opening and it was absolute carnage on the M6 that Friday night. It had taken me hours to even get as far as Wolverhampton, but then it was clear that the motorway was closed, so everything was diverted through Wolverhampton. It was sheer hell – moving an inch every 5 minutes at best, no chance of changing lanes when you needed to and added to that, the confusion of not knowing a town or how to negotiate it to get to where you needed to be.

I literally sat and burst into tears in the middle of Wolverhampton. I hadn't really stopped, hadn't eaten or even had much of a comfort break since leaving Kent and sitting in solid, blocked and immobile traffic, there was no chance of any of this. The journey took me 11 hours.

Despite this, I got up and got to Stoke as planned and the day went well, apart from the fact that Sir Stanley's kick didn't reach the net to set the fireworks off and the community officer had to do it. I did feel completely weary the following day, but that wasn't the worst of it. My radio alarm came on playing funereal music and I thought the Queen Mother had died, as press had long told me that all radio stations were geared up to do this, whenever the inevitable event took place. I was absolutely shocked and horrified when it proved to be Princess Diana who had died in a car crash in Paris. Having met her at Olympia, I just burst into tears and wept, on and off, for days, as every piece of footage of her and her boys was played out on TV.

A Green Flag event was staged just after Diana's funeral and I cried again as I drove back from Wembley to Hertfordshire and further up the M1, seeing every motorway bridge decked with messages and flowers for Diana. I was following the route her funeral car had taken.

Following the opening of the stadium, there were lots of plans for other things to do. P decided to leave the agency, having found himself another job and that was a relief. Laura and I had started tackling the maximisation of Britannia's corporate social responsibility programme, as well as the football sponsorship and were involved in all sorts of community and educational initiatives taking place around Leek and its environs.

We also worked with the football in the community team, who we equipped with a thing called a Footwall, which the FA had told me about. It was a target-shooting wall, with different target zones and loops and was a fantastic bit of kit for the community guys to have. Potamus turned up at the kids' sessions using the Footwall and the whole thing was branded Britannia. Graham Kavanagh launched it for us and it was a great on-going piece of branding.

Michelle was working on some PR for a Britannia initiative in Northampton and I was still involved with Green Flag and Yorkshire Bank. This is when things got really tough. There were many times when I would drive to Altrincham to open up the office there, then have to drive to Leeds for some ridiculous reason of 'being needed there more frequently', then have to drive to Stoke for a story, then back to Altrincham and back home. Often, I would be doing 500 miles a day and it was killing me.

I had started to arrange media post-match dinners outside of Wembley, as something changed with the Green Flag allocation for numbers in the conference suite. My account manager and I had enjoyed an absolutely fantastic evening at one of my very favourite restaurants, The House on the Hill in Hampstead. It was a night full of fun with the likes of Steven Day and, on that night in particular, Nick Gardner of the Sunday Times, who now lives in Australia. I can remember two taxis departing from the House on the Hill that night and Nick hanging out of the window of his taxi blowing me kisses as I sat in mine! We had really had a great old time.

The time after this, I had the likes of Simon Read and a few other journalists heading with me to a restaurant closer to Wembley. The relatively new Green Flag PR manager was with me and we only got away from the meal at around midnight, if not later. We went back to the Wembley Hilton, where we knew everyone would be in the bar until 3am. Sure enough, they all were.

What happened next changed my life. Within weeks it was time to move on.

Chapter 13
A NEW DAWN

I had never really thought of running my own agency. To me, I was just a single mother, with no maintenance or child support money coming in, trying to make ends meet. The idea of starting my own agency was actually my father's and it actually astounded me, while touching me at the same time. It was a massive risk, but probably the recognition I'd always loved getting from him from the time I would enter, and win, the Blackpool Library writing competitions!

It was November when I left Leeds and the first thing to do was to think of a name for a company, get it registered and design a logo. It wasn't anything to which I had ever given any thought and yet the idea came to me really quickly. People often ask me where I get my ideas and often it is in the bath. The idea for the name 'Catapult' came while wallowing in my oasis between the soap bubbles.

I devised it because it obviously communicated targeting and the idea of catapulting people into the limelight. I didn't want to sound like one woman and her dog, though as it turned out, I wish it had been in those early days. I wanted to sound like a company that could really achieve results. I think the plan worked.

My logo was designed by a former colleague of my father's from the Lancashire Evening Post – the very talented Ken Wignall. I suppose, being a big Manchester United fan, the combination of red and black was inevitable. I think I am a very red-centric person anyway, so I briefed him on the colours and on he cracked, producing something that I instantly loved.

I had quite a bit of time on my hands at this point and, when that happens, I do a lot of thinking and my mind goes into overdrive. I knew I had to devise some sort of mechanic that would be memorable and convey a bigger entity than just someone setting up on their own. Nowadays (2013) that is all the rage, with every Tom, Dick and Harriet setting up a PR consultancy, but back then it was rare, and preferable in my opinion, as I believe the quality of work turned out was a lot higher.

After a lot of pondering, I came up with the idea of Dempster and I owe Dempster an awful lot. Dempster was a character who I devised as the archetypal client, wandering into the PR world not really knowing what they are buying, or what to ask for, when they appoint a PR consultancy. Dempster was brought to life by my logo designer, Ken Wignall, in a series of postcard mailings built around cartoon scenarios that I devised for him. Each either highlighted an aspect of appointing an agency, or focused on a particular PR skill.

The six themes related to strategy, accounting, image raising, media relations, corporate community involvement and copywriting. The hapless Dempster was typically pictured looking baffled, having made a bad decision, or having got hold of the wrong end of the stick. He and his budget had suffered badly, because he had not checked out an agency's credentials, understood its pricing policy or worked out whether they were PR cowboys or cowgirls, prior to signing a contract.

Dempster was my means of drumming up business and these mailings were ready in the pipeline before I even found any premises. That in itself was a challenge and I must have trailed around 30 unsuitable offices, from St Annes and Lytham to Kirkham and Preston, before I finally went to see one that I had been resisting viewing. That office was at Marsh Mill Village in Thornton Cleveleys and the reason I had avoided it was that there was another PR consultant around the corner, by whom I had once been interviewed.

However, beggars cannot be choosers and I had seen so many unsuitable offices that the Marsh Mill option: a private office, outer office, kitchen and toilet, on a first-floor level overlooking a square full of flower beds and right next door to a pub, seemed like paradise. There wasn't too much thinking to be done about it, especially as it was, at most, 10 minutes from home.

The office shared a landing with a solar energy company and was above a fashion shop and the complex's toilet block. The toilet block didn't seem to mind my arrival too much, but I certainly ruffled the feathers of all the boas in the fashion outlet. I think this was down to three main reasons. The first was that they had been used to having things their own way and not having someone upstairs. The second lay in the fact that one of the men connected with it spent about 10 hours a day in the pub and eventually paid the price. The third was rooted in the fact that they were 'friends' with the other PR consultant.

A few things happened very quickly. The first was that the solar company did a moonlight flit, leaving me the sole occupant of the first floor. I would regularly get people knocking on my door asking where they were, because their solar system had gone wrong and they were worried that their warranty wasn't being honoured. I could do nothing to help them, having been given no forwarding address.

The second thing that started to happen was that racks and racks of clothes started to be strewn right across the entrance to my office door and out about ten feet in front of it. There was many a time when I couldn't even get to the door without fighting my way through hangers and hangers of leopard print, gold lamé and sequins. Over the course of several months, it became obvious that this was a deliberate ploy to try to force me out and polite requests for the racks to be moved, so that I and any clients could actually reach the office, fell on deaf ears. Only the intervention of the Fire Service got the racks moved.

The next thing that occurred was slanderous, but a little amusing nonetheless. The shop started telling people that I was a prostitute entertaining gentlemen callers! When I found out about this I was livid, but also paranoid every time someone came to see me!

Following this and a sharp warning, that if I ever heard this again there would be hell to pay, my mail kept getting stolen. The post office actually pointed the finger of blame at the shop and I believed them, as there was no other explanation. When my father went in to have words about this, there was a gap of about 10 minutes before the alcoholic owner came upstairs threatening to punch him, which I fully believed, as he nearly beat the door down in an attempt to get in.

It would seem that the final attempt to get me out was that of putting super-glue in my lock, so that I couldn't get into the office on a Monday morning and was locked out for hours.

Attempts to make the peace were enacted. During this conversation, we were spun a tale of how he had once arranged for Tina Turner to play a concert on the field next to Marsh Mill (between the failed craft village and the sports centre) and only Wyre Borough Council's refusal to pick up litter after the event prevented the 'Nutbush City Limits' star from performing there. One had to question whether Tina had been that hard up!

These early issues were not helped any by a feeling of a lack of personal safety sitting in an office by myself. This started when a knock at the door saw me admitting a guy who had read about me starting up and wanted a job. As the conversation progressed, I came to see how very odd he was and the worry deepened when he began telling me about an article he had had published, which revolved a lot around him having sex under one of Blackpool's piers.

I managed to rid myself of him the first time, with a promise to consider his CV, but was unprepared for a second weird visit. At that point, I started locking my door and wouldn't answer it if I though it could be him. Several notes were posted under the door, all of which I ignored. After a good few months, this very strange man went away and I breathed a real sigh of relief.

That wasn't the only pressure of those early days. Having registered Catapult with Companies House and then submitted my logo as a trademark, I received a phone call one afternoon from a business in London, who said that I was infringing another organisation's trademark. The man was very bullish and tried to really push me into saying that I would change the company name. The man foolishly uttered the words, 'You are just a little one woman band sitting in Lancashire and we are a big outfit in London', which proved a red rag to a bull. From that point, I resolved that, no matter what it entailed, I would fight to keep the name.

This instantly led to a search for a trademark lawyer and I was directed towards a company in Birmingham called Laurence Shaw and a remarkable lady called Ann Roome, who now has her own company

– Roome Associates. Ann was completely supportive and put together an excellent case as to why we should have a trademark in the categories for which we had applied. More importantly, she instigated some detection work worthy of my office ex-door neighbour in Altrincham and came across discrepancies in the account of what this London actually did and what they said they did. She also found someone who had been for an interview there, left his portfolio at the business's request while sent out to get some lunch, only to later discover that they had copied his work and were claiming it as their own.

Although it took several years to fully secure the trademark, this London company's business practices were such that they went to the wall. At that point, I secured the trademark for both Catapult PR and Catapult Design.

I had been very fortunate when setting up, as this coincided with the arrival of my ex client, John Grimbaldeston, at Abbey National Direct, where he was charged with setting up a direct motor insurance business in Bradford. I produced a proposal and carried out some work for John before, a few months in, the Abbey National Direct Press Office realised that I had been taken on and reminded John that employing external consultants was not company policy. Grimbles had, however, given me my first step on the PR consultancy ladder and, for that, I will be forever grateful.

I often wonder whether what I did one afternoon in those early months is what everyone does when setting up their own business. At one point, I thought it was just me, but years later, I spoke to a client, who told me that he did exactly the same thing one day – and I hadn't even shared my experience with him. I call this the 'What have I done?' moment and it's where the enormity of the risk that you are taking hits you between the eyes and overwhelms you. In my case, I was sitting at my desk in Marsh Mill, crying buckets. In the case of the man in London, he had his head in his hands wondering how he could have been so irresponsible when he had a wife and disabled child to support. The 'What have I done' moment comes out of nowhere and maybe it's linked to conscience. Maybe the little voices in your head hammer away whispering the word 'risky' over and over again until you succumb and can't take it any more.

Personally, I think the 'What have I done' moment is a good thing, as it shakes you up and makes you determined to prove that you can succeed. To assist this, I put two stickies on my computer screen. One was a quote from Winston Churchill – 'Success is the ability to go from one failure to another with no loss of enthusiasm'. The other carried a quote from Walt Disney – 'If you can dream it, you can do it'.

The 'What have I done' moment galvanised me into using the tools that I had at my disposal, which were basically my contact book and my Dempster cards. I started sending letters and postcards out and then found a telesales company, who could follow them up. This strategy was what got the business off the ground in those crucial first months after Abbey National Direct's departure.

In early July 1998, just three months after setting up Catapult, something marvellous happened. My telesales follow-up person spoke to a chap called Tim Berry, who was the managing director of a company called Direct Response Travel, based in Altrincham. They had been interested in my mailer and wanted to see me, which was fantastic news. I put together a strong presentation and went to see Mr Berry.

Mr Berry thankfully found my presentation exceedingly good, mainly because I had gone along and presented ideas and solutions, not just credentials. I had taken the time to examine the product, used my knowledge of the sector and communicated all of this. I got the account.

In the exact same month, I was called back in my Dial Direct – an insurance company that I had pitched to with my boss from Leeds. They were really pleased that I was now on my own and, again, I presented ideas based upon all of my experience in the insurance sector. Once again, I got the account.

With these two accounts under my belt, I took on my first part-time member of staff and really started to work full-time. At around the same time, I was appointed to handle the PR for Business Link, who had an office just across the square at Marsh Mill. I now had three valuable sources of income, in pretty much the space of six weeks.

The Direct Response account had an urgent need. The company had always done very well out of Which? Report rankings, but the times were a-changing and they were slipping behind other competitors, who were using PR to a much greater extent. Rules on publishing Which? rankings were tightening up, so having a higher profile was essential.

The first thing I did on this account was something that instantly hit the mark, resulting in a piece in the Daily Express's consumer section. There was an issue to latch on to in the industry and that was the levelling of Insurance Premium Tax across the industry – so that everyone paid the same amount of IPT on a policy, regardless of whether this was sold by a travel agency or by a direct travel insurance provider. The travel agents were cock-a-hoop about this, saying that it would make the industry a level playing field. The message I put out for Primary Direct was that there could be no level playing field given the huge amounts of commission that had to be paid to travel agents selling the product, which vastly inflated the price of the product.

To communicate this, I knew we had to make a bit of an impact, as Direct Response was unknown to many of the national personal finance journalists. I persuaded the client that we should do something quirky and create an 'unlevel' playing field, in the style of a blow football game. I worked with a designer to create something that would be as tilted as the pitch at Yeovil Town, with the travel agents' pricing in the more elevated goalmouth and the Direct Response pricing in the other. The green card creation was marked out with the centre circle, penalty areas, halfway line and goal mouths and was issue with a straw and a small plastic ball, all of which I sourced. I issued this to a number of personal finance press and the results were fantastic. Direct Response became a media spokesperson overnight and, on the back of this, I began to book media one-to-one lunches with my contacts on the national financial pages.

This was the first activity in what became known as the 'Passport to Pole Position' campaign, which ran in the calendar year to July 1999 and which then became my very first award winning campaign with Catapult PR. That year was full of interesting angles and hard work. Some of this revolved around finding case studies that we could use to illustrate the need for travel insurance, whether they had torn their cruciate ligament when skiing, or broken an arm while in Majorca. Using the shock figures of what their treatment would have cost them in Colorado, or a private hospital in Palma, really helped to communicate the need for travel insurance. As usual, the main issue was not in getting a case study, but in finding someone that wanted to be photographed. Somehow we managed it.

I say 'we', because all the business that had come in led me to have to take on an admin assistant and a full-time account manager. The former was quite a colourful character from Poulton-le-Fylde, who took a shine to almost every man who came into the office and who would shimmy out of her cardigan when the fax repairman arrived. Her job was reasonably well paid, but not that interesting. This was an age before e-mail and the web, so all press releases had to be physically posted out or faxed out, leading to a lot of trips to the photocopying shop, envelope stuffing and, even worse, licking stamps!

This led to her declaring one day that she found her job 'boring and mundane'. Apparently, my repetition of 'boring and mundane', with an exclamation mark, could be heard in the outer office!

My account manager came to me from a journalist's background and started working with me on all accounts initially, though it quickly became clear that Direct Response, which had now rebranded as Primary Direct, were jealously guarding me as their property. By now, Mr Berry had introduced me to Ms Dwyer, who was actually his wife! We all got on extremely well, as the pair of them were very ambitious young entrepreneurs, with a business dream that they were following with a great passion.

I was soon introduced to the brother-in-law – Adam – who was an avid Liverpool fan. However, Helen Dwyer was a massive Man Utd fan like myself, so we quickly put Adam in his place at every possible opportunity. Helen also had a link to Martin Edwards (though I cannot recall what) and was able to get tickets through this connection. This led to she and I and, later on, my son as well all going to matches together. As I said, Primary Direct jealously guarded me from other takers and it used to make me laugh how I would have to brief my son not to tell Helen whether Mummy had been to Coventry lately. She just loved to quiz him in the Pizza Hut queue!

One of the really stand out things that we did in that first year was what I describe as 'The Great Christmas Cake Drop'. This happened to include the afore-mentioned Adam, who was the driver and getaway man on this mission – one that he willingly chose to accept! Myself, Adam and Tim all set off, very bleary-eyed, at around 5.30am from Altrincham with a cargo of hand-made Christmas cakes, wrapped up beautifully in net and ribbon. Our challenge was to get around as many London-based personal finance and travel media as possible in the course of the day, driving down to the capital in an attempt to hand-deliver cakes to press that we either knew, or wanted to know.

I had planned a route that led us around key locations, such as Blackfriars Bridge for the Express, Wapping for the Times and Sunday Times, Kensington for the Mail and Mail on Sunday, Farringdon for The Guardian, Canary Wharf for several papers and then the City office of the Daily Telegraph.

As anyone who knows London will know, this is a pretty big area to get around in the city's traffic, especially when you've got a driver who doesn't know London and, to cap it all, is a Liverpool fan! The game plan was basically for Adam to drop Tim and I off, for Tim and I to clutch as many cakes as we could to our bosoms, according to how many contacts were in the building and then to abandon Adam on double yellow lines, pavements or wherever else he could manage to park a Range Rover!

This actually worked a treat, with a fair few press coming down to see us and having a chat, if they were in and not tied up on a story. We had been pretty surprised to be just waved into Canary Wharf's massive media tower without any check for Semtex in our cakes, but even more amazed when allowed to go up in the lift. However, this was nothing compared to what we found at the Telegraph's city office. There, the reception security man just told us to head to a certain floor, didn't bother ringing up anyone on the city desk and didn't even take our names. Off we headed in our by now familiar cake-to-bosom/chest-clutching way and soon found ourselves standing right next to one of the recipients, Nina Montagu-Smith! To say she was surprised was an understatement, but in a time of supposed heightened security, so were we!

Somehow we managed to distribute about 57 Christmas cakes in the course of day, before heading back off to Altrincham and then even further for myself, back to Poulton-le-Fylde. We received profuse thanks from recipients, especially once they'd tucked in and we had forged, or reinforced, some valuable relationships.

Another thing I did to really boost Primary's profile and its annual travel insurance policies was to create a press pack called the 'Primary Direct Annual', which was mocked up to look like a children's annual, with the bright orange of Primary shining throughout. This annual contained press information, but also highlighted key product benefits through unusual communications vehicles such as one of the twisted strings puzzles that you would follow in a children's annual, to discover which person ended up where. Through this means, we highlighted which cover was best for each type of traveller. There was much more to it than this, making it a really novel way of bringing travel insurance to life.

With regard to the Dial Direct and Bennetts account a real twist came along just after taking it on. This was down to the tremendous boom that had occurred in sales of motorcycles, which had brought about a shift in strategic thinking in the Dial Direct offices. Suddenly, it became more imperative to promote the motorcycle insurance product than the motor insurance product. This came as a bit of a shock, as I had never done anything with motorcycle insurance and, other than having had an uncle who was bike mad and an avid speedway and scrambling rider and having been on the back of a boyfriend's bike on a journey from Bristol to the Isle of Wight, I didn't exactly have much empathy with the sector.

This proves, however, that if you are prepared to do your homework and climb a sharp learning curve, you can promote anything if your strengths are creativity and commitment. These had to come into play really quickly, as the highlight of the motorcycling year – The International Motorcycle and Scooter Show was coming up in November 1998. Bennetts were exhibiting for the very first time, which was incredible, given that their main competitor, Carole Nash, had a massive stand at the show. In all honesty, Bennetts' stand was more like a shoebox that year – a basic shell scheme with blu-tacked posters on the walls and a small table. Bennetts had to get a foothold at this prestigious motorcycle show and this was it. The best thing that could be said for it really was that it was near the ladies loos and restaurant!

The early work we did for Bennetts in this first phase of their account was based largely around research and biker safety – a combination that was to prove a winner throughout the life of the account. From the early research I had done, it was clear that the motorcycle fraternity is a tightly bonded one and that bikers align themselves with companies that demonstrate that they care about biker issues.

On this basis, I put together some research questions, which were commissioned through a research company, as well as utilising some existing research held by Bennetts and created angles that were interesting, relevant and a little quirky besides. The NEC show was an opportunity to bring some of these to life.

The campaign itself was called 'Inside the Lid of a Biker' and we had a visual of a biker's helmet drawn up, with different thought bubbles emanating from it, which showed various statistics and research findings that were representative of bikers' viewpoints, according to the research that had been conducted.

We looked at research which related to biker prejudice and how many bikers had been refused service in a pub or restaurant, simply because they were wearing leathers and carrying a helmet or 'lid' in biker speak. By this time, I was extending my normal vocabulary to include words like rozzer and knee sliders, so that I could try to gain entrance to the fraternity.

We also asked various lifestyle questions and, above all, asked bikers to name who their most unpopular pillion passenger would be.

Using all of our research, we put together a biker safety guide that wove in some of the findings. This was called 'BEN's Guide To Staying Safe In Your Seat', Ben being a character that Bennetts had devised.

We released the details of the most unpopular pillion passenger in Britain on the day that the NEC show opened. The winner of the poll, by a long way, was Maggie Thatcher, so we had hired a Maggie Thatcher lookalike from a very colourful character, who ran a lookalike agency and who delighted in telling me that he could always get me a Madonna with conical boobs! He absolutely raved about his Maggie Thatcher, saying people just couldn't tell her apart from the real thing. Convinced by his spiel, we booked her.

As I have said, the Bennetts shoebox that year was very close to the ladies' toilets, which was just as well, because the minute the Maggie Thatcher lookalike turned up, looking less like Maggie Thatcher than we had thought possible, she was quickly ushered to the ladies loos, in the hope that she might perform some miracle and emerge as someone different. Bennetts had an employee called Chris, who never failed to amuse us, partly because of his broad Brummy accent, partly because he didn't like 'foreign food' and mainly because whenever we had a meeting in Coventry, he would invariably ring us about 30 minutes after departure from the Bennetts office and ask if we were back yet, even though the journey typically took 2.5 hours, if not longer when the M6 was gridlocked! He was one of those characters that you just had to love, because they were so different. I found him a hoot.

Chris was in a real flap about Maggie Thatcher. In his Brummy accent he said, 'Oy've never seen anyone look less like her. I hope she comes out of the loo a different woman'. We could hardly contain the laughter.

In fairness, she didn't look too bad when she emerged and she did create quite a stir when walking around the NEC. I didn't really care too much what she looked like, as we'd had a real coup that morning, with Chris Evans talking about the survey, along with Jonathan Ross on his radio show and a few others. Jonathan Ross had also come pretty high up the unpopularity poll, so a few DJs were making the most of the opportunity to bring it to his attention. All of this was great PR for Bennetts, so Maggie's appearance was just the icing on the cake and one that definitely got picked up by the show photographers. Considering we'd been working from a shoebox and not from an ultra-glamorous Honda stand, or Ducati den, we'd done pretty damn well to create waves.

A few other significant things happened in this early period, one of those being the arrival in my life of one Dave Nelson, a whirlwind who blew into my office one day when I was still on my own there and who then remained in my life for quite a number of years. I have always maintained, until very recently, that the only person who had ever taken a decent photograph of me is Dave, primarily because he has always had the ability to make me relax and be myself, because he is so damn funny.

Dave, when I first met him, was a DJ and a photographer, working mainly for the Blackpool Gazette as a freelancer. He first breezed in when I needed him to do a photo shoot for a company that was receiving support from Business Link and I instantly knew that we were going to have fun. Little did I know that this would involve all manner of strange occurrences, like him pounding up the stairs, opening the door to the office and throwing in a big plastic hand-held windmill in the shape of a flower – for no apparent reason. This once occurred while I was having a client meeting in my office, but had my office door open, so the client clearly saw this going on. I have no recollection of how I explained it!

If it wasn't an unexpected entrance provoked by Dave, it was one delivered by the rather temperamental cat that lived at the adjacent pub. For some reason, she took a shine to me, though I am definitely not a cat person, and although my office was on the first floor of the building, if the window was ajar on the latch, she would miraculously launch herself, with no warning, from the roof of the office below, which jutted out a little, and jump clean through the window and on to the office floor right by the meeting table. I have seen grown men leap out of their seats after this had happened, but she would just saunter around my room and curl up under my desk, or take herself to one of her other favourite positions, under the fax machine table and go to sleep.

She only every really bothered to try to show any sort of friendliness to me, though she was prone to scratch and bite when she was in a mood and I had to choose my moments if I tried to reciprocate with any form of affection. This made shifting her, if we wanted to lock up, extremely difficult and a job for only the very intrepid! Her time of being welcomed was well and truly up several years later, when she decided to eat the tinsel on the Christmas tree and promptly be sick under it. After that, my office administrator did anything she could to communicate to our feline visitor that she was most definitely not welcome.

In one of our early summers, we also had the strange incident of the wasps that fell from the sky! This started in around late March, with wasps suddenly appearing on the carpet, though at first nobody knew why. One then nearly fell on the head of the admin assistant that we had at that time and then more started tumbling down until we realised that we had an infestation in the loft.

This necessitated calling Wyre Borough Council, who sent out their 'Bee Inspector' (or maybe we just re-named her role!). Before we could do anything to try to rid ourselves of what was clearly a wasps' nest, this lady had to come for a site visit, which we presumed would entail her going up in the loft and inspecting what was up there. How wrong we were. What she actually did was draw our admin assistant a picture of a bee, asking her if that was the same shape as the things falling from the light fittings. Having satisfied herself that we all knew the difference between a bee and a wasp, she sanctioned wasp destruction and, thankfully, after a short time the likelihood of being hit on the head by an angry wasp became very slight!

A final peculiarity of the office was the lock on the toilet, which was very temperamental indeed, but we had all sort of worked out how to lock it in such a way that we could get out again. Unfortunately, this was not the case with a couple of our visitors, who found themselves locked in the toilet and seeking assistance before they could get out. One poor woman was in there quite some time before we even realised, but luckily she wasn't a client!

Perils seemed to lurk everywhere, even when I went out of the office. The chap who featured in the first photography I ever did with Dave Nelson ran a company that were pioneering the use of magnets with pipelines, in order to increase energy efficiencies. The head of this company invited me down to his office in the centre of Blackpool. On the day in question, I had some rather large metallic earrings in – something that I didn't bat an eyelid about until strange things started to happen!

On arrival, the three guys in this organisation all started to tell me about the office poltergeist, who liked to wreak havoc and always liked to have fun with visitors. I took all this with a pinch of salt, thinking what a strange conversation they had struck up. Suddenly, while sitting there all innocently, one of my earrings shot out and flew right across the room, landing about ten feet away. 'There it goes', they said. 'That's typical of the sort of tricks it gets up to'. Next minute, out flew my other earring, by which time I was rather embarrassingly scurrying around on the floor, trying to retrieve my jewellery. As I got up from my cat-like position on all fours, I looked at their smug faces and suddenly realised that actually they were using magnets to achieve this trick of the 'poltergeist'. I was semi-amused, but only semi! What a naïve and gullible PR girl I must have seemed! I would defy anybody to try it now!

My first near-death experience due to food consumption occurred just after my new account manager had joined me. We had both gone to a North West Fine Foods event staged in Manchester Town Hall and arrived to find various producers with stalls already laid out and with food samples on offer with which to tempt visitors. All were located in one big room, with stalls laid out in a U-shape, so you had to work your way down one side and then back up the other. On the second stand that we encountered, there happened to be a very keen cheese maker just desperate for us to try his goat's cheese. My account manager wasn't too keen, so I felt obliged to take a piece.

The sample that he gave me was so dry that it instantly hit the back of my throat and stuck there, causing me to instantly start to choke. Things got worse and I found that it was blocking my windpipe completely. The man annoyingly just stood there, watching as I turned purple and doing absolutely nothing to assist. I signalled to my account manager that I needed water, but other people in the room had already realised this and some kind woman had rushed to a water cooler to get some. Loads of people were by now fussing around, all bar the man whose cheese had caused the issue in the first place!

After several gulps of water, I finally loosened the chalk-dry cheese and began to regain a modicum of composure. I managed to thank those who had assisted and urged my employee to get us down the aisle of producers as fast as possible. Even then, the cheese maker said nothing. Having then worked our way right round the room, I decided I needed more water and dashed past the man who had nearly killed me as fast as humanly possible. At that point, he suddenly decided to spur himself into action, proffering the words, 'I hope it wasn't anything to do with my cheese'. At that point, apparently, if looks could have killed, we would have had one dead cheese maker and, surprisingly, no kind obituary written in honour of his goat's cheese patties!

The other real stand out event of these very early days of Catapult was the opening of a new Alpine-themed restaurant in Preston that was to be the sister restaurant to a long-established German restaurant in another Lancashire town. I was introduced to the owners of the restaurant by a contact at Business Link and having met with them, while I was still on my own at Catapult, put together a launch strategy for their new venture.

The restaurant was to be modelled on an Alpine chalet and located in the heart of Preston's solicitor-and-accountant-land. It was set to bring something entirely new to the city, with much more emphasis on Alpine fare than even the sister restaurant had tried.

My proposal was pretty whacky and creative and centred on something inextricably linked with the Tyrol and the ambience of Austria – The Sound of Music. I wanted to create a massive stir for the restaurant pre-opening, by devising a series of media stories that would be irresistible to the local press, even though, in truth, this was one of my first experiences of really doing something in Lancashire, as my entire career had been spent elsewhere, or had had a national focus.

The strategy started with a drip feed of press information relating to the future plans for the Preston building and the investment being ploughed in. To get the local businesses excited about the launch, a series of postcard mailers were devised, each carrying a Tyrolean image of some sort and a carefully worded message on the reverse. In these days, before the internet, building up the mailing list saw me walking around the neighbouring streets of Preston, noting down business names and then ringing them to ascertain who the key contact might be. Nothing was done at the push of a button in those days!

I planned a pre-launch photograph in Winckley Square in Preston, just a short hop from the new restaurant. This featured the owner and his wife in full Tyrolean costume and was a really eye-catching photo that the press lapped up. With this and other releases, I generated so much pre-launch publicity that a leading chef in the area put in an official complaint to the Lancashire Evening Post!

This, however, was just the aperitif for the campaign and the real sparkle was yet to come. The restaurant had wanted to have a grand opening and so I gave them a formula that would achieve that with style, panache and with a local 'celebrity' thrown in for good measure. The local celebrity in question was Andrew (Freddie) Flintoff, who was then a young player just at the start of his Lancashire career and certainly not the global persona or sporting royalty that he is these days. Freddie, who came from Preston anyway, was booked to officially open the restaurant, but I wanted something more special than that, given that he wasn't that well known, other than among members of the local cricketing fraternity.

Using the 'Sound of Music' theme, I managed to find a group of young am-dram performers who could act as the Von Trapp family and perform on the evening. Music licences were sorted out and, to make the opening really different, I decided that the typical ribbon-cutting ceremony would be somewhat transformed, as what Freddie would cut would be a blue satin sash tied around the waists of two 'girls in white dresses with blue satin sashes' – one of my 'favourite things' you might say, if you were Maria von Trapp!

I would like to think that Andrew Lloyd-Webber took some inspiration from my launch plan when he put together the concept for his 'How do you solve a problem like Maria', as I also planned for the troupe of girls to sing 'So Long, Farewell' to guests, on their departure.

My idea was based around the restaurant inviting a select number of guests and having a really good and well-planned seated meal for these VIPs. The restaurant and another business consultant that they used decided against this and insisted that they wanted to provide a buffet only and not a laid out buffet at that, but one which would be taken around the room by the restaurant waiting on staff. I could see this being fraught with problems, but could not make them budge.

The restaurant then got the brewery to agree to so many barrels of free beer and so many crates of free wine too, given all the promotion they were putting behind the event. A guest list was drawn up, according to how many the restaurant said they could serve with their buffet and invitations to local businesses were issued.

For me, the real genius of this campaign unravelled just before opening. I had created this whacky idea of having nuns seemingly breaking into the restaurant with the intention of grabbing a launch invitation. To bring this to fruition, I had managed, with the help of the account manager, who had now joined me just before the restaurant's opening, to find a team of abseilers from BNFL in Cumbria, who told me that they were up for dressing up as nuns an abseiling down the walls of the restaurant, to ham things up for the cameras. As you can imagine, this was media gold and the pictures were fantastic, rubbing more salt into the Preston chef's wounds.

All had gone swimmingly and everything seemed set for an absolutely fantastic night. At these occasions, there is always a fear that people who have said they will turn up will actually turn into no-shows on the evening, but there was none of that. My Von Trapp family all arrived on time, the restaurant's regular musician arrived on time, Alpine games were in full swing on the top balcony, people streamed in waving their invitations at myself and my assistant manning the signing in desk and Freddie and another Lancashire cricketer then arrived right on cue. Wine and beer poured from every quarter and merriment accompanied it. All that was missing, in this fabulous new restaurant, was food!

As I had been so busy on the signing in desk, I hadn't really noted this fact, presuming that the 'circulating buffet' had been circling around me. It was only when the person in charge of the Von Trapp family came over and told me that her girls hadn't had any food that I realised something was amiss. I summoned a waitress and was assured that food would be taken over. From that point on, all I personally saw on a circulating platter were tiny pieces of strudel, at which point, although I hate the stuff, I had to succumb to a mouthful. I kept asking if food was going around and was assured that it was.

By the time that Freddie came to cut the blue sash, I would speculate that half the guests were already legless, having made the most of the free wine and beer and been offered absolutely nothing to soak up their alcohol intake. The sash cutting occurred on the stairs and the picture was lovely, but a rather disgruntled leader of the Von Trapps then made her excuses very quickly and got the girls out.

With all the official stuff being out of the way and the staircase now open, I went upstairs for the first time and witnessed a scene worthy of a bacchanalia, featuring a load of rather merry builders, who had worked on the refit, plus other esteemed guests.

At this point, my account manager and I took a pew with Freddie Flintoff and his cricketing buddy. The latter proved rather entertaining to me, so I took my eyes off my account manager for a second and turned back to find her lolling on the bench on which she seated. I managed to get her to sit up, but realised that she too had fallen prey to empty-stomach-and-too-much-alcohol syndrome.

This general atmosphere, with still no food in evidence, went on for a good while longer, providing even enough time for the restaurant's Tyrolean musician to come and grab me around the waist in my little David Emmanuel little black dress with the full, swingy skirt, declaring, 'You look every inch the German Fraulein'. I disengaged him from my body with a disparaging glare and recalled the famous words of a bunch of nerds in Kenya who my sister and I had fobbed off for days, pretending we didn't speak their lingo. When we did declare our nationality, we were greeted with, 'Oh and we thought you were German bits of crumpet!'

After I had managed to extricate myself from the musician, I became conscious of the fact that people were beginning to drift away and shortly after that we bade farewell to Freddie and his friend. I decided, once all had departed, that my account manager and I should order a taxi and get away too, before she fell over and I had to carry her! At this point, I ventured into the kitchen to find all the staff sitting round a table piled high with food and stuffing their faces. What I had presumed to be a complete absence of food proved not to be the case at all.

In an incredulous state, I was just about to raise the question as to why all this food was still sitting here, when all hell broke loose just outside the kitchen door. I will never forget the angry screech that accompanied the words, 'Get your hands off my son', as the owner's wife dragged my account manager off the neck of her offspring and I looked on in absolute horror at the scene that presented itself. I hurriedly apologised, shoved my account manager out of the door and thankfully found our taxi waiting. I had it take her home, but she couldn't find her keys, and like some surrogate mother figure, I had the embarrassment of having to knock on her parents' door and pass her over to her father, like some lifeless parcel. With surprisingly no hint of irony in his voice he said, 'Is she drunk?' I found that quite remarkable!

I couldn't sleep a wink that night without thinking about how incensed the owner's wife had been, especially as I had to go and see them on Monday to collect a cheque for the work that had been done. I prayed that after two days of calm, the memory of their son's predicament might have faded from the memory. As it happened, my account manager had no recollection of this incident, or of me handing her over to her father and, I have to say, was more terrified when she heard the latter, rather than the former. I, on the other hand, had to go and face the music, praying that it wasn't going to be served up by any man calling me Fraulein and squeezing me tighter than an accordion.

My great hope that all would be forgotten proved very ill founded. I was, however, somewhat armed with information prior to this debrief, as I had received numerous calls from guests who had attended, telling me how great the evening had been, but how absolutely starving they had been on the way home. Some had been forced to head to the nearest fish and chip shop, others to curry houses and some even to the Preston chef's restaurant! Trying to communicate this message fell on stony ground, the piercing stare of the owner's wife never leaving me. Thankfully, I did get my cheque and the launch was over. My account manager never had to come into contact with her son again!

The other account that came on board during 1998-9 was that of Stringers department store in Lytham. This threw up one of those instances where you really cannot believe how small the world is. The client at Stringers proved to be a former part of the marketing team at the pizza company, who I had met when working in Cheshire. It now transpired that she was the partner of the MD of Stringers and needed some help launching her brand new cookware department and the re-positioning the store as a place where those in their 30s and 40s really could shop without feeling that they were 20 years too young.

The budget was not massive, but enough to stretch to hiring a bit of entertainment for the opening day and covering the cost of a low budget stunt. A jazz band was hired to play under the Victorian-style canopy of the store, located in the heart of leafy Lytham, but the stunt was a little more out of the ordinary. The plan was to have a giant rolling pin made, which a number of members of the public could carry like a battering ram, to portray the fact that they were so keen to see the new kitchen-ware that they were charging at the door. As a concept, it worked fantas-tically well for all the pictures relating to the department's launch: what we hadn't bargained for was the fact that we would all have to wear pegs on our noses for a week!

The giant rolling pin had been commissioned from a prop designer in Bolton, who was adept at making all manner of theatre props and found the making of a giant rolling pin no problem at all – no doubt it was just the sort of thing that Widow Twankey would run around a stage waving in the Christmas panto.

He and his wife made the journey from Bolton with the rolling pin several days before the launch date of the Saturday. By now, we had ex-panded to such an extent that I had taken over the office across the stairs, which had once belonged to the solar energy company who had done the moonlight flit. All had been redecorated and re-carpeted and, as it was just one open plan office, there was far more room within it in which to store a giant rolling pin!

This was a stroke of luck from my point of view, as within a matter of hours a truly revolting smell started to emerge. At first, we thought the cat had got in and decided to pee on the carpet, but using our noses as adeptly as Cyrano de Bergerac, or Steve Martin in 'Roxanne', we all traced the source of the smell back to the rolling pin.

The temperature at this time of year was high, which meant the smell seemed to get worse. Within an hour of the smell emerging, all windows had to be opened and numerous cans of air freshener used to try to com-bat the dreadful pong. Luckily, I could head into my office on the other side of the stairs and shut the door, which hardly made it detectable. This soon encouraged everyone else to ask if they could come and work with me!

On the day of launch, we reluctantly loaded the rolling pin into the car and had to drive with windows open wide all the way to Lytham.

Even in the open air, the smell was obnoxious, but we got the 'charging of the door' shot done as fast as possible and then sought to rid ourselves of the smelly object. It was promptly taken into the new kitchen department and laid down on one of the window shelves.

The rest of the day passed without incident and very successfully and it came to the point when we had to decide what to do with the rolling pin. To a woman, we all enthused about how good it looked in the window and how it would make a fabulous feature for the new department. Somehow, our passionate pleas paid off and we were able to scarper off without the pongy pin in tow!

All of this work, and more, naturally meant very long hours and much less time at home than I would have wanted to enjoy. Suddenly, completely out of the blue, my beloved dog, who was only seven years old, became terribly ill. At first, everyone thought it was kennel cough, but he quickly lost all of his appetite and was lifeless. The vet took an x-ray and found a strange shadow that he couldn't explain. He said he needed to send the photo to Edinburgh, to a specialist. I took Troy to the car, got him in the back and cuddled him round the neck, crying into his fur. I knew things were really bad.

This carried on for a few weeks, but on a morning when I had to go to Coventry, I was really encouraged. He seemed livelier and was trotting around the garden as if he was on the mend. By the time I returned at 5pm, he was no longer there. He had declined so much during the day that my father had taken him to the vets. He had arranged for me to go and see him, even though they were closed.

I walked in to find him wearing a massive white collar and with his head on his paws. He saw me and thumped his tail, making a sound of recognition. The female vet on duty said this was amazing, as he'd shown no energy at all, but was clearly delighted to see me. I got down on all fours and put my head inside the collar to kiss his nose. He licked my face in response. I hugged him for a while and then had to leave him. That was the last I saw of my beautiful dog and best friend. When I rang to check on his progress the next morning, I was told that he had passed away in the night.

To say I was heartbroken was an understatement. After all we'd been through together, I was totally lost without him. I would sit at my desk and just cry buckets, as unfortunately I had to start working on a new pet insurance product that Primary was launching. I can remember being totally incapable of focusing on the product details, as I was too raw to deal with this sort of subject matter. My father got really angry with me and told me to buck up for goodness sake, but I just couldn't. Without Troy, there was just a big empty hole and I felt guilt-stricken that I'd spent so much time at the office, setting up the business. My mother banned me from ever having a dog again.

He died in early December, about a week before I had booked to take my son to Lapland, with my mother and father also going. To be honest, I was still numb with grief and my son had a chronic cold, so it certainly wasn't the ideal trip. It was nice to ride on a skidoo, hunt Santa and enjoy an Arctic Circle Crossing Ceremony, but life just wasn't the same and wouldn't be for a very long time. To cap it all, although I had told the tour company that I couldn't touch the salmon they would serve for lunch, because of my allergy, the plate of mash that they gave me instead must have been in contact with salmon or salmon juices, as I was covered in a rash from head to foot by the time we arrived back at Manchester Airport. At this point, I was at an all time low. Christmas 1998 came and went, which meant it was time to move on.

Chapter 14
THE GREAT AWARDS HAUL

A lot of sacrifices were made during 1998 and 1999, with family life having to sit alongside the business. Still feeling guilty about having not spent more time with my dog in those last months, I wanted there to be something good resulting from the many hours spent at my desk. On this basis, I entered my first awards in July 1999, little more than a year after starting up.

By this point, we numbered five and had expanded so much that we did a photo call in which we all wore blow up fancy dress costumes to communicate how we had grown in size. I was a policeman with my very own truncheon! As autumn came along, we were delighted to find both the 'Inside the Lid of a Biker' campaign for Bennetts and the 'Passport to Pole Position' campaign for Primary Direct, nominated for awards. The Bennetts campaign was in contention for the 'Best Use of Research' Award while Primary Direct was in the category all agencies wish to win – 'Best Consumer PR Campaign'.

We hired a mini-bus to take us to Manchester for the awards and had invited two business contacts to come with us. There was rather an embarrassing moment en route, as one of our number had a terrible B.O. issue, which none of us had ever dared tackle head on. We had dropped all sorts of hints for months and even plugged in an air freshener to combat the odour, but all to no avail. Our hearts literally sank when this person came in to work wearing an outfit for the third day running, as we knew that the problem would be at its keenest.

One of our guests seated himself beside them in the mini-bus, at which point they started waving their arms around madly. Sitting in the row behind them, myself and my account manager just looked at each other in horror as we saw the man back away from the armpit as much as he could. We were totally mortified and made every effort to make our colleague sit still, so that the problem could be minimised for the rest of the journey.

That wasn't the worst incident of the evening however. One of our number also had a real penchant for snobbish behaviour and for bigging things up to a proportion that was way beyond their actual status. She did this on a daily basis, but we all took it with a pinch of salt.

On arrival at the hotel, we were very much viewed as infiltrators. The event, which supposedly covers the whole of the northwest, is fundamentally an event for the Manchester agencies and back then, at least, they were definitely not used to having outsiders from beyond their clique come in as nominees. The whole scene in Manchester is very incestuous, with employees desk hopping from one agency to another, meaning that everyone knows everybody else, one way or another. Nobody knew Catapult.

To me, this wasn't an issue then and isn't an issue now. I find the rivalry between agencies in Manchester quite entertaining, but also enjoy nipping in there and picking up the odd award or two, just to see the reaction.

Being viewed under this veil of suspicion, I discovered for the very first time that it really does pay to cross your legs and try not to have to go to the ladies toilets at these occasions. It's simply like a catfight waiting to happen, with prima donnas teasing their locks for hours, making it totally impossible to wash your hands, as they are too busy preening. Add to that the fact that they are all bitching under their breath to one another, while acting as if they are all bosom pals and I really can't tolerate these toilet breaks.

Having vague recollections of it being like this in the days when the awards were more civilised affairs, held over a lunchtime in Manchester, I decided to head to the loo as early as possible on this occasion, before the claws really started to come out. My employee with the penchant for snobbish behaviour and one-upmanship decided to come with me, but was waiting in a small queue, while I got into a cubicle straight away.

This was probably just as well, as if I had been outside in the queue, I would probably have throttled her.

I had just entered the cubicle, when she struck up a conversation with a girl from one of the other agencies. In her most plummy accent she asked, 'And who are you here with?' to this poor unfortunate. The girl gave her reply, only to be met with, 'Oh, I've never heard of you. I'm with Catapult and we are nominated for two awards. Our managing director is extremely talented and we are feeling very confident indeed'. At this point, I was literally wringing my hands behind the door, wanting to head out, but not wanting to face the girl who was on the receiving end of this. If it had been a phone conversation that I was overhearing and I had been anywhere within arm's length, I would have grabbed a pair of scissors and cut the cord! I cannot describe how totally cringeworthy it was and the best of it was that it continued, even though the girl was obviously trying to ignore this snotty intruder, who'd seemingly landed in Manchester from an alien planet.

I couldn't really delay my exit any longer and wanted to shut my employee up as fast as humanly possible by this point. I rushed out of the cubicle, swept her up and prepared to usher her out. Unfortunately, totally oblivious to what she had done, she decided to once again act like my agent, declaring grandly, 'This is the very talented boss of Catapult that I was telling you about'. I just wanted to curl up in a ball, as the girl eyed me up and down as if I was some egomaniac, who paid her staff to big her up on all occasions. I tried to offer a sympathetic smile and got the hell out of there. I swear that I could see the girl telling her colleagues the whole tale as we were having drinks and once again died an inner death.

We had made our box file entries superb works of art in their own right, by having a wrap design fitted around them and theming the subject dividers within the box. The 'Passport to Pole Position' box, for instance, was designed as a passport cover and it looked absolutely stunning. These days, there isn't the opportunity to make an impression in this way, as everything is done online. Personally, I think that removes the opportunity to demonstrate flair and creativity and communicate everything the award entry stands for, through professional presentation.

For me, this was potentially my favourite ever award ceremony, not because it was virgin ground for Catapult, but because it was run to a formula of one of my guilty pleasures – The Eurovision Song Contest! What the organisers had done was to create an electronic leader board, which the whole room could see. This awarded a certain number of points according to whether you won a gold, silver or bronze award. These days, bronze awards aren't even given – something to do with the tightening of budgets perhaps – but having three different score levels made it absolutely gripping fun – particularly for me!

All agencies were listed on the board, so the poor unfortunates, who won nothing, were very much the Norwegians, sitting at the bottom of the table with the indignity of having picked up the legendary 'Nil Points'.

Every time an award had been announced, the board scrolled as the points were added to it, leading to much anticipation and gasps as the new leaders were revealed. I loved this element, as it actually made everyone pay attention rather than just talking through the awards that they weren't involved with. It was genius!

Perhaps I remember this so fondly because Catapult was always in the top three places and actually leading at one point. We picked up the prestigious Gold Award for the Best Consumer PR Campaign for 'Passport to Pole Position' and then the Silver Award for the Best Use of Research for 'Inside the Lid of a Biker'. Our points rolled on to the leader board and had us right up there in contention, which was truly amazing given the size of Catapult compared to the big Manchester agencies. It goes without saying that the smaller you are, the fewer campaigns you have to enter for the awards in the first place.

My account manager and I had made an embarrassing walk to the stage twice, which was made extremely painful thanks to the fact that we were filmed on video all the way from the back of the room and beamed up on to a huge screen next to the Eurovision leader board. Having made the second trek in heels, I was very relaxed, thinking that the evening's events were all over for us. Little did I know.

Suddenly, it was announced, from out of nowhere, that there was another award in the offing – the 'Grand Prix Award' for the 'Best Overall

Campaign' conducted in the northwest that year. All Gold Award winners were in the running for this prize, which naturally ruled out the Bennetts campaign, but kept the Primary Direct campaign very much in the mix.

I'm pretty sure there has never been such a Grand Prix Award since, but the format of this event was really unique and I suppose the idea of having a Grand Prix Award was in keeping with us all believing we'd been getting the results from the Belgrade jury all evening!

Despite having won a Gold Award, I didn't think we had an earthly of winning the Grand Prix accolade, until that is the then President of what was then just the Institute of Public Relations (IPR) rather than having the Chartered bit tacked on the front as is the case now, took to the microphone.

I had sort of resigned myself to seeing someone else pick up this award, so wasn't concentrating that much until certain words made my ears prick up. The President was uttering words along the lines of, 'At face value, the product that this campaign was promoting could have been seen as rather dull, but this campaign brought it to life in a truly creative fashion'. At that point, having heard the word 'dull', I knew we had won. I looked around the table at the faces of my employees and could tell that they were thinking exactly the same.

'It's got to be us', one of them whispered and, sure enough, within seconds, so it proved. Up we trooped to pick up the award, but more importantly, off whizzed the Eurovision leader board again, moving us firmly into second place, just behind the massive and well-established Manchester agency Communique. Perhaps what I most loved about this board was that it clearly showed to all the great, the good and the giddy assembled in that room that Catapult had been runner-up as Northwest PR Consultancy of the Year and, who knows, if our neighbours in Dublin had been more generous to the Bennetts campaign, we could well have scooped that title at our first attempt! From that point on, this became my goal.

All of this makes it seem as though the latter half of 1998 and the early part of 1999 was a doddle and free of any rogue elephants rampaging their way through the jungle. This was far from the case. The first person to deserve the title of 'Rogue Elephant' in my Catapult career was a totally unfathomable creature who, in the end, we thought could be a compulsive liar, as none of his tales ever consistently fit together, when one examined the facts. When I first met him, he insisted that I go to his office on a Saturday afternoon and listen to his grand scheme. This was probably one of the most uncomfortable meetings I have ever had the misfortune to sit in, as he chain smoked non-stop for about three hours, the duration of the meeting being determined by all the faffing around that he did, calling up his mates, bringing in other supposed employees and messing around with them and generally conducting the whole thing in a really unprofessional manner.

I returned home that day absolutely reeking of cigarette smoke and had to immediately cleanse both myself and my clothes. On the plus side, his product sounded a reasonably good idea and he claimed to have reputable partners involved, who would give it credibility. On that basis, I wrote a proposal and he appointed us.

The weeks that followed were full of tales of him having his chauffeur run him all over the place, when not in his private chopper or chartering a plane to fly him to France. He was one of those people who could make you feel grubby just by uttering your name and conversations were full of him referring to me as 'darling' or 'doll' or something equally as objectionable.

My account manager felt exactly the same way, so my own thoughts were repeated back to me by her, making me very worried when the first invoice wasn't paid and was several weeks overdue. Despite many requests for payment, nothing came. He did turn up with his entourage one day and insist we go to the pub next door with him, which was a fairly painful experience and one we did not wish to repeat. There was also something quite threatening about his whole demeanour and neither of us would have relished being on our own with him.

All these feelings towards him suddenly erupted one day. I had rung his office and asked, yet again, for payment, this time being quite forceful and saying that it was essential that I get it. At this point, his tone changed from the, 'Darling, how are you?' one, to a decidedly different one. A short time later, the phone rang and neither of us wanted to answer it. We let it go to answer phone and got a message that said he would be getting his chauffeur to drive him over and would be there soon. At this, we looked at each other, remembered the last time we'd had to suffer sitting with him in the pub and decided, money or no money, the safest thing to do was to scarper. You have never seen two women pack their bag, lock up and run to their cars quicker than we did, with the excuse we gave later being that we had been at a meeting.

Somehow or other (and I have no idea how, given the tales we heard from other suppliers who never got paid by him) we got our money and, even more amazingly, the cheque didn't bounce. After that, he went very quiet after somebody had challenged a claim about his product and he said he had to put things on hold. He then disappeared for a while, which was even more dubious, and we, thankfully, never heard from him again.

The other rather unusual character of this time was a man who sold pet products. He was rather an intimidating man, but at face value the business itself seemed reputable. The worst part about this experience for me was that he insisted I go to Crufts with him. Still feeling raw after the death of Troy, I found this a really upsetting experience, which wasn't helped any by the way he behaved to the various stand holders with whom he struck up conversations in the sales area of the show.

The most embarrassing moment of all was when he put a take-way coffee down on someone's stand and proceeded to knock it over all over the poor stand-holder's wares. Rather than apologising to the poor woman, he just declared, 'Well, it was a pile of crap anyway!' I looked at the devastated woman's face and wished the ground would swallow me up. I tried to make out that I didn't really know him, hanging back as he walked away, but really just wanted to run and get away as fast as possible! Luckily, we didn't have many more months of association with him, after he rang up one day to tell me that he thought one of my members of staff 'illiterate!'!

Having had the big boost of the November 1999 awards and all the Eurovision excitement, we headed into 2000 full of beans and confidence. Business was really booming and by now we were writing some really fabulous, eye-catching employee magazines for Bennetts and Dial Direct. This then allowed us to scoop additional work, writing customer newsletters. When the HR department needed to communicate change to the workforce, with a leaflet needing to be turned around over the course of a weekend, I wrote that too!

Having worked for Primary Direct since July 1998, the back-end of 1999 saw us recommended to Primary HQ in Horsham. The Primary Group departments in Horsham really handled all the behind-the-scenes functions that kept Primary Direct running: underwriting, claims handling, accounts and the department that liaised with overseas medics, hospitals and hotels when a holidaymaker or traveller had been injured or fallen ill overseas. This department – the Assistance division – had a role that really intrigued me and I found the whole process of repatriation really fascinating, involving as it did, language skills, medical knowledge, great judgment, negotiation skills and much more. I loved sitting with this team and finding out about different cases, especially as these were the nuggets that we needed for press stories.

Getting down to Horsham typically meant flying down to Gatwick from Manchester Airport and then being picked up by our contact, who would then drive us to the Horsham offices. However, when we were asked to help Primary arrange a golf day, we drove down – a long trek, but the only way to really get there, given that everyone was too tied up to pick us up at the airport.

The golf day was being held at the Horsham Golf Course and was being attended by all of our new contacts in the Primary HQ offices, plus key clients to whom they supplied insurance services. We had invited people in a really innovative way, having discovered that it was possible to print an invitation on a golf ball!

Those who couldn't play golf, like my account manager and I, were put into the golf school for the day, first starting out with some tuition on the driving range and then moving on to the putting green. Having played a lot of pitch and putt with my family, I instantly knew that I would be appalling on the range and half-decent on the green. My predictions were spot on.

No matter what I did, I couldn't hit the ball off the tee without hitting the ground, the whole process being made far worse by the fact that a video was running, so that we could all take home something that would show us what we needed to work on. I think I could have summed that up as 'everything'! Not surprisingly, I never bothered to watch the video!

Despite all this appalling form on the range, I had enormous fun, as I found my tee next to a really lovely guy called Martin, who was a part of the sales team. We laughed all day, (he laughing not necessarily at me, but with me) and what I truly found endearing about him was that, as I showered him with dry soil towards the end of the session and apologised to him, I received the reply, 'Don't worry, you've been doing it all day!'

I was terribly relieved when this ordeal was over and I was able to get on the putting green. We were all given various putts to get and I kept holing one after another! I don't think anyone could quite believe this complete reversal of fortune, but they weren't aware how many hours I had spent in my childhood with my father teaching me how to hold the club, swing and line up the shot. To everyone's amazement, I won the putting competition by a country mile!

The best thing about this whole day for me was the fact that the evening dinner was to feature a special guest speaker, who I had been responsible for booking. It was the BBC sports presenter, Garry Richardson and, when he arrived, I had to look after him, sort out the PA system for him and make sure he had all he needed. We ended up having a really good chat, which proved of immense interest to me, as it brought up the topic of a fellow historian at New Hall, friend and, by this point, a BBC Grandstand employee. It was none other than my grinning friend, who had annoyed Dr Seal so much in Cambridge!

Garry told me this amazing story of how she had been covering an Olympic shooting event, at which all competitors had carefully set up their sights and equipment. She was apparently walking past and had hit one of the competitors' guns, putting the cat among the pigeons on a scale that almost caused another Cold War! I found Garry's tale hugely amusing and he must have found me quite interesting too, as he apparently went and told the Primary guys how much he had enjoyed talking to, 'Jane with the infectious giggle'.

This fact was relayed to me by someone that I found truly fascinating, – in my eyes, the most unlikely underwriter you could ever wish to meet in your life. This bright young thing in the Primary HQ, without fail, had me in fits of giggles every time I spoke to him, or opened an email from him, and I was fascinated by his whole persona, whether that was the way he dressed, or the fact that he had a model of the Millennium Falcon hovering above his desk!

This character was a bit like my colleague at British Gas HQ, who I would always end up talking to within a matter of minutes, as everyone else was simply too boring. It was not surprising, therefore, that I ended up in fits of laughter once again, as he wound me up about my infectious 'giggle' and what he termed my 'distinct twang' – apparently the 'bits of Bristol', which now invade my speech every now and then. I thanked God for the presence of my Jedi soul mate and his great line in conversation, which went on into the wee small hours.

The other really big plus of working with Primary HQ was the fact that it introduced me to another great friend in my life – Paul O'Sullivan, who ran an insurance product for ex-pats. Paul and I hit if off immediately and I instantly started working for his Goodhealth product and also a specialist insurance product that he sold to yacht crew. One of the great regrets of my life is that I didn't take up an invitation to go out to Majorca to meet one of Paul's contacts there. I think that would have been great fun.

Paul would come up north to see us and I greatly enjoyed working on everything that he put our way. The ex-pat health product was something that I found fascinating, as it opened up a whole world that I had never really thought about. Before I knew it, I was writing for English magazines and papers serving the ex-pat market.

Within a short space of time, I was generating a whole host of full page and double page features in insurance sector trade magazines for different parts of the Primary Group. This helped make many of their management team industry spokespeople, particularly when strong opinions underpinned the pieces that I was placing. Naturally, I got the biggest satisfaction from these articles when it boosted the profile of my Jedi master and Paul! I'd like to think that I put the Jedi master where he is today, but I actually know that it was all down to his natural genius! Paul ended up living in France and I can happily imagine him in the local village bar, enjoying a glass or two of 'vin' and walking home with a baguette under his arm!

Catapult's new business campaign was still ongoing, which meant bringing in the telemarketing company now and again for a ring round of different businesses that we had targeted with a variety of very innovative mailers, which I would devise from time to time. The upshot of this was that I, and whoever I took with me, would go to pitch in some weird and wonderful locations, given the fact that businesses came in all shapes and sizes. We once drove all the way to Stoke to see a man who made innovative toilet seats, only to arrive to find that he had forgotten all about the appointment. Toilet seats seem to have played a regular part in my career, as a few years later, I found myself pitching on one (in the PR sense that this!) while in a bathroom showroom!

One of the strangest meetings during this time was at the premises of a waterbed company in Wirral. Waterbeds had suddenly become high profile, thanks to the episode of Coronation Street in which Reg Holdsworth's waterbed had burst, sending gallons of water crashing through the ceiling below. At this particular point in time, my telemarketing man was replaced by a lady called V, who we didn't know and so could not really put a voice to the name. We arrived at the waterbed company and started to pitch, before the lady there stopped us in our tracks with the words, 'Neither of you sound like the person who rang me on the phone'. We thought this a very odd statement, but explained that, indeed, neither of us had rung her. We proceeded with the pitch, but couldn't help but detect an air of disappointment.

This really bothered me, so back at base, I rang the telemarketing company to speak to V. I suddenly realised why the waterbed woman had been so disappointed as, to put it quite bluntly, V's voice would not have been out of place on a sex line. It was extremely deep, to almost manly levels, pretty filthy sounding and extremely suggestive – obviously exactly what the waterbed company wanted. Having discovered this fact, I didn't do much marketing with this telemarketing company – I didn't want to shock the 99% of normal potential clients that she would be ringing!

There is always a Pollyanna moment in every sorry story and it came about four years later when our designer answered a call that was selling him print services. I happened to be in the room when he put the phone down and said he felt hot under the collar as the woman to whom he'd been speaking had the filthiest voice he'd ever heard. I instantly said, 'Was she called V?' at which he looked astounded and said, 'Actually, she was'.

Although our trip to the Potteries to see the toilet seat maker was not flushed with success, the year 2000 did see us picking up another account in Stoke – one that led to a really innovative launch strategy being devised for what was, fundamentally, a disability product.

A new product called Door Knight was to come on to the market, to help make life much easier for those with impaired mobility and movement. The product allowed an elderly or disabled person to open their front door by means of a remote control key fob, rather than having to try to get to the front door, manoeuvre their wheelchair and try to open the door. Furthermore, a security camera was integral to the whole device, allowing the fob holder to check who was at the door before opening it.

To bring this product to life, we suggested a London-based launch, to which key members of the press would be invited. However, presenting something as a disability aid was not likely to make people sit up and take notice, so we suggested a much more innovative launch strategy that had a synergy with the Door Knight brand and its associations with the chivalrous world of the Round Table!

A key part of the strategy was the making of a video to demonstrate how the product worked. We needed a house to which to fit the Door Knight system and a new account manager volunteered her parents' property. We then found a video maker from Fleetwood and brought in as many friends and family as we could muster as extras – all having to sign away their rights to future royalties if the film won an Oscar, or suddenly thrilled those beside the red carpet at Cannes! The video worked really well, demonstrating the usefulness of the product and the scenarios in which it might assist.

The mechanic with which to entice the media to the launch was a beautiful, invitation, which tumbled downwards when opened. The front panel showed Rapunzel in her castle, trying to see who was at the door below and as the invitation fell downwards, her long, flaxen hair ran down the turret's wall, until it reached a knight below. The invitation explained the need to know exactly who was knocking on the door, as well as the necessity of having a suitable device with which to let them in.

The venue we sourced for the launch was the Kensington Roof Gardens, which linked somewhat to the Rapunzel theme, being located high up above London. It also had enough floor area for what we called 'The Door Knight Wheelchair Challenge'. This was basically a race by wheelchair and the press who attended were each given a chance to try to manoeuvre a wheelchair around a set circuit, which included a door that they had to get through using their Door Knight fob and one that had no Door Knight device fitted. Each journalist was timed and a handsome prize made available for the winner.

To help them understand how to tackle this challenge, we invited along a paralympian, who showed them exactly how to go about things and tackle both doors.

We had other fun features such as a court jester to amuse and entertain and a compère in the shape of quiz master, Nicholas Parsons. Now, to be honest, we had hoped to be able to get some other options to fill this role, but budget did not permit. I had set my sights on Sean Bean (one of my missions at the time was to involve him in any PR campaign that I could). We almost secured Darren Day, but didn't feel that he was of an age to empathise with the more mature market. On this basis, the client chose Nicholas.

This was a little bit of a shame, as we had arranged a quiz for three journalists to partake in – the names being drawn from a hat. Successful answers allowed the participant to pull a fob out of a hat to see if they could open the door and reveal the mystery guest. I have to say that the winning journalist didn't initially seem that chuffed to see Nicholas Parsons, but he certainly swung that around during the course of the evening and they got along famously.

Nicholas then, to everyone's delight, took on the Wheelchair Challenge himself, revealing bright red socks under his trousers that definitely caught the eye of our photographer on the night – the mad

Dave Nelson, who had travelled down to the event with his twin brother Darren from Blackpool, to ensure that we had really good press photos of the event.

The whole thing was tremendous fun and we celebrated with the client, who insisted on us drinking copious amounts of champagne after all guests had departed.

With all this excitement going on, it would be easy to overlook what was happening on the key accounts of Primary Direct and Bennetts, but the answer is that there was an awful lot rolling out, month after month. Both accounts had massive campaigns being implemented and I say that in terms of the amount of activity being undertaken, rather than the budget. Catapult PR's main skill has always been rooted in allowing campaigns to box above their budgetary weight thanks to the fabulous ideas and strategies employed.

On the Primary Direct side of things, 2000 was the year of the 'Big Travel Cover Up'. The challenge here was to continue to grow the Primary Direct case count in a travel insurance sector dominated by the travel agents, who sold 90% of all policies. The PR campaign was geared at achieving the lion's share of share of voice, promoting all types of travel insurance policy sold by Primary, but doing it in Catapult's inimitable style!

To assist with the PR, I drafted some key questions for a consumer research survey and by 'key questions' I don't necessarily mean the obvious ones, but ones that would give findings that could become headline makers and which related to malpractice and illegal selling techniques used by travel agents selling insurance.

This malpractice was the cornerstone of the campaign, but there was far more than just this issue-based activity. I had known the Mirror's personal finance editor, John Husband, for a very long time by this point and introduced him to Primary Direct. I knew that John was the sort of journalist who liked looking after the interests of his Mirror readers and I knew that Primary would be the sort of flexible, go-getting company that would help him do that, if they could. What resulted was an absolutely phenomenal reader offer, exclusive to Mirror readers, which enabled them to get an annual travel insurance policy at an absolute fraction of the price they would pay an agent for even a single trip policy.

This high profile, Primary-branded reader offer ran twice in 2000, bringing in 5000 new customers. This offer continued to run in subsequent years and invariably meant me staying in the office until very late, as the Mirror sub-editors sent over the proof at around 7.30pm and I then had to amend anything that was wrong. Despite the late nights, it was worth it.

Different themes were explored and for Christmas that year we had a Christmas stocking mailer of a handmade stocking made from gold net, which contained some intriguing items, each with a tag attached. There was mistletoe, with a message of 'kiss goodbye to travel agents' prices', a betting slip for snow at Christmas, with details of the odds of having to make particular types of claim on travel insurance attached, and chocolate coins, with a message that stated that the much lauded E111 health cover scheme would do 'sweet FA' for you in some countries and in some circumstances. Additionally, there was a mini filing cabinet gift with Primary Direct's directors' business cards already inserted.

The ski product was supported with 12 different releases about ski insurance and brilliant cartoons drawn up by the very talented Ken Wignall. Meanwhile, we produced our own 8-page magazine about gap year travel, entitled 'The Wanderer', which gave useful tips and advice for backpackers, as well as full details of the type of travel insurance they needed to buy and the reasons why. This generated a really great piece by Anne Ashworth in 'The Times' as well as lots of other coverage and feedback.

One of the funniest parts of this year's campaign, however, was the Sun Awareness activity that we undertook. Primary had, by now, introduced us to their sales director, Stuart, who was a larger-than-life character of Spanish origin, who can just light up the room with his personality. He is also the only man to whom I have sung, 'Yes, Sir I Can Boogie', in a hammed up Spanish accent! We came to an agreement with the Imperial Cancer Research Fund to donate a certain sum per policy sold, to help raise awareness of skin cancer and to promote sun safety. To help launch this, we bought a sombrero for all personal finance and travel editors on the nationals and also hired a model to take promotional shots, clad in a bikini and wearing the same sombrero.

Apparently, when this photo started to circulate at Primary Direct, Stuart nabbed a copy and went around telling all his sales contacts that this was his wife, pinning up the picture by his desk, to add to the deceit! The fun of the sombreros also transmitted itself to London, where journalist Clare Francis told me that she and her colleague wore them out on the town and were asked continuously where they got their sombreros, to which they replied, 'Primary Direct'! To be honest, the Catapult office probably wished they'd said, 'Catapult PR'! Packaging up 50 sombreros is not the easiest task on earth!

Altogether, we had face-to-face meetings with 20 personal finance journalists, a 31% share of voice in the travel insurance sector and 31 appearances as a media spokesperson in national titles. Total coverage was to a value of £171,000, back in the year 2000!

The activity on the Bennetts' account was equally exciting. Our campaign for 2000 was called 'I'm the Leader of the Gang' and positioned Bennetts as being on the biker's side by demonstrating that it was aligning its vision with that of riders in the saddle. This was fundamentally important, as Bennetts hadn't traditionally pursued this kind of activity, whereas its competitors had.

From reading the motorcycling press over the course of many months, I'd picked up on the real issue of diesel spillage on the roads and bikers' annoyance and anger at this life-threatening peril. From there it was a question of generating momentum behind a campaign, fronted by Bennetts, to do something positive to tackle this issue.

Loads of desk research was undertaken to collate facts and figures and we discovered that no one authority was responsible for cleaning up diesel spillages under the terms of the Highways Act. Consequently, diesel spillages were often left untended, as death traps on the roads.

We decided to take this issue to the International Motorcycle Show. Bennetts had upgraded from a shoebox and now had a decent sized stand, though still nowhere near as huge as its competitor, Carole Nash. We worked with biking authorities the BMF and MAG, to get support for our diesel stance and launched a petition on the Bennetts' stand, which we presented to the BMF (British Motorcyclists' Federation). We also had the Gladiator 'Diesel' on the stand on press day, to promote the petition's launch and had diesel splodges made to position around the show, to help raise awareness. We secured an impressive 500 signatures.

Additionally, we produced the first ever booklet for female motorcyclists, which was called 'Born Free'.

One of the really significant things of 2000, however, was the launch of a Bennetts website, complete with online quotes and purchase facilities. This seems crazy to say now, but until this point, we had no internet or email. I can remember my client at Bennetts, the lovely Andrew Simpson, saying we would soon need to communicate by email and I also sort of recall dismissing it in my head as some sort of fad that wouldn't catch on. The more techy Chris banged on about it all the time, until we realised we were going to have to get into this new-fangled way of communicating!

So having a Bennetts website with all of this content was something massive back then and Bennetts had appointed a really keen and talented digital manager to sort everything out. She wanted a high impact launch – something that nowadays businesses wouldn't bother with too much, as the internet is everywhere, but back then it could be big news, if handled creatively.

I was in my element here and really wanted to do something fantastic with this. I had always been a fan of teaser mailers, but rarely got the opportunity to do any. I felt, here, that building excitement prior to the launch with teasers was the way to go.

The first teaser comprised a set of biker earplugs, which we mailed out in a little jewellery box, with a message that said that bikers could soon 'plug in and boot up'. The second mailer that went out one day later consisted of a pair of wind-up chattering teeth, with a message that said that 'bike quotes with byte' would be coming soon. The final mailer was a computer screen wipe, with a message that said that it was now time to go 'window shopping'!

Until day three, we had not revealed who the mailers were from, but amazingly, on day two, Post Magazine rang me and said they had been guessing in the office and thought that it had to have come from Catapult and Bennetts, because of its originality. I was so chuffed!

However, that was not all that we had up our sleeve. I had wanted to find a way of communicating the URL of the Bennetts website photographically and discovered a motorcycle display team called The Purple Helmets, who were a spoof display team who got up to all sorts of crazy antics. They happened to have a motorbike that seated around eight or nine riders, which they used in their shows. I thought it would be perfect to get a banner made, carrying the Bennetts web address, which could run the length of this vehicle, held by the Purple Helmets in their trademark trenchcoats.

As luck would have it, the Purple Helmets are based in the Isle of Man, to which we could fly from Blackpool Airport. They were up for getting involved, in return for a donation from Bennetts and Bennetts asked Catapult to fly to the Isle of Man to sort the photo out. To do this, we had to book a tiny little private plane, which only seated six. We had no idea, when we did this what this would mean. Our flight was scheduled for a Monday afternoon, with the shoot to take place as soon as the Purple Helmets could get away from work.

Something very strange happened to me on the Sunday night. I was tossing and turning and feeling physically sick about making this journey, which had never happened to me before when I'd been flying anywhere. Although it was spring, the wind was howling and I just didn't want to go to the airport. I told my account manager this and I think she thought I was being ridiculous, but something just felt very wrong.

We had booked a model and also a photographer called George Archer, who had contacted us just after we had taken on the Bennetts account. George travelled up from the Midlands and we all met up at Blackpool Airport. We were taken into a tiny lounge set aside for those who had chartered a private plane. I still felt terrible and, as I stared at the carpet, I saw fleas jumping out of it, which didn't help one little bit. Luckily, we were ushered out on to the tarmac shortly after that. Here, to our horror, we realised that the only way of getting into this plane was to climb on to the wing, walk over it and enter the cabin.

My account manager and I sat at the back, with George and the model in front of us – quite opportune, as she kept throwing up and I would have hated to be in front of her. We discovered at this point that George had a penchant for liquorice humbugs, though I'm sure that he chain-ate them throughout the flight out of sheer nerves at what we were enduring.

Our pilot arrived and introduced himself and that gnawing pain arrived again. It was truly terrifying taking this flight, as it was almost like sitting in a dodgem. I just kept thinking that there was hardly any protection at all, that anything could hit us and give us no chance of surviving and that the wind that was buffeting us was going to bring us down at any second. It was the most painful flight I've ever taken.

We luckily touched down and were picked up at the airport by one of the Purple Helmets. He'd come in a big transit van, so we let the model sit in the front and we sat on the floor in the back. The weather was dismal, but as anticipated, we got some great shots and had fun. All I could think about, however, was the flight back.

Again, that passed without incident, but around a week later, my account manager brought me the local paper. 'Look at this', she said, 'It's awful'. The pilot who had flown us to the Isle of Man had suffered a heart attack while flying and had crashed his plane into the Mersey. I couldn't help but think that my inexplicable fear on the day of our flight had something spooky to do with this. I think my account manager was pondering the same hypothesis.

As the summer approached, we set about what had become our now customary way of entering the Institute of Public Relations CREAM Awards, creating a whole strategy around the presentation of the A4 file boxes and their contents and wrapping the box in an eye-catching designed sleeve. This was, by now, becoming almost a military operation, played out to a battle-plan devised by myself. Somehow, however, no matter how many months ahead of the deadline we planned everything, the day of the deadline for posting would still see us frantically assimilating all the contents of the boxes, all the evaluations of coverage, copies of press cuttings, sample photography and a whole load of other supporting evidence.

We had, by now, followed a policy of getting all of our award entries photographed. This was a painful, all-day exercise, as we planned what examples of a campaign to put into a shot, chose a coloured backcloth, waited for lighting to be set up, placed props within the shot, adjusted heights and positions of different components, so that they would look good on camera and generally sat around. I was the one constant of all of these shoots, which would last all day. Other staff drew lots or did the shoot on a rota basis, changing over at lunchtime.

In 2000, our Leader of the Gang entry for Bennetts was, to me, one of the best ever. We had bought some mock leather to decorate the box and then stuck studs into it, so that it looked superb as a piece of art-work in itself. Despite having prepared our awards meticulously, we ran out of time to complete the entry yet again! I swear that one constant in Catapult's history has been that the day before the awards have closed, year after year, has been the most stressful day of the whole 365, with time flying by, lots of crawling around on the floor required to fill boxes and tempers frayed!

In 2000, I decided the only way to get the entries in before the dead-line was to physically drive them to Birmingham and hand them in to the offices of the organisers. This was a task that I undertook with my designer, Darren, and an account manager, as we had no idea whether we could park, who could carry the awards in and how far they would have to be carried, or how on earth to negotiate Birmingham's city centre to achieve this.

When we found the office, Darren took them in and came back beam-ing saying that the organisers had whooped when they saw our glori-ously designed boxes. That, and having made the deadline, made us feel much better, so we went to a canal-side pub and enjoyed a spot of lunch.

This was still summer, but time flew and it was soon awards time in November. The nominations had been announced in September and we were absolutely wowed to find that we had three of the 32 nominations in total. For an agency of our size, we were definitely boxing above our weight and some very big Manchester agencies were not nominated at all.

We arrived there with the usual apprehension and I had briefed all the girls on the toilet etiquette. We took our clients from Primary Direct,

Tim and Helen, and also invited another client – the marketing head of an online perfume company. He hailed from South Africa and was quite a charming young gent, so good company. Everyone gelled well and we were set for what we hoped would be a really good evening.

What I have invariably found at these award ceremonies is that you try to get a feel for whether you have won anything on the basis of how far away from the stage you are. However, as we had walked from the very back of the room the previous year, I couldn't really calculate whether we were in with a shout or not. Another thing I have learned over the years is to pace the drink, so that you are still pretty sober if you do have to tee-ter up to the stage on your heels. A final dead certainty is that, whoever is organising the awards will have slotted in some high step up to the stage and will have provided no handrail to cling on to, when coming down. On this basis, best advice is to try to take another person up with you and to ideally make it a man, who can help you down the steps without you falling flat on your arse in front of all the esteemed guests.

Being as self-conscious as I am, my worst nightmare is to have to brave the stage walk on my own, so I always used to try to make it a group thing – for team bonding and to have someone to hide behind, when the invariably awful award photo was taken (always by some man below you beneath the stage pointing his camera up to capture you at your very worst angle!)

I can remember Tim and Helen saying to me throughout the long drawn out build up to the awards, (when everyone is seated for hours until all tables have had their three-course meal and then has to sit through lengthy speeches and spiel), that I looked physically sick. I can safely say that this is something that has stayed with me at every award ceremony I have ever been to and I literally cannot relax at all until the results have been announced.

So clinging to my seat, following the one-sip-water-one-sip-wine rule and ensuring that I was, at all times, facing the stage, I was in such a panic that I didn't really pay too much attention to the compère for the evening, the BBC NW newsreader, Nigel Jay. I could hear words be-ing spoken, but throughout them, I was feeling more and more physi-cally sick, with butterflies leaping around my stomach and had hardly touched my food.

The awards always start with high drama, as shots of all the entries nominated for awards flash up on the screen to some upbeat music that the video production company has added as a soundtrack. There are whoops from around the room, as each agency's work appears on screen and this all adds to the general excitement or, in my case, nausea.

We were nominated in three categories. Primary Direct was up for 'Best Consumer PR Campaign' – the one they all want to win because of the kudos attached to this category. Bennetts was nominated, and quite rightly so, for 'Best Financial Campaign' and 'Best Integrated PR Campaign' – one which encompasses a variety of marketing tactics that can be brought together under the umbrella of 'PR'.

One by one, our categories were read out and, one by one, we scooped the top prize in each, being the category winner in all three. Three negotiations of the steps, no casualties and seemingly three encounters with Nigel Jay: little did we know that there would be a fourth. Amid the general euphoria of having gone to Manchester and picked up these spoils again, especially the top banana 'Best Consumer PR Campaign' Award for the second year running, and during the ordering of bottles of champagne to pop and imbibe, it suddenly became apparent that the 'NW Consultancy of the Year Award' was up for grabs.

I think it was almost a complete shock, perhaps because I'd been so busy being delighted about our success, that I hadn't really compared it to that of other agencies in the room. Given that I was feeling so nauseous and terrified of the stage walk anyway, all of that had sort of passed me by, particularly as we were this year deprived of the marvellous Eurovision board! So when we were suddenly announced as agency of the year, it was as if I was in some crazy dream. Off we all trooped this time, to pick up the award, with everyone absolutely beaming from ear to ear, bar me, given my still semi-nauseous state. Once again, there was Nigel Jay, smiling on and applauding as we scooped our top accolade.

We returned to our table and Primary Direct's first question was, 'Are you putting your fees up now?' Once I assured them that they wouldn't be, they relaxed and imbibed lots more alcohol!

At this point, a chap from CIS came over to the table to congratulate me and my clients started to heckle him saying he was a 'boring Volvo driver' if he came from CIS! I might have been merry, but I was also mortified!

Things were about to get worse. As we were waiting for the lift, we managed to call back the people who had only just got in it, who happened to be an agency called Mere Communications, who had also been up for awards. As the lift doors opened, one of our number shouted, 'Mere Communications, shove it up your arse!' I must, at that point, have looked mummified, with a mouth gaping wide open in shock! I just wanted to pretend I didn't know the people who'd shouted this and have the ground swallow me up. Thank goodness the lift doors closed at that point!

I have no idea why, but I found myself wandering around the car park of the Piccadilly Hotel a short time after all this, whereupon I found a man with a white waistcoat, who I recognised as the CIS man who had been called a 'boring Volvo driver'. I felt obliged to apologise profusely to him, as best I could and he graciously accepted my apology and asked me to contact him in the coming weeks. I did, indeed, do that and ironically enough, he became a client for around 5 years – boring Volvo driver, or not!

All that remained was for us to all stagger outside to find the minibus we'd hired to take us to the awards, so that we could, in a real stupor of excitement, take all of our awards safely back to base camp. The adventure was just beginning! Luckily, Mere Communications hadn't punctured our tyres!

When we rolled into the office (some time from mid-morning onwards, according to the hangover that each member of staff had), we had an email from Nigel Jay, congratulating us on our outstanding success. That's how Nigel suddenly became an adopted son of the Catapult family! There was no shaking him off after that!

Knowing that we needed to capitalise on our success in the press, we hired a stretch limo for a photo shoot and all got back into the clothes we had worn on the night, to make it seem as though we'd just arrived back carrying the spoils. A few feather boas and plastic roses were thrown in for good measure and beaming smiles conveyed our pleasure at having gone to Manchester, beaten the best and returned to Thornton Cleveleys as triumphant winners. The future was looking very rosy.

Chapter 15
TONY, TROPHIES & TERRORISM

2001 undoubtedly started with a bang, which continued the mood of a fabulous Christmas party night out that I had enjoyed with Primary Direct at a venue, near Stockport, called Elvis's Chinese Palace. It was the most amazing Christmas party I've ever had, with dancing on the chairs being expected rather than being frowned upon, and a white cat-suited Chinese Elvis impersonator touring the tables singing Elvis tunes in a Chinese accent and handing the mic over, whenever he spotted someone who looked like they could belt out 'Suspicious Minds' or 'You Were Always On My Mind'.

I had needed someone to take as a plus-one, so took the perfume client as he had already met Primary Direct's directors. He and I had the microphone thrust between us to the karaoke backing-track of 'You've Lost That Loving Feeling'. When I did the 'Baby, baby, I get down on my knees for you' bit, with real, hammed up and over-the-top sexiness and feeling, he just stared at me and said, 'Wow, that was good'. I didn't have too much trouble finding people to boogie with on the tiny dance floor after that!

As January came, we knew that on Australia Day, January 26, we would be getting ourselves down to Brum to attend the national CREAM Awards – an honour reserved for those who had won awards categories at a regional level. On this basis, we had three shots at a national award, two for Bennetts and one for Primary Direct.

The ceremony was at the ICC and we had booked rooms in a city centre hotel nearby. The whole Catapult team went, as usual, along with Helen, her sister and a new employee called Adele, plus our new lucky mascot, Mr Perfume. Helen nearly managed to take the top off her 4x4 entering the low-barrier car park, while for some of the team, the biggest headache was getting the big rollers into the hair.

We all walked to the venue, avoiding a load of drinkers in the streets standing outside the pubs and bars. The room was massive, with probably 70+ tables of agencies at this national awards ceremony. This was thanks to there being over 50 categories of awards to be handed out. It was just our luck that the PR awards came right at the end.

The room was largely full of what I would call 'ad men' – very different from the PR clan – much more all muscle and testosterone, attitude and anger: a heady mixture! Had we not had a really entertaining compère in the form of an Ali G impersonator, complete with yellow jumpsuit and streetwise humour, we would have probably fallen asleep by the time our PR awards came around. We did, however, try to stay active by adopting an ad agency in each category and cheering on our 'chosen one' with all the volume our lungs could muster.

As the results started to be read out, one of my account managers' faces fell. Neither Bennetts award scooped the national prize. We were down to the toughest of the lot – the 'Best Consumer Category', with our Primary Direct campaign of the 'Big Travel Cover Up'. At that point, our luck changed and we were amazingly announced as the national winner!

The Primary Direct girls, myself and my Primary account manager all trooped up to meet Ali G, who did Catapult a great honour by declaring to all and sundry that they should show us some 'respect' as we'd definitely been the loudest table in the room. We liked that recognition from the sunglass-wearing, banana yellow wonder. We grabbed our prize, before anyone changed their mind, and returned to the table.

As these were the national awards, the organisers had pushed the boat out and organised some very special entertainment – golden oldie, Tony Blackburn. Bearing in mind that this was in his pre-jungle, 'I'm A Celebrity' days, it wasn't that much of a draw, but having already exhausted ourselves by pogo-ing up and down to 'Come on Eileen', by the time it approached 12.30am and many bottles of wine had been consumed, we were up for anything. That included throwing ourselves into 'audience participation' during Tony's soul set.

As this progressed and as we whooped and raised our hands up in the air, hanging on to Tony's every word, he announced that he was going to scour the room looking for the 'lucky lady' who would become the recipient of his gold medallion – the one hanging around his neck. This was to be bestowed by him on the damsel of his choice, as he gyrated his hips and bared his manly chest in the shirt that was unbuttoned to the waist.

Everyone whooped even more at this news, as you can imagine! Tony's eyes roved around the room, to more gyrating of the hips and sensuous, velvety toned words of wisdom. To my horror, they suddenly alighted on me and, before I knew it, he declared, 'I am going to bestow my medallion on that blonde lady over there. Come up here and claim your prize'. Those on the dance floor turned their collective gaze on to me, as a spotlight fell on my face, doing nothing to spare my blushes. Up I had to trot, as the first DJ to ever broadcast on Radio 1 (this is how I console myself!) anointed me and let me kiss his medallion!

For services rendered, I received a signed postcard, which I promptly shoved down my bra for safe keeping, as the conga had now started and I was being swept up by a huge line of people all obviously wishing to 'connect' with Tony's golden girl! The photo stayed down my bra for the rest of the night, which is where I'm sure Tony might have liked it to be kept.

We all staggered back through the crowds of drunks on the street, mingling in nicely. We'd given Mr Perfume charge of the trophy, but he promptly dropped it, luckily with no harm done. We crawled back into our beds, with frostiness in the non-winning corners of the team and ecstasy in others. You can't win 'em all, but the one won was definitely la crème de la crème.

By this point, Primary Direct were attracting the attention of a lot of 'joint partners', or organisations wishing to find someone to underwrite their insurance policies. One of my account managers and I had the dubious pleasure of encountering one of these – a completely insane man from Denmark, who was wheeled into a meeting with us, to discuss his proposed media expedition to Greenland.

The moment this chap entered the room, you could tell that there was something not quite right, given his frenetic way of moving around, his mannerisms and the tales he was telling. This commenced with a tale of how the Russian mafia had been after him and had had him cornered in a hotel room, until he managed to convince them that he had no money and it would be best if they didn't shoot. The tale proceeded with some narration of an escape that sounded like something out of James Bond, but this was definitely no Sean Connery!

His next topic of conversation really just highlighted the extent of racism in Denmark, where someone had apparently had the idea of sending all 'New Danes' to the moon! This tickled him greatly, with a loud belly laugh filling the room as we all stared at him in a totally politically correct way. This 'New Danes' story was somehow tied up with a tale of a massive 10-foot tall stuffed polar bear in an exhibition hall, which it seemed that he wished to replicate, but by now I was beginning to lose any thread of what he was talking about!

We then got down to the crux of it – the marvellous media expedition to Greenland, with which he would launch the new policies that Primary would underwrite for him and on which my account manager and I, plus selected English journalists were invited.

The whole thing sounded like the Nightmare on Elm Street to me, with no mention of a hair dryer socket dropped in to the description of basic tents, no toilet facilities and below zero temperatures. We hadn't got to the best of it yet, but the mad Dane, in between his jumping around and banging his briefcase on the desk to re-enact how he had handled the Russian mafia suddenly said, 'Den dare eez de matter of de Polar bears'. At this point, pens went down, eyes were pinned on him and all ears were trained.

'What matter of the Polar bears?' asked Tim, laughing nervously.

'Well, de theeng eez, de Polar bears only come to dis part of Greenland once evverry ten years', said the Dane. We all exhaled – far too soon unfortunately. He sensed our relief, so decided to wreck it.

'De bad news eez dat it is ten years since de Polar bears came to dis part of Greenland'. Our jaws dropped open, visions of an angry Polar bear slashing its claws through our flimsy tents crossing all of our minds. The mad Dane began to smirk, awaiting a reaction, in a sort of masochistic way. By now the lack of the hair dryer socket had paled into insignificance.

'I don't think this is something to which we can subject the British media', I said, like the wise old owl that I am. Mad Dane looked crestfallen, as if I had taken a pin to his balloon and burst it in the cruellest manner imaginable. I'm sure he had fancied the idea of us all having to get into his embrace in a one-man tent, just to keep us safe from de Polar bears and any passing Russian mafia snipers! Needless to say, that was the last we heard of him.

Weeks whizzed by after that to March 2001 and another awards do at Park Hall, Charnock Richard. This was the LAWTEC Business Awards and we were nominated in the category of 'New Business of the Year'. This was a particularly special award, as there was a sizeable cash sum up for grabs, as well as a trophy – rather less glamorous than those we were accustomed to, by this point in time!

There were three or four other companies nominated in this category, but it was with some sense of pride that I went and picked up this particular trophy. We were on a roll and I also had the added pleasure of getting my programme for the evening signed by the guest speaker, footballer, Alan Hansen. He'd spent the entire evening before on TV declaring, 'It should have been a pen', when talking about a dodgy refereeing decision. When I pulled a pencil out of my bag instead of a biro, to allow him to sign the programme, I uttered the words, 'It should have been a pen', in my best Scottish accent. He just looked at me blankly!

Moving on to April, we were heading to another awards ceremony, this time at the Winter Gardens in Blackpool. These were the Blackpool Challenge Partnership Awards and we were up for 'Most Promising Company'.

I'd gone to town for this occasion and bought some glittery body make up, which my boyfriend of the time had decided to put on my back in some sort of pattern. Also nominated for an award was this rather colourful character from Blackpool, who went by the name of 'Mrs Sparkle'. She was literally larger-than-life and, on the night, had her long, black curly locks falling down a black gown-like dress well ahead of its time, as it would definitely have been the vogue at Hogwarts.

Mrs Sparkle was a mini-celebrity in Blackpool, as she ran a themed hotel close to one of the piers, which boasted, among other things, a Barbie room and a Jungle/Tarzan room. At this point in time, she was at the height of her fame. Unfortunately, I believe that a hotel inspector-type TV programme destroyed all that, but luckily for her, she did have her moment of glory at these awards. In fact, we cheered loudly when she went to claim her prizes.

Despite this support for a fellow woman in business, however, I was more than a little affronted when a man came over to me in the bar before the ceremony and said, 'Mrs Sparkle, I presume?' This was hardly a Stanley meets Livingston encounter and I fixed him with a stony stare.

'No it is not', I said. I then became wholly paranoid about how much sparkle had been applied to my back and what might have been written on it, trying to keep my back to the wall as much as M the Swinton security guard had done at my leaving do!

Despite this affront to my sensitivities, we once again scooped the top prize. This is still, to this day, the ugliest trophy Catapult has ever picked up, comprising a very large gold-coated piece of metal, shaped as paper dart, resting on a chunky base. I try to shove it at the back of the trophy display whenever possible!

The most notable part of that evening lay in the fact that a Radio Wave news reader made a very disparaging remark about us being the 'Popstars' of Blackpool, Hear'Say having just won that particular music contest. We all looked up at the stage and gave him a withering look at this point, but then realised that he obviously hadn't expected any winners to be that happy to pick up an ugly, fake gold metal dart!

One of the funniest days of 2001 was another Primary HQ golf day down in Horsham. I flew down to this one with one of my account managers and this time there was no need for me to humiliate myself on the driving range, as we two girls had a role. We were told to head out to something like the 11th tee and set up a table of refreshment, beers and snacks, so that guests could have something before moving on to the next hole.

We were popped on board a golf buggy and driven out to the hole, where we found boxes and boxes of drinks and snacks, a trestle table, which we had to erect, and some large parasols. Luckily, we also had two seats. This was particularly opportune, because we sat and we sat and we sat, waiting for any sign of life to show itself on the course. Eventually, we saw one group, so leapt into action and served up some drinks. That happy band of golfers disappeared over the horizon, leaving us quite alone, once again, trying to keep busy with games of i-Spy and other such nonsense.

After about half-an-hour of not seeing another living soul, the heavens absolutely opened and we had nothing with which to protect ourselves, or our stock, other than the two parasols. We tried to collect everything under those and tried to ourselves get shelter, wondering what on earth would happen if lightning struck up. We presumed, being girls of great optimism and belief in human nature, that someone would be coming to rescue us at any moment, but no shining knight appeared over the hillocks and we were already like drowned rats. After about another 20 minutes of more of the same, we realised that we had been well and truly abandoned, so we did what all self-respecting women would do, when in a now very pissy mood and opened two bottles of beer! Still we sat there, getting wetter and wetter, with virtually no chance of protecting anything under now soddened parasols, which were about to collapse under the weight of water they had accumulated.

Just as we were abandoning any hope of anyone ever remembering us, a golf buggy came bouncing over the course and the club course marshal appeared, looking absolutely amazed to see two PR girls now in a perfect state to enter any wet T-shirt contest! He told us to hop aboard, but for some reason couldn't take us back to the clubhouse, so took us to a tiny little shed, with no light other than a cut-out panel in the door. We were then left sitting in there for about an hour before we spotted one golf group on the course and shouted with all of our might as if we were the remnants of the Swiss Family Robinson stranded up a coconut palm. Eventually, we were rescued and taken back to the clubhouse, in not too good a humour, or state, to everyone's total surprise. Yes, we had well and truly been forgotten about! How we laughed about it later though, once we'd wrung our clothes out!!

The dinner at this event was not quite as memorable as the one with Garry Richardson, but this was the evening on which we discovered the total folly of ever going back to a hotel to have a last drink at the bar with Mr Bensusan and Mr O'Sullivan. We believe that they were found asleep somewhere on a landing or in some other public place and we have little recollection of how we made it back to our rooms, but suffice to say that I have never felt so sick on any flight, anywhere in the world, as I did the following day, when flying back to Manchester! I realised that these two gents should come with a public health warning!

Another account we picked up early that year was that of the Holker Garden Festival, held every year at Cark-in-Cartmel, Cumbria. Things were just being set in motion on this account, when disaster hit the countryside and, in particular, in Cumbria, thanks to the foot-and-mouth outbreak. That started in the February of that year in Essex and quickly spread to other parts of the country. British livestock exports were banned and in Cumbria the footpaths on the fells were closed, decimating the tourism sector, as well as the farming community, whose pyres of burning livestock could be seen everywhere.

Although the Holker Estate was free of foot-and-mouth, the owners took the decision to cancel the 2001 Festival, a huge decision, as they had lost the last day of the 2000 Festival due to torrential rain. The cancellation was due to their desire to show support for the farming community and not be seen to be celebrating, while their neighbours suffered. Rather than doing the all-out promotion we had expected to handle on this account, we had to swing into crisis PR mode, drafting news releases announcing and explaining the decision.

In the midst of the crisis, in April 2001, myself and three of my employees were really privileged to be given tickets to Ladies' Day at Aintree, thanks to the generosity of the photographer that Primary in Horsham used, Michael Cockerham. It was touch and go as to whether the Aintree meeting would be cancelled, because of the foot-and-mouth outbreak, but in true British racing spirit, it went ahead, with all attendees like ourselves having to wear plastic bags on our feet and be disinfected on entry into the racecourse.

We girls had really gone to town, buying hats and outfits and trying to look smart. When we looked around at some of the fashion crimes around us on Ladies' Day, we needn't have bothered. Leopard skin, plastic white mini skirts and white stilettos abounded and, if anything, we looked overdressed. I noticed Gordon Banks sitting in the stand, but didn't want to interrupt his day by asking for an autograph.

The really classic moment of this day for me was when we were watching a race and a rather vociferous scouse lady behind us started cheering on a horse called Historic. I will hear that screeching scouse voice, shouting out at goodness knows what decibel level, 'Come on 'istorick. Come on 'istorick. Whip the bastard!' for many years to come!

Foot-and-mouth was not, however, the only tragedy of 2001 to affect Catapult. The boyfriend and I headed off to Florida for two weeks, flying in to Tampa and starting our tour in Clearwater. The four days spent there was probably the best part of our holiday. I got up and went swimming in the most glorious pool each morning, on which a flamingo would land while you were in the water. He, on the other hand, wouldn't emerge until nearly lunchtime.

I had a new account to sort out shortly after arrival, but that done, we moved on to other parts of Florida, staying in places such as St Petersburg, Sarasota and Venice. From the word go, things were awful and I nearly didn't board the flight at Manchester Airport. The whole thing seemed doomed thereon in. When we were around Naples, I walked to the water's edge to find the sea full of dead fish floating on the surface. It was absolutely revolting and I had no idea why, until I saw the news and realised it was phenomenon called red tide – an algal bloom, which contains a toxin that paralyses the nervous system in fish. This was hardly what we'd come to Florida for.

It seemed that things couldn't get much worse, but we had the boyfriend's birthday to look forward to on September 11 and had bought tickets for an NFL game, so that we could see the Tampa Bay Buccaneers from the best seats in the house.

The night before, we'd had a typically strained night. We headed off to a diner in St Pete's for breakfast and I was pretty hung-over and not paying attention to what was going on around me. There was a TV playing in the diner, but I wasn't watching it. The boyfriend suddenly said, 'Have you seen this?' pointing to the TV. I could see lots of smoke and planes crashing into a building and thought it was a film. 'It's not a film', he said, 'It's what's happened in New York'. I then just couldn't believe what I was seeing. The whole diner was completely silent.

We had also bought tickets for the cinema, as part of the birthday treat, and there was nothing else to do, or that we could do about the situation, so we headed off there, partly to try to stop thinking about things back at the apartment. The audience comprised us and about three other people watching the film. By the time we came out, St Pete's was like a ghost town. Most shops, businesses, cafes and restaurants had shut up, with shutters down and nothing to even see in the windows. There was nobody on the streets at all. There was no traffic, no noise, no chatter … just an eerie silence and feeling of doom. It felt like High Noon and I expected Gary Cooper to step out of a doorway at any moment.

In the third block that we walked through, we found a very small café open for business. It only had around six tables and a row of barstools. We sat at the bar and quietly ordered a drink. Silence reigned even in here, with the TV again on, showing the footage of the 9/11 attack on the Twin Towers over and over again. A hippy-looking 30-something suddenly burst through the door larger than life and said something like 'Hey man, why's it so quiet in here?' He was greeted with no response and just a hand pointing towards the TV, as if he were being punished for irreverence, rather than ignorance of what had gone on. He watched the footage, stunned and silenced.

For the first time in history, all NFL games were cancelled, so our first-class tickets were never used.

We left there and went back to our apartment. All TV programmes had been cancelled, on every channel. All there was, for hour after hour, was more and more footage of the attack, accompanied by analysis and then, to our horror, an announcement of 'America Under Attack' and the declaration that US air space had been closed and that no planes would fly in or out of the US for the foreseeable future. Our flight home was scheduled for 2 days later.

This was when it got really frightening for me, because there was a real expectation that more attacks were on the way and that all major cities would be hit within a matter of days. My son was at home and I'd been desperate enough to get away from this horrendous holiday and get back to him as it was, let alone be stranded and not know when, or if, I would get home.

The following morning, I wandered out of the apartment, which was just a stone's throw from St Pete's Beach. The beach was completely deserted bar me and the birds. The eerie silence could even be felt here, amid the haunting screech of the gulls – crying as if they were mourning the dead. I looked up the beach to see a Star-Spangled Banner hanging at half-mast. It symbolised everything that had happened.

I will never forget driving to get some provisions and hearing a radio presenter saying that all Muslims or those of Arabic, Indian, Pakistani or Middle Eastern race should be rounded up and put into concentration camps. The mood was now very much not of mourning necessarily, but of out and out war, of revenge, of America fighting back and showing that she could not be beaten. It was terrifying, particularly when my boyfriend was of mixed Anglo-Kenyan-Indian race, pretty dark skinned having been in the sun and sporting a black beard.

We had headed back to Clearwater and the first thing my boyfriend did was to shave off the beard. He was scared what might happen to him and I didn't blame him. When we walked into restaurants, which were now opening again, I could detect the strange, almost intimidating looks as he was sized up and judged by paranoid eyes.

We had no idea what was to happen to us, as we had travelled independently and not with a tour company. We rang the company that had provided our flights, who told us to head to Orlando and make for a hotel that they had arranged for their clients to stay in until they could get a flight out. We hadn't intended going to Orlando, but had no choice. As we were about to leave Clearwater, a hurricane started to roll in, so we had to quickly pack our bags, as we saw buildings were boarded up and jump in the car.

When we arrived at the large, Orlando hotel, which was very plush, with a couple of pools and lots of amenities, we prayed that there would be a room. We were so lucky, as we were treated as if we were one of the tour company's own bookings and given lunch and dinner vouchers to use in the restaurant. Air space was still closed, so nothing could be done about getting us home in the short term. We were told to try to relax around Orlando, as even when flights started again, planes had to get back into position and there were several days of cancelled flights ahead of ours, so no likelihood of us getting away in less than about 4 days. Nobody knew when the decision to open air space would be taken. We were still very much in the 'America Under Attack' mode.

Being in and around the hotel was very depressing. The pool areas were rammed, because everyone in the hotel had expected to be home by now and so had already spent their holiday money. People were forced to draw extra cash on credit cards, if they could find a machine that wasn't already out of notes. There was little to do other than go to some theme parks and a couple opened up the day after the tragedy. Consequently, we went to Busch Gardens, which was almost deserted. Disney had been afraid to open up its attractions, believing itself to be a top terrorist target, so our second outing was to Universal Studios. We also managed a game of crazy golf, before resorting to sitting by the pool with everyone else.

Every day we trailed down to the tour company office and, after a few days, flights did start again, so they started pinning schedules on the walls. Ours was not on there for several.

Eventually, we were informed that we would be boarding a Manchester flight, not with the airline we were supposed to be with, but with another. Nobody seemed to be in the plane they should have been in and the flight system was in chaos.

We were told we would need to get to the airport very early, because of the heightened security. We expected the airport to be like Fort Knox, but if that was enhanced security, I would have hated to see it when it was standard. The only sign of any real authority came from a woman by the check-in desks, acting like a Gestapo officer, but only to make sure people stayed behind a line on the floor, when waiting to check their bags in.

I cannot explain how nervous everyone on that flight was. There was every expectation that more planes would be blown from the sky, more airports attacked and even bridges blown up. We all sat in silent trepidation for most of the flight, willing the hours to fly by and for our feet to be firmly back on British soil. Eventually, we got home, several days late, but in one piece. It was a very tearful reunion when Mummy finally saw her little boy.

A few weeks after arriving back in the UK, it was the North West CREAM PR Awards ceremony, for which Catapult was nominated for four awards. Our campaign for Primary Direct's new home insurance division was nominated for both 'Best Financial' and 'Best Consumer PR Campaign', while the ski-focused campaign we had operated 'Ski-daddling in Safety' was also up for the 'Consumer PR' award. The final nomination was for our work for Primary Direct Pet, with a campaign called 'Pet Projects'.

The Primary Direct home campaign had been a real hoot. The title of the award, 'The Lights Are On But There's Nobody At Home' referred to the fact that we had conducted consumer research to assess homeowners' attitudes towards home security and home insurance. While 33% felt their home was at risk of burglary if there were no security lights on, the vast majority were very much in the dark, as they didn't shop around for their home insurance.

We also discovered homeowners didn't have a clue how to value their home contents, so tied this in with a press pack and quirky folder based around TV game show, 'The Price is Right'.

Part of this campaign involved a very informal evening launch party in a venue called Navajo Joe's in Covent Garden, at which we presented the home insurance product to journalists face to face, but also involved details of the travel insurance product too. All financial services press, travel writers and many freelancers were invited and the evening started with a little icebreaker between 7pm and 7.30pm which saw journalists trying to 'Spot the Garden Gnome' on a big, blown up garden scene from which the poor gnome had been removed. It was the grown up version of pinning the tale on the donkey, mixed in with spot the ball!

The fun was all aided and abetted by the serving of Primary Direct cocktails – all specially devised and described in terms of different insurance scenarios and statistics that we had generated through a consumer research survey. For instance, 'No Way Jose' was a cocktail for the 83% of travellers who believed they would never cancel a holiday. The 'Latin Lothario' cocktail was for the 22% of us who have enjoyed a holiday romance!

After cocktails had been ordered and a fair few knocked back, Tim gave a speech about the launch into home insurance and more games followed before a delicious Mexican themed buffet was served. We then had a round or two of housey-housey, or Bingo, followed by a fun travel quiz. We also had several prizes to hand out, including one for the loudest Hawaiian shirt worn by a guest. This was won by freelancer, Stephen Ellis, who seemed to thoroughly enjoy the whole event. From 9pm to midnight, it was then party time!

Some journalists had sort of invited themselves to this event, one of whom was a very strange and exotic lady who took to draping herself around any available men she could find and talking about her split from her ex-boyfriend. There was simply no shaking her off and as guests left, one by one, she was still there perched on a bar stool. At that moment, the larger-than-life Mr Bensusan decided that it was time to order about six bottles of champagne, just to see off the hour between midnight and 1am! We all then took to the bar stools, with our new found friend, having to pander to Mr B's wishes and imbibe his fizz. Needless to say, there were some exceedingly sore heads the next day and I have no recollection of how we finally freed ourselves of the somewhat strange lady with the broken heart. She did, however, ring me up and email me for months afterwards!

The Ski-daddling campaign was also great fun. It encompassed everything from sending press a branded snowstorm, to having an 'Itchy Feet' mailer created, shaped like a foot and carrying a packet of foot powder. This mailer contained lots of facts and figures about the backpacker market and went out to all relevant press. It was one of my all-time favourites.

I also spent days of my time researching ski safety for this mailer, learning about everything from the debate about whether or not helmets should be worn on the slopes, to ski etiquette on the piste and why drinking yellow snow is not a good idea! All of this research tied in with ski claims information, provided by the Star Wars-mad Primary underwriter and enabled me to write an 8 page, A5 booklet about ski safety called 'Skidoos and Don'ts'. It was packed with funny cartoons, was vibrant and comprised a real eye-opener for the skier.

For me, the Primary Pet campaign was the weakest, as it had the least amount of money spent on it. Pet passports had been introduced and Primary had slipped out of national pet insurance coverage because its underwriters would not insure dogs travelling abroad. The PR had to re-launch Primary Pet, to remind media that Primary did offer pet insurance.

We created four doggy cartoon postcards, to highlight that Primary Direct didn't discriminate against breed, size of dog, postcode area in which an owner lived, or other factors commonly used by competitors as a pricing factor. We also had an innovative doggy toothbrush mailer for National Smile Week, to promote doggy dental cover and we created a yo-yo mailing, sending out a yo-yo to media, with instructions on how to do the 'walk-the-dog' trick, to highlight that while competitors' prices were always yo-yoing on their pet insurance products, Primary Direct's were stable. The rest was about themed and targeted press releases, case studies and media one-to-one briefings.

As the awards were read out, our chances of winning anything were waning by the minute. I had honestly felt that the Primary home insurance campaign was in with a great chance, but it picked up neither award. Then the ski campaign failed to do so. In the end, we scooped a Silver Award for the pet campaign, which I had never thought on the cards.

This was perhaps the most depressing award ceremony that I ever attended. It was such an anti-climax after winning the NW PR Consultancy of the Year Award the year before and I might have felt like that whatever we had won on the night. That title went to Spin Media and, I have to say, that I thought that Andy Spinoza showed great class in coming over and saying that he hoped his agency could follow in our footsteps and do it justice.

I don't actually think it was just the award results that were eating at me. I had never got over how awful the holiday in the USA had been and split up from my boyfriend. It was time to try to rebuild Catapult and ensure 9/11 did not hit the business for six, built as it was on financial services business based on markets that could suffer as a result of the terrorist attack.

By now, my account manager on the Bennetts account was a young chap called Chris and he and I had planned that year's International Motorcycle Show PR activity for November 2001.

Part of the activity was a Playstation Challenge, which saw a Playstation game being played on a big screen, with a prize up for grabs for whoever could get the best score on a motorcycle circuit while playing the Moto GP game. The Playstation itself was then to be donated to the charity of the winner's choice.

The NEC show was our platform for the launch of the second lady biker booklet, so we had invited all the motorcycle journalists to come along on press day and play the game. They were all nicely queued up in line, with Granada TV ready to film for their 'Men and Motors' programme, when I noticed that Chris was no longer taking names and recording scores on a whiteboard, but looking rather perturbed and flustered.

Chris was a Bury lad of great principles and a man who would tell someone that something was 'rhubarb' if he thought that was the case, 'rhubarb' being his favourite word in many different scenarios.

In fact, it was Chris who taught me the power of the word rhubarb and how, if you drop it in at the right time, in an argument that has you at odds with an opinion that is plainly wrong, your opponent has the wind taken out of their sails completely. It's not a word they can call offensive, but one that they really don't expect to hear you utter. I would recommend anyone to try it, as it really does work!

Anyway, at this point, we hadn't got to the rhubarb stage. Chris came over and I asked him what was wrong. 'This guy in the Ducati shirt has just jumped the queue and thinks he's better than everyone else', he said, clearly seething about having the rules of his game broken. 'I'm about to turf him off and tell him to get to the back and wait until all the journalists have had their go'. I could see that the words, 'Wait in line, pal', were not far from his lips. The guy in the Ducati shirt was exceedingly handsome and recording a very good score on the game and the queue didn't seem to mind: in fact, they were all watching with great interest. I told Chris to leave it, as I was quite enjoying watching this hunk show off his skills.

That was just as well, as after Ducati man had finished, Chris had to record his excellent score and ask for his name, which transpired to be Ruben Xaus. Having written his name up and watched the guy walk off, one of the members of the press told Chris that he might like to add the words 'World Superbike Race Champion' after that. He went on to explain that Ruben was a national hero in Spain and massive in World Superbikes. Suddenly, Chris's high moral ground went out of the window and Ruben's name, after jumping the queue or not, was put up

in lights, it having been proven that he wasn't some stage fitter wearing a Ducati shirt to grab a bit of reflected glory!

'Thank God I didn't turf him off', said Chris, breathing a sigh of relief. 'I also nearly joked, after he recorded his great time, that it was a pity he couldn't really ride a bike like that! Imagine that!' I've never seen a man look so grateful for having kept his ire and tongue in check!

We rounded off the year with a big Christmas party for all staff and clients and contacts at Guy's Court, located at Bilsborrow near Preston. Everyone seemed to thoroughly enjoy the evening – even myself in my newly single state. We had put behind us a very testing year. It was time to move on to 2002.

Chapter 16
ALL FOUR WON

2002 started with a bang of the bongos and another dose of Raymond Blanc and all thanks to the Hi-Life Diners Club. Although, when we had started work with this client, its network had been restricted to mainly Lancashire, with the vast number of eateries at which you could use your discount dining card being located on the Fylde Coast, by January 2002, it had reached Manchester and other parts of the country too.

The MD of Hi-Life decided that he wanted to create a series of awards for restaurants that accepted the Hi-Life card, these being divided into brasseries, hotels and other similar classifications.

He wanted to hold his awards at a new member's premises – the Gaucho Grill in Manchester – and was determined to invite Raymond Blanc along, to try to convince him that getting behind Hi-Life was a good thing to do. Now I like people who reach for the stars, but this client truly expected Catapult to find top celebrities to present these awards, despite this being their first year and there being no budget with which to pay anyone. This was more than mission impossible – it was mission inexplicable, as we did keep trying to explain that getting a top star just wasn't going to happen. What we did have up our sleeve, however, was our new best friend and adopted son, Nigel Jay.

Ever since our success in 2000 and his congratulatory email, we had kept in touch. I firstly sent two of my account managers on his media training course and then arranged for him to train all of us in presentation skills. We now needed a big favour, in asking him to compère these Gaucho Grill awards and, luckily, Nigel stepped up to the plate, in return for a small donation to his chosen charity, the National Deaf Children's Society.

Nigel was actually planning a charity bike ride to raise funds for his charity, so was pleased to give this a bit of profile. When it came to other presenters, however, the best we could muster was someone from one of the medical-themed soap operas, who was a friend of a friend of a friend and who kindly agreed to present. Apart from this, we had the MD's son, who was a young actor just starting his career, and his girlfriend, who had been a Bollywood actress. For other categories, we were struggling, so these two had to double up!

Three of us went from Catapult and we were given the task of selling raffle tickets around the room, fetching and carrying things and trying to raise interest in a charity auction.

This gave me a golden opportunity to do something I had pondered, as soon as I knew Raymond Blanc was attending. I had taken along the book he had signed for me at the Ideal Home Show, with the intention of asking him to sign it again, if he would. I suddenly found myself at his table, so presented the book and asked if he would add a note. I opened it at the page that he had signed 12 years previously and he was totally amazed to see his writing and the little chef's hat that he had drawn all those years before. I reminded him of the occasion and he seemed to re-call it. He wrote in the book. 'Let's not leave it so long this time'.

For whatever reason, the service at the Gaucho Grill was really ter-ribly slow on the night and the honoured 'celebrity' presenters and our-selves were the very last to get our food. In fact, we were still on starters as some were getting their dessert on the level below the stage, where we were sitting. Nigel kept joking that he would get chronic indigestion and not be able to compère the events at all, or maybe have an attack of the hiccups. The long delay, however, did enable people to have lots of time to consider their bids in the auction.

Eventually, we received our dessert and, by this time, all four of us (ourselves and Nigel) were in fits of giggles, because the much-acclaimed Nicaraguan Custard Cake was rock hard and pretty inedible. Somehow, within minutes of realising this fact, Nigel had to compose himself and stand at the lectern, ready to announce the awards, the presenters and the short-listed restaurants.

I have a pretty strong feeling that the fact that I put a bid of £100 against a Fabien Bartez shirt was purely down to the fact that I was in a Francophile mood, having been so generously treated by Raymond Blanc. Any other reason would defy belief, even if he was a World Cup winning goalie. Not surprisingly, I won the auction with my bid and left clutching the grey, signed shirt with true Gallic pride!

Nigel was by now, well and truly, one of us and we knew all about his special Children in Need waistcoat that only came out once a year and the fact that he would sometimes just wear shorts with a jacket on the top when reading the BBC news, because nobody saw anything below the waist!

Our next outing with Nigel was at the Blackpool Challenge Partnership Awards 2002, at the Winter Gardens in Blackpool. Once again, we picked up an award, this time for Employee Development. Nigel somehow became the target of a lot of party poppers and a picture of him, sitting looking very bemused with streamers dangling off his head, still amuses me now!

Shortly after this, I myself was handed an opportunity to become a TV star – and all thanks to my hairdresser! This chap, Anton, was a complete scream and ribbed me like mad, no matter what I did or said. We would end up in fits of giggles all the time, making the rest of the salon question what on earth we were laughing about. I would regularly have plastic tarantulas put in my hair, have a hair-clip thrown at me, or have a rumour spread about me that stated that I had gone on holiday with Anton to an Austrian ski resort. Supposed pictures would be brought out and shared around – that's if he wasn't asking me how my bongos were, or saying that a video of me attempting to salsa (which we had done as a work night out) was now circulating around Poulton-le-Fylde!

On this basis, when he declared he had entered a contest to try to win tickets to the World Cup in Japan and South Korea, which involved having to show why he was England's biggest fan, I wasn't too surprised when he asked whether I would come to the salon and take part in the filming. What did flummox me was when he told me that he'd decided to give me the 'lead' customer role, so I would feature in some of the main filming sequences!

Sure enough, when I arrived at the salon, which was swarming with film crew, I was instantly told that I would be filmed sitting in a chair, as if Anton was about to tend to my locks. I was told to chat to him and have a bit of banter. Anton set the thing going with a bit of chit-chat, as he supposedly messed with my hair, but was totally knocked sideways when I uttered some immortal lines that I had been mulling over in my head. These were, 'Anton, I said Madonna, not Maradona!' At this, Anton just gave one of his weird repetitive belly laughs that sounds a bit like a hyena and even the cameraman was laughing. We had to do several takes before we got the perfect facial expressions on footie-mad hairdresser and victim.

The rest of the filming was a hoot. I had to join in with a load of accumulated customers who were all sitting under fixed hairdryers and then do the Mexican wave from under them! The salon owner's son-in-law had shaved his head and dyed it in the colours of the England flag and my secretary, who I had taken along, pretended to ask for an appointment with Anton, only to find every date on which there was an England match blocked off. It was a scream.

Now as I don't like seeing pics or footage of myself, I've never watched the programme that finally resulted, but it was apparently very funny and my Madonna/Maradona comment was very prominent within it. Unfortunately, the famous England band won the prize to the World Cup, rather than Anton, and it had to be said that they probably deserved it. At the end of the day though, it had been a really fun thing to do.

Around the same time, we had some new excitement of our own, in terms of the opening of our own design studio, Thoughtfox Design. Although I had employed a designer for a few years, they had always worked solely on Catapult projects. Now, we had the opportunity to take another unit at Marsh Mill, Thornton Cleveleys, and make it a design and photocopying service for anyone. I bought a horrendously expensive top-of-the-range Canon copier and had the new unit redecorated and fitted with counter, shelves and other features. I then took the decision to give it a good launch by hiring artist, Tony Hart, renowned for his Vision On TV series and its famous 'Gallery'.

Tony visited us in May 2002, having been driven up from his home in the south by his friend and assistant. We also had a jazz band playing in the Marsh Mill Square on the day and had various competitions running too, with Tony Hart signed art kits and other prizes on offer.

The day was gloriously sunny and we had invited various guests, including Primary Direct and our now fully adopted son, Nigel. We had arranged drinks and canapés in local restaurant 'Twelve', also on the complex, and had different offers running.

Tony opened the shop in a marvellous way, attracting a crowd as he sat and drew different caricatures on the spot. We even had 'Vision On' music playing. A generation who had grown up with Tony Hart really loved it.

In the midst of all of this, my father, my son, Nigel and my cousin Howard, all decided to take themselves off on a tour of Marsh Mill itself, going right to the top of the windmill and finding out all about its workings. They were gone for what seemed like hours, but eventually returned in a bit of a panic, as Nigel had suddenly remembered he needed to read the early evening news back in Manchester! He dashed off at about the same time as Primary Direct, who said that he was stuck with them in traffic and that they could not believe that he did actually appear reading the news that evening. One can only presume he was wearing his shorts below the camera level and his suit above it!

May 2002 also allowed my Primary account manager and I to celebrate a massive achievement on behalf of Primary Direct. The independent Presswatch service, which evaluated financial services sector coverage month by month, put Primary Direct at the very top of the league table for May 2001 with a massive 18 pieces of personal financial coverage in just the one month. For a company of Primary Direct's size and budget, going head-to-head with big boys within this league table, such as all the major banks and building societies in the country and their massive marketing spend, this was incredible. It just demonstrated how our passion, ideas and contacts were continuously allowing our client to box above its weight.

Strange as it may seem, it was only in 2002 that Catapult got a website. Looking back, it was a very simple site, featuring pictures of the offices and a moody image of a catapult about to be fired on the home page, with the main colours used on the site being our brand's red, grey / black and white. We were able to upload press releases to a media centre and update our awards page – a real bonus as it turned out, as we were continuously winning awards.

We were also doing well on the account side, winning the business of BNFL's enterprise start-up scheme, Primary Direct Motor, a garden centre near Southport and a contract to promote various motorcycle shows – the National Motorcycle Show and Streetfighters being just two of them. To promote the latter, four of us headed to the Raceways motorcycle shop in Fleetwood and had our photos taken sitting on superbikes.

The final big thing of 2002 was the Holker Garden Festival, due to be staged again, having not taken place in 2001 due to foot-and-mouth. We recognised the real importance of re-launching the Festival and directed all of our attention to this, using a stunning magnolia image, which Holker had in its archives, to act as the symbol for what we called our 'Rebirth of a Festival' campaign.

The magnolia was used on special labels stuck on to envelopes carrying press information, on postcards and on a stunning press pack folder. It was decided that the strategy should be to take the Festival to London and to invite gardening editors to a press briefing in a London venue. I wrote a script for a film to showcase the Festival and also suggested we get an up-and-coming gardening celebrity to be the face of the 2002 Festival. I suggested Kim Wilde who, to me, was still the young girl dancing around in a stripy top singing 'Kids in America', but who now had a new career as a keen gardener and presenter. She was fresh, vibrant and everything the Festival needed to be that year.

We did all we could to generate exposure in national glossy magazines and created interesting photo calls, including one with a child in a flower headdress emerging from a massive pot. Advance ticket sales soared and we generated £121,000 worth of press coverage.

Simultaneously, we were pulling out all the stops for Bennetts and Primary Direct. Bennetts had decided to sponsor a Driving Standards Agency motorcycle safety video called 'What If?' and were struggling to know how to maximise this sponsorship. I suggested that we make motorcycle safety the focus of most of the PR for the year and pitched the idea of a motorcycle safety guide that could support the messages of 'What If?' which was all about hazard awareness and judging which scenarios could prove dangerous if not handled with caution.

To get this going, I conducted hours of desk research and then collated all information and drew out interesting and engaging snippets that could be presented in different ways within a 16-page, A5 handy guide, which was beautifully designed and illustrated. We launched this, with the support of Transport for London and the Metropolitan Police, at a motorcycle exhibition at ExCel in London.

As usual, the International Motorcycle Show at the NEC in November 2001 had been a big PR platform for us. We had liaised with the British Motorcyclists Federation to find an issue that was a hot potato and found that topic to be tinted visors and whether or not they should be allowed on helmets. This became the theme of our 'Lift the Lid' campaign, which we took to the NEC – we even had press packs carrying a helmet design on the folder front, with tinted opaque film in a cut out that represented the visor. Somehow, our press packs always stood out more than any other organisation's on the shelves of the show press office.

With a lot of campaigning, we managed to get 2700 motorcyclists to sign a tinted visors petition, which forced the Government to then publish research into the safety of tinted visors, which they had been refusing to make public. Another coup.

When we then commissioned research among both motorists and motorcyclists, to examine the perceptions that each held of each other and to assess how these might impact on safety on the roads, we began to bridge a void between the two sets of road users. I called this strand of activity 'Knowing Me, Knowing You', but did stop short of adding 'Aha' to the end!

But while all of this was very nice and worthy, there was one stand out moment in the promotion of Bennetts in 2002 that blew everything else out of the water. Va va voom hit the Catapult office the moment we heard that Bennetts had come to an arrangement to support a new stunt team comprising non other than the legend that is Eddie Kidd and his new display partner, Jason Finn. When we heard that Eddie would be coming to the Bennetts stand at the NEC, our mouths just dropped open.

There are probably relatively few people within the world of motorcycling that are household names, but Eddie Kidd is certainly one of them. Jason Finn was less well known, but in 2002 held the world-record for jumping over the greatest number of people laying down in a line – 23 in all – with this feat being achieved from a standing start. We thought that pretty damned impressive.

We were just embarking on a new campaign called 'Stop the Stripping', which was one of my personal favourites. I had thrown myself into still more desk research into the topic of motorcycle theft and discovered the huge need for motorcycle manufacturers, particularly Japanese ones, to apply security marking to various different parts of a motorbike, to prevent them being stolen (often to order) and then broken down so that different parts could be sold on. We made a play on the title of this campaign, by getting a Page 3 model to be the face of it, so the predominantly male audience would stop and take note of the word 'stripping', if nothing else!

To our great joy, we were told Eddie and Jason would be willing to officially launch this campaign on what was the biggest Bennetts stand we had ever had at the NEC and a far cry from the shoebox we started out with in year one.

I was really nervous about meeting Eddie, as I had always followed his career and thought him a legend, shedding more than a few tears when he suffered his horrific crash in 1996 at the Bulldog Bash. On that day, he had landed his jump, but his chin hit the petrol tank and he lost consciousness, resulting in injuries that doctors felt could leave him in a coma for 10 years. He regained consciousness in 3 months.

I wasn't sure how I would react when seeing this hero in his wheelchair, but found that it was a moment that I enjoyed sharing with him, as I could see the pleasure that he derived from being back at the heart of the motorcycling world. I have handled hundreds of press events in my time, but I have never seen so many cameras pop up and members of the public rush to get a picture of their hero as they did when Eddie Kidd arrived on the Bennetts stand. I could almost feel a wall of human emotion washing over us as people whispered his name, as if they were in the presence of a God and, to them, they were.

For some reason, Eddie wanted to talk to me and I wasn't going to miss the opportunity to do so. He kept grabbing my hand and telling me that he would be back on a bike very soon and there was going to be no stopping him. I could see the passion in his eyes, as he kept repeating this over and over again, though deep in my heart, I knew that this probably wasn't going to happen, at least not in the time-frame that Eddie had set himself. His language was somewhat colourful, with lots of swear words interspersed with what he explained to me, but it just added to the aura that he had, despite being confined to his wheelchair and having various physical and mental barriers to overcome.

Suddenly he decided that he wanted to have a picture taken with my account manager and I. We happily went to stand beside him, but he slapped his knees and insisted – and I mean insisted – that we both perch on there for the purposes of the photo. We looked to Jason Finn for guidance and he said it was what Eddie wanted, so we should do it. This counts as one of the proudest moments of my life. Forget all the awards and the accolades, I have sat on the knee of a man who took on Evil Knievel and triumphed, a man who was a stunt double for Timothy Dalton in 'The Living Daylights' and a hero who once jumped over the Great Wall of China on a motorbike. That's something to boast about. Furthermore, he shared his dream with me, which is even more precious.

While it was very much business as usual on the Bennetts account, other than this marvellous encounter, it was anything but on Primary's. The repercussions of 9/11 were being felt in the travel insurance world, with holidaymakers shunning the USA as a destination and so not buying the annual policies they might have bought for that destination. The PR campaign's focus had to switch away from the USA market completely, focusing on niche marketing of niche products launched by Primary Direct at this time, as well as European cover only.

Consequently, we found ourselves promoting a new Primary Active policy for the sports fanatic travelling overseas, a low-budget policy called Essentials, which was definitely no-frills and niche products such as travel insurance policy for golfers.

As usual, we did all sorts of creative and innovative things with these product launches, even creating a new social grouping within the world of travel, which I christened YASHMACS – Young, Affluent, Sports-mad, Holiday Makers And Committed Skiers! The press pack to launch this concept was designed around a scuba diver and the launch was supported with the heavy selling in of competitions in key sports titles.

Out of adversity comes triumph and we found ourselves getting the number one ranking in Presswatch in March 2002 for the first time ever for Primary Direct, which was truly amazing given the size of the company and our available budget. Added to this, we got 2nd, 3rd and 5th position in other months! In fact, between September 2001 and July 2002, we generated 90 articles in national press for Primary Direct – an outstanding achievement. We were actually never lower than 23rd of 162 companies monitored in the financial services sector that year.

We went to the NW CIPR Awards that year hoping for greater success than in 2001 and we certainly got it. We had the second highest nominations total of any Northwest consultancy or in house department, despite our size. To celebrate that fact, I hired a stretch limo to drive us to Manchester. This beautiful white vehicle cruised around The Midland Hotel before dropping us off as if we were film stars attending a film premiere. I thought it was the touch of class we deserved and a great morale booster for the team. The champagne we sipped en route was pretty nice too!

We picked up an amazing four NW CIPR Awards – two Golds for the 'Rebirth of a Festival' campaign in the categories of 'Best Use of Photography and Design' and 'Low Budget PR Campaign' and a Silver for Primary Direct and another one for Bennetts; 'Think Ahead' campaign. The compere on the night actually said, 'You just can't buy those smiles' and that was very true.

By this point, our Catapult adopted agency song was 'Reach for the Stars' by S Club 7 and we certainly had. How we weren't agency of the year again was a mystery, but we'd gone to Manchester and picked up four awards once again, winning awards for four years in a row, so weren't going to complain too loudly! Also by this point, we had learned the vital lesson that the only way any of us could get through the morning after the night before was to head to the butty shop and bring back bacon and sausage baps, to be served from 10am onwards. Religiously though, no matter how bad I felt, I always made sure that I was first in the office the day after the awards and that all awards would be on the trophy cupboard by the time the others arrived! That's what being the boss is all about!

Chapter 17
ON A STICKY WICKET

Having triumphed again at the NW CIPR Awards, we had very little idea how challenging 2003 would turn out to be. The first events off the block were both In January and were the National Motorcycle Show at G-Mex, which we had been appointed to promote, and the Hi-Life Diners Club Awards.

We'd worked really hard to promote the National Motorcycle Show and had generated a lot of interest, as well as fabulous advance ticket sales. The day the show opened, we went down to G-Mex and had arranged for Granada TV to be down there, to get footage for the Friday evening regional news, which would then help boost attendance on the Saturday.

As it was, the tickets were flying out of the door anyway. There was a massive snaking queue outside of GMex, stretching quite a way up the street as the doors opened, with many motorcycle enthusiasts clamouring for tickets. We had to work our way through the queue to reach the little room set aside for the press office, which to our horror we discovered was situated right next door to a mobile burger van. The smell of burger fat wafted over us all day, leaving us feeling grubby, smelly and decidedly ratty.

Granada TV were heading our way at lunchtime and were ready to do an interview with the representative of the Mirror group, who backed the events. At the very last minute, this girl decided she didn't want to do the interview and my account manager also refused. Although I was feeling a little under the weather, which I put down to the burger issue, I had the embarrassment of having to talk to camera for around 7 minutes, explaining all about the show and why bikers should head to GMex.

When I got home that night, I saw the footage and thought I looked decidedly washed out. My friend Simon called just as I was running a bath, to satisfy the massive need to rid myself of the aroma of burgers, and said his father was very impressed with my interview! I thought that the bath would make me feel better, but to no avail.

The following day, we had a meeting with a potential client and we went to what proved a really difficult meeting. I was feeling worse and worse and, on the way back, did a very rare thing and told my account manager I was too ill to go into the office. I went straight upstairs and went to bed. I woke up about four hours later to find myself covered in spots and, to my horror, realised that I had chickenpox – my son having had it a couple of weeks before.

I had kept telling my mother that I had never had chickenpox as a child, but she kept insisting that I had, but had only had a few spots. I knew she was wrong, but there was no arguing with her. In any case, the evidence was now here. This was a real killer blow for me, as I am absolutely useless at being ill. I had to advise all employees of the new developments and arrange for documents to given to my parents, so that I didn't spread the pox to anyone else. The frustration of not being able to get into the office was killing me as much as the itchiness of the scabs was driving me mad.

Luckily, the scabs and contagion disappeared in time for me to attend the second Hi-Life Diners Club Awards, which had been ramped up somewhat from our first event at the Gaucho Grill. This time round, it was to be held at the Lowry Hotel in Manchester and the client wanted bigger and better celebrities – again, for no fee, but simply the love of the charity element to the night.

My account manager did a great job of hooking up with the Coronation Street press office, aided and abetted by our hyper-active photographer, Dave Nelson, who was now moving in paparazzi circles and in regular contact with Corrie stars that he had photographed before. The hook for getting Corrie to support the event came in the form of a donation to Christie Hospital in Manchester, to support cancer care. On that basis, several Corrie stars said they would attend the event, including 'Ken

Barlow', policewoman 'Emma Watts' and the real bad boy in the soap at the time, 'Aidan Critchley', boyfriend of Rosy Webster.

I encountered 'Aidan' in the bar and got on really well with him, laughing about his story line in the soap and what my mad hairdresser had told me to say to him about it. I hadn't realised this was attracting attention, but later learned that our photographer for the night had said he could have a field day starting a rumour with the tabloids!

At the event itself, I had agreed to sponsor the 'Best Overall Restaurant' Category and had taken guests along in the form of some employees, plus honorary adopted son, Nigel Jay. We were sharing a table with the late Anthony Wilson, who was the compere and wearing his famous long black coat. Luckily, I had taken my son's Manchester United autograph book along, which Anthony loved, being an avid Man Utd supporter himself. He almost wrote an essay in it when I handed it over, to the strains of Nigel whispering in my ear, 'Why does he always wear that black thing?'

The charity auction came along and up came the lot of the signed Manchester United football. My designer turned to be and said, 'Aren't you going to bid for it?' I replied that it wasn't worth it, as there were only a few names on it, to which he responded, 'That's why I signed it'.

I looked at his face and could see no sign of lying written on it. He, however, told me later that at this point he thought he was going to be sacked on the spot, as I looked completely devastated by the thought of the sanctity of a Man Utd ball being desecrated by a Scouse fan.

My reaction to him was, however, 'Oh my God, what did you sign it as?' to which I got the reply 'Giles'. Thinking about all the ramifications of what he had done and halfway towards a panic attack, all that then came out of my mouth was, 'Oh, so it could pass as Giggs then?' At this point, my designer said he just wanted to crack out laughing at my thought process, but I was too busy looking up at the stage, where Anthony Wilson was about to start the bidding and debating whether to run up and stop proceedings. Luckily, my Giggs comment had proved far too funny for him to keep inside and he did burst out laughing, admitting that it was all a lie. That was just as well, as the ball then went for £400 and ended up in the hands of my newly renewed acquaintance,

Raymond Blanc!

The other bizarre occurrence of the evening occurred when I declared that I was going to go. I was acting as chauffeur of my Dad's Ford Galaxy, so had driven my staff there. Prior to the event, I had also treated myself to a new handbag, which was actually quite a lethal weapon, being a metal purse on a very long metal chain, which weighed quite a bit and could inflict some serious damage in the wrong hands.

As I stepped away from my chair and took one step on to the dance floor, Nigel decided to 'sweep me up', as my staff put it, suddenly whizzing me around and around, to try to prevent me from leaving. As he spun me round, he also set the lethal metal handbag spinning through the air like the hammer and chain of an Olympic hammer thrower, much to the fright of everyone within about three feet of us, in serious danger of being decapitated. I was muttering, 'Put me down for God's sake', while Nigel was far too merrily telling me it was far too early for me to go. By the time he'd come to his senses, I was as disorientated as a competitor on 'Total Wipeout', who's just been treated to the Dizzy Dummies!

When the room began to come back into focus and the sickness died down, I seem to remember smoothing down my skirt and bidding Nigel a rather frosty goodbye! I remember the open mouths of the frightened people, (those who had had to flee the dance floor), finally re-closing and I tried, with as much dignity as was possible after this public display of what could well have been my knickers, to exit the room with the minimum of fuss!

I must have been in the mood for sponsoring things that year, as my next decision was to get involved with some grass-roots sport, by sponsoring Thornton Cleveleys Cricket Club, where my son was playing as a junior. He had brought a leaflet home, which highlighted different options and I arranged a meeting with club reps. Before I knew it, I was sponsoring the First X1, but also erecting signage at the ground, buying branded 'Bumsters' for fans to sit on, purchasing One Day International tickets and signed bats as prizes and staging photo calls.

We all threw ourselves into this sponsorship – quite literally, in fact, when we had our Investors In People photo taken at the ground. Some bright spark of a photographer thought it a great idea if we and our IIP mentor, all laid on the ground, pretty much on top of each other, as if all trying to grab the award. It is possibly the most unusual IIP picture ever taken!

This was a year of real transition for Catapult, which started with the news that Primary Direct's directors, Helen and Tim, were selling up and going into very early retirement in their early 30's! This was a huge blow. After six years of taking Primary Direct to the top, it hurt a lot, but I had a cartoon-based picture drawn up by the talented Ken Wignall, which depicted the key things we had done over the six years, from Christmas cake deliveries, to using their dogs for the purposes of the pet campaign. They seemingly loved this.

Bennetts had been in transition for a year. The owner, Michael Bennett, had sold out to the Budget Group and hung up his boots, sending me a lovely letter to thank me for all I had done. We then started travelling to meetings in Peterborough, which was a long haul from Thornton Cleveleys. We were very lucky, however, in that we were embraced by the new PR manager there and very much appreciated, even taking on PR for Budget as well as Bennetts. I wrote a PR guide that every branch in the Budget network could use as their PR bible and it was all going swimmingly, even if a little incident nearly upset the whole Catapult apple cart.

This was all down to Brewster the Bear and, in fact, they could have put that on my gravestone. We had taken to stopping off for a late lunch on the outskirts of Leicester, on the way back from Peterborough and, on this particular day, I opted for white fish, which I thought would be nice and healthy cod or haddock. It tasted fine and I thought no more of it, driving everyone back to base as normal.

At 3am the next morning, I woke itching from head to foot and was scarlet. Very quickly, I realised that I was not breathing properly and had no option but to wake my son, who was aged 10, asking him to call an ambulance. Luckily, I took some Piriton before the ambulance arrived and reckon it was this that saved me. I don't remember too much about the journey to hospital, other than the fact that they suddenly put me on oxygen. My son says he was terrified at this point, as they switched on the siren of the ambulance and put their foot down. We'd been unable to raise my parents before leaving, so nobody knew we were there. They rushed me into A&E and stuck drips into me to pump me full of hydrocortisone and more Piriton. We stayed there all night, with my son having to sit by me, until 8am, when someone got hold of my father.

I was taken into a ward for observation and eventually discharged. None of my employees had known where I was, so were really confused as to why I hadn't arrived at work. When they found out what had happened, I think they were horrified.

The moment I got out, I rang the pub and asked them what on earth the fish was. I was told it was Butterfish from the Pacific. I explained what had happened and they referred to an allergies manual that each pub had. I asked them if Butterfish happened to mention iodine. They went very quiet and then said that it does, in fact, have a high concentration of iodine.

Funnily enough, the next time we went to Brewster the Bear, there was a sign on the counter saying that the white fish dish was no longer available! Perhaps I've saved someone's life, though as an iodine sufferer, there's a peril lurking around every corner. It was very nearly the end of Catapult PR that day and a huge shock for everyone involved. After that, one of my account managers became an official taster at all buffets, to highlight if it was safe for me to delve into a pasta mix, a sandwich or a vol-au-vent! I felt like the Queen, who I believe also has her tasters and even a shoe-breaker-in. At least I didn't go that far!

Shortly after this, we learned that Bennetts' new marketing manager wished to award the PR account to an agency he had worked with previously. The whole thing was very cloak and dagger and we were asked to pitch, but got the sense that whatever we had said wouldn't have made a scrap of difference.

Something kept nagging at me and I kept telling my account managers I was sure there was something more to this than there appeared. They all kept insisting that I was imagining things. My employees had to eat their words, as when we failed to retain the account, I insisted on being told who had won it. I was rather sheepishly told by the client, by now not our original contact, that it was indeed my former agency. My gut feel is seldom wrong. .

Losing two key accounts in the same month was really ironic, as six years earlier, they had come on board in the same month. I knew this meant tough times ahead, as the problem with PR accounts is that they don't grow on trees and can take months, if not years, to acquire. I was desperate to think of any way of getting replacement business and income on board.

Luckily, an approach to other travel insurance companies resulted in take up from a really nice company in Bromley called Flexicover Direct. We travelled down to meet Ivan, the marketing manager, and the charming MD, Mansukh Ganatra, and hit if off with them immediately. The fee was never going to replace Primary's, but it was a move in the right direction and we sealed the deal with a lunch, with Mansukh insisting on driving us to the door of the restaurant, even though it was virtually just across the road from the office!

Later that year, we also temporarily replaced the Bennetts account, in part, with that of Bikesure in King's Lynn. The trouble with both of these accounts was, however, the distance away from our base in Thornton Cleveleys. As luck would have it, Blackpool Airport started a Ryanair service that flew to Stansted, so that's how we managed, flying down for peanuts and then hiring a car for a much greater amount of expenditure!

Trying to keep our chins up, we took advantage of one of the perks of our Cricket Club sponsorship – use of the cricket ground for a corporate day. I imagine that the Club thought that a sponsor would wish to do something conventional with this and just hold a limited overs' match with cucumber sandwiches served at the change of innings, but Catapult and I don't do conventional. Instead, we decided that our corporate day would be completely different from anything ever staged before, starting with the setting of a Mexican theme for a 'Mexican Cricket Party'.

This party basically went on for most of the day and evening, starting with the arrival of guests and the playing of Tequila Rounders! We had tried for ages to find some rounders bats, but were eventually successful and decided that the incentive for someone trying to run to fourth base should be the opportunity to swig some Tequila punch when they arrived there. My secretary, Lisa, after she had nearly burned the clubhouse down by putting some gluten-free bread in the microwave to warm up, made some marvellous, yet lethal punch, that was certainly required to keep spirits high, as the weather Gods were not at all kind and we were playing our Tequila Rounders on a soddened field, while all wearing sombreros and trying to appear sober.

We had decorated the place with cacti borrowed from Granada Studios, with Mexican flags and streamers and balloons too, while also making up snacks of guacamole and dips and cucumber sandwiches for the day's events. We had also hidden some green plastic crickets around the grounds for a 'Hunt the Jiminy' competition, as we had invited Cricket Club members to come along and join in the fun and thought it would amuse the kids.

Also on the agenda was 'The Good, the Bad and the Downright Ugly' fancy dress contest, for which we created special 'Wanted' posters, which hung around the clubhouse prior to the event taking place.

We arranged a Mexican-themed music quiz, had a Salsa dancer booked to give everyone a Salsa lesson and had a DJ for dancing in the evening. We had even hired a Bucking Bronco, but this never arrived, due to the weather.

Amazingly, we attracted clients and contacts from right across the country for this madcap day in the rain. Messrs Bensusan and O'Sullivan both travelled up from the south, so we knew the bar would be drunk dry, and we had all manner of other people, from my accountant and his wife and our web designers, to my parents and the ever-present Nigel! That in itself was a bit of a feat, because although Nigel had turned up to various days at the club when we'd had sponsor's rights, he'd always moaned (to the extent of creating prose) about the midges that thrived at the Skippool Creek-based ground and which could eat a man or woman to death even if wearing the stinkiest form of jungle juice or the highest quality Tea Tree Oil!

Personally, I was really glad he turned up, as the Catapult XI only managed a rounders score of 24 and Nigel was first in to bat for the 'Tourists'. I was bowling and got him caught and bowled first ball, much to my delight – and all without dislodging my sombrero from my head. A picture was taken at just the right time to show a really smug look on my face!

ON A STICKY WICKET

As the afternoon moved on, we had bandits of all shapes and sizes turning up in the quest for a prize in 'The Good, The Bad and The Ugly' contest, and by the time the music quiz came along, I was happily shaking my maracas and reading out the questions. I do believe my Tina Turner impersonation may have been acted out on the dance floor too!

By the time the last guests left that night – Messrs Bensusan and O'Sullivan naturally – there wasn't a chance of them walking in a straight line back to their accommodation of The Royal Oak! A former admin assistant, Rebecca, and I were the last to leave, having bid the bar staff farewell and thanks. They were rubbing their hands with glee at the size of our bar bill.

This may all sound like a truly crazy day spent in torrential rain – and it was – but the comments we received were amazing. As one guest wrote, 'Thank you for a fantastic day; I have been telling everyone how good it was. I got a laughing fit when we left and just had a great time'.

This was one of the highs of sponsoring the club, while creating Catapult awards for the juniors was a truly memorable one. These were for the child in each group that had progressed most during the year and I will never forget the faces of some of the younger ones when they received their reward.

A few months after the amazing corporate day, I went away on holiday to a place called Limone sul Garda, at the top end of Italy's largest lake. Apart from the fact that there was a stifling heatwave that year, that took everyone by surprise, I had a great time. On my return, I wrote to some Italian firms that I had come across during my trip, one being a firm called Ferrari, who made a brand of sparkling water that I particularly loved.

A few weeks after sending these letters off, I received a reply from Ferrari, which invited me to go and visit their champagne-producing factory in Trento, as their guest. I took the plunge and decided to take up the invitation, contacting the factory to explain when I would be visiting. I booked myself back into the Hotel Cristina in Limone and made arrangements for flights to Brescia, tacking this on to one of my visits to King's Lynn, when I would already be at Stansted anyway and able to board a plane to Italy as easily as one back to Blackpool.

In October 2003, I made the trip out to Italy and enjoyed my tour of the Ferrari factory. In the process, I also found myself a new 'friend', who worked in Limone, but who was actually Macedonian. At that point, I wasn't exactly sure where Macedonia was. I soon would!

Shortly after this, we had a real stroke of luck. For years, I had created really innovative new business mailings on various themes and suddenly, out of the blue, the PR manager from Yorkshire Building Society rang to say he had a brief for a financial services campaign and would like Catapult to take a look at it. This was music to my ears.

The campaign was for a Children's Treasure Bond – a means of saving money in a children's account so that the youngster had a little pot of savings to set them on their way in life.

We created various innovative ways of communicating the fact that the Treasure Bond was a fund that grew with the child, due to interest payments and we had an absolutely gorgeous giraffe height chart made that plotted the age of the child against the expected value of their fund by that year. It was one of the cutest things ever!

However, it was in November, when I was writing another press release about the Treasure Bond and how it grows with the child, that I sat at my desk and had a brainwave. I was actually writing that the Treasure Bond was a much more useful gift than a football shirt, which a child soon outgrows and which then becomes of little or no use and I started focusing on all these outgrown shirts and all of those that are ditched and regarded as 'uncool' because a player has left the club, or because a sponsor has changed and the shirt looks dated with a former sponsor's name on the shirt. The thought kept running though my head, 'Why don't we do something with all of these abandoned shirts?'

I did something then, that I'm not sure I do enough of now and that is speculating to accumulate. I knew there was no budget set aside to conduct the sort of campaign that I had in mind, but was so convinced of its value that I sat down and wrote a PR proposal for it anyway. My idea was to collect as many football shirts as we could, using the YBS branch network as collection points, and then donate them to a worthy cause. Given the strength of football allegiances in this country, I knew it had to be abroad and by now I also knew how poverty-stricken the

Former Yugoslav Republic of Macedonia was, given that it had been free of fighting in the Balkan Wars, but had found itself absorbing thousand upon thousand of refugees from other Balkan states. With no system of social security or Government support, that was a massive drain on its resources and poverty was rife.

Having taken this decision, I found it vindicated, as if by fate. YBS's head office is in Bradford and amazingly, without any prior knowledge of this whatsoever, we discovered that Bradford is twinned with Skopje, the capital of Macedonia. It was almost as if it was meant to be.

Armed with this knowledge, approaches were made to the British Council in Skopje, to see if they would be interested in the idea. As it happened, they were delighted, as their work in Macedonia was very much restricted to Skopje alone, with no real vehicle through which to run an out-reach programme in the rest of the country. Our shirts could help provide opportunities for greater involvement with Macedonian communities and we were told that British army transport systems could be used to get the shirts to Skopje.

With all of this additional information, I pitched the idea to the YBS marketing team, who loved the idea enough to take it to their Board and get additional funding for it. One of my favourite campaigns of all time 'Send Shirts to Skopje' was born.

For me, 'Send Shirts to Skopje' was a labour of love from first to last. My man in Italy couldn't speak more than a few words of English, but I had started learning Italian in September 2003 and somehow, with the help of translation services and trying to teach myself the past tense way before the class got around to it, I managed to make him understand what I was attempting to do. From what I could understand, he was pretty proud.

I wrote my first press release about the initiative prior to Christmas 2003, focusing on the line that had first entered my head at the start of this voyage, relating to the fact that many former Christmas presents of football shirts would now be redundant and laying dormant in cupboards and drawers with no real purpose whatsoever, when they could be bringing joy, or simply clothing, to someone in need. I issued this story to a variety of press, but naturally to the football press on dailies and nationals. Christmas came and, to my delight, during the Christmas holidays, Henry Winter on the Daily Telegraph rang me at home and asked me further questions. Before New Year, I had a piece in the Telegraph to get the ball rolling.

This article and others in regional titles, football magazines and a variety of other media started to bring footfall into YBS branches, as mums and sons, dads and lads, pals and gals, all encouraged each other to dive into their wardrobes and haul out that old shirt. They started to arrive direct at our office too, in all shapes and sizes, colours and hues, with everything from tiny little toddler shirts, to those for XL men.

Locally, we had a man donate a shirt that he had held on to for 40 years, which was an absolutely charming story and such a generous thing for him to do. The generosity of spirit that this campaign evoked was truly touching and really restored a lot of faith in human nature.

I drew up letters to send to all football clubs in the league and we started to see donations coming in from individual clubs. Sometimes they would just send us a new shirt, while at other times we would get shirts signed by an individual player, or sometimes the whole squad.

YBS branches started to report a major uplift in customer visits, which was a key objective, as getting someone into a branch and introducing them to its environment and its product lines was a major reason for setting them up as collection points.

This went on through January and, by then, I had issued an update release to urge more people to follow the lead of those who had already generously donated a shirt, but something was really starting to bother me. A voice in my head was saying that I needed to do something else, as I couldn't keep sending out an 'appeal' release.

I sat and let my mind wander, mulling this over in my head. The lucky part about all of this was, of course, that I had all my football sponsorship experience behind me, but that I also love football and always have done. Without this passion for the sport, I'm not sure I would have come up with the idea of the 'Send Shirts to Skopje Cup'!

This, in essence, was my version of the FA Cup and its goal was to tap into all those intense football rivalries that surround local derbies, or as

Arsene Wenger would say, a 'durby'. Using my knowledge of both geography and football teams, I worked my way around the country, identifying all the local derbies that could exist around the country in Round 1 of my 'Send Shirts to Skopje Cup'. Effectively, my competition's first round would have been a TV channel's dream, with passionate, do-or-die ties in every location imaginable, with fans urging their team on to victory, just to get one over on the team from over the other side of the tracks! The difference was that in my competition, the winning side would be the one whose fans donated more shirts than their arch-enemies. It was a numbers game and focused solely on shirt donations.

So on this basis, I had Blackpool playing Preston, Man Utd drawn against Manchester City, Everton v Liverpool and Chelsea v Fulham. The same formula occurred in every possible location and I wrote press releases to go out to each of these places, advising their local media about the need to gee up fans, to see who would win the battle and get through to the second round.

We also informed football clubs and the message really took root, with teams like Blackpool inviting us to attend training and get a publicity shot that might enable them to encourage Blackpool fans to out-do Preston supporters. The whole idea was simply capturing the imagination of the football world.

The FA Cup idea proved a massive success. Shirts started to pour into the branches and our offices once the gauntlet had been thrown down around the country and we had to build several large home removal boxes to house the shirts we were now amassing. Once the deadline for donations for round one had ended, we counted all the shirts and asked the branches for their figures and announced which teams had progressed to round two.

By now, YBS were really seeing the benefits of this campaign, to the extent that they asked a real football manager, Peter Jackson, of Huddersfield Town, if he would officially draw a round of the competition. Peter duly obliged, so we had still more momentum behind the campaign.

By now, two clear factors were beginning to emerge. The first was the absolute passion of the Scottish club, Raith Rovers, who desperately wished to win the cup overall, but who definitely wanted to win the Scottish cup that we had also had created. The reason for this was that they had a Macedonian player in their ranks, defender Goran Stanic, and he was acting as a sort of ambassador for their efforts in the contest. The club itself donated shirts, but was also really pushing the contest all it could and promoting heavily to its supporters.

The second trend related to what was going on at Rushden and Diamonds. There, they had a supporter who had first-hand knowledge of the situation in Macedonia. He rang me several times during the course of the campaign and advised that he had set up a display of photos and information about Macedonia at the club's ground, in order to inspire supporters to donate their shirts. This was truly impressive, but I never thought they stood a chance of winning the competition, given their size.

By the time we got to about the third or fourth round, we drew the names and found that Rushden and Diamonds had to play Chelsea. I wrote a press release about giant killers, pointing out how minnows could triumph, if they put heart and soul into what they were trying to achieve. Guess what – Rushden and Diamonds proved to be the giant killers that we all feel a secret affection for, unless they've knocked our own team out! Chelsea were dumped out of the cup and the road to glory was a lot smoother for Rushden and Diamonds now.

As things unravelled, Goran Stanic got more involved, writing us a message of support in Macedonian, which we had translated into English. We used this to start creating a noise amongst Macedonian media and allowed the British Council to use it for their own promotional purposes. Shirts kept rolling in and the postman looked more puzzled with each passing day, as he handed parcels over, done up with string, half ripped, protected with cardboard, or just stuffed into a large envelope.

We now had so many shirts in the Catapult office that we had to create extra storage space in the loft. The whole thing was just an outstanding success and as we headed towards the final, it was clear there were only going to be two winners – Rushden and Diamonds as the overall winner and Raith Rovers as the Scottish winners. Both were presented with trophies, to create the final wave of publicity for this Cup initiative.

Pride comes before a fall. Our pride came from knowing that we had collected a whopping 13,000+ shirts in total – an amazing achievement, as we were not Children in Need with the power of a TV programme behind us ... just Catapult PR. The fall came when the British Council turned round and said they could no longer get the army to take the shirts out to Skopje.

The day that I received this news, I was completely devastated. I thought that all our efforts could have been in vain. I tried to look up former contacts from my freight forwarding days, but it was clear they would have to put the idea to their Board of Directors and it could take months to get a decision as to whether they could send a consignment to Macedonia as part of their CSR activity.

I had to go to my Italian class that night and was, by now, in year 2 and sitting next to a pilot. He was a kind, mature chap and asked me if I was OK, as I didn't seem my usual chirpy self. I told him the whole sorry tale and he instantly said, 'Leave it with me; I'll see what the RAF can do'. I was completely taken aback by this, but he was true to his word and contacted me the next day to say that it was all very hush hush, but if we could get the shirts to the local airbase, they could probably be flown out to Macedonia, en route for some other destination in which operations were taking place.

We now didn't have long to get the shirts packed up and they had to be sorted into different sizes, teams and colours, to suit what the British Council wished to do with them. I had to think on my feet here, as this needed a massive amount of manpower. One of the chaps who worked at my web design company was heavily involved in his local church, so I asked him whether there was any chance of getting assistance from the people there. My pleas did not fall on deaf ears – I was told that the youth group would donate its time on a Saturday, if we could get the shirts down to their Methodist Church in Cleveleys.

Therein lay the issue. We couldn't get the shirts out of the loft much before the Saturday as we would have no floor space, I couldn't get all staff to assist and once we got a box down, we had to carry it down the stairs, out of the front door and a good 100 yards to where I had arranged for a friend's van to wait. All morning and right into the early afternoon, the Marsh Mill team and our client from YBS were carting shirts out to the van and, for most of the day, the van was driving back and forth to the church. The youth group leader kept ringing to ask for more shirts, without seemingly realising what a nightmare we were having at our end.

To make matters worse, the British Council had uncovered a young Macedonian film maker, who they had sent over to the UK to film this exercise taking place. By the time the Marsh Mill team finally got to the church to assist with packing, it was panic stations, as we had a house removal team turning up at 5pm to take the shirts to a warehouse. We were all literally sorting shirts, stuffing them in boxes, grappling with packing tape and scissors, as fast as humanly possible, apart from her. She occasionally got up and stuck her camera up someone's nostril for the odd 30 seconds, but apart from that sat on her chair making no attempt whatsoever to assist. It was clearly beneath her.

This became more and more irritating as the deadline loomed and it really looked like we were going to miss it. It really was like a 'Challenge Anneka' moment, with the clock ticking down and hundreds of shirts still not packed. All the kids, my son, my account manager and anyone we could collar were frantically trying to get everything packed up. We made it by the skin of our teeth. Everyone sank to their knees giving thanks to God that we'd managed it, apart that is from one person, who seemed to have let the whole high adrenaline moment pass her and her video camera by.

She was focused on more lofty ambitions, as we had arranged for her to interview Goran Stanic. She had to get to Edinburgh on the Monday and my account manager and I were heading up to Moffat that day to arrange for a launch there. We foolishly offered to give her a lift to Lockerbie station, from where she could get a train to Edinburgh.

For the whole of that journey, trying to get any conversation out of her was like pulling teeth. I did my best: my account manager tried to be jolly in his usual affable way, but nothing worked. In fact, between Blackpool and Cumbria she hardly responded at all, though she could speak English perfectly well. It was only five-minutes after crossing the Cumbrian border that we realised she had the capacity to converse, when she uttered the words, 'I like the architecture here; it is not poor like in

Blackpool'.

I have never been so relieved to have someone leave my car as I was at this point. We sped away from Lockerbie station just in case she decided that she'd forgotten something. The utter relief that we then felt on the rest of the journey to Moffat was just immense.

A short time after this, we got the call-up from my pilot friend and were told to get the boxes transferred to the airfield. This was truly a boy's own mission and so I sent two of the boys. They left as lads and returned as men, describing the fun they had had loading the belly of a Hercules with our boxes of shirts. They even had a photo to prove it, both striking a real 'Top Gun' pose for the cameras.

So, after all the trials and tribulations, trophies and minnows triumphs, our 13,000 shirts reached Skopje – something I myself still hadn't done.

When it came round to the PR Awards of 2004, the 'Send Shirts to Skopje' campaign won a Silver Award for 'Best PR Value'. Personally, however, I think it was potentially the best of all my campaigns over the years and only suffered because of its timing and how that fit into the awards' dates criteria of when campaigns had to have been conducted, in order to be eligible. We had to enter the awards before any of the packing and flying out to Macedonia had been arranged: had we mentioned that we had a Hercules at out disposal, I am sure the 'Best Value' accolade might have been upgraded to a Gold!!!

News of this exhilarating campaign makes it sound as though 2004 was a fabulous year. The YBS campaign apart, it was anything but. By this point, we were trying to bring in accounts to fill some of the void left by Primary and Bennetts. As a result, we seemed to attract a series of clients who were, to put it mildly, a lot of trouble and who left us with a lot of bad debt. Added to this, some of my best account handlers left, for various reasons, leaving me with younger and less committed employees. This was a bad mix of circumstances and one that we had managed to avoid up until this point in time. Undoubtedly, 2004 was a watershed year.

The bad luck started really as part of our promotion of the Hi-Life

Diners Club. Through that, one of my account managers somehow had contact with a man who had developed a range of wines for the Indian market. He asked us to go and see him about PR and we duly travelled to his office on the outskirts of Manchester.

With the benefit of hindsight, and it's been said that we all have 20/20 vision when it comes to that, I should have got up and left the room half-way through that meeting. Instead, I sat there and listened to this man tell me how it would be beneficial for Catapult to work on a big brand like his and it would give my consultancy some profile. I had to bite my tongue, as I wanted to point out that names like YBS, CIS and BNFL were hardly small names. The condescending nature of the conversation really got to me, but I didn't want to rock the boat too much.

His big plan was to not only have the PR exposure from press releases, which we started work on immediately, but to also stage restaurant awards, with entrants being those eateries that stocked his wines. He wanted a series of regional events and then a grand final. He asked us to source venues across the country and put together an awards event action plan. Foolishly, I did, as I knew that several of my staff were very keen to get involved with event planning and would relish this brief.

These keen wannabe event planners spent days pulling together quotes and details for venues around the country, for staging and presentation equipment, food and drink, video production and much more. All of this was compiled and presented to the client.

Given that he had been so keen to push this idea forward, there seemed to be very little attention paid to the document. He said I could go ahead and book some venues, but then moved on to the sale of his wines. He said that he wanted to offer us a sales patch, in which we would recruit restaurants and generate sales within them and then earn commissions on those sales. Our patch would cover the Fylde Coast, including Blackpool, and Preston. He said this was a gift to me, as I was like his sister!

At this time, I was so keen to generate income by whatever means possible that there seemed no harm in giving it a go. That was fatal mistake number one.

By this point in time, I had embarked on another project that I thought would be a way of utilising our motorcycle sector experience to good effect. The idea came to me while sitting in a café in Knott End, near Fleetwood, where lots of motorcyclists were calling in for cooked breakfasts. Part of our work for Bennetts had concentrated on anti-biker sentiments and prejudice against those who turned up in leathers and helmet. It occurred to me that we should create the first guide that would tell bikers where they could call in, around the country, and find a warm welcome. The idea of the BUG Guide was born in my head – Britain's Ultimate Guide to Biker-Friendly Stop-Offs.

This guide was destined to be unique in the biking world and it received massive praise in the bike press, but was, undoubtedly, a labour of love rather than a moneymaking exercise. It had to be financed through selling advertising space and that necessitated taking on telesales people and therein lies a tale in itself. A variety of telesales people came, stayed a couple of weeks and left or, in some cases, went out at lunchtime and never came back. One threw a strange turn in the middle of the office, terrifying us all to death, while another came out with the classic line, when asked to do something, 'The last thing Jane wants me to do is wade in with my size 9s and f*** it up!'

We had them all. Colourful characters, odd personalities, disreputable people, others with the inability to wash their own clothes and someone who left a syringe behind them when they left! The most colourful was undoubtedly George – a Greek-American who was an award winning cocktail bar attendant. He amused me greatly with his slow drawl and almost genteel way of talking to me with a degree of respect that only an American could bring to the table.

George really amused everyone in one way or another, which is probably why we made him get into a role as a bike thief, to photograph him for a new campaign. He also delivered the ultimate dose of sarcasm to the local post-mistress, who had the look of Mo Mowlam and a terrible attitude towards her customers. When she tutted at George putting a pile of post on the counter, he answered in his American drawl, 'Hey, sorry man, am I obscuring the light or something. Let me move man and give you some rays'. She was not amused.

The fact that we had this 'sales team' of sorts on the books meant that the wines sales patch idea wasn't too bad a concept at face value. I went out touring various restaurants with one of the guys that we had at the time. We visited a variety of different Indian restaurants together, with some but limited success, but we did get a few orders.

In the meantime, our events planning for the wine awards was getting signs of agreement from the client and I was being asked to book venues and pay deposits. Luckily, I refused to do so and insisted that the deposits come from the client. They never did.

Other PR work was being carried out, however, and we gave the company a free cover advert on our BUG guide, as well as an advert inside.

Invoices were raised and not paid and invoice chasing produced nothing. Two sales guys went out on 'our patch' and discovered that other reps had already been in there to sell wine. They came back angry and full of warnings. When asked about it, the owner of the company fudged and gave no clear answers.

After several months of working on this account, it became clear we were not going to get any payment without taking Court action. Consequently we resorted to that and a solicitor rang up to request that we go to discuss the issue before the Court hearing. An undertaking was signed that stated that his client would settle out of Court and that the solicitor would ensure that this happened. We never received a penny and are still, to this day, owed thousands, though the boss of this outfit has spoken at London conferences about how to run a company!

Not being paid proved a common theme during this awful year and, again, we never received money awarded at court in some cases. We wouldn't have received any payment from another client, had I not taken drastic action. This company produced a speed trap detection device, which we promoted in motoring press and to national motoring editors. As a result of this, I managed to get the offer of a reader offer in the Daily Telegraph, which was a massive coup. The client had said we could get a commission on each unit sold, which we accepted in return for work on the account.

We knew that the offer was going well, because we kept getting calls into the office from people wanting to buy the device, who couldn't get through on the sales line, had tried all day and resorted to ringing us to see if they could place an order through us. The MD's son also told one of my account managers that he'd been flat out taking orders. When it came to asking how many units had been sold, however, we were told 'hardly any'.

We then innocently went along to a client meeting and I had a new employee, who had just started, called David. David was with me on work experience, because I had known his sister for a few years and she had asked if I could offer him any on-the-job work. I thought it would be a good thing if he came to the client meeting, to see how things ran. If only I had known what was to happen!

The moment we got there, the MD started going off at the deep end and saying he didn't want our services any more. The crux of his argument was that my account manager had sent a fax header saying she was attaching one page, but had actually sent two. The whole thing was absolutely ridiculous. It was clear that this was all tied up with the commission situation and a fabricated argument to get us out of the door before we asked for our earnings. In fact, after five minutes of ranting he told us to get out of the building and promptly left the room.

David looked white at what had gone on and my account manager confused and upset. They got to their feet. I don't know what came over me, but I sat firmly rooted to the seat, turned to my two companions and said, 'Sit down'. They looked baffled.

An employee told us that we should leave. Again, I don't know what came over me, but I said, 'I am not leaving this building until you pay me the money that I am owed and I will stay here all night if I have to'. The guy looked amazed and went scurrying off.

I wasn't budging. I was incensed by his cock and bull story about the fax header. I could tell that there was all sorts of kerfuffle going on outside the meeting room, as the message that I wasn't moving was relayed. The employee came back and said it would be best if I left. I again reiterated that I wasn't moving. Eventually, after about 20 minutes of me making my stance, the same employee came in waving a cheque. I took it, looked it over and got to my feet. 'Thank you', I said and ushered my employees out of the room. We'd been paid fee, if not commission. It was something. 'Are all client meetings like that?' asked David innocently!

By this point, I was doing whatever I could to find some reputable clients and joined a BNI group in Preston (a networking group that has the insane policy of meeting at 6am or 6.30am in the morning). I can't say I ever got much pleasure out of attending BNI, but I did meet a few really good people, some of whom became clients after we'd all left the group!

In the midst of the BUG edition 1 hassle, which had its ups and downs, mainly due to the telesales issues, we hit a big, immovable object in the form of a angry rhinoceros of a Zimbabwean running a hotel in Moffat, Scotland. One of my account managers, who had suddenly discovered a love of putting adverts together for those establishments advertising in BUG, had somehow managed to cock up the advert of the angry rhinoceros big-time, lifting details from another establishment in Scotland with the same name and not sending off a proof pre-publication. I wasn't in the office when the angry rhino rang up, but David and the at-fault account manager soon brought me the news, as they shook ever so slightly, saying that the angry rhino wanted me to call him. That filled me with dread, particularly as he referred to himself as an 'irritable bastard' – a point they kept re-iterating to me until it was well and truly made!

I made the call to him, in total fear and trepidation if the truth be known, and apologised profusely, suggesting that I travel to Moffat to see him and discuss how we could rectify matters on his behalf. This was a brave move on my part, but it did seem to appease him. I was filled with dread as I drove up to see him, but actually quickly realised that I liked him a hell of a lot. I encountered a short and squat, highly intelligent and articulate guy, who was clearly at home at the heart of a rugby scrum and who did have a touch of the rhinoceros about him, in a certain light!

His story was amazing, which was the first thing that engaged me, as he had given up a fabulous job in Zimbabwe in order to get his family out and keep them safe when political turmoil descended. They had stuck a pin in a map one night, to decide to which country they should flee. It ended up in Scotland and he decided that sounded OK, as every Scotsman he had ever met had a good sense of humour and he knew he liked a tot of whisky. This compelling story won me over and his lack of political correctness also amused me greatly, as he referred to women as 'birds' and uttered the odd expletive here and there, not to mention other references that the nanny state would no doubt frown upon. The fact that his father was still somewhere down a gold mine, unaware that his family were no longer around, also touched me, particularly when he described how his father – a man used to dropping molten metal on his skin without flinching – would die a slow death in any other environment.

Little did I know, at this time, that this man would become a friend and that his venue would become the site of a PR launch. All I knew was that I had walked into the lion's den and lived to tell the tale, sorting things out to his satisfaction and calming the rhino. When I walked back into the office and relayed this tale, I'm not sure the boys could believe that the 'irritable bastard' had proved relatively easy to tame.

On the plus side, I had started working for a local company that retailed the best Omega-3 products on the market, selling both fish oils and flax, plus lots of other products too. I started writing a monthly e-newsletter for them, which they loved, as I tried to make the subject matter lively, and which I really enjoyed creating each month.

It was this client who gave me reason to return to Moffat and once again engage with the 'irritable bastard'. The local client wanted to promote the world's healthiest porridge – porridge topped with one of their Omega-3 products – flax oil – and the moment I thought porridge, I naturally thought of the not-so-angry rhino. I rang him up and told him that I would like to launch this porridge at his hotel and he, having been into promotion himself in Zimbabwe, was well up for it.

The whole plan developed until we had a really attractive formula – inviting the whole of Moffat's rugby union team to come to the hotel for breakfast, to tuck in to their healthy porridge, serenaded with bagpipes, as if it were the mighty haggis! I took David up to Moffat with me and a serious case of man-love developed when he met the 'irritable bastard'. He found everything about him as appealing as I did, not to mention the fact that he found his steak and Guinness pies the best and biggest he'd ever tackled – something upon which the 'irritable bastard' prided himself with his two sizes of pie 'The Earl' and 'The Duke'.

We also had a fabulous stay and dinner at the hotel, to which the client invited a doctor that they worked with as an expert voice. He hailed from Glasgow and was a specialist on diet and nutrition. I will never forget his tale about shitake mushrooms and their beneficial impact on cancer. David will never forget the venison that he tucked into or the 'irritable bastard's' tale of the old woman from Moffat, who took him to task over his cranachan!

The launch itself attracted Border TV and we had a really lengthy piece of coverage on there, with interviews as well as footage of the rugby boys tucking in. It was great exposure for the 'irritable bastard' and also for the Omega-3 product. My rhino friend also found himself a new regular guest in the form of my client, who started making Moffat a regular stopping off place.

By the time we progressed to BUG edition 2, we had created BUG Awards for the best biker-friendly stop-offs in the country, as voted for by motorcyclists. The 'irritable bastard' liked a good competition and had thrown himself into attracting bikers, being a keen biker himself. He even devised special route maps for them and would head out into the Moffat square to talk to passing riders and tell them that they and their 'birds' were very welcome in his establishment. To my great pleasure, the 'irritable bastard' won the top prize in the BUG Awards. Also, somewhat ironically, when the account manager who had cocked up his advert decided he was leaving, to travel to Canada, I drove him, David and myself up to Moffat for the day, so that he could meet the rhino he'd irritated in person! This lad had a big appetite – he was even banned from the all-you-can-eat at Pizza Hut – but even he couldn't finish the 'irritable bastard's' steak and Guinness 'Duke' – a mouthful too far for even his stomach. I think the 'irritable bastard' took satisfaction from that!

Chapter 18

A WATERSHED

2004 was not a year I like to look back upon. The bad debt, the continuous chasing for money, the need to bring in more business to sustain a massive wage bill and a total lack of business being brought in by the design studio were draining resources with each passing month. Luckily, some employees decided to leave, for various reasons, and as they did, I took the decision not to replace them and assess what the impact on the business was. There was no perceivable difference at all and my workload remained constant, which made me wonder.

The aim at this point was to try to produce a European version of the BUG Guide and, with this in mind, I stumbled across a Peruvian chap who could speak Spanish. He started to come in at weekends, to start researching possible stop-offs in Spain. We liked to hear his tales of how guinea pigs are a delicacy in Peru and his other unique slants on life. I have always been renowned for attracting any nutter in the neighbourhood, wherever I go and, when relaying this fact to this Peruvian chap received the response, 'That's because you have the kind of face that people want to talk to!' I've often wished I didn't!

My romantic attachment in Italy had by now returned to live in Macedonia, to care for his sick mother. That fit in with my desire to discover more about our shirts' campaign at that end. I therefore took the rather bold step of flying out to Macedonia alone. I had no idea what I might encounter, but had read about the corruption, the Mafia and theft issues, so packed my possessions in the most battered old suitcase I possessed – the one I had taken to Sri Lanka many years before.

The flight was from Manchester to Milan, picking up another Al Italia flight at Malpensa, which would fly me to Skopje. The first part of the flight was absolutely fine, but I was somewhat taken aback to find that the flight to Skopje was on a tiny plane, seating roughly 30 or 40 and seemingly serving mainly business people flying into Macedonia with briefcases and a wheeled hand luggage bag for the hold. I feared I would never see my battered suitcase at the other end.

Out of the window, I saw Venice and then mile after mile of snow-covered mountains, above which we didn't seem to be flying that high. After my Isle of Man experience, I could only imagine what would happen if this tiny plane plummeted into the peaks.

I disembarked in Skopje and prayed I would see my suitcase emerge from the bowels of the Skopje carousel. Thankfully it did. I walked through to arrivals and was collected, as arranged. I was driven to the Holiday Inn in Skopje and was quite pleasantly surprised by how swish the hotel was and even more delighted to find an Irish bar next door. I was constantly advised to watch my bag, not leave it on a seat or table without my arm through a strap and be aware of thieves at all times – I began to appreciate that theft was an ever-present part of life here.

Exploration of the shopping arcade close to the hotel enabled me to discover the joys of eating pizza in Skopje, in a very trendy pizzeria overlooking one of the main squares. Skopje's architecture was somewhat concrete and 1960s, with dramatic Orthodox churches suddenly plonked in the middle of a soulless area of the city, but it was more than I expected.

After a night at the Holiday Inn, we headed to Gostivar.. I took up residence in what was described to me as a Muslim establishment, so I was advised to cover my neck and chest at all times. The hotel was surprisingly plush, with a big marble staircase and nice bar area in which they even served alcohol. The food wasn't too bad either, with nice salads and meat dishes, which I wouldn't order at home, but they sufficed.

Snow had fallen extremely heavily and the roads were impassable. There was an attempt to take me to a ski resort, at which wealthy Americans (ready to exploit the potential future riches of Macedonia) were creating a bit of a playground for themselves. There was a beautiful Swiss lodge type hotel in the resort, into which we trooped in search of room at the inn, but to no avail. The place was already swamped with dollars.

This meant staying on at the Muslim hotel, where the waiters and barmen viewed me rather suspiciously, as I was the only female guest. I had taken plenty of Sudoku puzzles to occupy me, so it was fine.

On the Sunday of my stay, I was taken down to Lake Ohrid, which I thought stunning and one of the most peaceful and serene places I have ever visited. It forms part of the border with Albania and I was constantly scouring the horizon wondering where the border might be. It was explained to me that, prior to the Balkans War, this had been a thriving resort, but now restaurants and hotels had mostly closed down and disappeared, leaving the beautiful lake with little more than a ghost town as its infrastructure. There was almost an eerie quality to the lake, as if communicating the calm before the storm.

The inevitable departure for the airport soon loomed, but I had no idea how painful this experience was going to be, as I had now seen my man for a few days – the first for a long time. It was actually a long, drawn-out farewell, which started with us walking over the bridge just outside the Holiday Inn, which led to the Turkish quarter in Skopje. Everything started to change in a cultural sense the further we progressed over the bridge, beginning with the craft stalls set up just over the water, which sold handmade slippers, Turkish style embroidered items, tablecloths and other paraphernalia. The cultural switch then intensified in a busy, bustling market area, surrounded by crammed alleyways and kids kicking footballs in the streets. It was as if we had gone through the wardrobe and ended up in Istanbul rather than Narnia.

Despite the cultural shock to the system, I really loved the vibe of the Turkish quarter, the aromas coming from the street-side eateries and the complete contrast to the somewhat static, concrete feel pervading the rest of Skopje. Here there was life rather than sterility and vibrancy rather than a rather Communist approach to everything, from filling in the hotel's check-in form, to ordering a drink.

We headed to a very small bar, which graced a corner of this old part of town. It had only three or four tables alongside the counter, from which a variety of deli style items seemed to be available and where the meat for shish kebabs was being carved. We received a signal to head up some rickety stairs and found a small dining area. I hadn't realised food had been ordered during the enquiry about where to sit, but there soon arrived some of the tastiest lamb and fresh tomatoes I have ever tasted. I was instructed to pile some salt on the plate and then sprinkle it on the tomatoes, something I had never done in my life. Luckily, these fresh tomatoes were sliced and the impact of the salt made my taste buds zing. Since then, I always do the salt trick when eating tomatoes, but they have never since tasted as good or as unique as in that little Turkish café.

The meal was my last taste of Skopje and we were soon at the airport and counting down the hours to my flight. The departure lounge at Skopje airport really wasn't too bad. There was a small café, in which to while away the hours until flights were called. Service was quite relaxed, no matter how fast or slow one drank one's coffee. It wasn't as if they were in a mad panic needing tables to be cleared and bums taken off seats. The driver, who had transported me us all over the place and who was a kind man, the kindness communicated through his eyes and gestures as he didn't speak a word of English or Italian, sat with us around the table as if it were the last supper. I was trying to hold my emotions in check and managing not too badly, until I was led across the departure lounge to check the departures board.

At this point, we found ourselves standing in the midst of men dressed in extravagantly rich costumes of all different hues and all distinctly zingari in nature, which to anyone in this country translates as something like 'gypsy', but which doesn't really explain the real ethnicity of these men with their wild hair, olive skin and dark brown eyes. They were all intensely studying the scenario between this blonde English girl and her Macedonian man, as it unfolded around them and between their guitars and gypsy violins; drum kit and mandolin.

My man in Macedonia started to cry, right there in front of all these piercing eyes and that was the thing that broke the camel's back for me and I too started to feel tears rolling down my face. I discovered at that moment in time that there is absolutely nothing worse than leaving someone behind that you cannot physically take with you, because the law will not allow it. It leaves you feeling completely helpless and numb, experiencing a terrible sense of injustice about a world that hands visas to a sullen filmmaker at the drop of a hat, but which will not allow someone, who has tried to go through the proper processes, to board a plane. All of his visa attempts had failed spectacularly.

Realising that the band of zingari men had for once stopped talking ten to the dozen, as they were all too intrigued by what was going on, I pulled myself together, picked up my suitcase and decided that if I didn't take myself through passport control at that point, I never would. I had to turn my back and walk away, which was an absolute killer, but I knew I couldn't look back, no matter what.

I found myself in a relatively deserted lounge, which was just as well, as it allowed me snivel into a tissue in my quiet corner. The peace and quiet of the lounge was then completely shattered as, to my horror, the whole troupe of zingari musicians piled in, not just waking everyone up with their colourful garb, but playing all their instruments at full volume too. Not content with just making an entrance, they decided to perform a full circuit of the departure lounge, playing their wild gypsy tunes and encouraging some of the departees to stand up and start clapping along. As the procession snaked its way around the lounge, it dawned on me that there was a strong possibility that these guys would be on my flight, as I didn't recall seeing many other flights on the board. My heart began to sink, recalling how small the plane out to Macedonia had been, but then I looked at all the instruments and paraphernalia that they were carrying with them and told myself that there was no way they could be on the tiny Al Italia plane.

I kept checking my watch, getting more and more het up, as it was clear that the flight would not depart on time. I knew the time available for getting the connecting flight at Malpensa was limited and, to cap it all, the instructions were that you had to go to a certain desk at Malpensa to find out the details of your connecting flight. All of these factors were weighing on my mind when a cheer went up. The Al Italia pilot, complete with smart blazer emblazoned with pips and stripes, had entered the departure lounge, much to everyone's relief. But rather than heading towards the gate and shooting down to the plane, he took himself off into the duty free shop, from which it took him a good 15 minutes to emerge.

The fact that he was then clearly carrying bottles of alcohol didn't really make anyone feel any better, but was greeted with cheers. Although I couldn't speak a word in the tongue of my fellow passengers, I could clearly see what they were all thinking!

Eventually, the flight was called and, as I expected, only about 25 people got to their feet – namely myself, a few waifs and strays and the whole of the zingari band. A man, who I had clearly identified as the ringleader of the group, started clapping and singing and setting the whole troupe off again with some gypsy melody. He kept winking and grinning at me and I think the words, 'Pray God in heaven he's not sitting next to me', sprang to mind.

It was only as we queued to get through the gate that I realised just how many instruments the band had – including a branded drum kit with their name on it. Many of the instruments had no case or protection at all and it crossed my mind that they must have had great faith in Al Italia to place their instruments in the hold in such a way that they wouldn't get damaged.

We trekked across the tarmac to board the plane and the few other passengers that were there handed over some baggage to the aircrew. I prayed someone had managed to get my battered suitcase on board, but had little faith in the efficiency of the system, being even less certain that there would now be time to transfer my case to the connecting flight from Malpensa.

As we reached the plane, the zingari chatter reached full volume and it was clear to me that the topic of conversation related to the instruments. I had no doubt that the baggage handlers were pointing out that instruments should be in cases and that they couldn't be held responsible for any damage. I walked up the steps and got on to the 'compact' plane, finding my window seat and looking back at the terminal to see if I could see any sign of a teary face at the window.

A hullabaloo shattered that thought as the musicians piled on to the plane and, to my total amazement, brought all their instruments and kit with them. Violins started to be pushed into lockers, mandolins under seats, flutes and smaller items into the seat pockets in front of them. I stared at this scene in stunned silence – which wasn't difficult given that

I had nobody with whom to converse. The only thing I couldn't see being brought into the cabin was the drum kit, but as that thought entered my head, a massive tuba was heading towards me, shoved up against my legs and then straddled by one of the gypsy musicians.

I know it's rude to stare, but I must have done. I remembered all those safety announcements about how important it is to keep the aisles and seat area free of obstacles, ensuring everything is stowed under the seat, or in the overhead locker. Clearly, the tuba couldn't be put in either of these places, but the mere fact that the flight crew were allowing it to completely block me in just left me incredulous. I kept telling myself that when the air hostess came to check the seatbelts had been done up, she would perhaps notice this man's instrument, which must have been a good five foot high and pretty damn wide too. My hopes were dashed. She gave a cursory glance at the seatbelts in a typically, 'I'm Italian and don't do red tape', kind of way and didn't seem to notice the massive obstruction pinning me into the corner!

The only silver lining I could derive from this situation was that the tuba owner seemed a fairly reserved member of the group. He seemed quite content just straddling his instrument and paying no attention to me at all. I was very happy that this was the case and felt almost smug. But then, the ringleader jumped out of his seat the moment the seatbelt sign went out and started raising a chorus on board the plane.

As he got everyone clapping, singing and stomping their feet, his wild eyes darted around the plane and alighted on me. Unfortunately, I made direct eye contact with him and knew I was in trouble. Sure enough, he came sauntering along, made a 'hop it' like finger gesture to the tuba owner, (who slid out of his seat and into the aisle without a word, leaving his tuba behind him), and then the leader became the cuckoo in the nest, plonking himself next to me. I was well and truly trapped!

Within seconds, he started to speak to me in pigeon English, giving me his name and asking me my name in the way that a lot of foreign people like to do. I answered politely, but with no real commitment in my voice to an on going dialogue. He didn't seem to pick up on that, firing question after question at me. In the end, I felt obliged to ask where they were going and was amazed to find that they were on a tour of Europe and would be heading to England in the coming weeks.

My big mistake was taking some sort of interest, because it presented him with the opportunity to take things to a new level of intimacy and he began asking me about the man in the departure lounge. I really didn't want to get into this conversation, which was making things ten times worse, but he kept pushing me until I had to give a few curt answers. This line of questioning then filled the conversation, which I had to have with him all the way to Malpensa. I was counting down the minutes to landing, partly to escape from tuba prison and mainly because I was so concerned about the connecting flight. There was no way of getting off the plane speedily when one had to negotiate a load of musical instruments barring every means of exit, so I found myself having to queue behind my inquisitor. Just before we exited the plane, he shook my hand and wished me well. Perhaps he wasn't too bad a sort underneath all the bravado and rabble rousing.

Somehow or other, I did manage to catch the connecting flight at Malpensa and my suitcase miraculously arrived with me back at Manchester. Thanks to the lunacy of the visa laws and the fact that Macedonia was not an EEC state, my man in Macedonia did not.

During 2005, one of the most unique characters I ever worked with entered my life. I was introduced to him by two guys at an advertising agency, with whom Catapult had tried to work in the past, but usually to no avail. This new client of theirs was a surgeon, who had, unusually, due to his own particular circumstances, set up his own branded business as a private surgeon. This was a bold and enterprising move for someone in his profession, but then I was to discover that he was a bold and very unusual man.

The first meeting I had with him was an evening affair, at his flat and with one of the guys from the advertising agency. I had some prior knowledge of this gentleman, as he had operated on my mother a few years before, but I had never met him. What greeted me was a chap of Caribbean descent, fairly dashing and wearing a casual white T-shirt and jeans – not at all the sort of figure I had expected to meet, or the sort of image I had held of a surgeon.

We sat around his dining table and discussed the situation with his

352

new company and the brand that he wished to create and promote. I was immediately captivated by his very unusual sense of humour and mannerisms and have to say that he was one of those people that you meet in life that you really do get hooked on, because they always have something unique to offer to you – good or bad.

Within weeks, he had fallen out with the advertising guys, feeling that they had ripped him off. By now, he was on the phone to me quite regularly and he invited me down to his flat in the daytime, to talk about the PR. On this occasion, I learned some key things about him: he loved hot cross buns, he couldn't get enough of maple syrup and he was a genius within his own world, but pretty hopeless at coping with the more mundane aspects of life.

His tale of falling out with the ad guys amused me greatly. 'Jane, let me tell you', he said in his heavy accent, with a touch of Michael Holding mixed with Dwight Yorke, 'There are only two types of men in this world who compliment you on your vase: they are either a pufta or they are after your money'. In this case, he had decided that it was the latter.

So somehow or other, I found myself becoming pretty much his marketing lynchpin. I wrote his advertorials, which he absolutely loved, telling me that I had a rhythm of writing that was lyrical. He said his patients brought the copy into the consulting room with them and could repeat back to him what it said and that it was of massive value to his business.

I quickly learned all about the type of surgery that he performed, swotting up on the terminology of the medical profession, the types of injury that could provoke a need for surgery of this kind and the various procedures that he could perform.

His tale of how he upset the hospital radiographers was another piece of sheer gold. He had trained in radiography, unlike most surgeons, and had pointed out to the radiographers that they were doing everything wrongly. The story goes that the radiographers were taking their X-rays from way too far away from the patient, causing the dangerous rays to be bouncing all round the room. His way of expressing his discontent about this was to say, 'For Christ sake man, you'z-a frying me balls!' The radiographers allegedly didn't take kindly to this!

Another classic piece of amusement came when he fell out with a secretary he felt to be a little dim. 'Jane', he said to me, in his deep, mumbling Caribbean voice, 'That woman will always be a lemon and will never be a mango'. One couldn't help but be fascinated by someone with such a turn of phrase.

Life was certainly never dull. When I told him that his advertising sign was much bigger than other people's, the reply came, 'That's because it's a West Indian sign!'

I would frequently be called by him at midnight or later, as he was an insomniac and would talk to his American web designers during the night, as that was their daytime. He seemed to assume he could do the same with me!

Invariably, whenever I went on holiday, he would ring me up – even though for weeks I had pre-prepped everything and told him that I would be unavailable while away. The most memorable example of this came when I was struggling to reverse back up a one-way street in Portugal, among non-amused market traders into whose midst I had arrived, while he was rabbiting on about some advert he had just decided to place on a whim!

He was a man that definitely polarised opinion. In his case, it was all black or all white, with nothing grey in between, but I wouldn't have been without him, purely for the pearls of wisdom that he could impart and the totally unpredictable things that he would do.

One of these was done to the psychological harm of a photographer we regularly used. He was asked to go down to the surgeon's hospital for an outdoor shoot, but was hauled into the operating theatre and ordered to take pictures throughout an operation. The poor man wasn't good with the sight of blood and had to be brought a stool – but he was still told he had to stay there until the end and capture the whole thing on camera. I took one look at the resulting photos and had to delegate any future dealings with them to my assistant. I was far too squeamish to even contemplate viewing them ever again. How the poor photographer coped, heaven only knows.

One day, the surgeon rang up in an absolute panic (which was typically the case no matter what) but on this particular occasion said that a photo of him wearing his face mask in theatre has led to his enemies telling patients that they thought he looked like a terrorist. From that point onward, we could no longer use that picture!

For me, however, the most classic example of his eccentric but addictive behaviour came when he rang me up, while lost in Cumbria and trying to make his way to Sellafield, asking me to guide him as he continued his journey. When I asked why on earth he was going to Sellafield, he said that his daughter's favourite TV character was Homer Simpson – who worked in a nuclear plant. You see, in his mind, everything made sense!

Our working relationship came to an end when a stranger arrived and said he had bought into the surgery business and no longer needed PR. After around two years of doing everything for my quixotic surgeon, I felt very sad that he never picked up the phone to do this himself. For once, I wouldn't have minded a 1am call!

When I look back on 2005, I will always remember it as the year that a little sunshine fell upon Catapult. The sunshine began around May time. By this point, there was only David and my Peruvian chap employed in the business, my secretary having left to have a baby. Out of the blue, I received an invitation to tender for the PR for the North West Farm Tourism Initiative.

Although we had done some tourism PR for festivals and I had worked for visitor attractions in my former life and handled some farming sector PR for Rural Insurance, part of the Primary Group, it wasn't something we majored in, as most of our experience had been formed in financial services' PR. Nevertheless, I put a response to the tender together, recognising that we really needed the money and some fee income through the door.

I wasn't over-confident of being called to pitch, so was delighted when we received the invitation to head to Windermere and present my thoughts to the NWFTI panel. I took David with me and off we set for Windermere, with our pitch documents in hand and a few answers up our sleeve to questions that we thought we might be asked.

At the time, Cumbria Tourism were based in a charming old house in Holly Road, Windermere, where we sat in what would have been the hall, I would imagine, waiting to be called into the presentation room. When we entered, we found three people around the table – the Cumbria Tourism PR officer, the NWFTI representative from Lancashire and the NWFTI project manager, who was heavily pregnant.

We began to pitch, crammed around a tiny table made even fussier by the addition of cups of tea and coffee. I really didn't sense that things were going too well, but tried to ride out the feeling that they weren't that interested in us and poured a load of passion into the pitch, as always. We reached the end of our presentation slides and the pregnant lady suddenly said to me, 'Haven't we met before?'

I was totally thrown by this, staring at her face and then moving down to her very big bump and left feeling as clueless as when I had started this visual voyage. 'I don't think so'. I said, still nonplussed.

'I'm sure we have', she said very defiantly. 'Weren't you at the opening of the Royal Armouries Museum in Leeds?' I almost fell off my chair at this, wondering how on earth she knew that and where she had been on the night. She wasn't letting go now she had me on the ropes.

'I was there with my friend', she continued. 'We'd both travelled up from Taunton, where I was the Tourism Officer'. My mind started to race to the opening event at the Royal Armouries, now trying to picture two women together. I had got as far as being outside, in the cold, watching a firework display, when she jumped in again.

'We asked you a few questions while we were watching the fireworks', she stated in a matter-of-fact way. At this point, an image of talking to two women outside appeared in my head in a sort of very nebulous way.

'Well, I was there', I said, not committing too much to what I remembered. To be honest, I was staggered that she should remember me at all!

Having gained this position of one-upmanship, she seemed very much in the driving seat for the rest of the pitch and the questioning didn't seem that positive, so I left feeling very down indeed, sure that there was no way we had won this account. David seemed to have been absolutely terrified throughout the whole ordeal, with great fear seeming to come over him whenever he talked to the pregnant project manager. I drove back dismissing any hope that I had held of picking up this account.

On this basis, I was simply amazed when I received a call to say that we had won the pitch. David seemed really chuffed that he had played a part in this and we were ecstatic at having brought a fairly sizeable bit of fee income on board. We were asked to travel to Windermere for an inception meeting with the project manager and her assistant.

At this meeting, everything became as clear as mud. Suddenly all sorts of random information was fired at us, in no really logical way and all we could do was to scribble down notes and hope that we could fathom it out when we got back to base. Added to all this confusion, there was a real atmosphere in the room and it was clear that the project manager didn't really like us that much and probably hadn't wanted to appoint us.

What we did leave with were some NWFTI projects to explore. The NWFTI was an initiative funded by the NWDA, to help farmers cope with the devastation of foot and mouth by diversifying into tourism. This could mean setting up a farm attraction, doing something in the sphere of equine tourism, opening a tea room, creating visitor accommodation, or getting involved with marketing farm fresh food. The initiative spanned Cumbria, Lancashire, Cheshire, Greater Manchester and Merseyside and a PR agency had been on board for the first year, but was now no longer retained. Our job was to start promoting individual businesses and funded schemes, making sure we drove visitor demand.

To this end, we left our first meeting armed with the names of some of the new businesses. One was the Lakeland Maize Maze, based in the South Lakes. Another was a new cross-country horse course in Endmoor just outside Kendal. The third was built around a tarn, being transformed into a nature reserve, particularly for birdlife.

To show how keen we were, we quickly arranged a day of visits to these businesses. This was the day we learned all about the geography of Cumbria and just how long it takes to get from one part of the county to another. We had set off fairly early, but what with not knowing how long to allocate each business for their facility visit and the slow, windy roads of Cumbria, we found ourselves way behind schedule practically from the word go.

The other things we learned to appreciate on this day were that the best way of getting anywhere with the promotion of the NWFTI was to park yourself at the kitchen table in the farmhouse, accept offers of tea, tuck into home baked cake graciously offered by our hospitable hosts and get into the mind of a farmer. I quickly changed the way I dressed to attend site visits, abandoning really formal suits and suddenly developing a penchant for dresses and nice cardigans, or smart jumpers with trousers. Wellington boots entered into my wardrobe for the first time for donkey's years and I had to start to really get acquainted with dogs again. Nearly every farm had one and they would always make a beeline for me, perhaps sensing that I was a dog lover who would pat them, stroke their ears and talk to them in a sympathetic way. Going home covered in dog hair, with muddy paw prints on the clothing and a filthy muck-strewn car became par for the course.

At the Maize Maze, we learned all about the hi-tech satellite-guided way in which a pattern would be cut out of the infant crop when it was just a few metres high. At the cross-country course, we discovered how difficult it could be to get some cross-country training in if you were a keen horse rider. At the bird reserve, we found that people could just wander past the farm window and take themselves down to the lake, with a seeming lack of commerciality about the whole thing. Having been taken into the hen huts, we also discovered just what a reek could stay with you all day once you'd been counting your chickens!

This was definitely a formative experience and one that paved the way for many site visits over the years of handling this PR account. Having visited these businesses, we fed back our news and started work.

I was pretty hooked on the idea of using satellite technology to carve out the maize maze, as there were very few examples of this type of attraction in the country at the time. I suggested that we invite TV down to film the process, as a teaser for what would be coming to the farm when the maize grew to its 8 or 9 feet in height. This scored an instant coup for us, as Border TV were keen to take up the offer and sent a crew down to the farm. David and I travelled up on the day and attended the filming, excited that our ideas were already taking root.

Unfortunately, our pregnant client was not so amused. She felt that her assistant should have been there to supervise, even though there was absolutely no need. She gave us a really hard time at our second client meeting, treating us like naughty children. David left the meeting seething and muttering under his breath!

The days were counting down to her maternity leave, but we had one more significant encounter before that. This was when she called a number of four and five star farms together for a presentation on a new concept on the cards called 'Luxury in a Farm'. This was to be a cluster group, which we would have to launch and promote, but at the time of this presentation, it wasn't looking hopeful that there would be enough farms to make a 'cluster'.

We attended and sat in the audience, a row in front of a farmer's wife, who never stopped knocking the idea and rubbishing everything very vociferously. Other farms then piped up and voiced their concerns about trying to target Londoners and folk from the south, while others then contradicted this view and said that was exactly what they wanted, as they were in self-catering and Londoners would make the journey to Cumbria, if they were then going to stay a week or a fortnight.

The whole thing was descending into near anarchy and the very pregnant project manager was looking very fatigued standing at the front of the room in a brightly coloured summer maternity dress and pink sandals. For some reason, I thought she needed rescuing, so I shot my hand up and asked a question that I knew would feed her a line to give an answer that would really make the room think about what was on offer. She almost smiled at me when I asked my question, picked up on what I wanted her to do and gave the answer I had wanted her to deliver. The room shut up and took notice.

I think this was a watershed in our relationship, even though she was off on maternity leave shortly after this. I think she had noted that I had shown great support and loyalty in asking my tactical question, though she never actually said this. It was definitely a turning point. David never understood why I bothered to come to her rescue!

A brand new category appeared in the NW Chartered Institute of Public Relations Awards in 2005 and it was that of 'Small PR Team'. We were most definitely that and though I debated the whole thing for ages, trying to decide whether being classified and boxed off as 'small' was a good thing or not, I decided that we might as well go for it.

I was absolutely delighted when we were short-listed for this award and David was over the moon. He had never attended a PR awards ceremony before, so he was instantly mulling over what to wear and deciding that he wanted to re-define 'black tie'. I left him to it, thinking that my days of worrying what my employees wore to these events – and goodness knows there had been some eye-openers – were well gone. In any case, I was more worried about what I would wear!

We decided that we ought to invite some guests and so I opted for the ever-present Nigel – by now almost a permanent fixture at any of our awards ceremonies – and the surgeon – who I thought would at least add some amusement. In actual fact, I was totally wrong about that and I discovered that he wasn't quite as social as I had imagined. Nigel on the other hand, as per, was life and soul of the party.

We were up against another agency for the title of 'Small PR Team' and I had no idea how we would be judged for this award. What I had hoped was that, once the awards started to be announced, David would be there to head up with me to collect any prize that might be coming our way. Ironically, having sat all through the dinner and the preamble, he had taken himself off to the bar or gents and was nowhere to be found. The compère was rattling through the awards at a rate of knots, as the timing of the event had slipped horrendously.

I studied my programme and could see that the 'Small PR Team' award was looming. David was still absent without permission and I was by now panicking. Nigel, himself now rather merry, slurred a sentence that I took to mean an offer of tracking down the employee I hadn't tagged and I virtually pushed him towards the door, encouraging him to scour the bar and bring him back at all costs – and very fast.

Thinking that Nigel would be a man on a mission given the urgency in my voice, I began to feel a little calmer, but with false hope. Our category came up on the screen and the small PR team was feeling very small indeed, comprising just one woman with a fear of falling flat on her arse while negotiating the stage steps. This was now a very real prospect given the unsteadiness she felt in her stilettos! I was so het up about having to fly solo that I almost overlooked the fact the compère was announcing Catapult as the winner. I did know, however, that there was no escaping having to go up to receive the award, so in my panic-stricken state, got to my feet and walked about three yards.

At that moment, my knight on a shining white charger – or rather employee in a brown jacket – came bursting through the door leading from the bar as if in slow-mo, his jacket flaring out as he positively sprinted towards a point that I would reach within a few seconds. Hot in pursuit came Nigel, doing a very good impersonation of a sheepdog that had just rounded up a wayward lamb. David met up with me down the centre aisle and, as if it had all been a very well planned albeit dramatic PR strategy, we headed up to the stage.

David was more than a little inebriated and was positively gushing about how brilliant it was to win this award, even while we were having the obligatory pictures taken and I was suffering my frozen gum look as I tried to smile. I then couldn't shut him up for the rest of the evening, which led to one of those episodes a little like the 'Mere Communications shove it up your arse incident. This time, however, it involved David talking to staff from another PR consultancy and telling one girl that I had taught her boss (my former assistant in my first agency job) absolutely everything that she knew about PR. Not for the first time at a PR awards event, I wanted the ground to swallow me up!

Nevertheless, we had another trophy in the cabinet and one of which David was truly proud, once he'd sobered up. Catapult had now not only been NW PR Consultancy of the Year (and runner-up twice) but the Small PR Team as well. In some ways, this lesser title meant more, as I could truly see how much it meant to my assistant. But then, isn't that often the case.

In the December of 2005, I returned to Macedonia. If my flight back from Skopje with the band of zingari had been eventful, this flight was to be even more memorable – for all the wrong reasons! I arrived at Manchester Airport early in the morning to find that the Al Italia flight to

Milan had been cancelled. All hell had broken loose around the Al Italia desk and very little help was being administered.

When it came to my turn to make a plea for help, I must have looked particularly distraught, because I was offered a lifeline that could get me out to Skopje. I was told to take myself off into another terminal, brandishing a voucher and head to the Lufthansa desk, to take a flight to Frankfurt, rather than Milan, and pick up a connecting flight there. This threw the cat among the pigeons somewhat, but I had no option. Sure enough, I found myself booked on to a flight to Frankfurt.

The first leg of this journey was really quite pleasant and then I was more than impressed with the facilities and size of Frankfurt's airport on arrival there. It was a pity that I couldn't buy any Italian books or magazines, but at least I was en route to my destination. I mooched around for a while, grabbed a bite to eat and then headed to the gate. I quietly sat myself down and took out something to do.

As I relaxed there, I increasingly realised that I was becoming the object of someone's attention. I would like to say that this was a handsome Adonis of a man, but unfortunately the person who couldn't take their eyes off me was a long, dark-haired woman in a fake fur. Every time I looked up, I found her staring at me, to the extent that, in the end, I shifted myself, after purporting to walk off and look at a board.

Luckily, the flight was called just after that, so I boarded and plonked myself down in my seat. The plane had relatively few passengers on board and was way bigger than the tiny Al Italia planes that I had flown on previously. This meant that seat allocations went out of the window and it was more a case of sit where you please. This was definitely the message that had filtered through to the head of my dark-haired, fur-coated 'friend', who suddenly left her seat and slumped into the one next to me. To say I was now on edge was an under-statement.

She started to talk to me in an accent that mixed Teutonic tones with a little Russian-style twist. At times, I couldn't make out a word she was saying to me, which may have been just as well. She tried various languages on me, but didn't speak Italian, so couldn't make any progress with me there. Instead, however, she started to resorting to silly gestures, to try to make herself understood. What with these and the odd word of

German that I understood, plus a little English here and there, I sort of deduced that she was going to meet family in Macedonia. I did my best not to reciprocate with any information that could lead to a prolonged conversation, desperately hoping that she would take herself back off to her original seat and leave me alone.

To try to make this point as tactfully as possible, I did what every girl should do in such circumstances and got my Sudoku book out. I started to ponder over the numbers, developing a wrinkled frown that was supposed to communicate sheer concentration, but instead of taking the hint and buggering off, she virtually stuck her head between my head and my book, grinning at me in a ridiculous fashion. At this point, I realised that there was going to be no shaking her off. The face that people 'want to talk to' had landed me in it once again!

Little did I know, but having her buzz around me like an annoying mosquito that you can't quite swat, was the least of my worries. We hit a spell of turbulence flying over the Alps and jolted around a little. It became a huge drama for my unwanted travelling companion. She suddenly started pulling faces like a child and simpering and acting scared, but in a totally unconvincing fashion. Now I'm not known for my ability to hide my feelings when I think someone is a complete fool and my face must have portrayed this, but still she carried on, with me staring at her as if she were the angel of death!

Having passed through one pocket of turbulence, I thought we were over the worst of her antics, but how wrong I was. My heart sank as I tried to sort out my Sudoku squares realising we'd hit another patch. The angel of death wasted no time in making the very most of this, grabbing hold of my arm, linking hers to it and cuddling up to my shoulder, on which she started to rest her head, while looking up at me like a child and simpering anew. I tried to shake her off, but to no avail. I again tried the 'get the hint, I'm doing my Sudoku' strategy but it was hopeless. Within seconds, I felt her squeezing one of my tits, which made me jolt upright and fix her with the most awful stare that I am sure would have turned anyone else into stone or a pillar of salt within seconds. I shook her off and semi turned my back on her, to signal rejection. A thought ran through my head that I should call the stewardess, but I didn't want the rest of the plane knowing that I'd found myself saddled with a randy lesbian.

She sulked like a child for a good half hour, until we started our descent into Skopje and we had some more unstable movement. She now began to act as if she had never flown before, with mannerisms worthy of Kate Bush in her 'Wuthering Heights' video. She over-dramatised every single expression on her face, clearly trying to signal to me that she was terrified. Her arm clamped around mine once again and she went in for a second grope. By now, I couldn't even be bothered to push her off, having virtually lost the will to live. I could see us descending rapidly towards Skopje and therefore realised that my ordeal was almost over. The minute we landed, I was out of my seat and grabbing my possessions, while she had to make her way back to her own seat to be re-united with hers. I knew this was my chance to try to get someone between us as we disembarked and succeeded. I could, however, hear her calling to me and doing what appeared to be inviting me to meet her mother. 'Fat chance of that', I thought!

On arrival in the airport, I couldn't see my welcome party anywhere. I rang and rang mobiles, but got no reply. By now, I was well and truly cheesed off and even my lesbian lover had departed, so I couldn't even bag a room at hers. Instead, I found myself surrounded by a ring of 'organised' taxi owners, all trying to take me to various hotels in Skopje. I kept reiterating that I didn't need a taxi and was waiting for someone. A very tall man, clearly the leader of the gang, took me to one side and started to probe as to what I was doing in Skopje. He said he would, 'look after me', if I needed to find somewhere to stay. This was almost as terrifying as my other option, knowing what I knew about all the Mafia links.

Eventually, my welcome party turned up, telling me they had been cautioned at a motorway patrol for not having the right papers with them. I was rapidly realising what a very communistic country this was. I was ushered out into the snow, which had fallen even more heavily than the last time I had visited. Many villages could not be reached and snow ploughs were out everywhere, including one belonging to DHL, who were nobly trying to maintain a normal service.

We headed down to Gostivar and checked in to the hotel I had visited previously, with all the rather strange Muslim waiters who did good impersonations of zombies, speaking almost never, having few facial expressions and certainly not providing even a shred of evidence that they welcomed this westernised woman with her blonde hair and blue eyes.

Over dinner, I explained my ordeal on the plane, which caused, on the one hand, great amusement and on the other consternation, as same sex partnerships are not legal in Macedonia.

I had kept this trip as brief as possible, as appeal of Macedonia was most definitely waning. This left little time for seeing much, other than tall walls of snow that had drifted by the roadsides. I also managed to see the inside of a Macedonian supermarket, which was an experience similar to Lidl, but ten times worse, and was then taken up into a tiny mountain village, approachable only by the iciest of roads, to have lunch with some of the family.

This actually comprised only men – a cousin, a brother-in-law, an English-speaking nephew and a few other faces, whose familial relationship to the others I knew not. The brother-in-law was quite interesting as he was an 'imbianchino' – or painter and decorator, apparently working in Italy where the only colour he was ever asked to paint in was white!

We all piled into an otherwise deserted mountain log cabin, which was the 'acclaimed' restaurant that I had been told I had to experience. The assembled men folk all studied the menu and the nephew asked me if I liked a dish that he said was chicken. I replied that if it was chicken that would do fine and awaited my delicious meal with anticipation.

What actually arrived at the table, however, was a totally indescribable white modge on a plate that lacked colour, presentation and pizzazz. It would have got precisely nowhere on any of the TV cookery programmes. Unfortunately, it was as bland as it looked and completely tasteless and devoid of anything pleasant in terms of texture. I hate to be impolite and leave food, but there was absolutely no way I could eat any of this having tasted my first few forkfuls. I pushed it around the plate, trying to summon up some enthusiasm for this Macedonian bush tucker trial, but simply could not contemplate another mouthful.

'Jane, this is not chicken?' asked the nephew, with a furrowed brow and worried look as he observed me playing with my food rather than purring over it.

'No', I replied, 'this is definitely not chicken!'

I was keen to keep my visit to Macedonia short, but hadn't legislated for the fact that an accident could befall me. The hotel had a big marble staircase surrounded by massive mirrors, giving it quite a luxurious feel considering that it was little more than a motel with a nice restaurant. Going down the stairs in the morning, a chambermaid was heading up the flight carrying a load of bed linen. This meant manoeuvring out of her way as she struggled with the sheets, but her reflection was everywhere in the mirrors and I'm sure that was what threw me as I tried to clear a path for her. Suddenly, I fell down about five of the marble steps, landing on a little landing area and nearly crashing my head into the marble wall. My hands took some of the impact, but as I came to my senses, I could feel a terrible pain in my leg and thought I had broken it for sure.

The incident had caused a real load of noise, but the zombiefied men didn't move a muscle to come and assist or see what had happened. The chambermaid smiled and left me splayed on the stairs and other guests just stared.

Gingerly, I got to my feet, but the pain in my leg was immense. My man scurried off for a load of ice, which we wrapped in a napkin and stuck on my leg. For several hours, I just sat in the bar area with an ice pack on my leg, still not convinced that nothing had broken – a true miracle in fact. All that went through my head was that, if I had broken something, I would be stuck in a Macedonian hospital, unable to say a word to make myself understood and, more importantly, unable to fly home.

When it came to getting up to make the journey to the airport, I was so grateful to find that I could walk, even though this was pretty painful. I made it into the car and continued to apply ice as the snow splashed up through the hole in the bottom of the vehicle, drenching my shoes as we rode along the motorway with its Cyrillic traffic and place signs. We were stopped by a patrol but thankfully allowed to pass through and then we arrived at the airport and the departure lounge, where yet more ice was requested from the café.

This time, the departure was extremely painful, with tears and guilt tripping that I had spent so little time in Macedonia. That did spark a flood of tears on my part, but all I was really certain about was that my leg was killing me and I wanted to get back home, in case I needed any treatment. Undoubtedly, it was time for me to move on, even if that meant hobbling on to the plane.

It was just typical that I very nearly missed my connecting flight at Malpensa again, due to Al Italia's late departure and then the fact that we had to keep circling Malpensa waiting for permission to land. Luckily, the flight had waited for transferring passengers, which I was coming to see as being part and parcel of Al Italia flights. Even more remarkably, my battered suitcase made it too. I got back home in the early hours of the morning, tipped the clothes out of my suitcase, zipped it up and put it away. It wasn't going to Macedonia any more and, in my heart, I knew that neither was I.

Chapter 19
WRONGS, WETSUITS AND WEIRD OCCURRENCES

By the time 2006 reared its head, Catapult had already been left with a load of bad debts, but more was to come. The troubles of this year were rooted in my trust. That trust was placed in someone who I had met when getting my website launched. I had thought we had become friends. We went out for meals together, he shared his personal demons from his school days with me and I provided an ear that listened and tried to help. We bought each other presents for Christmas, even though he was Jewish. I thought we had a bond.

He came to me, after not having seen him for a few months and told me of a new venture with which he was involved, which related to speed trap detection. His father was also part of the set up, though there was also an MD, who I never actually met and an accountant too, who I did unfortunately meet.

My friend asked me to do some PR for the product and we commissioned a research survey to understand the consumer's views on speed traps and speeding. I wrote a series of press releases and threw myself into the account. The first invoice was not paid on time, so the standard chasing letter was sent out. The response was a letter back from the MD asking how we dare issue such a reminder. Eventually, that invoice was paid.

Work continued and other invoices were not paid. The amount being invoiced was significant enough for this to have a massive impact on cash flow, the whole situation being made worse by the fact that we were moving offices and leaving Marsh Mill to go to a new, much better equipped office on the outskirts of Blackpool. This meant a host of expenses – removal expenses, joinery charges to create an office/meeting room for me within the open plan new office, new stationery, rent up front and much more.

Prior to leaving Marsh Mill, we had down-sized from three units to one, having to close the design studio, as it brought in no business and then relinquishing what had been my very first unit, to move everything in to the one across the stairs. This almost broke my heart as I sat with my Peruvian chap and David crammed into one space that now held all of our files and years of press cuttings and most of the furniture.

Luckily, my half Italian friend had shifted some of our furniture to my house, getting his work colleagues to dismantle it all and transport it. That saved me a stack of cash, but now, the rest of our possessions had been moved to the new office and people wanted paying.

I rang my web friend's office and asked to speak to him, being sure he would sort out payment for me. His colleague, who I had also known for years, told me to bring another copy of the invoices down to the office. I went down there and did just that, but on arrival was told to go into the boardroom, as my friend was in there. I went in, chatted to him, explained how much I needed the money and was told to ring the accountant and tell him that my friend would authorise a cheque.

Mid-afternoon, I received a phone call from the accountant, who absolutely tore a strip off me, ranting and raving and saying it was a disgrace that I had forced my way into their office and then 'barged' into the boardroom. I explained that I had done neither and had been asked to drop the invoices off and then invited to go into the boardroom. He didn't want to listen. He just left me in tears, with David standing over me calling the guy all the names under the sun for upsetting me so much.

I called my friend again, explained what had happened and was told to go down to another office and collect a cheque. I did that and did collect a cheque. Unfortunately, within a few days it had bounced and I was back to square one.

By now I couldn't sleep at night. I found I had a total inability to switch off from cash flow issues. The amount of total debt created by all the bad debtors was now huge. I desperately needed to get this money from my friend, so had no alternative but to draw up court papers. By the time this happened, we had reached November 2006. I was told that a payment plan would be set off to pay back the money so that the Court case could be dropped. By early January, I had a letter to say that the debtor's company had been put into liquidation.

With all of this, I am surprised I derived any joy from 2006 at all. Surprisingly, however, I did, which I think goes to show what an optimist I was when it came to getting this money paid by my friend. I never believed that he would stitch me up. I will never, ever do that again. It's not the mistakes you make in life, it's the lessons you learn from them.

So the first rays of sunshine that I enjoyed in 2006 had their origins in late 2005. Having won the North West Farm Tourism Initiative account, I realised that something bigger and more groundbreaking needed to be done to reposition farm tourism in the eyes of the consumer. Farm tourism was seen as a dirty thing, taking place in muddy, smelly farmyards that offered little fun and which were associated with very downmarket holidaying experiences. Add to this the stigma of foot and mouth and there wasn't a lot of good news on the horizon.

I had been racking my brains as to what we could do creatively to shake up the image of farm tourism and make it relevant to everyone, regardless of social class or age group. I wanted to do something dynamic, which would make the media sit up and take notice, but I hadn't quite formulated an idea as to what that might be. Then, I visited Crake Trees Manor in Crosby Ravensworth.

David and I had been despatched to Crake Trees Manor to meet the owner, Ruth, who had created luxury B&B accommodation by renovating a barn, fitting it out beautifully with green oak, designer touches and a gorgeous and massive dining table that just put the homely touch on a stay here. Ruth was, and is, a very unusual farmer's wife, having a real passion for interior design, dressing in the trendiest clothes and just being very quirky and unique in a way that really engages me, as part of me wants to be her.

She is also quite a formidable lady, who knows her own mind and isn't afraid to speak it, which again I appreciate. Perhaps all these factors put me into a state of receptiveness when we were standing outside in her courtyard. I had noticed a sheep's skull on a bench in the garden – a stark reminder of foot and mouth and all that had been lost, so maybe this too had an effect. There, outside, Ruth started telling us how she had had a Motown party at the barn and how much everyone had loved it. David was well into this tale, as he too loved a bit of Motown. I didn't know that much about Motown music, but from the moment Ruth mentioned it, I sure as hell knew that I had my big idea for the NWFTI re-positioning campaign.

I shared my thoughts with David and he loved it. My idea was to create an old 45rpm style album sleeve entitled 'Mootown Classics', which would contain themed press releases, each based around the title of a Motown hit and housed on a CD. This would sit inside the sleeve, along with an accompanying booklet, detailing the businesses mentioned in each 'track' and carrying images of farm tourism.

David threw himself into the concept, telling me that Motown was the sound of young America that made music accessible and attractive to all cultures, just as farm tourism needed to be. With this backing, I pitched the idea to the client and gained a big thumbs-up.

I went to my designer, Quentin James, and briefed him to source a really funky image for the front of the CD sleeve and he came back with a fantastically engaging image of a cow on a psychedelic background. This was exactly what I wanted for the initiative, so it was now down to me to find suitable Motown hits to comprise the titles and then dissect different strands of the farm tourism offer to sit within a particular theme.

Things panned out really well, with a suitable title for all strands of farm tourism found, whether that was 'Too Hot To Trot' for the equestrian focused farms, or 'Reach Out I'll Be There' for those offering teambuilding experiences. The mailing, when issued, not only generated lots of requests for press trips, turning David into a travel agent for half his week, but also created editorial coverage in its own right, as press wrote about the novelty value of what they had received in the post.

This was just part one of our repositioning of farm tourism and the next task was to launch the luxury farm cluster that had finally come together. The aim was to time the launch around Valentine's Day and create a sense of the luxury farm being the ideal bolthole to which to head for romance.

I'd racked my brains as to what to do here and the concept that I came up with drew a little on my experience with the 'Great Christmas Cake Drop'. However, it also provided some nostalgia and retro-type romance that epitomised the spirit of going the extra mile for a loved one. It was based around the hunk that every girl once wanted to be wooed by – the Milk Tray Man.

I decided we would launch our own version of this iconic figure, which would become the farm stay man and that we would create a campaign that combined teaser mailer tactics with a media relations exercise targeted at the national travel writers in London. I wanted to be able to take Cumbrian romance to them, quite literally, and have the farm stay man present them with something in person. What I needed was someone who could think on their feet and wing it when they arrived in a London media office's reception. One photographer and one photographer only sprang to mind – the crazy Dave Nelson, now 'papping away' as he put it and selling his 'pap pics' into many national news desks.

I called up the crazy one to ask if he was man enough to carry out this mission and he leapt at the chance. All I then had to do was organise the farm stay man himself, in the shape of a hunky male model, decide what he would present to journalists and sort out the teaser mailers.

I thought that the gift that the model handed over really had to be chocolates, but wanted to do something more than just give handmade Cumbrian chocolates to the journalists. Instead, I organised a box that had just the right number of chocolate compartments to ensure that one space could represent one of the luxury farms, until all 15 were covered. While an accompanying slip detailed the flavours of the chocolates, I had an insert produced that carried 15 pen sketch images – one of each of the farms – so that every chocolate related to one of the luxury accommodation providers. All of this was presented in a gold box tied with a red bow.

The thorny question was how to possibly afford to get the same male model to tour London and also feature in the teaser mailer pics to be taken in Cumbria. I decided there was no way the budget would stretch to this, so the only alternative was to find a volunteer to do the Cumbria end. Funnily enough, as I sat in the office, with just one other occupant, who happened to be male, a name did spring to mind – David!

I think being asked to step into the role of a dark, mysterious demigod that could make women swoon at just the sight of his calling card and who could scale walls, climb through windows, sneak into bedrooms and swim across lakes, just to please a lady, could be said to have appealed to David – immensely! He lost no time in ringing a mate to organise a wetsuit and then was on the phone sorting out the second prop needed – a quad bike.

I would hazard a guess that in his eagerness to become a 1970s icon, he forgot one simple fact – that he was going to have to get into Windermere up to his thighs, in the middle of January, pretending to be emerging from the lake brandishing chocolate box and flowers. I did chuckle about this to myself, not realising, of course, that his borrowed wetsuit had a hole in it, so he would feel the icy water even more than expected – as if I would be that cruel!

The pictures of a brave man bearing the pain like a Trojan came back to me, along with the same hero, goggles affixed, tearing across a Cumbrian fell with his quad bike – and all because the lady loves a farm stay! David took one look at them, studied the portfolio shots of the male mode and uttered the memorable line, 'I think those journalists will be really disappointed when they realise it's not me that's come to see them!' I did have to stuff my hand in my mouth to prevent a loud guffaw!

The initiative worked a treat. Top travel writers actually emailed back in response to the email teaser to tell us at what time they might not be there, as they didn't want to miss the farm stay man! Others said they were very annoyed to not be in the office on that day, but asked if they could nominate a female colleague to collect the chocolates in their place!

Off went Dave Nelson with camera in hand to hook up with the male model and we kept receiving fantastic reports all day, telling us how overwhelmed various travel writers had been by our male model and how delighted they were to receive the chocolates. Subsequent photos of journalists like Lisa Minot of The Sun, Jo Morris of The Times and Nicola Iseard of The Express, to name but a few, proved the point.

The results of this launch were phenomenal. A piece in 'The Guardian' proclaimed 'Cumbria is the New Paris' and pictured a couple rolling in the hay. A double-page spread in 'The Independent', featuring the formidable yet impressive farmer's wife's dining table, ran under the heading of 'Cool Cumbria Down On The Farm'. The URL featured in 'The Times' 'Website of the Week' box and they also praised the idea as one of the best ICT projects they had ever seen.

Requests for press trips snowballed after this, with every paper from 'The Sun' to the 'York Times' wanting to visit a farm. Coverage about individual operators also rocketed, whether they offered an experience such as riding on the beach like Murthwaite Green Trekking Centre, or allowed children to be firemen for the day, as at The Firefighter Experience. Somehow, with the help of a psychedelic cow and a man in a wetsuit with a hole in it, we had repositioned farm tourism.

But we were far from over with this campaign and the next thing to which we had to turn our attention was a cluster of teashops on rural farms called the 'Tea Trail Cumbria'. The summer of 2006 was remarkable for two things. The first was the World Cup in Germany. The second was that it was actually, for once, a pretty hot summer.

Catapult moved into its new offices in April 2006 and we had literally only just got everything sorted out when David dropped a bombshell and said that he was leaving. This was a huge blow to me on several counts. Firstly, I hadn't wanted the continued overhead of an office rent and had stated to my father that I wanted to work from home. He said that wasn't practicable because I had David. I signed a 5-year lease and was now stuck with it.

The other reason why it knocked me for six was that of sheer emotion. I had become hugely attached to David, who had become probably the most loyal and kind employee I had ever had. He was what you could call a 'fine young man', well mannered, polite and very helpful. However, I did understand his decision. He had found a girlfriend in London and thought that, if he moved down there, things might develop further. More importantly, he told me that he had to know what it was like to work in London, or he might always regret it. He said he was sure I would understand, having worked there myself. I did. It was time for

David to move on.

We had a month to sort out his replacement and I approached UCLAN, who had a student placement programme. Various candidates turned up for interview – some very late – and both David and I decided that the best of the bunch was a foreign guy, who was so tall he had to stoop to get through the office door! On that basis, we offered him David's post.

However, there was an idea in development as part of the promotion of the tearooms. This was a stunt involving a reader of tea leaves, who could head to one of our rural tea rooms and predict the winners of the World Cup. The client loved it.

Neither David nor I were particularly well connected with readers of tea leaves, so we decided to call upon the expertise of the Blackpool Gazette's entertainment and food editor, Robin Duke. Robin immediately pointed us in the direction of a psychic called Paula Paradaema, who worked in Blackpool. Now I personally have always steered well clear of anything to do with the Ouija board, or psychic readings and tarot. It makes me feel really uncomfortable, to the extent that I didn't even want to contact Paula Paradaema. I left David to call her and assess whether she could do the reading and at what price. An answer came back that was within budget, including travelling expenses, so we now just needed to select a tea room.

We chose Low Bridge End Farm tea garden, at St John's in the Vale, Cumbria. It is located in a truly idyllic setting, offering views to Blencathra, Helvellyn and Castle Rock and overlooking St John's Beck. Neither of us had ever been to this tea garden before, but it was one of the more centrally based tea rooms on the trail.

The day of the media call in the tearoom garden, it was gloriously sunny and hot. David and I arrived at the tea room early and awaited the arrival of the ever energetic Dave Nelson, who was going to take the pics and then sell them in to the national picture desks. We had all sorts of World Cup paraphernalia decorating the tea room tables and all was set.

Once again, I was edgy. I knew that I didn't want to speak to Paula Paradaema or have any reason to be put into a position where she offered to read my palm, or do anything else for that matter. For this reason, I positioned myself, very tactically, in a corner and behind the wooden trestle table on which we had dumped all of our materials. Bags blocked me off from anyone quite frankly and I felt really safe and tucked away.

Paula breezed in flamboyantly in a colourful frock and with her strawberry blonde curly, long hair glistening in the sun. I didn't try to attract any attention and David had gone to say hello, so I stayed put. To my horror, despite there being a few people around on different tables, she made a direct beeline for mine, pushed past the bags that were on the seat and plonked herself right next to me. I was also in total shock.

I kid ye not, as Frankie Howerd would have said, within a matter of minutes she turned to me and said, 'You are owed a lot of money aren't you?' My jaw dropped open, as I was in the midst of my troubles getting the money out of my friend's company at this point, but was also carrying the other bad debts. None of this was documented anywhere, but Paula suddenly gave me a figure. 'Give or take', she said, 'That's what you're owed isn't it?' I started to tot it up in my head and discovered that 'give or take' a few hundred pounds, she was right.

I was un-nerved by this. I, like many others, assume that many psychics pick on very general aspects of life about which they are likely to be right. What she had said, both in terms of topic and figures, wasn't something I assumed a psychic would comment on.

More was to come, though at the time, I didn't understand its relevance. I was, at this point, just a trapped little butterfly unable to escape from her corner. 'Someone passed away from your life when you were 14 didn't they?' she said. I started to think about it and wondered if it were my grandmother – my mother's mother.

'She loved bluebells, didn't she?', continued Paula. I honestly didn't know whether she did or she didn't and by now was getting spooked, so didn't really want any more of this. 'I don't know', I answered.

'Oh yes, she did', stated Paula in a matter-of-fact way. 'Anyway, she says that she's happy but to tell someone close to you that they have an illness that hasn't been diagnosed yet, but it's not that serious'. I didn't have a clue what she was talking about.

'And someone that you loved has died recently, haven't they?' she continued.

'No', I answered, in a very definite way, as if pleased to prove her wrong. 'You might not know it', she said, 'but they have'.

After having spoken to only myself, she got up and started to wander over to the table where she would read the leaves. I was racking my brains trying to make sense of her words.

A reporter and cameraman were there from a local paper and the reporter was complaining of chronic backache. Paula said that she could find the source of the pain if he wanted. He looked sceptical, but told her all else had failed. She put a hand on him and he triumphantly told her that wasn't where it hurt. 'I know that', she replied, simultaneously jabbing him in part of his back much further away. He yelped like a dog. 'That's where it hurts, isn't it?' she said. After that, he let her put her healing hands on him.

Then we came to the main event – the reading of the leaves. She dramatically swilled her tea leaves around her special cup and looked puzzled. 'I see a lot of people crying', she said. 'And there's someone who is running but something unexpected stops him'. We all looked at each other for divine inspiration.

She then swilled more tea and started to talk about colours. She kept saying that all she could see was maroon and then red. The press leapt on to this and immediately wrote up that she had predicted an England win. In fact, she hadn't. She kept coming back to this crying, something red and someone being stopped in their tracks.

To be honest, the reading of the leaves was a big relief for me, as it meant getting away from the really unnerving stuff. Unfortunately, it was to return. Paula said she had sensed a presence ever since arriving at the farm, which also had a camping barn. She could sense some unhappy soul there. When prompted, the farm owners revealed that many guests who had stayed in the camping barn had reported seeing a ghostly figure of a girl and having their possessions thrown around. Paula said she intended returning to investigate more.

No amount of conversation in the car on the way back home could make me forget the bluebells issue. I went straight round and told my mother what had happened. She immediately said, 'Well, when I was young, my mum always liked to take us on the Bluebell Line'. My mother lived in Sussex at the time, so this was her local railway attraction. My mother continued, 'And she used to like it if Brian (her brother) and I collected bluebells in the woods for her'.

My mother then talked to my Nan who further revealed that whenever my grandma came north, she liked to go out for the day into the countryside and see the bluebells. We were all completely spooked.

Within weeks, my mother had been diagnosed as being diabetic – though borderline rather than really serious. Later that summer, I tried to ring my old friend from my days at Swinton. I asked to speak to him and a girl said I couldn't, as he wasn't there any more. I asked where he now worked. She said, 'I'm awfully sorry to have to tell you this, but he died last November'. At the World Cup, Wayne Rooney was stopped in his tracks by a red card in the game against Portugal, leaving thousands of fans in tears as their dream faded away.

David left literally days after this event. Our parting was awful. I knew that I wasn't going to be able to hold it together when he went and he was also a really sensitive and emotional person and I'm sure he felt the same. I'd organised a really nice surprise leaving 'do' for him in a restaurant called the Thai Mews in Poulton-le-Fylde and, because he had become so close to the guy who had stood in for the NWFTI lady during her maternity leave, had invited this chap to come to the meal as a surprise guest.

David was totally overwhelmed that I had done this. Our poor guest was overwhelmed when the waitress tipped a bowl of Thai food tipped down him, but all in all, it had been a great night out, sitting on the floor with the cushions and generally being really daft. Now, however, it had come to the end of David's very last working day and we had to say goodbye. I knew that if I walked down the stairs and out with him, I would dissolve into tears in front of him and it didn't look like it would take much to set him off either. I made some excuse about needing to just check something before he left and let him give me a kiss and then head off. The moment he had gone down the stairs and out of the front door,

I sat on the stairs, sank my head in my hands and blubbed for England.

After this, I was then left with my foreign student. To say he drove be completely insane is an understatement. He took it upon himself to re-organise my filing system, to tinker with the settings on my online media database, to say ridiculous things to people on the phone and to go home, without permission, when I was out of the office in London, because he'd had a nosebleed!

My NWFTI client, now returned from her maternity leave, had started to get really pally with me, asking me to prepare materials for a trip she was making to Poland and commissioning me to write the annual report. Her comment on my new office worker was that, 'He is just so European', having caught him lethargically leaning by the car and having a crafty cigarette.

I nearly exploded one day, when he done his usual re-organising of everything and messing things up all morning, to the extent that I had no choice but to leave the office to calm down. I returned to have him saunter to my door, loll all around the doorframe and announce, 'You rrr een-vited to go to Paree'. I just looked at him as if he had landed from another planet.

'What?' I replied abruptly.

'I zed', he continued, 'you rrr een-vited to go to Paree to see my seester's jewellery launch'.

I was absolutely seething. In my head, a voice was saying, 'how dare you try to get around me with bribery after all you've done this morning'. Instead, I said, 'I haven't even got time to go out on a Saturday night, let alone go to Paris. I don't think that will happen, thank you'.

From that moment, I knew he had to go. I resolved to ring the University and say that they would have to have a word with him.

I did that, but the outcome was not as expected. The moment I mentioned his name, it was as if the person on the other end of the phone had caught his sighing virus. 'He shouldn't even be there', she said angrily. 'He needs to come back and re-sit his exams!'. I somehow gathered, perhaps from the angry tone in her voice, that he wasn't her favourite person on earth, which made me feel a whole lot better. I gave him the 'bad' news, trying not to look too pleased about it and that was the last I saw of him.

From that moment on, I resolved to manage, no matter how hard it was to cope with everything on my own, because my nerves just could not stand another walking disaster area. I suppose, in a way, he was responsible for my very bold, but in hindsight, fantastic decision to go it alone as a 'freelancer'.

Those PD days, as I call them (Post David), were some of the toughest of my working life, as I suddenly had to know every single aspect of running an office that I had been 'managing' for 8 years. I spent hours crawling inside our massive design studio's photocopier, ages trawling through various computers trying to find photography and documents and regularly had to call on my parents when there was a mailing to get out in the post.

I found a temp to just come into the office a few times during my holiday in Portugal, though that was a little unfortunate, as she couldn't even switch the computer on, let alone use it!

Just as I was about to depart on this trip, I received a really frenetic phone call from a chap in the South Lakes. I didn't particularly understand what it was he wanted at first, but it transpired, once he'd drawn breath a few times, that he was asking me to pitch for the account of a body called the South Lakes Tourism Action Group.

This group had set itself up to generate exposure for the South Lakes, rather than the rest of Cumbria, believing that other parts of the county were now attracting funding and resource at the expense of the traditional honey pot areas such as Windermere, Bowness, Ambleside, Grasmere, Rydal, Hawkshead and Kendal.

I threw a pitch together as fast as possible and went to a business centre in Windermere to present it to a panel of four – a lady called Dawn from South Lakeland District Council, a man named Peter from Rydal Mount and a chap called Stephen from Mountain Goat, plus my original contact. Little did I know that I would come to work for each of these people within their own individual businesses in the years to come. Somehow or other, I won the account and was duly appointed by SLTAG!

One of the really fabulous things about 2006 was encountering a lady called Alison O'Neill. I was asked to get in touch with her, because another PR consultant had told her that she would never make a go of her business and ought to give up. In my capacity as the PR person for the NWFTI, I had to try to give her a launch.

I rang her and, to this day, think that the key to what happened lay in listening to her – for a full 45 minutes. She described her life to me in detail, explained how her free-range walking holidays would allow people to not just walk in the Howgills, but live her life, going to sheep auction, looking after her fell pony, baking scones, dropping in to have tea with a neighbour. I took her words one day later and created a powerful piece of copy, which described her as a latter day Catherine Earnshaw. I didn't even know that her roots lay in Yorkshire!

This piece of copy, in which I tried to encapsulate all there was about a woman I had never met and her farm at Shacklabank, created a platform from which Alison became a media star. Double-page spreads in national titles followed, I was invited to sit around the tea table and make friends with her adorable old sheepdog, Moss, and Alison started to see bookings rolling in from around the world. I continued to work with her, getting her gypsy wagon experiences in The Guardian and seeing key media figures picking up on copy and booking their holidays with her. Suddenly, this woman, who would, 'never make it', had become a national and international personality.

My work with Alison continued beyond the NWFTI. A few years later, again just sitting around the kitchen table with her in Sedbergh, she dropped into the conversation that she did something called 'barefoot walking'. She also showed me her new treehouse (only reached by a walk across the meadow in the wellies) and her new shepherd's hut. Despite the novelty of these, I homed in on the barefoot walking, declaring, 'Why have you never told me about this before?' Over a cuppa and home baked scones, I had picked up on a theme that I knew would go big and so it did, with more double page spreads in national travel sections resulting. Sometimes, you have to take the hit on your fee, do something for free like having a cuppa and simply chat, in order to find the gem that will help your client really bring home the bacon.

Immediately after David's departure, I had also picked up three accounts in London – all three in insurance. I was particularly delighted with one, as it meant hooking up again with Mr Stuart Bensusan, who had set up his own company working from swish offices in Carnaby Street. My last trip to Carnaby Street had been on a school trip in the punk era and my memories were all about Mohicans, tight leather trousers bound with chains and safety pins through the nose. Thankfully, Stuart hadn't adopted any of these!

Suddenly, trips to London were back on the agenda, which was a little expensive, but at least bringing in good income. On one of my trips to see Stuart, I decided to kill some time prior to my train home by having a coffee and snack in a little coffee bar that I'd found a few streets away. I was totally absorbed with my coffee, so hadn't immediately noticed someone sitting on a table diagonally opposite me. When I did look up, I died a death, realising it was my ex graphic designer boyfriend from Bristol. I suddenly shuffled some documents out of my bag and pretended to be hugely interested in them, sneaking a peek now again hoping that he was making a move. I was virtually pinned to the back of the café and I knew that, if I stood up, I would be immediately noticed.

This whole incident was absolute torture. I was sure he had to have noticed me, but it was clear neither of us wanted the embarrassment of having to strike up a conversation. I kept pondering what the chances were of this happening in a statistical sense and again sneaking a peek to check that I wasn't just hallucinating, but it was most definitely him – he even had a portfolio case!

In the end, there was nothing for it but to plan a dash to the door. I knew this was going to need precise planning, given the number of bags I had, so shuffled along the seat at about 3 cm a time, over the course of about 10 minutes, and strategically placed my hands on the bag handles ready to make my move. I was up and off the seat faster than Usain Bolt, slapping some money on the bar and making a dash for the door. Not surprisingly, I never ventured into this part of the area on subsequent visits!

Toward the end of 2006, I also acquired a client that I thought might be with me a few months, but which has actually been with me for the whole of the last 6.5 years! He came to the office for a meeting, which was always very strange in the PD era, as it basically entailed me sitting in the middle of the massive outer office at the meeting table, surrounded by lots of empty desks, filing cabinets and equipment. One woman playing Queen Bee in an employee-less empire!

I showed the man – Darrell – what I had done for various other pubs and clubs and was asked to put together a proposal. I then went and presented this at Darrell's house in Hambleton, about four miles away, meeting his wife Debra and a somewhat crazy-mannered guy called Johnny, or Jazzy John B as he was also known, who was going to be the manager of Darrell and Debra's new dining pub, which they were totally refurbishing.

I started issuing my first press releases about the plans around October time, building up to a big official opening for selected guests and media just before Christmas 2006. This was quite a glitzy night and I was charged with running around taking captions for the local press photographer and the one employed to take shots of guests during the evening.

The biggest gaff I made on the night was to not recognise the local millionaire – Karl Crompton. I'd found this couple by the bar and realised that the photographer had just snapped them. I dutifully took my spiral-ringed notebook out and asked the man his name. When he gave me his Christian name, I wrote down Carl. The woman stepped in and put me straight. 'That's' Karl with a K', she said. Both obviously then assumed that I knew who he was, so weren't expecting me to ask for the surname. When I did, I got a bemused 'Crompton', at which point I wanted to crawl under the bar and hide! It was time to move on!

Chapter 20
TEA & SYMPATHY; LOVE & COCOROSES

As I headed into 2007, I had one thing on my mind – how to achieve as great a coup for Luxury in the Farm linked to Valentine's Day 2007 as I had achieved in 2006. With no man willing to don a wetsuit, in the spirit of some of my favourite film characters, 'The Three Amigos', I was just going to have to use my brain – damn it!

As per, I think the idea may well have come to me in the bath. At the time, maybe still even today, it was possible to buy silver replicas of a Rolo chocolate, housed in a lovely red tub, almost like a jewellery box, emblazoned with the words, 'Do you love anyone enough to give them your last Rolo'. I decided to use this as the basis of a media mailer to travel writers, but with a twist. In my case, the message would be, 'Do you love anyone enough to give them a Rolo in the hay?'

This slightly cheeky message could only be carried through, however, if we had some hay, so I despatched my father to a pet shop and back he dutifully came brandishing real hay. By now, I had all my Rolo boxes and Rolos, so all I had to do was removed the black foam insert, replace it with hay and shove the Rolo inside it – simple! The trouble was, that the hay was far too long to be scrunched into the small box, so the scissors were needed.

For hours, I lovingly cut up the hay and shoved little pieces into all the boxes, ensuring that a label that I'd produced, to mention the North West Farm Tourism Initiative, was also inserted. This took even longer, the whole exercise taking me the best part of a day. I stuffed jiffy bags, labelled them up, took one to the post office to get it weighed, so that I could buy stamps for them all, and then licked and stuck on the stamps.

A labour of love for Valentine's Day, if ever there was one.

It worked a treat. Instantly, the Sunday Telegraph rang me up and asked for images of one of the farms, so I chose one of my favourites – a picture of the free-standing bath at Ann's Hill near Cockermouth, which had a stunning white Victorian bath set against deep red walls, where a plasma TV was fitted. A champagne bucket sat on a small table next to the bath.

With this instant success for the NWFTI so early into 2007, I was on a roll, continuing to generate fantastic coverage. When the Jeremy Kyle show wanted to visit a farm in Cheshire that offered a 'Farmer for A Day' experience and other national coverage poured in for farms across the northwest, it was the icing on the cake, or so I thought.

Soon after the Valentine's Day successes, the mood plummeted rather dramatically. We were invited to attend the creditors' meeting being held after the insolvency of my friend's speed detector device company. My company secretary and I decided we had to go. We assumed that lots of creditors would be there, but on arrival, were staggered to find we were the only creditors in attendance. The people in the room, the horrible accountant and my friend, looked equally shocked to see us. My friend then attempted some chit-chat asking me how I was. I tried to ignore him, in total disgust.

Sheets of paper were thrust at us across the table. Just as we started proceedings, the accountant – who made no attempt to apologise for the way he had treated me previously – told us that a company 'employee' had landed them in deep trouble, as we may have read in the local paper. We had no idea what they were talking about, so they elaborated and said that their 'freelance associate' had been arrested for carousel fraud and likely to serve a very long prison sentence.

At this point, I produced the rude letter I had received from the supposedly non-employed associate, in which he had asked how dare we chase an overdue payment. I pointed out that it was signed MD – hardly indicative of being someone who had no formal connection with their company. They said they had no idea why he would have claimed that.

Their argument was that they had unwittingly become associated with this fraudster and that this had led to HMRC withholding VAT refunds that were due. This was said to have brought the company down.

As we were being rushed through the whole proceedings, we didn't get a chance to ask many questions. We did, however, study the list of creditors and asked why it was that people owed nearly a million pounds, or hundreds of thousands of pounds, were not at the meeting. Again, shoulders were shrugged and they said they hadn't heard from these people.

We drove home almost in silence. To us, there seemed to be a possible reason why creditors supposedly owed so much had not bothered to turn up given the rest of the tale we had been told. Nobody else seemed to consider that.

It was around this time, that I realised that I was going to have to get through the five years of the lease come what may, however hard it became and however difficult the financial situation was. I needed something to get me through the rain, but Barry Manilow was too obvious. I selected the Dido song 'No White Flag', which I know is about a relationship, but the symbolism of it appealed to me. I imagined myself standing there, refusing to raise the white flag, no matter what came my way. I am sure it was this alone that got me through certain times during the 5-year rollercoaster.

For much of this time, I had a real source of comfort and a lady who frequently prayed for me. Her name was Carol Fowler and she cleaned my office once a week. To be honest, there were many times when I couldn't afford to have Carol cleaning, but I juggled the finances and scrimped and saved elsewhere to try to keep her on. Only towards the very end did this become impossible and I felt terrible at that point. Her support and probably her prayers combined with my no white flag resolve saw me through.

It was damned hard putting on a brave face when I was alone in the office. I can admit to sometimes having had a really good cry, knowing that nobody would see. Once I'd done that, I somehow managed to find some strength again.

In the spring of 2007, while still working for the South Lakes Tourism Action Group, I received a call from one of its members – the Aquarium of the Lakes. I thought I was going along for a cup of coffee and a chat, but when I got there realised that the marketing manager, Cathy Burrows, wanted me to do some PR. I was shown around the attraction, which then told the story of water, from its falling on the Cumbrian fells as rain, to its journey through the lakes and out to the sea at Morecambe Bay. I suddenly had another tourism contract and was taken on to create PR around the Aquarium's 10th anniversary year.

What I loved most about this revolved around furry, adorable creatures that make you feel all warm inside simply by looking at them. The creatures I'm talking about are otters and they had long been one of my favourite animals thanks to the beautiful but weepy film, 'Ring of Bright Water'. I suddenly had two little, highly inquisitive and mischievous 'Mij's' of my own to promote and I couldn't have been happier.

Around May 2007, I also suddenly had a call from a lady that I'd been helping for quite some time. I'd never met her, but she had found my details on my website probably a good 18 months beforehand and had asked for advice on PR and indicative PR costs. I had never really expected to hear from her again, as she was based in London, but when the call came, completely out of the blue, I arranged to travel down to London and meet her at Euston.

The lady was one of the kindest and sweetest clients I ever had – Janan Leo of Cocorose London. She wasn't at all what I had imagined from our phone conversations and much younger and nicer. Despite this, she was an inspired entrepreneur and had had the genius idea of creating foldable ballerina pumps that could be housed inside a dinky little zipped purse and whipped out of a handbag whenever the heels began to cause agony. At this point a carry bag could be formed out of the lining of the purse and the heels popped inside.

Since that meeting at Euston, Janan's shoes have saved my life a hundred times over. In May 2007, however, the aim was was to get her launched, particularly as while she had been developing her product, a similar one had appeared on Dragon's Den. I created a big blitz launch strategy, on the smaller budget that she obviously had as a start-up business. I created some launch materials and was successful in targeting some key fashion editors on the Daily Express and Marie Claire online, which made the shoes their 'buy of the week'. These early successes helped Janan to move on with her plans, so I would like to think that I helped shape the amazing business that is Cocorose London – a brand I worked with for a good few years after launch.

The farm tourism initiative was, of course, in full swing throughout 2007. In the early months of 2007, we launched a new cluster group of farm shops that I had suggested. The farm shops were all passionate producers of local, farm fresh food, from meat reared on the farm with a full provenance and traceability, to full meals, fresh fruit and vegetables, Jersey milk ice cream and delicious sausages.

We named this 'The Natural Producers' and we all crammed into a farm shop tea room early one morning, as food was rustled up for the Border TV cameras and for hungry press photographers. I'd written all the copy for a Natural Producers leaflet, to go out into the tourism racks in venues across the NW and had already set up a 'BBC Good Food' piece well before launch.

The next cluster to which to turn my attention was the Tea Trail Cumbria. In September 2006, I had played on it being a long hot summer by suggesting we had discovered a new breed in Cumbrian tourism – the 'tea trail groupie'. I'd had black T-shirts made with the names of all the Tea Trail tearooms printed on the back as if they were venues on a rock tour. These were expertly modelled by my client and new best friend, the once fearsome Katie. The venue was the Gincase, near Silloth and Katie threw herself into the shoot, wearing her pink Hunter Wellingtons and striking her very best poses for the camera. You'd never have known she had once been offered a place at RADA!!

I had also commissioned a massive giant, green inflatable teapot, which we used to launch a limerick competition, based around scones and highlighted in the Tea Trail Cumbria leaflet. The first time this was erected, we were in the front garden of the idyllic Greystoke Cycle Café in the village of Greystoke. The owner, Annie, was a remarkable woman, who had taken advantage of her position on the C2C cycle route to open a tearoom and cycler-friendly stop-off, at which they could dry out and enjoy a refreshment in her barn, before setting off again..

But the real coup of 2007 for the North West Farm Tourism Initiative luckily coincided with the work experience stint undertaken by my son, or 'Young Padawan Learner' as I like to call him. My YPL had always maintained that I did virtually next to nothing in my job and greatly exaggerated all the stresses and strains involved in coping solo (or Hans Solo, if we want to keep the Star Wars theme going!). He was about to watch and learn!

The stroke of genius that coincided with my son's fortnight in the office was again focused on the Tea Trail Cumbria. I had been asked to generate publicity around the fact that the Tea Trail Cumbria leaflet had been translated into Japanese for the first time. In the PR profession, this is what we call a 'so-what' story. Telling the media about a Japanese translation was hardly likely to set the world alight. However, what I came up with did go global.

My idea involved creating and placing a job advert for a geisha to come to the Cumbrian tea rooms and teach the owners how to make the perfect cup of green tea, to serve to all those Japanese tourists about to descend on the tea rooms, now that they had their vital bit of Japanese information to guide them. Now, as you will recall, if you've been an attentive reader, I've had my own trials trying to make the perfect cup of green tea and I also knew that a fair few Japanese would never sacrifice this for a cup of our own rosy lee, so this knowledge fuelled my idea and enabled me to sell it in to the client.

I briefed my designer Quentin James on what I wanted from the 'job advert', which was a very dramatic poster, full of vibrant red colour, with hues of green in the background forming a very dramatic contrast. The words, 'Geisha Wanted' were printed in bold white lettering across it, with the description of the skills needed by the tearooms listed below.

I created a press release to accompany the poster and issued this to a very targeted list of media, not just in Cumbria, but across the UK too. Having just issued it, I had a call from a lady at BBC News 24, who said that she loved the story and wanted to persuade her editors to use it. I thought that sounded great, but had no idea of the magnitude of the consequences.

As it happened, the following day I had agreed to take my son to Lakes Aquarium, where we needed to do a bit of tour and take down some notes. At around 10am, while touring the Aquarium, my phone started ringing with press calls and I had to keep scurrying out in order to answer them. I had then told my son that we would go to Lakeland in Windermere for a bite to eat, before going on to Kendal for another appointment.

Throughout the whole of our lunch, the phone never stopped ringing with press enquiries about my geisha and if it wasn't a journalist on a phone, it was some Japanese girl or other not wishing to serve green tea, but rather, to get herself on the next poster! One, in particular, was determined that she was a better geisha than the one we had depicted!

As we drove into Kendal, my son had to keep answering the phone, writing down messages and then getting me to stop where I could, just to answer the press calls. For a good 7 hours, the phone rang non-stop.

When we eventually got home that evening, my son said, 'I used to think you exaggerated how stressful and busy your job is, but I now see that it is!' The one word entering my head was 'result'!

As it happened, I had already secured a geisha and shoved her up my sleeve, ready to pull out as deftly as a magician produces a white dove. I had somehow stumbled across a Japanese-focused organisation, which celebrated all things from the Land of the Rising Sun and had contacted the main person there – a lady, who I quickly realised was not so much passionate about Japan, but rather obsessed by it!

I had a lot of email and phone exchange with this lady, who told me that she had a Japanese friend, who was well versed in the Japanese Tea Ceremony and who could come and perform this for us, just as we wanted. This was music to my ears, as she didn't live too far away and the travelling time wouldn't be too great. The whole plan came together very nicely.

Around a week after announcing our 'Search for a Geisha' as we called it, we revealed that we had a geisha who would be performing the Japanese Tea Ceremony at the Greystoke Cycle Café (for media at that end of Cumbria) and then heading down to Low Sizergh Barn, on the outskirts of Kendal, to do the other photo call.

I had hired a photographer from the west coast of Cumbria and he, as you might imagine coming from that neck of the woods, was a nice, but no-nonsense sort of person, who had branched into photography after a long career in another sector. He wasn't a frills and fantasy kind of guy and neither is my son, so their faces – and mine I suppose to some extent – were an absolute picture when our lady from the Japanese organisation emerged looking a little like a cross between the Vicar of Dibley and Jo Brand and wearing an enormous black frock, which looked as if it would have been at home in the wardrobe of Demis Roussos. She also had the brightest orange hair I'd ever seen.

Her partner had come with her and was almost hanging on to her coat-tails all the time, as she faffed around laying out her tea utensils for the ceremony in the stunning back garden of the Greystoke Cycle Café, which looks out over Greystoke Castle, home to none other than the fictional Tarzan! However, more importantly from her point of view, she started extolling the virtues of some tea that she wanted to sell to Annie at the café.

After about ten minutes, I felt duty bound to enquire where the Japanese lady was and was informed that she was hungry so had asked for some food to be given to her and was inside the café. Everything else was set up ready to roll and Annie had even organised a silkscreen painter friend, who could work in Japanese styles and patterns, to be creating something special in the gardens for the press cameras to film.

Press started to arrive, including a BBC reporter / cameraman and the Japanese lady was still not in situ. I had to go and ask her 'agent' to fetch her out, as we had to keep things on time. In the meantime, I caught up with the photographer, who was in fits of laughter, as the 'agent' had told him that she had once been 'regressed' and discovered that she was actually Japanese! In Brian's world, people just didn't go through the regressing process and it was clear that he had really struggled not to guffaw loudly in front of her. My timing in sending her off in search of her charge seemed to have been perfect.

The kimono-wearing star of the show shuffled out of the café and took her place, with her 'agent' at the Tea Ceremony table. None of us really had a clue what was going on, but cameras rolled and clicked and her 'agent' kept fussing around her, encouraging her to do the next part of the ceremony, by handing her various bits and pieces.

When all of this was wrapped up, we really had to hit the road and head down to Kendal, as I explained to the 'agent' and her partner, who was the chauffeur. My son and I set off and got there well within the hour, as expected. We met the owner of that tea room and explained that the others would be there shortly. We waited and we waited and we waited and they didn't arrive. I rang and was told that they had been delayed because the Japanese lady had again been hungry and they had needed to find her food. By now, she was being talked about as if she was some Chihuahua that needed cosseting all the time and I was beginning to panic, as the press photographers had already turned up. To cap it all, the Japanese envoys had decided to take a different route to the one I'd told them to take and were lost!

When they eventually arrived, it was unbelievable. The Japanese lady – slim little thing that she was – was again hungry and in need of food. I did wonder whether a load of sandwiches were actually being stashed under the Demis Roussos outfit, to maybe feed the five thousand back at home, but just had to do that old trick that Grimbles had taught me in Trafalgar Square – smiling through gritted teeth.

Once we had got over the hurdle of it being too sunny for our geisha to have her photo taken outside, by finding a parasol to shade her, it was a wrap! More cakes were devoured by the star of the show, while my son and I beat a hasty retreat. It was definitely time to move on!

This exercise had phenomenal success. The story went not just all around the UK, but to the USA, Canada, India, across Asia and, not surprisingly, to Japan, where the likes of Kyodo News and others picked it up. It even featured on the Lipton tea website!

It was a pity that all of this success could not be communicated in an award entry for the NWFTI that I had submitted back in February, to meet the CIPR Excellence Awards deadline. Amazingly, despite this, our little, low budget campaign for the NWFTI became one of the few campaigns conducted by agencies or in house departments from north of Watford to be shortlisted for one of these most prestigious national awards.

I had attended a panel interview in London and had left it thinking that I had really messed up. That was because they had asked me what winning the national award would mean to me and I had uttered the words, 'Getting this far is more than I could have expected'. I immediately wished I could grab that sentence and shove it back in my mouth. I knew it was exactly the wrong thing to say.

The London event was very high profile and staged in a venue that was a bit of a security risk given the bombings that had hit London just two years before. The venue was the Artillery Garden at the HAC and it was truly magnificent. I took my NWFTI client and new best friend and we arrived by taxi, to find a red carpet awaiting us, a stunning marquee and a drinks area ready to welcome the esteemed guests. We were then shepherded into the main room in which the awards would be handed out and took to our seats. As fate would have it, we found ourselves sharing a table with my former client from CIS.

Catapult was one of only four agencies short-listed for this award – the CIPR Excellence Award in the Arts, Sport, Tourism and Leisure category. One agency had two entries, so we stood a one-in-five chance of winning. When we read the programme, and the words the judges had used to describe the NWFTI entry, to us and to the others on our table, it looked as though our entry had really ticked all the boxes. The comments were far more commendatory than those given to other entries and the entry read:

'Catapult's brief was to reposition farm tourism by helping attract visitors to the North West and win back consumer confidence after the foot and mouth outbreak. As British farm tourism is not pretty destination tourism, where the media clamour for press trips or exotic pictures, creativity was this campaign's lifeblood.

'This was a campaign where the creativity instantly brought a smile to the face and the results brought an amazing return on fee investment. Under the banner of 'Welcome to Mootown', Catapult produced a 'Mootown Classics' CD press kit. To promote Valentine's Day stays in farmhouses, a 1970s style all-action farm stay man visited female travel journalists with hand-made Cumbrian chocolates. A tea shop trail used a psychic to read tea leaves and predict the winner of the 2006 World Cup.

'The comprehensive 31-page evaluation report set this campaign apart from other entrants and brought thoroughness of approach to a new level'.

As it turned out though, the programme notes were deceptive. Our entry was a runner-up to a campaign that had involved sending a man to around 60 different countries in the world to see how blue the sky was in each. With our budget, we hadn't even been able to bring the farm stay man male model up to Cumbria to get into Windermere in the middle of January! That's what often annoys me about these awards: nobody seemingly cares a fig about what the budget was and what was comparatively achieved in terms of the budget available. On that basis, the bigger the budget, the more likely you are to win, in many cases.

This whole exercise had been very good for me in one respect, however, and had I not been to these awards in 2007, I very much doubt that I would achieve what I did in 2012. Knowledge is power!

There were other big plusses to the night. I had really had no idea who was nominated in each category, but suddenly up bobbed my former account manager, Chris – the one who had nearly turfed Ruben Xaus off the Playstation game at the NEC. He didn't quite know how to approach me, so I just went up to him after he had won an award with his new employer in Leeds and told him I was very proud of him. He said that my words meant a lot to him.

The other really big plus of the night was the fact that my companion abandoned me for a while. At this point, my former client from CIS sat next to me and had a heart to heart. He said he had never understood why I employed account managers, because all CIS had ever wanted on the account was me. To my amazement, he went on to say that I was, without exception, the most creative PR person he had ever come across, in any agency in the country, and he would hope to hire my brain for ideas in the future.

I was really shaken by this conversation, as I had never imagined a big financial institution like CIS would be interested in working with a freelancer. I knew they had always valued us being an extension of their team, but had never realised how much they had thought of me as an individual. At this point, I was still reeling from my last disastrous staff appointment and still trying to battle my way through all elements of office running. This conversation now strengthened my resolve to go it alone, as a positive and definite business strategy. It was the foundation of my becoming a fully-fledged PR freelancer, not because I was trying to earn some money between jobs, or having been made redundant somewhere, but because I wanted that freedom and lifestyle, free of HR, squabbling staff and red tape. This awards ceremony was possibly the most influential of all of them in shaping my career and I hadn't even won!

2007 was also the year in which I had some further challenging encounters. Having won the PR account for the Western Lake District, I was told that one of the main events to promote was the Whitehaven Maritime Festival – a fantastic sounding event that involved the arrival of Tall Ships into what was once the third largest port in the country and one renowned for its rum and spices.

I was asked to go and see the organiser of the event, to see how the tourism partnership could help him promote the Festival. What I wasn't told was that he had no dialogue with them other than rows over the way Whitehaven was promoted!

I instantly fell in love with Whitehaven and could almost smell the stench of the sea mariners on the dock and the whiff of rum on the breeze. I think Whitehaven brings out the pirate in me and, every time I go there, I am overawed by the sense of history.

When I got to the festival organiser's wine shop, it was full of press reporters wanting quotes from the main man and I had to wait quite a while before he could see me. When he did, it became clear that I had, once again. been sent into a lion's den, here almost in the role of an envoy waving a white flag.

The 'lion' explained to me why he felt so aggrieved by the website's policy of only featuring businesses that paid a membership to the Western Lake District Tourism Partnership. He felt it detrimental to the town to have a section on shops that only showed three, with similar misrepresentation of cafes, hotels and so on. I had to agree with him.

I think my attitude surprised him. As we talked, we got on well, coming to an understanding of the different viewpoints. I told him I would create press materials to promote the Festival in national and regional press and left feeling that we at least had an accord.

I did promote the Festival and with great success, with an excellent piece appearing in The Observer and some whopping pieces in regional titles. I attended and had a fantastic time there, boarding a Tall Ship, seeing cannon fire and enjoying activities such as riding on board an RAF simulated flight. There was also a BBC tent there, in which my son had a go at giving some commentary to a piece of football footage. He had created his own football commentaries from the age of about five, so I wasn't at all surprised when the BBC chap told me he was really good and that he should try to get into a radio station and get some experience there. He is still excellent, but that hasn't yet happened.

My luck with another character wasn't as good. The ad men, who had first introduced me to the surgeon, asked me to go and see a recruitment consultant. This was one of my very many classic experiences where I find that the person's voice does not match their body whatsoever. Imagine my surprise when actually the first signs of the body, in the shape of a very large belly, appeared before the voice by a good 10 seconds as it rounded the corner! I'd been expecting a very distinguished, lithe man with a slick suit and smart appearance, not someone in white shirt and braces.

This man was a true character, repeating the phrase 'I'm global and international' around 20 times in the course of 20 minutes! Those words will always stick in my head when I think of him, as exactly the same thing occurred, with the same regularity, in subsequent meetings.

Although this was a short-lived relationship, something very strange happened for years afterwards. Somehow, I must have acquired about 10 of this chap's business cards and they have haunted me every since. They fall out of filing cabinets, seem to appear in files that have nothing to do with him, crop up in archive boxes and more. What spooked me most, however, was that he was with me to the end, clinging like a limpet. When it came to packing up my computer to leave my office and re-locate, there was his business card, stuck very firmly to my desk, in the remains of a sticky deposit caused by spilt coffee many moons before. He was global, international and literally immovable!!

Chapter 21
ANGELS & DEMONS

2008 was definitely a year of angels and demons. The North West Farm Tourism Initiative had already come to a magnificent end, with the North West Development Agency (NWDA) funding having ceased. I wrote a legacy report for the project, which became the blueprint of how to do farm tourism and it was suddenly time to do other things.

One of these things involved judging the NWDA's Sustainable Tourism Award as my new best friend, Katie, had started working on the promotion of natural tourism in the northwest. Judging entailed going to visit the four different county winners of their local tourism board's Sustainable Tourism Awards, to assess their performance against set criteria. One was a large golf and country club hotel in Cheshire, another the SAS Radisson at Manchester Airport. The third was the Palace Hotel in Manchester and the fourth a 'green' B&B in Cumbria.

This, however, is not the purpose of this tale, interesting though the different approaches to sustainability were. The main thrust of this part of my tale involves the award ceremony itself, held in Liverpool's magnificent King George's Hall. The ceremony was compèred by Laurence Llewelyn Bowen and was followed by a grab-your-own-food-from-a-market-stall dining experience, which was a little tricky, requiring the balancing of meat pies and Eccles cakes on the same small plate as mushy peas and hotpot. In the end, I ate next to nothing, purely because of the logistical issues involved in the whole process.

What we hadn't been told about this grand Liverpudlian occasion related to the 'star turn' booked for the night, who suddenly descended from the heavens playing the organ and the dramatic notes from Phantom of the Opera. It was none other than the X-Factor's Rhydian, whose hopes of fame and fortune in the West End must have nose-dived if he was playing this gig!

Some of the people watching, including the lady from the Cumbrian B&B that we had judged, didn't have a clue who this platinum blonde male bombshell with the deep voice was, so I had to explain. By this point, Rhydian was circulating around the dance floor like a spinning top that was out of control, trying to do that hand-slapping thing that pop stars do with their groupies, only failing miserably, as nobody was interested.

I, however, knew that I would be in deep trouble, if I didn't take a picture of him on my phone to show to my son, so started fiddling around with the picture taking facility, which I didn't have a clue how to work. All of this meant that I was seemingly standing by the side of the dance floor, taking picture after picture of Rhydian, as if I were some sort of stalker fan. Given that I was the only one doing this, I stuck out like a sore thumb and was quickly noticed by the Welsh wizard, who started to belt out his notes right in front of me, lingering in front of the camera like a moth In front of a flame. I quickly put my phone down, made some sort of gesture that signified, 'you're OK, you can move on', and scarpered as fast as I could. The thought of being stuck with someone who sings Shirley Bassey numbers in a long, white fur coat kept me awake for weeks!

Given that these awards covered the whole of the northwest, I was particularly keen to see some winners from my local area and felt obliged to write to them, after the event, to congratulate them on their success. This proved a mistake.

Within a day or so of receiving my letter, an accommodation provider rang me up, wanting to talk to me about exposure, as they felt they were constantly being overlooked. I went along to see this couple and found their business as proficient and lovely as I had expected. What I hadn't bargained on was being given their life history, as a couple, including the fact that there was a massive age gap between them, with the wife being far older than the husband.

It was clear to me that the husband was keen to use my services, but not the wife. A certain expression was fixed on her face, communicating that she wished I'd never been invited into her inner sanctum. This became even more apparent when she kept calling me Vanessa instead of Jane, deliberately, it transpired, as she was actually trying to compare me to Vanessa Feltz!

I explained at length what I could do to assist this business and was taken on, returning to further meetings to explain the activity I had carried out. The wife's feelings were made crystal clear, when at one meeting she uttered words now entombed in Catapult history, 'To be honest, I'd rather have a tram than you'! Knowing that a metal, gaudy advert driving up and down the promenade, and only seen by people already in resort, was deemed preferable to the PR I was generating across the country, really was the last nail in the coffin.

In the spring of 2008, I was given a referral and asked to go and see the owners of what would be a new themed hotel. My thoughts on this instantly went back to the days of Mrs Sparkle and her Blackpool themed hotel that was destroyed by the TV documentary programme that featured it. I really hoped for much better.

At face value, it was going to be far more spectacular, though there was nothing for me to see when I first visited, other than the empty building that was being renovated and the logo – a rather unfortunate one featuring a bikini clad woman. Somehow, the local paper got it into their head that the name had connotations with a brothel and started writing about this with great gusto. This echoed the thoughts of my mother when I had shown the logo and name to her and I did recommend to the client that they think about changing the name and logo prior to opening. They simply didn't want to.

As with all of these projects the time spent on the building work dragged on and on, with a summer launch put back, in the end, to October. By then, the themed rooms were looking good for the most part, with some more spectacular and others just plain quirky. There was no doubt that it was a very different concept and, by enthusing about the various rooms, I managed to get a magnificent turn out for the official press launch – two TV crews, three radio stations, all of the local papers and local tourism officials too.

The idea for the press launch was to have the owner speak about the project and take the press on a tour of the rooms. I had invited them all for a drink and canapés and stated the time at which the owner would give the introductory speech. All went well in terms of press arrival ... the only problem was that the owner went missing!

Attempts to find him failed miserably and journalists started looking at their watches, murmuring about time getting on. By this point, I couldn't find the wife either, so was left with a young chap who had designs on being the marketing assistant at the hotel. Given that we could find nobody else to lead the tour, we had to scrap the speech idea and have this rather flamboyant chap lead us around the hotel.

We had probably visited six of the rooms before we walked into another and found the owner sitting in there chatting to a friend. It was obvious that the media found this very bizarre, but having now found him, took the opportunity to fire questions at him. By the time we left the room, at least some of the murmuring had stopped and we completed the tour leaving a real wow factor to last – the bridal suite.

This launch generated some absolutely fantastic coverage for the hotel, on TV, in the local and regional press and lifestyle titles and also nationally. Best of all, however, the owner's wife revealed that she had been in the local pub the night before launch and, even then, an ex journalist had told her that whoever was doing her PR must be 'bloody good!'

Having now won the accounts of Lakes Aquarium, SLTAG, Ullswater Steamers, Ravenglass & Eskdale Railway and a few others, to name but a few tourism sector businesses, I decided that in my new status as a freelance PR person, it would be a good idea to focus on a particular niche within PR, to back up my financial PR experience. I believed tourism was the niche to go for.

For a few years, I had been toying with the idea of studying with an organisation called Capela for a CIM Tourism Diploma. I had put it off and off, due to Italian GCSE exams in 2006, workload and other factors, but by October 2008 was ready to take the plunge. Had I known how difficult this was going to be for me, I probably wouldn't have bothered!

At the time, there were four different modules to study: Marketing

Planning, Hospitality & Service Marketing, Marketing Management in Practice and Tourist Behaviour and Motivation and these were staggered across a two-year period. Each required background study on the topic under scrutiny, plus attendance at two-day sessions in Manchester given by the distance-learning tutor. What I hadn't realised was that, in my case, I would have to 'become' one of my tourism clients in order to apply theory to a practical scenario. In everyone else's case, they could be themselves!

Throughout the two years of this course, I had the constant dilemma of who to be. I didn't have access to all the insights, facts and figures that someone actually employed by a tourism organisation had, so was always at a disadvantage. To get through, I really had to do what I do best and throw in loads of ideas and inspiration, to make up for any lack of key data.

This seemed to bemuse rather than amuse the tutor, without whose guidance, I wouldn't have passed. His name was Gary Grieve and I'm sure he won't mind me saying that for me it was often Gary Grief, particularly when I got feedback on what I had sent to him and read his comments! Much grief was indeed suffered, particularly in module one, not so much from the point of view of study, but because I suddenly had to learn how to use those weird little symbols on my Apple Mac called drawing tools, which absolutely drove me up the wall, as I tried to insert and design my own charts, putting text boxes in impossibly small places and trying my best to make it look as if I knew what I was doing. Add to that having to master the Harvard referencing system and it was a very long way removed from the walk in the park that I had actually thought it might be, in my naivety and blissful ignorance when signing up.

I was almost driven over the edge in module 1, by the strange incident of the linked text boxes, which I just couldn't get rid of, no matter what I did. In the end, I opted for the most sensible course of action that any woman of my age can take and picked up my laptop and transported it to where I knew I would find my son. It was a mystery for the younger generation to solve and, thankfully, he did!

My first module saw me becoming extremely innovative when it came to the marketing of the themed hotel. It was all about choosing the right marketing strategy (the theory) and then applying it to the hotel's scenario, which was extraordinarily difficult for the questions on distribution and pricing – and even parts of the general marketing plan for relationship management – as I wasn't privy to figures and facts needed. However, when it came to the product development question, I excelled and had some great ideas that even Gary thought were top drawer. I'm pretty sure it was this ideas-led part of the paper that saved me from the total doom and despondency that would have accompanied an ungraded mark!

From the word go, I got on really well with fellow seminar attendees, the lovely Emma Foster from Salford Council and now Media City, Carol from Port Sunlight and, on later seminars, Jo from the National Trust in Cumbria. We were a little gang of four, and Emma and I went through the whole process together from start to finish.

When it came to servicescape (and by now I was drawing interlocking spheres!) customer loyalty and relationship marketing and ICT papers, I had to be visitor attraction, Lakes Aquarium. When we focused on authenticity and festivals I became the Appleby Horse Fair and when the paper was destination marketing, I became the Western Lake District.

For my final paper, I was lucky enough to have a question on sustainability and could be the very committed sustainable tourism operator, Ullswater 'Steamers', accessing some real data via my client Rachel. Clutching at straws, I became a travel insurance operator for the 'Market Research and Information Needs' topic and to round things off, ended up being Lakes Aquarium again for the final paper. I suspect never before in the history of this course has one student been so many different organisations!

After more than two hard years of slog and trying to squeeze all of this in while not only running the business, but also studying for an Italian A' Level, I managed to earn my qualification – a fact of which I am very proud. I also met some lovely people along the way. It was certainly 100% tougher than I had imagined, but I got a hell of a lot out of it, not only to the benefit of tourism clients, but for all clients.

The more observant among you will have noted that I referred to Lakes Aquarium just now. This is because in early 2008 it rebranded and completely changed its theme, no longer focusing on the journey of life within Cumbria, but comparing and contrasting life in Windermere with that in other lakes of the world.

My client had gone on maternity leave late in 2007, appointing an interim marketing manager to fill her role during her absence. A fairly new marketing assistant was also in place and both were now in charge of re-launching the Aquarium in its new guise.

As I already held the PR contract for Lakes Aquarium, it was with some surprise that I took a phone call at 10am one morning to say that the group operations manager was in the Lakes and asking PR agencies to pitch for the PR account! I was absolutely dumbfounded, but told to get to Lakes Aquarium for 2pm to meet him!

I had never put a PR proposal together as fast as I did on that day, even though I had no PR brief and just sketchy information about something called the Virtual Dive Bell, which would be a world first and transport people to the bottom of an African lake to face Nile crocodiles, bull sharks and angry hippos. I threw all I could into this, got it on to paper as fast as possible and drove the 75-minutes to the attraction.

When I arrived, the stand-in marketing manager took me into the restaurant, where I found a man and woman who were introduced to me, but who looked a little bemused by my arrival. I introduced myself as Jane Hunt. The marketing manager left me there and so I started to take them through the proposal I had written, seemingly getting quite good responses.

The 'pitch' for the account I already held then ended and the main man looked at me and said, 'Sorry, who are you?' At that point, I realised neither of the people I had just sold my soul to had an inkling that I was their PR consultant. On that basis, I had to drop that in.

'We didn't have a clue', said the lady. 'How long have you been our PR consultant?' I explained that I was appointed 9 months before.

'Who appointed you?' asked the man. I explained that too. I then explained that I also had a contract, wondering in my own head who had been signing my cheques off each month!

Luckily for me, and not for the first or last time in my career, the ideas had won the day and I started to tackle the launch.

There were two distinct sides to this. On the one hand, there was a public launch to be created. On the other there was a need to introduce all the local hoteliers, B&Bs, campsites, pubs and restaurants to the new-look venue and encourage them to tell their guests and customers about it. Together the campaign I devised was called 'Crocodiles Rock'.

I went into this campaign a little blind, quite literally, as I hadn't been present at any meetings at which the new interactive feature had been discussed. I knew where it was going to be situated within the attraction, but apart from that, I only ever saw drawings and sketches. Somehow, all of this had to be brought to life, to attract the general public and the Lake District visitor. It needed something exceptional to ensure that as many people as possible knew about it.

It was a no-brainer to have a drip feed campaign running up to the opening of the Virtual Dive Bell and I tried to make that as exciting as possible. The first thing I did was to get one of the Aquarium's divers to take part in the publicity. A team of divers regularly cleaned the tubing through which the visitor views the fish in the Aquarium's amazing underwater tunnel. I managed to persuade the Aquarium to cajole one of this team to wander up to the Aquarium in his wet suit, as if emerging from Windermere, on which the attraction stands, to collect his invitation to the VIP launch. The pictures worked a treat.

My next mission was to create an innovative April Fool's stunt, for which I had to find some musicians. I asked around various music groups and eventually found a few youngsters willing to turn up at the attraction after school with their instruments in hand. The junior musicians were then situated inside the Virtual Dive Bell in such a way as to make it look like they were playing Handel's Water Music deep under the ocean. This was labelled 'The World's First Underwater Chamber Music Concert' – a real April Fools trick, if ever there was one.

However, to make a real impact, for a technical feature that didn't have the cute appeal of a brand new creature moving in to the Aquarium or the wow factor that new cute babies might attract at an animal attraction, I decided that we had to look beyond working with animals, children and men in wetsuits and actually bring in a real, live celebrity.

To that end, I started researching options, mainly based on two things – involvement with wildlife and countryside programmes and celebrity fee. Having been down this route before, I was determined to shop around amongst agents and find the very best affordable option available. I am very pleased to say that this strategy resulted in me hiring the lovely Michaela Strachan and finding an agent in Jo Sarsby, who was truly helpful, professional and worth their cut of the fee, thanks to their refreshingly honest and considerate attitude to all negotiations.

Naturally, I wanted Michaela to have a purpose beyond just cutting a ribbon, so in advance of her appearance at the Aquarium, I created a 'Junior Reporters' contest. All local schools in the South Lakes, Lancaster and Morecambe areas were sent information about the contest, which asked children to write an imaginative piece of copy leading on from a given opening paragraph, which related to the Virtual Dive Bell.

Short listed children were to be given a pass to come to the attraction with their reporting 'crew' – up to four friends – to interview Michaela Strachan and get all the information required for a report on the day and the Virtual Dive Bell as a feature. Entries duly came in and the reporters whittled down to a manageable number, who could compete for the prize on offer of a trophy and goodies.

The day of the official launch came round really fast and it was decreed that, to get Michaela to the Aquarium on time, it would be best if I picked her up at Preston railway station and then drove her up. I was a little nervous about suddenly becoming a chauffeur to a celebrity, but was equally relieved that I had just bought a new car! I was accompanied in my chauffeuring mission by Hayley, a part-time helper, who I had taken on for a few hours a month.

Hayley and I set off for Preston station that day not having a clue what to expect from this celebrity. We parked the car up and walked into the station keen to escort her as quickly as possible to the car, as we had an over-the-phone interview set up with BBC Radio Cumbria and the timing was tight. As the train pulled in, we waited to see people disembark and I luckily caught sight of Michaela, in casual cream pants and looking exactly as she does on the TV. I made the introductions and then whipped her off to the car, where we awaited the call from radio presenter Val Armstrong.

The interview went swimmingly, even though it was over 10 minutes long. I was watching the clock the entire time, wondering if we could make it to the Aquarium in time for the designated hour of arrival. I really had to put my foot down to get us there, but just about made it. As one might have predicted, it was absolutely pouring down at Lakeside, with Windermere hardly visible through the driving precipitation, so I had to whip out a Catapult golf umbrella and shepherd Michaela into the building, where a row of press photographers and reporters were waiting to interview her.

This gave me time to reflect on what a thoroughly nice and normal celebrity she transpired to be, with no airs and graces whatsoever. She had chatted continuously to myself and Hayley and it was almost as if we'd known her for years, as she explained about her life in South Africa, where she lives for much of the year, when not working in the UK.

By now the acting marketing manager had greeted Michaela and directed her towards the canteen for a quick sandwich and then the ladies toilets. I was occupied greeting parents and junior reporters and crews, so just assumed that Michaela would be brought back the same way that she had been taken out, but Hayley and I waited and waited and began to wonder where on earth she had gone.

Suddenly, the marketing assistant appeared on the stairs, so I asked her if she knew where Michaela had gone. 'She's in the Dive Bell', came the reply. I had been holding a reporter back, awaiting Michaela's return, so was mystified as to why nobody had thought to tell myself, or the waiting press, that she'd been brought back through the rear entrance. Hayley and I piled up the stairs and found a scene of pandemonium. Poor Michaela was standing in the midst of a sea of clamouring children, with all the procedures we had put in place for organised interviewing having gone completely out of the window.

She looked over at me and seemed totally relieved by my arrival. 'I was just left here', she said. 'I don't have a clue what's supposed to be happening'. Given the number of people in the room, I hadn't even realised she had no Aquarium representation with her. I felt truly sorry for her, but she carried on like a trooper, as I now tried to create order out of total chaos.

Any thought of stringing up the ribbon that she was supposed to cut had been completely absent, so we now had the very hard task, of clearing enough room to get that in place while the people, who should have been outside the Dive Bell observing, were actually inside the Dive Bell creating bedlam.

Once we'd managed to somehow get the official opening shots, Hayley and I quickly established where the winning junior reporters were and called up one crew after another to come and take their turn at interviewing Michaela. As this process evolved, two things occurred. The first was my realisation that boys are from Mars and girls are from Venus, even at the age of 10 and 11. All the girl reporters had brought clipboards and had a list of carefully thought out questions. All the boys were shooting from the hip and conducting their interviews in a totally haphazard and impromptu way, just as things came into their heads, with no preparation at all.

The second thing that became obvious was that there was something weird going on with a man in the crowd. Michaela made some comment about her child's birthday to a group of children and he responded by naming the dates of that birthday and Michaela's. I then realised that he was snapping photo after photo. I collared an Aquarium manager and asked who he was. She said that he'd rocked up hours before Michaela's arrival and had said that he was a real fan who had travelled especially from Lancashire to see her.

Once all reporters and the TV crew and press photographers had got their stories and all had, in turn, had their pictures taken with Michaela for the records of mums, dads, grannies and granddads, we began to take Michaela on a tour of the attraction, with Dave the education officer explaining all about the different creatures. At this point, the avid snapper had been in and out of the Aquarium shop countless times buying new rolls of film. All staff were now getting rather concerned by his behaviour. In the end, we had to take measures to get Michaela away from him.

The hours whizzed by and the whole thing had been truly successful. Children – both winners and others – had had a great time and were fired up to go away and write up their reports. Their faces were soon to appear as the lead banner on the North West Evening Mail, which did a fantastic spread on the whole day. Younger brothers and sisters had been entertained with drawing and craft activities in the Seashore Discovery Zone, where a pretend mermaid was watching over things. Parents were simply gushing about what a fantastic day their offspring had enjoyed – perhaps to influence the judges' future decision about the articles that would be written, but let's not be too cynical.

It was time for me to drive Michaela back to Preston for her train and, in the car, the topic of the snapper came up. I asked her if she had been alarmed by it and she said that it had been a little unnerving, as police had recently interviewed her about another very serious 'stalker' related case, as photos of her and other celebrities had been found in someone's home. She said incidents like that day's now made her think a little more about things. It made me think that it's really isn't all fun being a celebrity – especially one abandoned in a room with around 70 children all clamouring for attention!

We dropped Michaela back at Preston, exchanged numbers with her and secretly breathed a sigh of relief. All at the Aquarium launch had gone swimmingly, to pardon the pun.

All that remained was to organise the pre-view night for local tourism operators, accommodation providers, tourism chiefs and others. For this event, we had the marathon hero, Lloyd Scott, in attendance, in the famous diver's outfit and helmet in which he completed the London Marathon, despite having leukaemia as a result of inhaling toxic fumes while working as a firefighter. He proved to be another truly lovely person, but the events of the night took a very strange turn that resulted in someone's stints on the microphone and 'dance floor' (actually the middle of the restaurant) costing them dear. Luckily it wasn't me, or my rogue elephant-fighting companion Hayley. We were too busy smarting at having had our efforts in the launch of the Dive Bell described as 'stuffing a few envelopes'.

Luckily, our efforts were recognised as being more than this by the Chartered Institute of Public Relations and we picked up a Silver Award in the 'Best Consumer PR Campaign' category of the NW awards. That was a really good way to end 2008 – a year that had definitely seen encounters with both angels and demons.

Chapter 22
SUNGLASSES, STICKS AND STONES

2009 started on a real high, thanks to another bit of farm tourism PR. This was on behalf of a northeast farm attraction that I really got off to a bit of a bad start with, having got hopelessly lost en route. Being lost wasn't made any easier by the fact that nobody answered the phone when I rang the attraction and, having stopped and hailed dog walkers, women with prams and various other passers-by, it was by sheer luck that I found it at all. It was about this time that I created the golden rule of being lost – finding a postman. Since then, it's really spooky, because I always seem to manage to do that – but only if I'm lost en route to a morning appointment!

My first piece of activity for this farm attraction involved promoting their stunning Christmas barn, which they were decking out with thousands of twinkling lights, a Santa's Post Office, a fantastic sleigh and even live reindeer. I sold this story to their local TV stations and they were inundated with visitors. Off the back of this, I had to next promote Easter at the farm.

I vividly remember a conversation that I had with the owner, who told me that she didn't feel promoting the attraction in the national press would be beneficial to her at all. I tried to persuade her otherwise and just about got permission to go beyond local press, probably on the basis that it wasn't costing her any more for me to do that anyway.

For Easter promotion, she sent me an absolutely gorgeous picture of two little girls in flowery, country dresses sitting on a farm fence and cud-dlng lambs. Off I set, attempting to prove that national coverage would work. Using all my farm tourism experience, I picked publications to target and issued details of the activities available at the farm. Four different national travel sections ran with the story, with beautiful usage of the picture in all cases. I hoped that this had had an impact.

Immediately after Easter, the owner rang me up and I prayed that she'd had good footfall. Over the years, I've become more and more involved with my clients' businesses and shared their hopes and dreams, so their success means as much to me as my own, in many ways.

She told me that she was ringing to say that she had been wrong and that I had been absolutely right about the nationals. She had trebled her gate on Easter Monday and when she'd asked parents why they had visited, they had mainly said that it was because they had seen the farm mentioned in the Independent on Sunday's '50 Best Spring Days Out'. They had also driven their little darlings a fair distance just to visit this particular farm.

That was a great start to the season and more promotion throughout the year generated further fantastic coverage. I was really enjoying what I was doing and also getting more involved once again with farm and natural tourism.

That continued through the promotion of five demonstration projects funded by Natural Economy Northwest. One was actually my brainchild, as I had a vision of a Cumbrian wildlife cluster in what I called the Wildzone. This went down a treat with the powers that be and it became one of five funded projects. Others were a farm accommodation cluster in Cheshire, new trails and birdwatching resources in the Forest of Bowland, a sustainable trail at WWT Martin Mere and a woodland play experience in Cumbria.

All of these were to have their own bespoke activities provided through PR, but my new best friend, Katie – had set her heart on having a stand at the 'BBC Countryfile Show' at the NEC – part of BBC Gardeners' World. Not only that, she wanted it to be created as a bird hide.

In theory, this was all marvellous. In practice, there was no budget for this. It was also decided pretty late in the day that the stand space would be booked, leaving me with the headache of trying to create a bird hide out of peanuts, complete with videos running behind supposed viewing slits in the back of the hide!

It is no exaggeration to say that I lost sleep over this for very many weeks. I tried numerous exhibition companies, who all failed to get back to me the moment they learned of the available budget. On the other side of the fence, (or bird hide perhaps), my client wouldn't budge or down-size her dream. I was just left in an impossible position and the weeks were ticking by, as one exhibition design company after another let me down.

In the end, I called a joiner into the office and explained to him what we wanted. He could have done something to assist, had he had time, but didn't know anything about the exhibition regulations, with regard to aspects such as health and safety and lighting. He would have had to climb a big learning curve.

After this, I was truly desperate and less able to sleep than ever. With very little time to go, I somehow stumbled across a company in Manchester, which said it could help. It came up with some plans – more than I'd managed elsewhere – and downgraded some of the brief to suit the budget. I was totally relieved and managed to get the downgraded plans passed.

The next bombshell dropped on me was that I would have to man the stand, for at least some of the day, on most of the days of the show, including my son's birthday. This entailed a very long trip to beyond Birmingham and back each time. I also had to be there for 7am at the latest, so I spent virtually a whole week getting up at the crack of dawn to be on the road for 4.30am at the latest. As five different projects were sharing the stand – one on each day of the show – I was invariably cart-ing one project's materials off the stand at around 7am, before another project arrived to put theirs up. My route to and from the car park be-came well trodden, but I had wisely invested in a little carry truck and handle (which sold like a bomb at Gardeners' World) on day one and wore my trusty Cocorose foldable ballerina pumps, so that my feet sur-vived the daily ordeal!

Life on the stand with different stand partners was very interesting, with each having completely different approaches to the way that they wanted to use the stand as a sales tool. I did many shifts of manning the stand while stand partners went off to get lunch or tour the show, so certainly earned my money. I also came to realise that the Countryfile viewer of that time was already an avid birdwatcher or nature lover, not the kind of nature virgin that some of the projects were trying to attract.

Some interesting things happened to me during the show. Being the early bird that I was, I would remove the previous day's mess and then head off for my breakfast, in the form of a cappuccino. One morning I had my eyes fixed on a chap, though in reality I was just daydreaming, but it occurred to me that his face was very familiar. The coffee bar was empty bar the two of us, so he asked if he could join me. At that moment, I realised that it was the Olympian, Geoff Capes.

He chatted to me for ages, after I'd acknowledged that I knew who he was. I learned all about his love of budgerigars, his fear of flying (which prevents him from taking part in 'I'm A Celebrity' and his work for various security firms. He was a really interesting chap and he gave me his card, in case any future work came up, for which he could be suitable. That morning went with a real zing.

The other big plus for me came on the very last day. The stand was very well manned that day by the Cheshire farm ladies, so I was a bit of a spare part, but had to hang around a bit, to see that all was well. I suddenly became aware of a big stir on the BBC Good Food stand. I wandered across and found that the hullabaloo was down to the fact that Gino d'Acampo was appearing later and signing copies of his book. At this point, he wasn't as big a name as he is now, as it was pre-jungle and he was just an up-and-coming chef, but I decided that I wanted to queue and get two books signed.

As the rope for the queue opened, there was a mad dash to get into it and I was quite a way back. I heard the staff on the book stall saying that Gino had instigated a cut off point in the queue at his last signing session and that lots of people had been disappointed. As an official looking chap walked up and down the queue, I prayed he wouldn't cut it in front of me.

I quickly grasped what was happening. Gino was at a table and women (there were no men in sight) were going up to him and getting one kiss on the cheek. Most of them were absolutely swooning as he then put his arm around them, brought them in towards him and let friends take their picture with him. As I had no friend there to take my picture and could hardly holler over half the NEC to my Cheshire farm ladies, I decided I had to get my share in some other way. I decided to call upon my Italian.

Now, by this point, I'd been learning Italian for about six years, so I could confidently converse a bit with him on arrival at the table, after receiving my token kiss. This seemed to impress him and he gabbled back to me in Italian while signing the books, as I explained that one was for a friend. I could see women hovering around the enclosure looking increasingly jealous and others hoofing the carpet waiting to get into the enclosure to get their hands on Gino. We finally finished our chat and he gave me another kiss. As I walked away from the table, I heard one woman on the perimeter fence say, 'She got two kisses and everyone else only got one', in a most disgruntled tone. I smiled sweetly to myself thinking that all those hours of Italian study had not been in vain. At least I could flirt well in italiano!

Almost immediately after all my days spent at the NEC, I did two of the slightly crazy things that I sometimes do. The first involved twigs and was to launch the Wildzone to the outside world. I'd come up with an idea of a mailer that was a designed label attached to a twig. The label was to read, 'Have you twigged yet?' and was to direct people to the Wildzone website, to get information about various wildlife experiences that they could enjoy across Cumbria.

Katie's two twin boys apparently spent a very happy few hours in the woods collecting twigs for 'Auntie Jane' and 'Auntie Jane' spent many a long hour attaching them to the mailer tag, putting them in envelopes and posting them out! They did look really good, however, so the effort was worth it and it was a truly novel mechanic with which to hit press between the eyes.

The second crazy thing involved the promotion of a new guide to sustainable holidays that I had painstakingly researched and written. The idea was to utilise a piece of research which showed that visitors to Cumbria would park the car up for a day or two during their holiday, if they knew what transport options were available and what they could do without a car.

I spent days on this, as the best way of approaching it was to pick one area of Cumbria and concentrate on sustainable transport and things to do within it. I chose the east of Cumbria, which is perfectly named as Eden.

I had suggested that we could name this the 'Give Your Car A Holiday Guide' and so launch it with a photo of a car wearing a giant pair of sunglasses on its windscreen, as if parked up and catching some rays, while its owners walked, caught buses, hopped on boats and hired bicycles.

I roped in my client Mrs B from Ullswater 'Steamers' and asked if I could take pics by the shore of Ullswater. Mrs B and I first took some shots in the car park of the Inn on the Lake and then headed back to the shore by the pier house. The fact that I managed to take any shots was a miracle in itself. There was a very stiff breeze blowing across the lake and I would have just perfectly positioned the giant sunglasses on the windscreen, when a gust of wind would spring up and blow them half-way across the car park, necessitating me running around like a blonde madwoman chasing ginormous, cardboard sunglasses.

Eventually, we managed to get some shots where the sunglasses stayed on, if a little wonkily placed and publications did actually print them!

This, however, was not the only skirmish by the water that Mrs B and I would have with the forces of nature! Our very finest moment came in July of that year and involved the 'All England Open Stone Skimming Championships' – something that I religiously support, to this day by offering my services for free.

South Cumbria Rivers Trust had devised the 'All England Open Stone Skimming Championships' as a fundraiser. The event allows both adults and children to have a go at skimming a stone and attempting to become an official English champion, whose score goes into the record books. The stones have to be skimmed within lanes marked out in the water and, to record a score, a stone has to bounce a minimum of three times before sinking. It is then the stone that travels the furthest, taking these rules into consideration, which wins.

The previous year, I had been hugely successful in getting the Cumbria-shy Granada TV to travel up to Windermere to film the stone skimming. A very long piece of broadcast coverage resulted, which was then followed by Border TV coverage and lots of press and radio too. So, consequently, when it came to summer 2009, I wanted to find a fresh angle to again entice the cameras. I opted to create the inaugural 'All England Open Mascot Stone Skimming Contest".

This is something that I shall certainly never forget and I think it's one of those events in life that will always make one chuckle! The mascot stone skimming was intended to act as a pre-view piece for the main competition on the Saturday – which happened to be the day on which I was going on holiday. With a late morning photo call, I knew that I would be fine for time, so set about rounding up some mascots.

I wrote to various attractions, many of whom had nobody to go into their mascot costume, but did manage to secure the services of La'al Ratty (Ravenglass and Eskdale Railway), Sammy the Squirrel (Ullswater 'Steamers'), Oscar the Otter (Lakes Aquarium), a new Bear on the block – Plumpton – (Lakeside and Haverthwaite Railway) and a visiting mascot from afar, who represented a northwest sporting club. I had thought that securing the services of the latter was quite a coup. We all know what thought did!

That year's competition was held at Coniston and I arrived in glorious sunshine in a thin-strapped bohemian flowing top with a plunging neck-line, cream casual pants and sandals. I ordered a coffee at the Bluebird Café on the lake and sat on its decking sipping contentedly while working on my laptop. Suddenly, out of the blue, the heavens opened and all 'deckers' had to dive for cover. At that point, the visiting mascot from afar turned up, demanding a cooked breakfast for him and his partner.

This was the first example of what proved to be quite diva-like be-haviour throughout his time on the lake. He took himself off into a ca-noe at one point and almost tipped over, before then insulting all the other mascots by highlighting how superior his costume was, with its breathable materials and ventilation. By this point, I was recalling some incident involving fistycuffs and Cyril the Swan at Swansea and praying that none of that would go on at Coniston. There was obviously great snobbery and rivalry in the mascot world and let anyone who thinks differently cast the first stone!

All the mind games had stoked the mascots up for a fight by the time they got to stone skimming's equivalent of the 'oche'. To get two of them that far, however, I had to lead them by the hand, like Dorothy leading the Tin Man and the Lion down to the shore. Neither of these mascots could see through their heads, so I had to be their eyes, traversing the bumpy pebbles on the lake's shore in my sandals, with my ankle turning over every few seconds, as I held one mascot with one hand and the other with my other.

My client with Oscar the Otter could see all of this perfectly and was chortling behind me as a Border TV camera filmed my backside and the very strange sight of a grown woman taking two mascots out for a promenade by the lake! The folk holidaying by the lake also seemed to find it highly amusing, but a girl's got to do what a girl's got to do, backside being filmed or not! To this day, the client, who was bringing up the rear (no pun intended), says it was one of the funniest things she's ever seen.

Having got both of my charges safely to the shore, I didn't feel responsible for their actions. Perhaps I should have been. As might have been predicted, the visiting mascot charged in to show the others how to do it, whilst most were still working out how to hold a stone in their paws, let alone how to skim it! Having seen the visitor's display of confidence, however, all went up to take their turn, with Plumpton suddenly revealing local knowledge, having skimmed stones many times here in his youth. It was clear that the cocksure interloper would have a bear-and-a-half to beat before he could walk away with the title.

Sammy the Squirrel, Oscar and La'al Ratty were, however, rather more reticent, the fact that two of them could hardly see a thing not helping at all. Oscar skimmed bravely: Sammy followed suit. Next up came La'al, aka my client Mrs B.

At this point, a rather unfortunate incident occurred. Having got his stone in his ratty little hand and then managed to get his balance and sense of direction more or less sorted, a rather dumb Coniston duck decided to paddle over to see what all the fuss was about. The stone squirted out of La'al's hand rather feebly, but somehow managed to land right on the back feathers of the Coniston duck, which scarpered quickly, making quite a racket as it went.

As everyone knew that La'al couldn't see a thing and as a colleague of Mrs B's was being Sammy for the day, the colleague turned this whole incident into a melodrama. There was an, 'Oh my God, what's happened to the duck?' pronounced in a dramatic Welsh accent, as we all followed suit and suggested that it was perhaps still under the water, having maybe been concussed by the stone that had so unfortunately coshed it on the head! La'al began to panic, believing that a duck had truly become a fatality of this most innocent of pastimes, while the visitor from afar splashed about in his canoe again, extolling the virtues of his costume and ignoring the banter completely.

All three stones were thrown by all of the mascots just before the heavens opened once again and we all had to take cover under a gazebo that was helpfully erected on the shore to cover schoolchildren having a watersports' lesson. It was determined that years of practice as a boy had served Plumpton well, as he proved the winner by a mile, with a rather disgruntled visitor having his feathers ruffled at having to take second place, despite his superior costume. It was, I recall, suggested that the bear done good because of his more human-shaped hands. Maybe someone's costume had a defect after all!

At this point, the Border TV cameraman/interviewer decided that he wanted to interview the stone skimming organiser, Ben, and some mascots. By now, I was absolutely freezing and decided that putting on a rather oversized navy cagoule, that I'd had for years, was the only way forward. My hair had frizzed up into curls and coils in the rain and I had a strong suspicion that mascara was running down my cheeks.

The interview with Ben went swimmingly, Ben not being known as 'booming Ben' for nothing. Next came the request for an interview with a mascot. 'I can't do an interview', said the visitor from afar, much to my surprise. 'I'm not allowed to speak'. I witnessed all mascots turn to face each other at this point, their big, furry heads literally in their hands, as if their animal existence had suffered some decapitation.

'Well, I don't think I'm allowed to speak either', said another, 'as sometimes it's a woman in me and sometimes it's a man'.

417

'Thinking about it, I don't know if I am either', said another, as the others also threw their doubts about their contractual obligations into the mix. Stuart, the Border TV man, then uttered the immortal words, 'Well is there anyone else who can speak for you?' The only people without a head in their hands at this crucial moment in time were Ben and I, and Ben had already been interviewed. All eyes turned on me with expectation. I, with my cagoule, straggly hair and mascara-ridden face was the only option!

'You'll have to act like an interpreter', Stuart suggested, as my mouth fell open realising that I not only had to be interviewed, but had to act at the same time – multi-tasking with a mascot! My only consolation was that the visitor from afar had taken himself off to get more food, so I wasn't going to be heckled or told that my costume was totally inferior! I didn't need telling!

As we determined that I should be interviewed with La'al Ratty, I led him (actually Mrs B) by the hand to stand under the trees that were providing a modicum of shelter from the rain. I had to hold Ratty's hand throughout the interview and must have looked like some over-protective carer. It was probably the most bizarre thing that I've ever done in my life and I decided that the only way to go was to make it really tongue-in-cheek and play it for laughs.

Stuart would ask me a question, at which point, I would have to turn to Mrs B dressed as Ratty and say, 'What's that Ratty? ... oh yes, Ratty says that he did try his best, but other mascots were much better than him', or equally ridiculous phrases. This is how the interview proceeded, with not a word uttered by Mrs B, who just shook her head or made a gesture at times, with me having to deliver the answer, as if I had picked it up from my mascot friend through divine inspiration.

A fair few questions proceeded like this, until I received the killer one and the look on my face must have been a picture, as Stuart delivered it with a triumphant look on his face. 'I believe, Ratty, that you hit a duck while you were stone skimming. What have you got to say about that?' I could feel Mrs B clench my hand and knew it was all down to me to get her off the hook.

Now, I've never seen this bit of footage, though I believe the whole thing, from the parade across the stones to this moment of TV gold, was hilarious. I can categorically state that I never want to see this footage! I can remember suddenly taking on the persona of a truly humbled La'al Ratty and saying that I was extremely sorry and just couldn't see what I was doing. By now, I was totally in character and I can vividly remember putting my chin on my chest before raising my eyes to the camera and saying, in a truly mortified and please-forgive-me kind of way, 'Sorry Coniston. Sorry Coniston duck!'

Stuart just looked as if he wanted to burst out laughing as I delivered these lines with such fake sobriety. He decided it was a wrap – I suspect because he would have developed camera shake. A very grateful Mrs B decided I'd done La'al's reputation proud and he wouldn't be carted away to mascot jail and I, thankfully, went away on holiday and didn't get to see the programme. Somewhere, in the Border TV archives, there's a repentant looking bedraggled woman pretending she can talk to the mascots in a truly Dr Doo-lally way!

On that day at Coniston, there was no thought in anyone's head that just a few months later, the Bluebird Café and its decking would be decimated by the most terrible of natural occurrences, that would not only wreck Cumbria's tourism trade, but also lead to loss of life.

As seems to often be the case in my life, I was at the heart of the action during the November 2009 floods, which would sweep away piers, property, cars and bridges. My new best friend was giving a presentation to tourism businesses at the Trout Hotel in Cockermouth and I had been asked to go along. The Trout Hotel sits right on the river in Cockermouth and I pulled into the car park, having arrived pretty early, and drove to park at the bottom end, right by the river.

I have never seen a river look like this one did. It was more like a sea, with water moving faster than I had ever witnessed a river flow. A man with a dog was walking on the opposite bank – about 100 yards away, as the river was pretty wide at this point. He urged his dog, which was off its leash, not to go near the river. A small gull landed on the water and within seconds was out of sight, swept along by the fast-moving current.

The thought running through my head was, 'this doesn't look good at all'. I contemplated moving the car, but there were no other spaces. I resolved that, if I saw one spot of rain falling, I would leave the event and get out. Even I knew that the river was likely to burst its banks if that occurred.

I watched the weather from inside the hotel throughout the event. No rain fell, but at the conclusion of the day, I packed up quickly and went. The following morning, reports of the loss of life and devastation that had befallen Cockermouth and Workington were all over the news. The very hotel that I had been in was under feet and feet of water and most shops in Cockermouth were ruined. A major bridge had been swept away and homes destroyed. I had been remarkably lucky to get home safely.

While this was a tragedy for lovely Cockermouth, there was also extremely bad news for some of my clients. Ullswater's piers had been badly damaged, with a pier house also affected by the flooding. Luckily, all of the vessels were fine. Down at the Aquarium, however, things were much worse. They were under water by several feet, with damage to various pieces of operational equipment. Thankfully, the creatures were safe, but it was clearly going to be months before they could re-open, with a full refurbishment necessary, whenever the floodwater cleared. How anyone got near the place to even check it out is beyond me, given the pictures that I was sent of the flood outside the front door.

I was extremely worried about the impact this might have on my own business, if the visitor attractions could not open and so did not need PR. I spent many days worrying myself sick about this, but was powerless to do anything. I just had to hope and pray.

Within a few weeks, I was approached by Cumbria Tourism and asked to deliver some PR seminars/workshops at the Shap Wells Hotel in Shap. Their PR team were too busy to deliver these, so I was drafted in instead. The atmosphere at this event was a little sombre, as you might expect, with tourism operators wondering how on earth they could attract visitors to the county.

As a result of my seminars, I managed to gain a new client, which made the effort worthwhile. Luckily, I lost no fee as a result of the floods, but what it had proved was that we are powerless against the forces of nature and the impact that these can have upon our lives and livelihoods.

On a lighter note, as part of my Natural Tourism brief, I visited the Wirral, to look at its natural tourism assets. While on New Brighton promenade, I was asked if I would pose as a disabled person, being pushed along in my wheelchair. As there was nobody else to do this, I agreed. Little did I know that somehow, when getting dressed that morning, I had managed to put on my pull-on skirt inside out, with the label on the outside!

Having discovered this while in West Kirby, I dived into the Sailing Club and was told I could change it around upstairs. No sooner was my skirt off, than a load of sailors starting trooping up the stairs, causing me to panic and get dressed as fast as possible. In my eagerness, I put my skirt on inside out once again!

Despite all the embarrassment, the great thing was that, when telling my Nan about this, she suddenly revealed that she had lived in West Kirby during the War and had often taken my father, as a baby, on to the beach. She then told us this amazing story about how she was catching a train from Liverpool, just as the station was being bombed and she had to be swept up, with her baby, by two soldiers, who got her on to the train just in time. Without this trip to West Kirby, we would never have known that – or the fact that 'nobody loved stiletto shoes' more than her!

During 2009, I decided to do something that had long been in my mind – to try to find the man who had made such an impact on my life as a 19-year-old-approaching-20-year-old in Sri Lanka. I found the card I had saved for decades and scoured the internet, praying he was still alive. To my relief, I found details of him via a Rotary website. I had no direct email for him, but managed to email someone who put me in touch. I sent an email and he e-mailed back.

This was monumental for me. I started to receive the most uplifting emails, in line with Buddhist thinking I suppose. Spookily, it has always seemed that whenever I was most in need of emotional support, an email would arrive from Sri Lanka. At times when my world was in a state of collapse, I received comfort and emerged stronger. I owe a massive debt of gratitude to that man in Sri Lanka for the huge impact he had on my life and still has.

'When we meet again, we shall have lots to discuss', he says. I love the use of the word 'when' and not 'if'. I hope to see him before fate removes either of us from each other's lives forever.

Chapter 23
SHREDS OF SUCCESS

2010 started in a cute and cuddly way with the arrival of the first baby reindeer born in the north of England for between 8000 and 10,000 years. This wonderful story of new life on my northeast farm attraction was at true heart warmer, as the mother of the baby reindeer had, only one year before, had her life saved by the dedication of the farm owner after she slipped on ice and dislocated her leg. Rather than having her put down, the farmer made her a special sling and lovingly massaged her leg for many weeks, to try to give her a chance of survival. This dedication paid off and she made a full recovery.

This story demonstrated fully how remarkable acts of human kindness really are the stuff from which great PR stories are made. There was nothing calculated or 'spin' orientated in the farmer's actions, which came from the heart and from his genuine love for his animals. These same qualities shone through again a few months later, with another story that even eclipsed that of the baby reindeer.

This one evolved from the farmer's discovery of two lambs, which he found suffering from hypothermia and at death's door because their mother's milk had not come through. He thought they only had about 15 minutes to live, so rushed them into his kitchen and, with the assistance of his two young daughters, inserted a stomach tube into each lamb, to allow warm milk to reach them fast. The family then held an all-night vigil, feeding them several time more. The lambs were showing signs of recovery the next morning and the family set up a lamb cam that took the viewer through their journey. This was a PR story that really captured the imagination and drove lots of viewers to the website.

My work for Cocorose London was still ongoing and new foldable shoe collections were launched every season. The business had really taken off and I had set a trend of naming shoes in innovative ways, so as to give a PR dynamic to each range. In 2009, I had created names for what became the 'Bond Girl' collection – from Domino to Vesper. In 2010, I suggested a link to thriller movies, naming shoes after actresses that had appeared in classics by Hitchcock and other directors. This collection had shoes named Tippi, Grace, Demi, Ingrid, Nicole, Mia and Glenn.

Through the Cocorose connection, I picked up another retail client in the form of a trendy bag-for-life company, but also won the account of a cupcake company in London, whose owner seemed to be continuously baking and creating the most fabulous cake designs I'd ever seen.

During this year, I discovered that I have a cyclical relationship with the man better known as Grimbles, my compadre at the Trafalgar Square shoot and my first ever client. Grimbles emerged again this year, this time working as a consultant for a debt adviser in Lancashire. I was invited to go along and talk to the marketing manager about carrying out some PR activity, similar to some that I had undertaken for a Blackpool insolvency firm for six years. I found myself back in the Grimbles fold.

Retail PR seemed to rule the roost for much of this year, as I was also asked to carry out promotion for Peter Rabbit and Friends shops in the Lake District and York. I found this truly frustrating, due to the very onerous approvals system operated by the copyright company. It seemed to me that they were more concerned with making changes to words in press releases than selling the product, this thought being compounded by the fact that I was told I could not use the phrases 'little ones' to refer to children and must instead substitute the phrase 'loved ones'. To me that wasn't the same thing at all, but this set a trend and the only way to seemingly get anything passed was to make it as bland and unappealing to the journalist and consumer as possible!

I enjoyed a fabulous day in York as part of my promotional activity – a city I had only ever had a few hours to see with a Dutch penfriend. I spent hours at the shop, learning about their promotional needs and range and started to work with them quite closely, to help generate more trade.

Unbelievably, at this time, a child attacked 'Peter Rabbit', who entertained passers-by in the street outside the shop. It beggared belief.

Luckily my faith in nature – in a truly literal sense – was restored by an experience that I created at the divine Rydal Mount – William Wordsworth's beloved family home for 37 years. Peter, a lovely South African chap, had been on my interview panel when I pitched the SLTAG account and I had worked with him indirectly, on stories relating to the destination as a whole. Now, he wanted something bespoke, which would highlight the stunning gardens and other facets of Rydal Mount. I suggested a Dawn Chorus experience.

This was to run on the May Bank Holiday Monday and entwined bird song, in the gardens that Wordsworth himself landscaped, with poetry read in the gardens during the experience. The key poem to be read on the morning was 'To the Cuckoo' – one that referenced an elusive cuckoo which William often heard in his stunning gardens, but which he failed to detect with his eyes.

Driving to Rydal Mount that morning (departing at 3.30 am!) and what unravelled at Rydal Mount thereafter, will always be one of the favourite memories of my career – even surpassing an evening cruise on Ullswater with the Eden Celiidh Band, which played the most atmospheric music, as we cruised between the fells and mighty Helvellyn and as the sun set over the lake.

On this May morning, there was virtually nobody on the road to Rydal except me. Light was being to create cracks in time and space, as Dr Who would say, in a charcoal-coloured sky, shedding just enough illumination to bring the bobbing, moored sailing boats at Low Wood, on Windermere, into view. The strains of Andrea Bocelli on the CD seemed a fitting accompaniment to this first early morning glimpse of the lake, contributing a touch of the theatrical to a dramatically impressive landscape.

I drove up the very steep hill to Rydal Mount, passing the church and heading into the small car park at the top. In the semi-gloom, an eerie figure appeared in the headlights. Luckily, Peter had provided ample warning that he isn't a morning person and it became evident that he hadn't been exaggerating! Nevertheless, hospitable as ever, he ushered me into the Rydal Mount tearoom, where the wood burner was being stoked up.

The group set out at around 5.40 am, more light having now appeared and a cacophony of birdsong already audible in the tranquil setting. Walking across the lawn and terraces that Wordsworth laid out, almost tame robins followed in our footsteps, literally hopping just inches behind as if eavesdropping on the conversation. Blackbirds struck up as we moved to the picnic area, with wood pigeons and chaffinches also in full song. What we all wanted to hear, however, was the cuckoo and I was absolutely determined to hear the one that lives in the gardens today, all these years after William immortalised it.

Peter dutifully read us poetry, as we moved around the gardens with little illumination and then headed up towards the Summerhouse and Coffin Route, passing rocks in a small pool. Peter told us how William would tinker with these, to create different sound sensations in the gardens. He then read 'To the Cuckoo', which created a few goose bumps.

A slightly less bleary-eyed Peter then granted us around 20 minutes in which to explore the gardens at our leisure, before heading back to the tearoom.

This was my last chance to attempt to hear the cuckoo and I abandoned the group and headed back to the summerhouse, to dwell a little longer. Suddenly, in the still of the dawn, I heard the unmistakable call of the famed elusive cuckoo. It was amazing, puncturing the silence in a magical, almost fairytale manner. Although it was proffering directional clues as to its whereabouts, true to form – and to the memory of Wordsworth – it simply could not be seen, no matter how much I looked. It didn't matter, however: I was so thrilled to have heard my first-ever cuckoo call that I couldn't wait to tell Peter and tuck into the bacon rolls!

Without a shadow of a doubt, however, the main event of 2010 was related to marmalade and a charming festival held at a historic home and gardens near Penrith. I had first been approached about working on this account, while at the NEC with my Natural Tourism projects and had subsequently held a meeting with the organisers. I had then put together PR ideas for sponsors, to help sell sponsorship packages. From there, it was all about promotion.

Now I did have a great advantage in running this campaign, namely my near addiction to marmalade! Suddenly, a girl who, as little more than a toddler, would run round her Nan's hotel, trying to find marmalade pots to empty and into which to stick a finger, was being asked to spread the love of a food dying in popularity and no longer of appeal to the children of today. This was a dream come true.

The campaign started with me trying to fill in pieces of a map that wasn't entirely coloured orange by any means. This was a map showing where previous entries into the marmalade competition had come from, which showed big pockets of the country to which the love had not yet been spread. Thinking along these lines made me decide to call this campaign 'Spreading the Love' and that was the theme I kept in my head throughout.

Press releases were issued to all these non-marmalade-making counties, to urge people to grab hold of their Sevilles, give them a squeeze and get those shredders going. This resulted in interviews on radio stations like BBC Radio Gloucestershire and lots of regional coverage, but more had to be done.

I discovered, during the course of my research, that D H Lawrence suffered from bouts of severe depression and would use marmalade making to lift his mood. Knowing that the third Monday in January is known as 'Blue Monday', I decided to urge cooks to make it an 'Orange Monday', to keep spirits high. More coverage resulted.

However, in my own mind, what I wanted to do was communicate with children. In a previous year, a young girl living near Penrith had submitted an entry based around romantic marmalade – with hearts cut out of peel. Tiptree, who were sponsoring the Festival, said they would make a batch of this marmalade up and put it on sale in outlets such as Booths supermarkets. Armed with this, I targeted children's TV, with great success. Blue Peter said they wished to film the young girl at the historic home and the BBC's Newsround also put her story as a main lead on its website. Both of these were major coups.

However, I wanted to generate still more interest. I had a photo taken of a couple both eating marmalade at once from a double-ended spoon, to tie in with Valentines Day. I then tried to gee up more marmalade entries by challenging England, Wales, Scotland and Ireland to try to beat their Six Nations rugby rivals in the marmalade making stakes, so as to not have to pick up the wooden spoon. My favourite idea, however, involved the seaside, as you might expect from a girl born in Blackpool.

My idea was one that I dubbed the 'Battle of Tastings' and this saw me building lists of media titles in each of Britain's most famous seaside resorts, from Margate to Morecambe and beyond. I went right round the coastline, listing everywhere from Brighton to Blackpool and then wrote tailored materials for each resort, to urge its landladies to try to win the 'Best Bed and Breakfast' marmalade at the Marmalade Awards. This category was only for those running B&Bs, so was ideal for the seaside resort route.

All that then remained was for me to do some international targeting, which even saw me discovering two avid marmalade makers in Australia, who came up during one of my many surfing sessions in search of marmalade fanatics. I contacted them and asked if they would spread the word in Australia, which I believe they may well have done.

All of this activity combined to generate a mass of publicity, but more importantly dramatically increased the number of entries to the competition and the number of people coming through the gate on the day – tangible evidence of how successful the PR had been. Being there, in the drizzling rain, as TV crews interviewed winners and photographers snapped away was one type of satisfaction. Seeing a long queue snaking around and trying to get in to see all the marmalades produced was something else – particularly as the event raised vital sums for Hospice at Home.

My love of marmalade served me very well, to the extent that I was nominated for three awards at the North West Chartered Institute of Public Relations Awards – in the categories of 'Best Consumer PR Campaign', 'Best Not-for-Profit PR Campaign' and 'Best Campaign Under £10k'. In one of these, I was up against Cumbria Tourism, who had entered their post-flood campaign, which I thought the judges would view very sympathetically. On that basis, I was pretty sure I didn't have a chance, in that category at least. As usual, in every category the competition from Manchester consultancies and in house teams was fierce.

I had no idea who to invite to these awards, as Nigel was now ensconced on his houseboat with a lady in his life and, in truth, I didn't really wish to have to buy two extra, extravagantly priced tickets for a gala dinner at the Manchester Deansgate Hilton. I booked a room on receiving news of the nomination, thinking I might stay over, as I had done in a previous year. On that occasion, the hugely impressive hotel that dominates the Manchester skyline had only just opened and I managed to leave half my clothing in the wardrobe, necessitating a trip back on the following Sunday with my son in tow. As luck would have it, we were given a trip up to the top floor bar, from which you can see the whole of Manchester – including Old Trafford and Coronation Street, which greatly impressed him!

However, this plan was to be replaced by Plan B – one that unravelled in my Italian A' Level class. I arrived for class a little early and just happened to mention to my teacher that I would have to miss a lesson due to the awards, which were on a Wednesday night. I also mentioned, in passing that I didn't know who to take to the awards with me. If truth be known, I was half trying to pluck up courage to invite a chap in my class, but everything was whipped out of my hands in one fell swoop. As various students arrived, some of whom I hardly spoke to or knew very well, my teacher took it upon herself to start asking them what they were doing the night of the awards. Given that it was a class night, the answer should have been plainly obvious!

I was wishing I'd never mentioned it and was relieved when the lesson started and she had to turn her attention to teaching rather than guest sourcing. Little did I know, however, that other thoughts were whirring through her brain. When it came to the time when we had to get our heads down and start doing some writing practice, she suddenly said, 'You know Gianna, I think I could come with you that night'. I almost snapped the lead of my pencil!

'It's a Wednesday night', I said, reinforcing the point that I would be missing class, while trying to infer that she would be teaching it.

'Yes, but I could make arrangements', she said, in a very determined way.

At this point, I could tell there was absolutely no point arguing. She had a steely look in her Italian eyes and I knew that she really wanted to go and sample some of the glitz and glamour of this gala evening (I hadn't briefed her on the bitching in the bogs!). I sighed a little, wondering what on earth this was going to be like, but then thought that at least I'd got a companion. My fate was sealed.

I cancelled the room at the Deansgate Hilton and hired a cab from Cleveleys instead. The evening arrived and when I got into the taxi, I could see that she'd really gone to town with glamming up, which was quite something, as she always looked like she'd stepped off a catwalk at the best of times. I felt quite dowdy in comparison, despite having had my first ever spray tan!

We arrived at the Hilton, and went to the bar with which I was pretty familiar after various award ceremonies in the past. It started to heave and eventually we were called through for the dinner. We were pat of a very amiable table comprising a few sponsors and a few PR consultants. All were mesmerised by this 50-something woman who was a cross between Nancy Dell'Olio and Sophia Loren, with her heavy Italian accent enthralling all the men, who instantly asked her to teach them a few words of her lingua madre.

I developed my usual incontrollable sickness as the nerves kicked in, which was all made worse by the fact that my companion probably ate only two mouthfuls of food throughout the meal. I had never realised what a faddy eater she was, as she had always waxed lyrical about her love of fish and things that she cooked.

It transpired that she didn't like smoked salmon, only fresh salmon, didn't eat lamb and didn't like the vegetables served and didn't much like bread either. In the end, I ordered her an extra dessert so that she could take three mouthfuls of that and cast that aside too. Guilt was eating me up and I couldn't wait for the proceedings to begin.

One of the first categories called was 'Best Consumer', which always has a lot of nominees, as was again the case. The Silver winner was called and then the Gold winner, leaving me trophy-less. At the moment of delusion, I became even more depressed. I suddenly realised that the trophy situation had changed once again this year. Over the years, I have learned that you never know what you're going to get as an award until you turn up and see all the trophies lined up, waiting to be presented. Some years, as in 1998, we had magnificent, chunky glass trophies that could easily do a burglar some damage, if you used them as a defence weapon. In other years, the trophies were so small and lightweight you dare not sneeze for fear of breaking them in half. One year, a bright spark decided to make them charcoal coloured instead of clear – a trend that never took off – while my most recent trophy was a half-decent, triangular shaped one with nicely shaped edges.

However, at around 9.30pm on this night in Autumn 2010, I realised that, despite all of the highly priced tickets sold and all of the entry fees collected, someone in events HQ had deemed that Silver award winners would not get a trophy at all, just a certificate! I was mortified and my level of nausea rose a notch.

Now I suspect some of the Silver award winners that night would have been chuffed with their certificate, but I knew, as a dead cert, that I would not. Over the years, I had won so many certificates as a winner and runner-up, that I stopped framing and displaying them by 2001, just shoving them in a cupboard, where they dwelled in not a particularly cared for state, out of sight and out of mind, never to see the light of day again.

I was by now really agitated, seriously thinking that I would rather not win anything than just go home with a piece of paper rather than a solid, chunky (or even just-about-sneeze-proof) trophy in my eager little hand. 'Look at that', I said to my teacher, 'They don't even get a trophy if they've won Silver'. She smiled in blissful ignorance and I realised that it was just me with my high expectations that was viewing this as a potential disaster in the making. I suspect I would have accepted my certificate with as much happiness on my face as when my mother-in-law presented me the green velvet, old-fashioned standard lamp shade that was immediately consigned to the loft!

Luckily for everyone responsible for the awards that night, this tragedy did not occur. The next category in which I was nominated was called and the Silver Award winner was announced. I breathed a sigh of relief, knowing that I'd at least avoided the certificate. Next thing I knew, Catapult was declared the winner of the Gold Award. I tried to get to my feet, but a rather excitable Italian woman next to me was going into raptures about this success, looking truly amazed that her 'Gianna' had managed to scoop this top prize. I eventually extricated myself and made it up the stairs to collect my TROPHY – and a very nice, substantial one it was too, crafted in the shape of a flame.

I returned, but had hardly sat down again when I was called up again for my next Award – something that really tickled the bella donna with the kohl-rimmed smoky eyes sitting next to me. By now, she was well into the spirit of the event and telling everyone around the table what a good student I was and how hard I worked. My second departure from the stage with my Gold TROPHY was by no means as smooth as my first. The staging had gaps between planks of wood just before the stairs and, as might have been predicted, I got my stiletto heel caught in it. I gave it as hard a tug as I dared, as the last thing I wanted was to then live up to the company's name and be catapulted headfirst. My thought process wasn't helped by the knowledge of a friend who had suffered a broken leg at an awards ceremony by tumbling down as she left the stage! I tried my best not to look perturbed and gave another little tug at my shoe. Thankfully, I extricated it and made my way back to the table.

Things had gone truly swimmingly, but it was almost time for Cinderella to depart. The taxi had agreed to pick us up at around 11.30pm and, as usual, the awards hadn't run on time. My teacher and I had to virtually run out of the hotel to try and get to the driver as fast as we could, praying he hadn't abandoned us and gone.

To this day, I wonder whether my teacher took more pride in those awards than I did. She posed with me for some shots with the trophies and never stopped talking about my success in class when we both returned. In a way, I was glad that I'd taken her – at least she now understood the world that I worked in and had an inkling of what PR was all about. It was no longer the topic you couldn't explain to your teacher, but a charmed circle, which I suspect she would secretly have liked to frequent herself, if she had her time all over again.

Chapter 24

COOKING ON GAS

2011 came along and filled me with excitement. I had just four more months to stick it out in the office and then I could be free of the overhead, the rent and lots of associated expenses. I'd waited for this moment for five years and employed nobody, other than on a freelance or work experience basis.

From the first week of January, I started to fill bin bags, to clear out absolutely anything that I could get rid of. I now had 13 years of paperwork, filing, merchandise and much more to sort through and dump. I set myself a target of four bin bags a week, which I religiously either took away for burning or took to the tip. By keeping to this target, I hoped I could make the final move as painless as possible.

This was foolish thinking. My son, father and I made so many trips up and down the stairs that I feared for my father's health. Consequently, if he departed with a load of boxes, I would bomb up and down the stairs carrying items of incredible weight, just to make sure he wouldn't have to do it on his return. Removal men were brought in, but it was all the little stuff that caused the issues, along with thousands of cables, computer disks, files, and papers. It was actually a complete nightmare and I had to try to balance this with practice for my Italian oral exam for my A2 Italian!

Despite the big plus of getting out of the office, some rogue elephants decided to charge my way. I made various trips to the southwest to talk to an attraction there and work eventually started to come through and I was appointed. I then discovered that planning permission for exciting plans wasn't even close to being granted. I raised an invoice for what had been done, but didn't receive payment.

Before I knew it, I was introduced to an HNLP and training organisation across the Pennines. Here, I should have trusted my gut feeling, as something didn't feel right. I worked for three months, having already granted some free time as the chap's mother had died and we couldn't get things off the ground, but despite being promised payment and emails claiming that he would send me my pennies, I received nothing. I then learned, from a debt collection agency, that he had loads of CCJs in his personal name. He now has a CCJ in his company name too, as I took my claim to Court and got judgement. He hasn't bothered to clear that one either.

The big decision this year involved where to work. I had been to see a cookery school owner the previous year and the dialogue with her struck up again around April. They wanted me to do something that I had never contemplated before, but which made sense now I had no office. They asked me to work from the cookery school, initially two days a week.

My first introduction to the team there was at an open day and I'm not entirely sure that any of them had been told that I was on my way. There were puzzled looks as I was introduced and an existing marketing lady clearly didn't have a clue why I was there. I left with a slightly heavy heart, wondering if I would be accepted and brought into the fold.

My first days working there were actually spent in the tiny office of the sister restaurant and with the owner, not the staff at the cookery school. I was sat in front of a computer and asked to trawl through past correspondence, press releases, pictures and emails, as well as working through the website and coming up with different story lines related to the different courses. Calls came in from the young front of house manager at the cookery school and I could just tell that she wasn't that keen to have me around. It was, therefore, with some trepidation that I turned up to work there for the first time.

I decided all I could do was be me, though I knew I was being judged, almost as if I was the owner's spy. This wasn't helped by the fact that a shareholder, who came in once a week, was clearly viewing me as a complete luxury. 'So what are you actually going to do for the cookery school', she asked me one day. It reminded me of when the air cargo journalist had asked me the same question back in the 80s. This time, however, I really knew what I was going to do.

After a few initial ropy days midst the air of distrust, the front of house manager and myself became a great team and good pals. The owner announced one day that my new pal really hadn't wanted me on board – hardly news to me – but now really loved having me around. She also felt I was bringing out the best in my new workmate. I felt very proud.

I think this was partly because I made her laugh so much with my antics and she quickly realised that I wasn't an all tits and teeth PR girl, but someone very normal and one of them. This was aided and abetted by the fact that I sat on a chair with a wonky wheel, which had to roll over a very uneven slate floor. I would frequently shoot my chair back and almost end up flat on my back as the wheel struck the raised slate. This amused my new workmate enormously and my reputation of being a 'girl who would fall off a chair if she could' soon grew.

This intensified when I went into her cubbyhole and sat on the other chair, holding a full mug of tea that had just been brewed. Suddenly, the seat shot down, leaving me drenched with tea. I honestly thought that she was going to wet herself.

Other things also amused her, such as the time I desperately needed an internet signal, so went out at lunchtime to drive 3 miles up the road, to get online. Somehow or other, I locked myself inside the car and couldn't get out. I had to crawl into the back of the car to try to use the back door, which I managed, but this whole process took me ages. Even worse, when crawling back into the front, I must have hit the overhead light and the following day my battery was completely flat – the day before my Italian exam!

Everything I did seemed to make my pal laugh, even when I wasn't trying to be funny. The young chef soon joined in with the banter and we had a great atmosphere within a very short space of time. The existing marketing manager, who dealt mainly with affinity and group bookings, didn't resent me at all and I was soon writing copy for both her and my new mate, which helped them with their projects. Before I knew it, I was entrusted with a key.

At first, it was very strange being there, as it felt like being an employee, though I was never on the payroll. I sat in meetings as if I was an employee, shared their vision as if I was an employee and experienced the rollicking, as if I was one of the staff! I sort of understood the latter, as I know how hard it is to employee people.

I was also privy to a meeting with a new head chef, when he came for his second interview. The owner hadn't mentioned him coming – he just sort of appeared in the bar we were in, at the very same time that I had realised I was sitting opposite a man who had just appeared in the 'Britain's Got Talent' final!

This bespectacled, very serious looking guy with a moleskin notebook, left us in no doubt that he would shake the school up when he joined. He had a steely look in his eye and a spirit of determination that was actually quite attractive. I went straight back to my desk and googled him!

What I found was actually very surprising. Rather than discovering a serious CV, I found a piece that highlighted what a 'bad boy chef' he was, having been a rising star of the chefs' world in his early 20s and having acquired a 'reputation'. He openly admitted to this in the editorial I was reading and actually seemed to relish this label. I couldn't wait to quiz him about it!

I headed off on holiday shortly after this, so didn't get the opportunity until my return, at which point he was in situ and seemingly ruffling everyone's feathers. He came and asked me what I was working on, so I tried to explain, but quickly realised that he wasn't the best listener in the world. He was much better at pacing up and down the reception area, as I attempted to talk to him.

The girls were very worried by the fact he would go missing for a time when it got to midday and then come back completely hyped up. On that basis, I didn't know what to expect when he came up to me on that first day with him and said, 'Let's go next door' – that was, of course, the bar.

We sat outside and I took my opportunity to ask him the direct question that had been on my lips for weeks, 'So why are you a bad boy chef?'

I certainly got my answer in a very rock 'n' roll kind of way! He did, however, claim those days and antics were now history!

He was definitely one who'd been part of the Manchester scene and our conversation moved on to Manchester bands and Madchester. We actually saw many things at the cookery school the same way and I got the impression that he really wanted me to boost his profile, rather than necessarily focusing on courses. We returned to the school to raised eyebrows and I could tell that my ladies couldn't wait to tackle me, given the way he'd whisked me off my wonky chair completely out of the blue.

Shortly after this, I was sitting in the tiny office – which I call the cubby hole – with the marketing lady and we were both innocently engaged in a conversation about star signs – which involved revealing my Leo-Tiger status. He happened to be passing the door at this moment, heard the word tiger and suddenly dropped his trousers, to reveal much more than just the scar on his leg where he claimed a tiger had sunk its teeth! Any observer would probably never have seen two more shocked faces on women at work! It just reinforced my view that I really was now charged with promoting a bad boy!

My days there were filled with bad boy baiting for a while, as he was very easy to wind up and I was never in the mood for any rhubarb. At the same time, I met lots of new people, shoppers who just popped in to the cook shop, wannabe cooks who I would take on a tour of the premises, course delegates that I would sometimes have to sign in, caterers delivering meat, fish and wine and many more people.

Coverage poured in – from having TV and the Manchester Evening News covering a students' course, to generating lots of editorial in national dailies and Sundays, big lifestyle magazine pieces and even a place in the 'Five Best Baking Courses' feature in the Daily Mail! I absolutely loved every minute of being there and not just because the expert baker lady would leave her lemon drizzle with blueberry cake in the kitchen for us all to tuck in to! I just felt truly part of the furniture and the team and loved having people that I could interact with at least part of the week. Going it alone as a freelancer, I discovered, could be a really lonely life and the banter I got at the cookery school was a real antidote to this.

One by one, the joint owner, marketing lady and the bad boy chef all left, leaving just our happy band of three to manage things. We ploughed on with ideas, had new chefs sent over to join us and tried to battle on. In my own case, I lasted to March 31, 2012, at which point I had no choice, but to throw in the towel and stop my visits, for good business reasons.

The last months were the time when something, which never failed to amuse me, started to occur. It involved the arrival of a new cleaner – an Eastern European lady, who was absolutely barking mad! She was a lovely woman to talk to, if you could set aside half-an-hour, and as with many mad people, she decided that I had a face she wanted to talk to.

Her antics just made me chuckle all the time, whether she was kicking over a bucket full of water right across the stone floor in reception, or singing at the top of her voice to a pop song upstairs in the cookery area, in her very strong European accent and tuneless manner, not hitting a single note and seemingly oblivious that the whole building could hear her!

She was a mistress of the dramatic sigh – in fact, I wish I could perfect her art. A massive sigh would typically proceed her launching into one of her tales, whether that was about the shoes that were falling apart, or her back pain. She apparently had the clocking in system down to a fine art, to exact the most hours out of the system, which drove my friend mad and always needed a lift to the school, which was said to be a nightmare for the driver, as she would sit groaning and saying she was going to be sick throughout much of the journey, or else bounce up and down claiming she needed to wee.

She would tell me about her life back home, her desire to buy a house, sending money home and her son and I would listen and try to converse with her, without then being pinned down for the next hour. She would just make me smile the moment I saw her, as you never knew what might happen next. I also developed the habit of counting to 30 as she went upstairs to clean the workstation drawers, as the most almighty banging and clanging would then emerge as she chucked utensils into sinks and crashed drawers.

What I particularly couldn't get enough of were her crocodile tears. She would just stand looking at some disaster, which she had herself invariably created, such as her spilt bucket of water on the floor and then shriek loudly and pretend to sob at a great decibel level, but without a single tear ever emerging. It was like seeing a 40 or 50-something woman suddenly become a four year old! I love people watching and, for me, she was the ultimate in fascinating behaviour and I was almost addicted to her antics!

Just before I decided to call it a day – and it had no bearing on my decision – I was graced with perhaps the most incredible thing anyone's ever said to me. My workmate decided to go and tidy the cookshop, which was more or less in front of my desk. She suddenly turned round and said, 'Do you know who you really remind me of?' I was absolutely dreading the answer, thinking it was going to be something dire, but she was in full flow and I couldn't stop her. I did, however, almost fall off my wonky chair when she declared, 'Abi Titmuss'!

I was still in a state of shock when she continued. 'It's just everything about you … the way you look, your mannerisms, the gentle way that you are and then the funny things that you say'. I realised at this point that this was a real compliment she was trying to give me, so stopped trying to flatten my boobs and gave in to it. It could have been far worse!

Life at my aquarium got really interesting in 2011. For a start, I'd suggested we run a young aquarist's apprentice competition for kids and this was taken up with a lot of success. Kids from Lancashire and Cumbria applied for the contest, detailing their love of animals, and then a grand final saw six compete for the trophy, by handling animals and giving a presentation.

The other great news was that my darling otters got a new swimming pool, being allowed to swim, after diving off a little plank, in the underwater tunnel. Seeing them doing the doggy-paddle at a really great depth in the tunnel really gladdened my heart and watching them on a little island, communicating with visitors, was the cutest thing ever, despite the smell of otter pee, which was now filling the attraction!

In the rest of 2011, a few things came my way, which were really a result of my dedication to certain things, free-of-charge, in the past. The first, was winning an account that was geared at helping to make Eden in Cumbria a sustainable tourism destination. That came about, in part, because I had shown commitment and attended an initial brainstorming day, at my own expense, before any funding application for the project was submitted.

The second project involved the renovation of the old Clocktower in the village of Haverthwaite into office accommodation. That account came my way through my dedication to the annual stone skimming contest, as the person behind the renovation was one of the stone skimming organisers. The third involved work on a planning application in Ulverston – which was won through a recommendation from the local Council, for whom I had handled a truly successful launch of the revitalised Sir John Barrow Monument in Ulverston.

It has become clear to me over the years that if you do kind deeds for people and help them out, they invariably then remember you – even if not immediately – and try to return the favour, whether that is by giving you business directly, or recommending you to others. It may seem like a mug's game to provide free PR, but I have found it has done me a great service during my career.

In 2011, on this same theme, I was auctioned twice, providing free PR time to the lucky bidder, whose money went, in both cases, to a good village cause. The upshot of the first auction was that someone who had bid, but didn't win me, took me on to handle his PR anyway, proving the point that I've made above. I suddenly found myself promoting crazy hats and knitwear and getting national coverage for products that would never have landed on my doorstep had I not supported a village cause.

The most significant event of the year, however, only took place in November 2011 and I wasn't even present! That summer, I had debated long and hard whether to enter a new category at the NW Chartered Institute of Public Relations Awards – 'Best Freelance PR Practitioner'. The debate in my head was a replication of one that I'd had when entering the 'Small PR Team' Award, that is, would it be detrimental to be seen as being too small? I thought about it for days on end and, at the last minute, decided to enter. I was, after all, what I was and there was now no way of entering the 'Small Team' category, as that was for agencies of around five people.

I didn't really think any more about this and decided it was pointless booking any tickets for the event, given the price of tickets, plus all the other expenses.

Shortly before the awards night came along, I had been asked to give advice to the son of a secretary, who worked for one of my clients. She asked me to tell him what I would do, if I had been offered the PR role with which he had just been tempted. I did what I could.

The day after the CIPR NW awards, this young chap emailed me to congratulate me on my award! I told him that I didn't have a clue what he was talking about and he advised me that I'd won the title of 'Best Freelance PR Practitioner' NW. I was absolutely stunned!

It took me weeks to get hold of my trophy, but I eventually managed it and did a teeny bit of marketing, which didn't really get off the ground as it was just before Christmas when the trophy eventually arrived, making it a bad time to get publicity materials out. It did, however, give me another tough decision to make in February 2012.

Chapter 25
RECOGNITION

My big decision of early 2012 involved the national CIPR Excellence Awards. I was faced with the same dilemma: should I enter and be classed as small, or not enter and maybe miss out? Again, at the very last minute, I decided to enter.

I was pretty busy at the start of 2012, with a new client in London, which was a singles and dining club, a second promotion of a local festival called Bikes & Barrows in Scorton Village, and the acquisition of the accounts of both Lindeth Howe Country House Hotel in Bowness and its sister business, Mountain Goat – a tour operator which, as I said in my PR proposal, makes the inaccessible accessible, for those who do not know the Lake District terrain.

Additionally, I pitched for something I should have avoided like the plague. I was early for this pitch, so stood in the corridor. I could hear a very loud woman discussing candidates' proposals, including mine, in very disrespectful terms and instantly thought she would not be an easy client with which to work. So it proved!

Despite this error of judgement, everything else went well. I was still at the cookery school until March, had a new and lovely Italian teacher in Horwich and was going great guns in promoting Mountain Goat's 40th anniversary. The start of this really began by re-enacting 'The Goat's' very first journey back in 1972, which had seen a bus leaving Bowness Pier and travelling over the Kirkstone Pass to Glenridding. On what appeared to be a nice sunny day in March, the little group gathered at Bowness for the off.

It was really warm at Bowness Pier, with everyone sporting summery clothes and drinking up the rays. By the time we met a Border TV crew at the top of the Kirkstone Pass, it had become a freezing cold, wind-blasted day, which played absolute havoc with my hair, just as the Border TV cameraman decided he wanted to film me cheering the Goat on! I had foolishly left my coat in the car and must have looked just as awful as I had on my last Border TV appearance with the mascots!

We all trolled down to Glenridding, where my client Mrs B was waiting to greet us on the shore. A stunning cake carrying a picture of a Mountain Goat bus was cut, with the Border TV crew and press photographers capturing every moment. Eventually, we all managed to pile into the pier house to warm up and eat cake!

As April approached, I had something in the diary. I had been shortlisted for the 'Best Freelance PR Practitioner' Award and had to go to London for a panel interview at the CIPR – just as I had done in 2007. Having been through this once, I wanted to put right anything I might have been done wrong on that occasion and I was determined to have a very good answer, if they asked me what winning the award would mean to me.

I had worked out that the other shortlisted consultants were a London-based consultant working in travel, who had been shortlisted the year before as well, and a Liverpool-based consultant specialising in legal PR. I instantly felt that it was highly unlikely that I, a non city-based consultant, would stand any chance against consultants, who probably conformed to the norm and didn't sit around the kitchen table listening to a farmer's tales of sheep woes, or have to pack wellies when she went out to most meetings (pink and spangly though they are!).

I had a strategy and it was all based around relaxation. I would get a very early train to London, hop off to the newly moved Italian bookshop and then have an early lunch in Soho. My interview was at 2pm, so I would leave plenty of time to get there by taxi, arrive early and sit in the waiting area, which I knew would have a water cooler and easy chairs! This was the plan.

It was all going swimmingly. I had a relaxing train journey in First Class (also booked specially to add to the air of calm), arrived and caught a taxi to the Italian Book Shop, bought a few books and ate in an Italian restaurant, ordering a plain salad with a little tomato and parmesan and lots of sparkling water. I then walked out and hailed a taxi and asked to be taken to Russell Square. I got in, thinking that it was very clammy and wondering if it was going to rain. I had sported a black and red dress, my best black jacket and black shiny heels. I was chilled.

The traffic may have been a little heavy, but we were down back-streets, where it tends to build up, so I didn't think anything of it. The driver fiddled with his radio. We sat there. Suddenly, he turned round and uttered the killer words, 'I can't get you there'.

I sat bolt upright. 'What do you mean?' I asked in total shock.

'The police have cordoned off Tottenham Court Road', he explained. 'The radio says there's a man throwing computers off the top of a build-ing. The traffic's just not moving, so I can't even get you down to Oxford Street and round. You're best getting out and walking down until you can cross somewhere'.

Two things went through my head. One was the fact that Tottenham Court Road seemed to have played far too big a part in my life over the years. The second was that there was no way I could walk in my heels. 'Give me a minute', I said. I dived into my bag and whipped out my Cocorose London 'Mia' black patent, foldable ballerina pumps and whipped my heels off. I then gathered my computer, books and shoes and jumped out of the taxi, paying my fare and not having a clue what to do.

The driver was absolutely right. All side streets leading into Tottenham Court Road were closed off with yellow tape, but there were no police to be found anywhere. Crowds were gathering by each strip of yellow tape, but no officials. I walked about four blocks and found the same thing there. Time was ticking by and I knew I had to ring the CIPR. I made the call and explained the situation. They knew nothing about any incident and clearly thought I was exaggerating. It was suggested that I could maybe ask to cross, but I could see men with guns. I wasn't going to try that one! They then suggested that I get the Tube, but then rang back instantly and told me they'd discovered the Tube stations were also closed.

I was, by now, desperate. They asked me what time I had to get back and I explained which train I was booked on to. They said they would try to re-jig the interview schedule, but by now I was in a really defeatist frame of mind. Having thought I had little chance anyway, I was now convinced that the whole day was a waste of time and that I would simply be turning round and heading home again, without any interview at all. I could see no way of getting there.

I kept walking down the road, praying it wouldn't rain, as I couldn't manage a brolly as well as all my bags. Suddenly, I spotted a policeman by a tape, so I ran towards him and asked for advice. This is what I was told. 'If you really leg it, and I mean really leg it, you might just get down a few more blocks before we extend the cordon. If not, you won't be able to cross at all'.

Not surprisingly, I legged it, running with all my bags and heels in hand, as fast as I humanly could, wondering why on earth they had to close off so many streets just for a man throwing computers off a roof way back up the road. The policeman was right: I suddenly found a road with no yellow tape, so ran straight across an eerily empty Tottenham Court Road, which was completely traffic-free. By now though, I hadn't a clue where Russell Square was!

I started to walk back north, stopping numerous people to ask for directions. Many were foreign and just looked at me blankly. Eventually, I found a chap, who told me to walk through what looked like a building, but did actually give access to the other side. Eventually, I found myself in Russell Square and had to then scour building numbers trying to work out where the HQ was.

I arrived hot, sweaty, a nervous wreck and totally harassed. I had to switch shoes in CIPR reception and ask if I could go and try to cool down in the toilets. I splashed cold water over my face and tried to regain some semblance of calm. The candidate from Liverpool had gone in ahead of me. I knew a computer-throwing madman had blown any chance I'd had.

It took me ages to get my heartbeat back to anything like normal and I drank cup after cup of water from the water cooler. I tried breathing techniques, to try to get back to a pre-taxi state. I saw the other candidate come out looking all calm, cool and collected and was more convinced that ever that I didn't have a hope. A voice in my head told me that all I could do was show how passionate I am about my clients' campaigns. It had to be all or nothing.

I entered the room to find four people awaiting my arrival. I apologised for being late, but they hardly listened and didn't seem to have any knowledge of the incident. I sat down feeling very small. I felt even worse when the only man on the panel told me he had two global PR consultancies. I did wonder what on earth he would know about a freelance consultant with pink spangly wellies.

The questioning began and I just answered everything honestly, while trying to communicate my philosophy, justifying why I charge little or nothing at times and describing my sample PR campaign in such a way as to paint verbal pictures that brought it to life. I was then asked the question about what winning the award would mean to me. I gushed and explained that it would mean absolutely everything, while secretly hoping that they were focusing on my wrinkles and realising it was probably my last chance of scooping this prize. I hadn't wanted to verbalise that, because the last thing I wanted to do was bring the violins out.

As I explained how little I charge at times, I could see the global PR man looking at me with incredulity and I shrank a little. I wasn't going to lie though, which is when I came out with the words, 'You see, my life is a little like PR's version of 'It Shouldn't Happen to a Vet'. It was suggested that maybe I should write about it, which is how this book was born!

I left the room after no more than 20 minutes, maybe less. I felt exhausted, as I'd poured absolutely everything into it. A lady who had sat in on the interview took me out and stopped me on the stairs. 'You really communicated your passion', she said. I was gratified. 'I work in PR', she said, 'And I know how hard it is to get a decent fee'. She'd obviously picked up on the fee incredulity. At that point, raucous laughter broke out in the room I'd just left. I shrank inside and wanted to burst into tears. I was sure they were laughing at a stupid girl, who charged peanuts and often worked just for the love of it.

I retained that feeling inside, not just on the way home, but for another month and a half besides, right up to the award ceremony. I have never felt so depressed on a train journey home. By then, I had learned that the man in Tottenham Court Road had been aggrieved at not being granted an HGV licence and had taken people hostage, while strapping explosives around his body. The road closures at least made more sense.

I got back into the swing of work feeling thoroughly depressed. All that kept me even slightly buoyant was the fact that I achieved a dream and won an account that involved chocolate, promoting wonderful, London-based chocolate tours. Other than that, I was really being to question what the point of it all was.

Tickets for the glorious gala dinner at the Park Lane Hilton cost an arm and a leg and I couldn't justify taking anyone with me. I even debated whether to go at all. In the end, I thought I would go, but stay at the Park Lane Hilton, so that I could make a quick exit once the awards were over and escape upstairs and probably have a good cry. That was the plan.

The event was being staged on a Monday night and was to feature compère, Colin Jackson, an address by Lord Coe (receiving a special CIPR Award) and various other Olympians. I travelled down early again and had a lovely female taxi driver, who chatted to me all the way from Euston and who really made me think that just being nominated was a great thing. The only trouble with that was that I had been down that route before.

I checked in and took pictures of the view from my room, which featured the Gherkin, the London Eye and other famous landmarks. I'd had an absolute dress disaster leading up to the awards, having been unable to find one for ages, then busting the zip of the one I found, while running a last minute dress rehearsal. At the very last minute, I'd had to get a new zip put in by a wonderful dressmaker in Preston, so had run to and fro, praying that I would get my dress repaired in time. I decided to put it on really early at the Hilton, just to check there were no further disasters.

By that time, I'd managed to get in the shower, not realising the water came straight down from a round shower head fitted into the ceiling, so had drenched my carefully curled hair! My computer cable was on its last legs and would only power up my Mac if strategically forced in at a certain angle. I knew not what to expect of the evening.

I left it really late to go down to the drinks party, then positioning myself away from everyone and by a window, which at least allowed me to watch traffic going up and down Park Lane. A man from the Institute of Directors came to talk to me and explained that he was part of the ceremony. He asked who I was, heard my name and showed no recognition. I was sure that, if he'd been in rehearsals, as he claimed, he would have heard my name read out, if I had won. I felt even gloomier, only being shaken out of this when I saw a tall, blonde Greek God of a man and realised it was Mark Foster, the swimmer.

Dinner was eventually called, after several painful moments on my own. I made my way to the table to meet my fellow professionals and found myself between a man with his own agency and three lovely people from a London agency – an account handler, a lady and the Olympic sprinter, James Ellington. There was also another PR on her own from Stockport Council, two ladies from the RBS and another two people across the table from another agency.

Everyone was very chatty and friendly and I began to think it wasn't too bad being on my own after all. However, we all speculated about our table position and felt that it wasn't good. We were in the far right back corner of the room, tables and tables away from the red carpet that led up to the stage and which Colin Jackson told everyone they would have to run up, as time was short between awards. We all reckoned it would take a good five minutes for us to even reach the red carpet, squeezing between chairs and bodies, so the chances of our table having any winners were extremely slim. We really cheered each other up there!

Our next group motivation topic concerned how awards were starting to be allocated. We suddenly got over our 'we're in a really bad position' idea and decided that other tables at the back were winning prizes, but that it looked like each table only had one winner on it! By now, I had determined that the RBS ladies were involved with in house magazines and that the sprinter was there because he'd been the only one in the Olympic team not to have a sponsor. He had dated the daughter of the lady that was with him for a time, so she had asked her PR agency to help him get funding.

Most of us were in categories that were way down the programme, mine being next to last. This gave plenty of time for more analysis of how awards were being allocated around the room. I had my usual nausea problem by this point and was feeling even worse when the two people opposite me scooped an award. The one-award-per-table concept seemed to be further endorsed when nobody else on the table was successful in their category.

By now, my award was looming, but I'd written off any hope of winning it. There had only been one award per table and there was no reason why that pattern should end. The category came up and the three names were read out. I was fully expecting the girl from Liverpool to have won, but suddenly I heard my name announced – I was rooted to my chair with fear. The guy next to me and sprinter James got to their feet to hug me and clap as I tried to make the impossible walk towards the red carpet. A member of staff obligingly cleared a path for me and I eventually hit the end of the VIP flooring. It was a very long red carpet and I could see Colin Jackson standing in front of me like Frankie Valli in the 'Beauty School Drop Out' song from Grease. I sort of sprinted towards him, as if in slow motion, taking care not to bounce out of my strapless dress!

Colin greeted me, hugged me, offered congratulations and thrust my award in my hand. It was a very disappointing plastic thing, but it didn't matter – at least it wasn't a certificate! I was then told to exit stage right and head to the photographer, who snapped me and the award sponsor. I left that area in a daze, wondering what on earth this would mean for the business.

That didn't last long. I suddenly developed this completely different feeling in my body, in my posture and in my head. I felt that I was floating on air and I suddenly had this perception of being unstoppable. I walked back to my table a different person from the one who had left her seat 10 minutes earlier. I think it's called recognition and I think it's also the signs of self-confidence! I had suddenly been through the exact same process that I had seen a junior chef experience in the Café Royal many years before. The butterfly had found her wings.

My table were ecstatic and I ordered champagne for everyone. The RBS ladies were particularly lovely and kept telling me that the award would be amazing for my business. In my head, the words, 'But I work in

Poulton-le-Fylde' kept repeating, so I wasn't as convinced as they were, but inside I definitely felt different.

I went back to my room still floating and was far too excited to sleep. The following morning, I got on the wrong train at Euston, plugged in my Mac and only realised at the last minute that the train to Preston was the one opposite. Luckily I managed to quickly unplug, half stuff my computer into my bag and leg it across the platform. I then later ended up on a train from Preston that didn't stop at Poulton-le-Fylde and arrived in Blackpool instead, from where my family had to 'collect' me! One cannot be a PR guru and a sensible girl at the same time!

Later on that day, I reflected on what I had achieved. After 27 years of plying my PR trade, I had been adjudged the best in the country. After years of unhappy jobs, personal issues, broken marriages, life as a single mother and a struggle for survival, I hadn't waved that white flag and given up. I had listened to Dido and made it through the rain with Barry Manilow. I had only survived, because, in the words of Anil Seal, I hadn't pussy-footed around and had always taken the risk, whatever it was, and gone for it. I had raised my chin from my chest thanks to the uplifting words of a man I had met in Sri Lanka at the age of 19. Who says we are not a product of our past and the people that have graced our lives along the way.

As Winston Churchill said, in the 'stickie' that has stayed with me on my computer screen for the last 15 years, 'Success is going from failure to failure without loss of enthusiasm'. Whoever you are and whatever you do, carry that thought with you.

4228588R00253

Printed in Great Britain
by Amazon.co.uk, Ltd.,
Marston Gate.